Anent Hamish Henderson

Portrait of Hamish Henderson (Tom Hubbard, 2015)

Anent Hamish Henderson
Essays • Poems • Interviews

[

anent/ə'nɛnt/
preposition
1. concerning; about.

]

Editor
Eberhard Bort
University of Edinburgh

ANENT HAMISH HENDERSON EDITED BY EBERHARD BORT

First published 2015 by Grace Note Publications
in collaboration with the Carrying Stream Festival
Grange of Locherlour, Ochtertyre, PH7 4JS, Scotland

www.gracenotepublications.co.uk
books@gracenotereading.co.uk

ISBN: 978-1-907676-65-9

A catalogue record for this book is available from the British Library

Front cover painting by Timothy Neat, 2014

Typesetting by Grace Note Publications

Dedicated to the memory of
Jean Redpath (1937-2014) and Sheila Stewart (1937-2014)
two of the finest singers and tradition bearers
of the Scottish Folk Revival

Contents

(iv) Culture and Politics

II Poems

III Interviews

List of Illustrations and Photos

Acknowledgements

Thanks are due to a number of festivals for commissioning talks and lectures: TradFest Edinburgh Dùn Èideann 2014 for Raymond Ross's and Alison McMorland and Geordie McIntyre's contributions; StAnza 2014 for Lesley Duncan's; Edinburgh People's Festival 2013 for Paddy Bort's Annual Hamish Henderson lecture on Nelson Mandela and Hamish Henderson (also thanks to *Living Tradition*, where a condensed version of the talk was published); Edinburgh Folk Club's Carrying Stream Festival for Sheena Wellington's and Dolina Maclennan's Annual Hamish Henderson Lectures of 2013 and 2014, respectively; also to Edinburgh City Council, especially Jo Navarro and Cllr Richard Lewis, for hosting the Hamish Henderson Lectures at the City Chambers; and the Edinburgh Festival of Ireland 2015 for Paddy's talk on Hamish and Ireland.

Luath Press for Donald Smith's 'Man and Boy' (from his *A Long Stride Shortens the Road: Poems of Scotland*, Edinburgh: Luath, 2004); *Scottish Review* (16 Dec 2010) for Keith Armstrong's 'Stella of Rose Street'; Smokestack Books for 'The Divided Self', from Keith Armstrong's *Imagined Corners*, 2004; *Bella Caledonia* for George Gunn's poem 'The Bones of Scotland'; Tony Troon's *The Best of The Scotsman* Diary (Edinburgh: Mainstream, 1992) for the three stanzas of the poem by David Daiches; John Lucas and Shoestring Press for John's contribution which is a modified extract from his *Second World War Poetry in* English, 2013; Polygon for Colin Nicholson's interview with Hamish Henderson; *The Melody Maker* for Andrew Means's Hamish interview; *Textualities* for Jennie Renton's; and BBC Radio Scotland for Archie Fisher's 'Travelling Folk' interview with Hamish – also thanks to Dave Binns for providing the tape, and to Jennifer Meiklejohn for transcribing it; *New Edinburgh Review* for Geordie McIntyre's interview 'Risurgimento!'

Margaret Bennett's tape recordings of Sheena Wellington's and Dolina Maclennan's Carrying Stream Festival lectures came in very helpful. We are also grateful to the Islands Book Trust – Dolina's lecture is partly based on extended passages of her *Dolina: An Island Girl's Journey*, which in turn is the result of her conversations with Stuart Eydman and Jim Gilchrist.

Photo credits go to Alison McMorland (for Willie Scott and Howard Glasser photos); Dolina Maclennan (for the snapshot of Hamish, Kätzel and herself), Allan McMillan (for a number of contributors' portraits), Margaret Bennett (for Martyn Bennett and Hamish), and David Pratt for the picture of Nelson Mandela in Glasgow. Illustrations, facsimiles, etc courtesy of Alison McMorland, Geordie McIntyre, Dolina Maclennan; reproduction of paper cuts and calligraphy with kind permission from Howard Glasser.

We're particularly grateful to Timothy Neat for the cover painting and the sketches of Hamish in the book, to Tom Hubbard for the frontispiece portrait, and to Jan Miller for her drawings of Hamish. And to all contributors who have made this book possible and such a joy to work on.

The quotes on the back cover are from Margaret Bennett, 'Continuing the Living Tradition', in Sarah Dunnigan and Suzanne Gilbert (eds), *The Edinburgh Companion to Scottish Traditional Literatures*, Edinburgh: Edinburgh University Press, 2013, pp.144-152; p.146 – and from Daisy Chapman (1912-1977), *Ythanside (MT CD 308)*, 2000.

I personally would like to express my gratitude to the following people who have responded to my emails, talked to me over the phone or met up with me for a chat while I was researching my two pieces in this book: John Barrow, Margaret Bennett, Owen Dudley Edwards, Brian Filling, Kätzel Henderson, Cathal McConnell, Geordie McIntyre, Dolina Maclennan, Alison McMorland, Robin Morton, Hayden Murphy, Maggi Peirce, Raymond Ross and Donald Smith.

Last, but certainly not least, a big thanks as always to Gonzalo Mazzei of Grace Note Publications – the Perthshire home of this and the previous three books on Hamish Henderson and the Scottish Folk Revival. His enthusiasm, commitment, and creative skills are peerless, and without him and his productive cottage industry these volumes – and many other fine books – would simply not happen.

Anent Hamish Henderson: Introduction

Eberhard Bort

I'll always be waiting
Where streams are afore me.

I

These two lines are taken from an early 'Love Poem' by Hamish Henderson.[1] They could be seen as programmatic, expressing a curiosity, sense of adventure and life force that would again be reflected in his last poem, 'Under the Earth I Go',

> While my love lives, I'll dance with the Mayers
> Teasing the Old Oss till there's new life in him
> Chasing sweet lusty Spring with pipes, goatskin and
> bones.[2]

If Timothy Neat's two-volume biography of the man has shown us anything, then how crammed with incident his life was. And charting, as in the previous three volumes – *Borne on the Carrying Stream* (2010), *'Tis Sixty Years Since* (2011) and *At Hame wi' Freedom* (2012) – the life and work of Scotland's foremost folklorist of the twentieth century, the songwriter, poet and political activist Hamish Henderson (1919-2002), this collection has been put together to fondly remember *and* critically assess the continuing influence he exercises.

---

[1] Hamish Henderson, 'Love Song', in *Collected Poems and Songs*, edited by Raymond Ross, Edinburgh: Curly Snake, 2000, p.14.

[2] *Ibid*, p.154.

Hamish Henderson has received quite a bit of attention recently. He has had a good press, as it were. Remember the Commonwealth Games in 2014? Particularly the Opening Ceremony on 23 July? Only a week later, the BBC reported that 'The haunting rendition of Freedom Come All Ye performed at the opening ceremony by South African singer Pumeza is now topping the UK i-tunes classical charts.'[3] More than 44 years earlier, when a seventy-year-old Hamish Henderson sang 'The Freedom Come All Ye' at the Pearce Institute in Govan, Glasgow in January 1990, it was, according to Neil Cooper, 'the ultimate folk-song cabaret'.

> Henderson sang it ... in his own slightly cracked tones not as part of some officially sanctioned flagship event for Glasgow's status as European City of Culture that year, but for a low-level grassroots initiative that brought together art and activism in an event that would prove to be of huge trickle-down significance.[4]

That 'trickle-down significance' could, perhaps, be seen in the Scottish independence referendum campaign and the 2015 UK general election. 'There's a roch wind blowing through the great glen of Scotland this morning,' Alex Salmond, the former leader of the SNP, adapted Hamish Henderson after he was declared winner in the Gordon constituency on 8 May – in an election in which the SNP swept the board in Scotland, gaining all but three of the 59 Scottish seats.

Alan Taylor used his column in the *Herald* to espouse the 'Freedom Come-All-Ye', Hamish's best-known song, in the recurring discussions about a Scottish national anthem. He introduced his plea for 'the one to go for' with a short character sketch of its author,

> Tall as the Eiffel Tower, he cut an imposing figure with his bulbous nose, wiry moustache and ever-present hound. Ignorant interlopers might mistake him for a barfly but

---

[3] 'Glasgow 2014: athletes, crowds and visitors breaking records', *BBC News Scotland*, 29 July 2014, <www.bbc.co.uk/news/uk-scotland-28547874>.

[4] Neil Cooper, 'Agitate! Educate! Organise! The Day Noam Chomsky Came To Town', May 2011, <http://blog.linemagazine.co.uk/post/7187994979/agitate-educate-organise>.

> regulars knew better. Given a roving brief by the university's School of Scottish Studies, Hamish used Sandy Bell's to hold seminars, for students and anyone else within earshot, discoursing on everything from Gramsci and Italian fascism to the travelling community and the obscenity of nuclear weapons. When he died in 2002 at the age of 92 [*sic*] it was as if a Scots pine had been felled.[5]

Note how Alan generously gave Hamish an extra ten years. But that can easily be forgiven for a choice phrase like this about the song: 'Like its composer, it is nationalist by formation, internationalist in outlook, and socialist by inclination.' It, Taylor persuasively argues, 'springs from the memory of a boy brought up in Blairgowrie but it is the opposite of parochial.' Attacking apartheid and the military aggression of imperialism, 'its ambition is for a world free from prejudice and exploitation. In short, it's an anthem for everyone.'

Yes – but it would also go against the grain of Hamish Henderson to 'elevate' it to officialdom by making it Scotland's national anthem. It was conceived, as he said in the interview with Colin Nicholson (reprinted in this volume), as an inofficial, 'alternative' anthem:

> I have always privately opposed the idea of 'Freedom Come-All-Ye' becoming an anthem because if there's one thing I don't think would do that song any good at all would be for it to become official. The whole idea is that it is an alternative to 'official' attitudes.

For him, 'the world of folk-song and story ... forms a kind of underground.' He loved to quote Antonio Gramsci:

> That which distinguishes folk-song in the framework of a nation and its culture is neither the artistic fact nor the historic origin; it is a separate and distinct way of perceiving life and the world, as opposed to that of 'official' society.[6]

---

[5] Alan Taylor, 'An anthem for everyone, not just Scots', *The Herald*, 7 January 2015.

[6] Hamish Henderson, '"It Was In You That It A' Began": Some Thoughts on the Folk Conference', in Edward J Cowan (ed.), *The People's Past: Scottish Folk, Scottish History*, Edinburgh: Polygon, 1980, p.13.

Having 'The Freedom Come-all-Ye' blaring out at every official occasion is nearly as bad as envisaging drunken football crowds mangling the words and swaying to the tune of 'The Bloody Fields of Flanders'. Maybe Hamish's intentions ought to be respected, and his song be allowed to keep its 'alternative' credentials. It is doing fine, not just in folk clubs and sessions. Here is Lesley Riddoch:

> Recently, I've taken to singing Hamish Henderson's Freedom Come all Ye before book events and campaign meetings. It's become surprisingly popular. The first time, only a handful of other folk knew all the words. The second time, there were more...[7]

'This is,' she contends, part of 'the conscious remaking and revitalising of Scottish culture – every bit as important as the expression of the nation's political will.' And, in her column in the *National*, she hailed Hamish as a role model for his civic courage to reject the OBE offered by the Thatcher government in 1983, in protest against its pro-nuclear arms and foreign policies.[8]

In his aptly titled *A Work of Beauty*, a splendidly produced Edinburgh photo album, Alexander McCall Smith paints an affectionate little pen portrait of Hamish:

> Henderson was a lovable and gentle figure whose message resonated powerfully with Scottish egalitarian sentiment. His 'Freedom Come All Ye' is perhaps one of the most stirring indictments of exploitation ever written, sitting comfortably in the company of that other great Scottish humanitarian statement, 'A Man's a Man for a' That'.[9]

---

[7] Lesley Riddoch, 'Cultural connection is vital', *The Scotsman*, 5 January 2015.

[8] Lesley Riddoch, 'Refusing gongs is the honourable thing to do', *The National*, 8 January 2015.

[9] Alexander McCall Smith, *A Work of Beauty: Alexander McCall Smith's Edinburgh*, Edinburgh: Royal Commission on the Ancient and Historical Monuments of Scotland (RCAHMS), 2014, p.65.

Dolina Maclennan's memoir is studded with fond memories of her 'big pal' Hamish.[10] And Stuart McHardy and Donald Smith remind us how Hamish set markers on the *Scottish Democracy Trail*: how he represented the Regent's Road Vigil (for a Scottish Parliament) at the Democracy March on 12 December 1992 (where he sang 'The Freedom Come-All-Ye'), which also rang out often during demonstrations and rallies on Calton Hill.[11]

Wednesday night session in Sandy Bell's, 2015 (photo: Eberhard Bort)

It will come as no surprise that due homage is paid to Hamish in Gillian Ferguson's short booklet on Sandy Bell's – after all, it was not just Hamish's 'favourite "howff",' he often referred to it as his 'office'.[12]

On the academic side, *The Edinburgh Companion to Scottish Traditional Literatures* has been a wee milestone.[13] Hamish is featured

---

[10] Dolina Maclennan, *Dolina: An Island Girl's Journey*, in conversation with Jim Gilchrist and Stuart Eydman, Laxay, Isle of Lewis: The Islands Book Trust, 2014.

[11] Stuart McHardy and Donald Smith, *Scotland's Democracy Trail*, Edinburgh: Luath Press, 2015, pp. 86; 116.

[12] Gillian Ferguson, *The Story of Sandy Bells: Edinburgh's World Famous Folk Bar*, Kibworth Beauchamp: Matador, 2014, p.2.

[13] Sarah Dunnigan and Suzanne Gilber (eds), *The Edinburgh Companion to Scottish Traditional Literatures*, Edinburgh: Edinburgh University Press, 2013.

prominently, particularly in the contributions by Margaret Bennett and Corey Gibson. In Chris Wright's edited volume on the *Kist o Riches*, Alison McMorland introduces Hamish, the fieldworker and collector.[14]

Fiona Ritchie and Doug Orr trace the transatlantic connections between the living traditions of Scotland and Ireland and Appalachia in *Wayfaring Strangers*, correcting some misconceptions of Cecil J Sharp's *English Folk Songs from the Southern Appalachians* (1917), by focusing on today's tradition bearers 'and the music they share ... immersed in Hamish Henderson's "carrying stream".'[15] Later, they refer to Hamish Henderson, who

> reminded us that folk tradition neither stands still nor exists in isolation. It is the same with identity – Scottish, Irish, or American. Culture becomes a platform upon which we construct our concept of identity. As people move and ideas are shared, so their identities become more fluid, overlapping and blurring around the edges. Openness to new ideas and cultural exchange are at the heart and soul of social music. [16]

Gary West's *Voicing Scotland* offers a practitioner's insights – as a teacher at the School of Scottish Studies and as a piper – into Scotland's traditional music and song culture. He pays tribute to his teacher, Hamish Henderson –

> He opened my ears to what folk culture is all about, what makes it tick, how the best of it stands in its own soil boldly looking outwards, not tamely looking in.

and to contemporary musicians, singers and poets, driven by the need for 'an appreciation of where things have come from, where

---

[14] Alison McMorland, 'Hamish Henderson (1919-2002): Fieldworker and Collector', in Chris Wright (ed.), *Tobar an Dualchais: Ulaidh Nàiseanta/Kist o Riches: A National Treasure*, Teangue, Sleat: Sabhal Mòr Ostaig, 2014, pp. 71-75.

[15] Fiona Ritchie and Doug Orr, *Wayfaring Strangers: the Musical Voyage from Scotland and Ulster to Appalachia,* Chapel Hill, NC: The University of North Carolina Press, 2014, p.3.

[16] *Ibid.*, p.283.

we stand within the stream ... and to embrace the future with the confidence that comes from knowing where we've been.' [17]

Ian Spring has recently published his collection of essays, *Hamish Henderson and Folk Song*, which contains an essay on 'Hamish Henderson: Man and Myth'.[18] He sets out to debunk some myths and generally feels that much that has been written about Hamish has been 'uncritical and anecdotal'. Apart from failing to break much new ground himself – that Hamish Henderson never produced that great book of Scottish folklore or folksong and did not fulfil the promise of the *Elegies* by producing a great 'epic poem or song sequence'[19] can be found, among other places,[20] in Tim Neat's biography of Hamish Henderson, much maligned by Spring as 'tainted by unwarranted and sometimes bizarre speculation' and 'a strange mixture of hyperbole and euphemism, or exaggeration and evasion'[21] – he ignores serious scholarship – like, for example, Corey Gibson's work on Hamish Henderson and Antonio Gramsci or Ewan McVicar's on Alan Lomax, Hamish Henderson and cultural equity, Gary West's inquiry into folk, culture and nation, Margaret Bennett's on the impact of Hamish Henderson on international folk collecting or, to add just one more example, Steve Byrne's work on digitising the School of Scottish Studies archive. Spring cannot quite avoid the anecdotal either – and why should he? He tells this one well:

> Even after his death ... Hamish's spirit still seemed to remain in Bell's. One strange thing happened in Bell's on the day of Hamish's funeral (many of us had decamped there).

---

[17] Gary West, *Voicing Scotland: Folk, Culture, Nation*, Edinburgh: Luath Press, 2012, p.13.

[18] Ian Spring, *Hamish Henderson and Scottish Folk Song*, Edinburgh: Hog's Back Press, 2014.

[19] Ian Spring, 'Hamish Henderson: Man and Myth', in ibid., pp.142-175; p.158

[20] 'There is no single great literary work, and no seminal piece of folklore scholarship with which his name is popularly associated. Indeed, it is through his songs that he is usually celebrated.' Corey Gibson, *Endless Flyting: The Formulation of Hamish Henderson's Cultural Politics*, PhD Thesis, Edinburgh, 2012, p.122.<www.era.lib.ed.ac.uk/bitstream/handle/1842/8025/Gibson2012.pdf;jsessionid=F3899ECD8BF0AA8CC6CAA0440302379C?sequence=2>.

[21] *Ibid.*, pp.145; 147.

> I was standing at the bar with Raymond Ross when I saw someone come in. 'That looks like Eddie Linden,' I said, 'I thought he was dead!' 'So did I,' said Ray (a newspaper had actually, accidentally, published his obituary). Eddie had 'come back to life' for Hamish's farewell; Hamish would have appreciated the irony![22]

And so it is not really surprising that his 'nudging Hamish from the pedestal on which he had been placed'[23] ends up in a very similar place to those he seems to attack: 'If you count also the poems, songs, essays, etc that came from those he nurtured, supported and championed,' he concludes, 'his achievement is immense.'[24]

Ian Spring may crave more academic scrutiny. Maybe he will find it in Corey Gibson's forthcoming *The Voice of the People*, based on his award-winning PhD thesis at Edinburgh University.[25] Or in Richie McCaffery's recently finished PhD thesis on the Scottish Second World War poets at Glasgow University. Or even in this volume? Both Gibson and McCaffery are too young to have known Hamish Henderson. Gibson sets out clearly what is at stake:

> On one level, Henderson's 'legacy' will be short-lived if it relies on personal reminiscences and kind-hearted sketches of a tall, ambling, slightly shabby intellectual who was gregarious, opinionated, always ready to burst into song, and frequently holding court in the unofficial headquarters of the Scottish folk revival, Sandy Bell's Pub. On another level, he cannot simply be cast as a folk-hero whose worth is in the example of his life, and in the readiness with which others invest in him as an embodiment of the values or ideas to which they ascribe. (...)
>
> My intention is not to dismiss out of hand the fond anecdotal picture that is often portrayed, nor to overlook the range of Henderson's interests and talents and, therefore, the variety of roles in which he might be cast; it is to show

---

[22] *Ibid.*, pp.167.

[23] *Ibid.*, pp.169.

[24] *Ibid.*, p.171.

[25] Corey Gibson, *The Voice of the People: Hamish Henderson and Scottish Cultural Politics*, Edinburgh: Edinburgh University Press, 2015.

how his life's work is underpinned by an ambitious moral-intellectual programme to reconnect and reintegrate the artist within society.[26]

II

Very much in Gibson's spirit, we continue in this volume what we started with *Borne on the Carrying Stream* five years ago: bringing together personal perspectives, memories and reminiscences with more detached and analytical pieces exploring the life, work and legacy of Hamish Henderson.

In this volume, Sheena Wellington and Dolina Maclennan, two fine singers and tradition bearers who knew and were inspired by Hamish Henderson, give us glimpses of the man. We can count ourselves lucky to have people putting on the record how they worked with and were influenced by Hamish Henderson. But – as in the other volumes – we do not leave it there.

Here, we put Hamish's *Elegies* centre-stage. Joy Hendry, Mario Relich and Tessa Ransford had already explored them in *Borne on the Carrying* Stream, and Fred Freeman in *At Hame wi' Freedom.*[27] Now, Lesley Duncan draws parallels between Hamish and the Scottish First World War poet Charles Hamilton Sorley, before John Lucas and Richie McCaffery engage in close readings of the award-winning poetic sequence – 'Henderson's finest achievement,' as Roderick Watson has called the *Elegies for the Dead in Cyrenaica*. In his view, 'this long poem, more than any other in the literature of the period, catches something of the strangely special nature of the desert war.'[28] And Douglas Gifford saw Henderson as arguably the greatest Scottish poet of the Second World War.[29] Hamish's *Elegies* as well as his war songs

---

[26] Corey Gibson, *Endless Flyting*, p.2.

[27] See also Corey Gibson, 'In the Midst of our Human Civil War: Hamish Henderson's War Poetry and Soldier's Songs', *Studies in Scottish Literature*, vol.40, issue 1 (2014), pp.146-166.

[28] Roderick Watson, '"Death's Proletariat": Scottish Poets of the Second World War', in Tim Kendall (ed.), *The Oxford Handbook of British and Irish War Poetry*, Oxford: Oxford University Press, 2009, pp.315-339.

[29] Douglas Gifford, 'Literature and World War Two', in Ian Brown and Alan Riach (eds), *The Edinburgh Companion to Twentieth-Century Scottish Literature*, Edinburgh: Edinburgh University Press, 2009, pp.94-95.

'came out of grim direct knowledge of that war which had to be fought, as well as deep disgust at later, colonial wars which did *not* have to be.'[30] Ray Burnett sums up Hamish's achievement in the words:

> The primacy of the moment was the utter necessity to defeat fascism. But in this struggle of total war, a profound sense of the human had to be retained if humanity itself was not to be consumed by it. Not least there was a need to retain an enduring commitment to the removal of want, injustice and inequality as the prize they were fighting for.[31]

Folk-collecting and song-writing are also being focused on in this section. Ewan McVicar, already established as an expert on Alan Lomax's collecting, gives a critical guided tour of Lomax's recordings of Hamish Henderson which are now all available online. Very apt, as 2015 marks the hundredth anniversary of the birth of both Alan Lomax and Ewan McColl. He makes some important annotations and corrections – alas, one anent the photo we used for the cover of *'Tis Sixty Years Since* and which, he persuasively argues, is falsely dated to 1951. Alison McMorland and Geordie McIntyre give insights into the evolution of the 'Underground of Song', reminding us of the ambiguity of that term – the fact that folk song often has been 'submerged', even threatened in its existence, but that it also has been and remains 'the music of the people', in the Gramscian sense, the voice of the subaltern. Their conversation shows what Hamish meant when he said:

> 'But what on earth are you going to do with all this stuff once you've collected it?' comes a parting shot from the opposite camp. The answer is: give it back to the Scottish people who made it.[32]

---

[30] Stephen Howe, 'Dying for Empire, Blair, or Scotland?', *The Guardian*, Open Democracy, 12 November 2004, <www.opendemocracy.net/conflict-iraqwarafter/article_2223.jsp>.

[31] Ray Burnett 'Man of the Folk', *Scottish Review of Books*, vol.3, issue 4, 2007.

[32] Hamish Henderson, 'Enemies of Folk-song' [1955], in Hamish Henderson, *Alias MacAlias: Writings on Songs, Folk and Literature*, edited by Alec Finlay, Edinburgh: Birlinn/Polygon, 1992, p.50.

In his discussion of the 'flytings' between Hamish Henderson and Hugh MacDiarmid in the letters pages of the *Scotsman* in the early 1960s, Raymond Ross (who in 2000 edited and published Hamish's *Collected Poems and Songs*), pitches Hamish's 'humanitarianism' against MacDiarmid's 'elitism', following on from a piece he contributed to Joy Hendry's *Chapman* twenty years ago.[33] Margaret Bennett reminds us in her transcription on the pioneering collaboration between Hamish and her son Martyn Bennett – which also comes up in Archie Fisher's interview with Hamish later in this volume.

The politics of Hamish and his lifelong interests in Ireland and in the struggle against apartheid in South Africa are foregrounded in the next section of the book. Ray Burnett corrects some misrepresentations in Tim Neat's biography in his contribution, while I try to trace Hamish's engagement with Irish culture and politics as well as his role in fighting apartheid and for the freedom of Nelson Mandela.[34]

That Hamish continues to inspire is not just evident from the reminiscences of Sheena Wellington and Dolina Maclennan. We have included in this volume a number of poems – some of them directly addressed at Hamish, as in the poems of David Daiches,[35] Donald Smith and Willie Hershaw, others about him, like Mario Relich's and Donald Meek's. When Alison McMorland mentioned to George Gunn that Hamish Henderson was, for her, 'the bones of Scotland', it inspired him to write the present poem in the run-up to the Scottish independence referendum. Keith Armstrong's poems are more loosely connected to Hamish Henderson and the poetic scene of Edinburgh – but, as a performing poet, Keith is an example of what Edwin Morgan called the 'links between the folk revival and the spread of poetry-readings, a link of per-

---

33 Raymond Ross, 'Hamish Henderson: In the Midst of Things', *Chapman*, 42 (1985), pp. 11-18.

34 It has recently been announced that Nelson Mandela will be honoured with a lasting memorial in the new St James development in Edinburgh. See Brian Donnelly, 'Site for permanent memorial to Nelson Mandela in Edinburgh revealed as St James development', *The Herald*, 19 March 2015.

35 Thanks to Owen Dudley Edwards for pointing me in the direction of this little gem.

formance, of a sense of the public…'[36] He thought that Hamish Henderson's folk-poems were a bridge that brought poetry and song closer together, and had an effect on poetry:

> The poem is jumping off the printed page into the gramophone record and the concert hall, and with it goes the poet. Performance – the poet's voice – becomes significant instead of being a mere curiosity. The concept of a living and reacting audience revives. Qualities weakened for centuries – vibrance and warmth, immediacy, tonal indication, subtlety of emphasis – are being regained … this is life entering again through the ear.[37]

At the opening of the Scottish Parliament to Sheena Wellington's memorable rendition 'A Man's A Man for a' That', wrote Ray Burnett,

> the spirit and the 'voice' of Henderson was there alongside Burns. At every gathering against wars, injustice and inequality, every celebration of Scotland's national culture, the songs he composed, the old songs he recovered and the new songs he inspired can always be heard.[38]

Hamish's inspirational power can also be seen in the art work that peppers this volume, from the cover painting by Timothy Neat – and his sketches of the young and the dying Hamish – and Tom Hubbard's frontispiece portrait to fellow Fifer Jan Miller's drawings and the paper cuts and calligraphy of Howard Glasser.

The book closes on a handful of interviews with and about Hamish Henderson. They cover the 1960s, '70s, '80s and '90s. All but Margaret Bennett with Howard Glasser's and Archie Fisher's 'Travelling Folk' interview have been previously published, but we thought it might be handy to have them together in one

---

[36] Edwin Morgan, 'Letter to Alec Finlay, poet and publisher', 31 January 1995, in Edwin Morgan, *The Midnight Letterbox: Selected Correspondence, 1950-2010*, edited by James McGonigal and John Coyle, Manchester: Carcanet, 2015, p.406.

[37] Edwin Morgan, quoted in Robert Alan Jamieson, 'In memoriam Edwin Morgan (1920-2010)', *Bella Caledonia*, 23 August 2010.

[38] Ray Burnett 'Man of the Folk'.

volume. There are overlaps, but they are also complementary, all illuminating different aspects of Hamish's life and work.

When talking about his interview with Hamish, Archie Fisher told me that he gave Hamish a lift afterwards from the BBC's Edinburgh Queen Street studio to Sandy Bell's in his Landrover:

> 'Why a Landrover, Archie?' asked Hamish. 'It's for the horse trailer,' I said. 'Last time I sat on a horse, I had requisitioned it from a German general.' Top man, Hamish!

The book ends as it starts, with fond reminiscences about Hamish. In between, there is what we hope will read as an exciting journey, with some new discoveries, and incentive for further research.

With Sheila Stewart and Jean Redpath, the Scottish folk scene lost two of the great voices of the Scottish Folk Revival last year – both good friends of Hamish Henderson's. We were lucky to have Sheila Stewart giving the Hamish Henderson Lecture at the Carrying Stream Festival in 2010.[39] She was also part of the 60th anniversary celebration of the first Edinburgh People's Festival Ceilidh in 2011, organised by Edinburgh Folk Club. Unfortunately, our invitation to Jean Redpath to give the lecture was to late. In 2012, Jean felt she could, for health reasons, not commit to attending the Carrying Stream Festival. It is a small consolation to have heard her sing at the 2011 festival. We dedicate this volume to the memory of these two fine tradition bearers, who bore testament to Ray Burnett's dictum: 'Wherever Scotland comes together in music and song, Henderson is there.'[40]

---

[39] Sheila Stewart, 'Hamish Henderson: A Traveller's Tale', in Eberhard Bort (ed.), *Borne on the Carrying Stream*, pp.46-52.

[40] Ray Burnett 'Man of the Folk'.

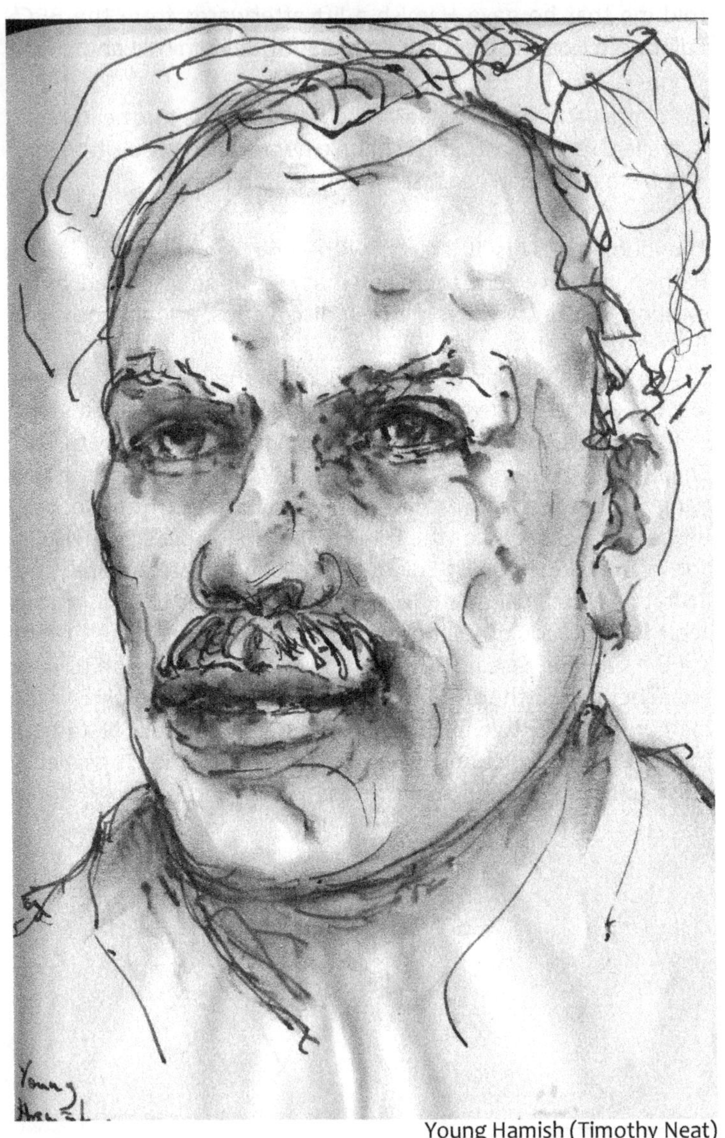

Young Hamish (Timothy Neat)

Essays

- Reminiscences
- Poetry
- Folk-Song
- Culture and Politics

Dolina Maclennan at the City Chambers, 2014 (photo: Allan McMillan)

Sheena Wellington at the City Chambers, 2014 (photo: Allan McMillan)

Hamish Henderson – Inspiration

Sheena Wellington

Thank you Edinburgh Folk Club for inviting me to pay tribute to someone who was hugely influential in my life, although my friendship with him was of fairly short duration. It was just the last twenty years or so of his life that I knew him as an advisor, a supporter, as an encourager and inspirer and a friend, but he dropped in and out of my life as a personality long before.[1]

I First Encounters

I can recall the first time his name registered with me and where I was. Well, when I say where I was, it was somewhere between Dundee and Glasgow, or Glasgow and Dundee to be precise. But I like to put Dundee first! I was on my way home with the rest of the Young Socialists and members of the Labour Party and CND Dundee from a CND demo in Glasgow. It was in 1961 and quite late in the year, because we had overcoats on which made sitting on a crate in the back of the van even less comfortable than it might have been. But, we were singing, as you did in those days, all the songs of the day, when the driver of the Corporation van we had 'borrowed' for the weekends suddenly began 'Roch the wind in the clear day's dawin'...

Now, whether it was the tune, or the language or his voice or the fact that I was high as a kite on the adrenaline of my first 'real' demo, the song hit me in a way that few songs have done, before or since, and I demanded to hear it again and again. For the rest of the weekend, I sang the first verse, which I had managed to pick up, over and over, driving my father to say, 'It's a fantastic song but it must have more than one verse.' And it occurs to me that I never did settle down to learn 'Freedom Come-All-Ye', just absorbed it in that wonderful traditional osmosis.

---

[1] This is a slightly revised and edited version of the Hamish Henderson Memorial Lecture held at the City Chambers at the 12th Carrying Stream Festival on 9 November 2013.

The driver had said to me, 'It was written by Hamish Henderson, great man, great Scotsman, he's the School of Scottish Studies in Edinburgh.' Not, note, that he is *in* the School of Scottish Studies, or that he works *at* the School of Scottish Studies, it was 'he is the School of Scottish Studies!'

I was still at school, of course, studying for my Higher English exam, and my English teacher at the time was Miss Dunbar, younger and much more approachable than most of the teachers we had. I told her about the song and ventured to ask if she had heard of this poet Hamish Henderson.

She had, and admired his work greatly. My reply, of course, should have been to ask why we did not learn about him in school. Apart from the obligatory Robert Burns, in January, and for the Leng Medal, Walter Scott's *The Lay of the Last Minstrel* and Stevenson's *A Child's Garden of Verses*, Scottish poetry, as far as school was concerned, was non-existent.

Miss Dunbar had a copy of the *Elegies for the Dead in Cyrenaica*[2] and very generously lent it to me. She was an English teacher with degrees and everything, and I was a lassie from Lochee, so it was a generous act! I took the book home and read:

First Elegy

End of a Campaign

There are many dead in the brutish desert,
who lie uneasy
among the scrub in this landscape of half-wit
stunted ill-will. For the dead land is insatiate
and necrophilious. The sand is blowing about still.
Many who for various reasons, or because
of mere unanswerable compulsion, came
here
and fought among the clutching gravestones,
shivered and sweated,
cried out, suffered thirst, were stoically silent,
cursed

[2] Hamish Henderson, *Elegies for the Dead in Cyrenaica*, London: John Lehmann, 1948; republished by EUSPB in 1977 (with an introduction by Sorley MacLean), and by Polygon in 1990, 2008.

the spittering machine-guns, were homesick for
Europe
and fast embedded in quicksand of Africa
agonized and died.
And sleep now. Sleep here the sleep of the dust.[3]

And that first stanza of the first Elegy reduced me to weeping where I sat because we had 'done' the War poets. We had 'done' Wilfred Owen, Siegfried Sassoon and, God help us all, Rupert Brooke. We had not, and it has annoyed me to this day, done Joseph Lee, the Dundee-born poet who in the day was considered on a par with them.[4] But we had nothing that seemed to be Scottish apart from songs my father and my uncles and their friends sang.

Have you heard of a place called Benghazi
Where most of the fighting was done
It was there that a poor Scottish laddie
Was killed by an old Eyetie[5] gun.

As he lay on the battlefield dying
The blood from his wounds flowing red
He raised himself up on his elbow
And turned to his comrades and said

'Oh bury me out in the desert
My duty for Scotland I've done.
Oh bury me out in the desert
Under the Libyan sun.'[6]

---

[3] Hamish Henderson, *Collected Poems and Songs*, ed. by Raymond Ross, Edinburgh: Curly Snake, 2000, p.52.

[4] See Frank Urquhart, 'Tribute to "forgotten" Scots war poet', *The Scotsman*, 12 November 2005; and Steven Brocklehurst, 'Joseph Lee: Dundee's forgotten war poet', *BBC News Scotland*, 9 July 2014 <www.bbc.co.uk/news/uk-scotland-27602625>.

[5] Eyetie was the common slang name for Italian.

[6] A Scottish version of 'Under the Libyan Sun' by George Smith. Ewan MacColl recorded a version of this as 'The Dying Soldier' on *Bundook Ballads* (Topic TSDL130, 1965).

And, of course, my two uncles who had been in North Africa, Sicily and Italy sang the 'Ballad of the D-Day Dodgers' and, though they did not always sing Hamish's text – and I cannot repeat some of the words they did sing in this respectable Edinburgh establishment – I am pleased to realise that I have had at least a tenuous connection with Hamish since my infancy.

And they had a song which touched on the events of June 1940 when so many of the Highland Division were captured and only a few of the wounded escaped. I looked for a recorded version of this for years. A few years ago I was cataloguing for the *Kist o Riches* and found that Hamish had recorded this.

Down by St Valery (3'43")

That night on the clifftops we'll never forget
As we lay on the ground and it was soaking wet
And we were surrounded with tanks and guns
Down by the silvery sea.

With their planes high above us kept dropping their bombs
While we on the ground kept on singing our songs
They thought they had got us but they were wrong
Down by St Valery.

Then way across the sea we spied the boys in blue coming to let us free
The debt that we owe them we'll never repay
and we'll talk o'er those heroes for many's a day
Each night in our prayers, we'll always say
God bless the boys in blue.

We lost many comrades on that fatal night
And when all seemed lost we then signalled a light
To the boys of the Navy out on the sea
Down by St Valery.

But now we're back once more and we'll never forget
the boys who keep guard on the sea

Good luck to the Navy those heroes in blue,
here's a toast that we drink in the honour of you
For you cheered us up when we were blue
Down at St Valery.[7]

The singer is a traveller called Andrew Stewart who was himself rescued, wounded, from St Valery, and who co-wrote the lyrics. I got quite annoyed when I was cataloguing it by a comment from someone who had looked at it before that the song was 'sentimental'! I think if you are lying there injured, with the Wehrmacht at the door, the Luftwaffe bombing the hell out of you, and the Navy is fighting and doing its best to rescue you – you are entitled to feel a bit sentimental about them.

But the *Elegies* revealed to me that there were still people in Scotland who wrote poetry of a kind which was powerful and challenging, and though the *Elegies* are not written in Scots for the most part, I felt then, and feel now, that the thought and the cadences have a very distinctive Scots sensibility, and I warmed immensely to it:

Interlude

We'll mak siccar!
Against the bashing cudgel
against the contemptuous triumphs of the big
battalions
mak siccar against the monkish adepts
of total war against the oppressed oppressors
mak siccar against the leaching lies
against the worked out systems of sick perversions
mak siccar
against the executioner
against the tyrannous myth an the real terror
mak siccar[8]

I had found modern poetry from Scotland, and it was a wonderful thing for a seventeen year old to discover. I could not afford to buy

[7] See <www.tobarandualchais.co.uk/en/fullrecord/31630/5;jsessionid=D18B1F6275087C509B9D5FAFAAD88AB3>

[8] *Collected Poems and Songs*, p.61.

the book, even if I could have found it, so I copied several poems from Miss Dunbar's copy. I was spotted carrying it by the head of the English department, a man whose voice could make the finest work of Shakespeare sound like an order for bread. His dismissive 'Henderson, Hamish Henderson, like that reprobate McDiarmid fellow, another Communist agitator and versifier.' Oooh – who is this McDiarmid? I was off to the library in search of McDiarmid, and I found him and a treasure trove – Sydney Goodsir Smith, Violet Jacob, Helen Cruikshank, Marion Angus, Sorley MacLean – and all inspired by 'finding' Hamish Henderson!

If I had not heard that wonderful song I would not have found Jeannie Robertson, because I went round to the house of the friend who sang it to listen to this record which had come over from America:

Jeannie Robertson – The 4 Maries

Yestreen there was four Marys
This night there's only three
There was Mary Seton and Mary Beaton
And Mary Carmichael and me

A knock come to the kitchen door
It sounded through a the room
That Mary Hamilton had a wean
Tae the highest man in the toon

Where is that wean you had last night
Where is that wean, I say
I hadnae a wean tae you, last nicht
Nor yet a wean today.

But they searched high and they searched low
An they searched below the bed
And there he found his ain wee wean
It wis lying in a pool o blood.

Yestreen there was four Marys
This night there's only three

There was Mary Seton and Mary Beaton
And Mary Carmichael and me

O little did my mither ken,
The day she cradled me
The lands I was to traivel in
Or the daith I wis tae dee

For aftimes hae I dressed my queen
An pit gowd in her hair
But little I got for my reward
The gallows tae be my share

O happy, happy is the maid
That's born o beauty free
It was my dimpling rosy cheeks
That's been the daith o me.

Yestreen there was four Marys
This night there's only three
There was Mary Seton and Mary Beaton
And Mary Carmichael and me.[9]

It is a stunning, outstanding, amazing version. It struck me because, though it was not really like my granny's voice, it was the way my granny sang. And it was a song I knew, having had the awfully twee version you get at school and having heard it played as a waltz at the Scottish country dances. Suddenly there was this power and there was the real story and I thought 'God, I need to find out more about this woman and if there are other people who sing like this.' And, you know, five decades, and more, now I have been kicking myself mentally because Jeannie Robertson actually sang in the Art Gallery in Dundee's Albert Institute in July 1961. She was brought there by Maurice Fleming and there was also Belle Stewart, Sheila Stewart, Alex Stewart, Charlotte Higgins – and I was down at the Caird Hall watching a gymnastics show. They were both part of the city's Civic Week and my father had free tickets through his work for the gymnastics. It was recorded

[9] *The Folk Songs of Britain*, Vol 5 – The Child Ballads (Topic TC 1146, 1961).

and I think it is online. One of these days I shall write a book entitled *Opportunities I have Missed* or *Open Doors I Have Decided Not To Walk Through*.

So after all this, I got involved in traditional music and the driver of the van said to me 'There's a few of us going to meet in the union rooms at Bain's Square for some singing.' So I went there and that was my introduction to folk clubs. Then we moved to the York House and then the excitement of everyone clambering on the bus to go to the Woodlands in Barnhill. But life happened, things happened, I went off to see the world and ended up in Lossiemouth, but I kept in touch.

So how did I eventually meet this man, this towering figure in my imagination? Well, it was Auchtermuchty festival, either 1982 or '83. It was the one and only time that I entered a TMSA competition and I came second, but when I tell you the winner was Maureen Jelks you will understand why I was still chuffed! Hamish was in the audience, which made me very nervous. I was in the Square later when he came up to me, grabbed me in one of those bear hugs and said, 'Sheena, dear Sheena, your Sheath and Knife! Wonderful!' I nearly fainted with the shock and the honour.

My two most vivid memories of Hamish were also at Auchtermuchty. The first, a sad one, was when we were in the middle of a session at the Cycle Tavern and Hamish burst in, distraught. Betsy Whyte, the great storyteller and ballad singer, had been found dead in her bed in her caravan. We were all shocked – I had spoken to her in the morning and she had been fine. We serenaded her with a gentle 'Yellow on the Broom'.

The other is happier. My son Michael was wee at the time and he loved Auchtermuchty, the music, the freedom, rampaging round with his friends! We happened to be staying in the same guest house as Hamish. I was putting Michael to bed, it was about one in the morning, and the wee monkey was still not ready for sleep. Eventually, I got him tucked in, then I heard a strange rumbling sound. I opened the door and looked over the balcony. One of the things Michael had been really excited about was the household's two dogs, an Alsatian and a Labrador cross, beautiful, big, good natured beasts. And there was Hamish and the dogs and he was declaiming to them Burns's 'The Twa Dugs'. So I thought 'Oh, this is historical!,' got the bairn out of bed, having just got him bedded down, and said 'You must see this, you will remember it forever.'

When he was coming to the end of the poem I whipped Michael back into the bedroom for, if Hamish had spotted us, it would have been 'Ah, let's have a dram and a song' and I was not ready for that! We both got into bed and a couple of minutes later it was 'Mum?', 'Yes, darling?' 'Hamish was reciting poetry to these two dogs!' 'Yes, I know, darling.' 'Mum!', 'Yes, darling?' 'The dogs were listening!' It is a memory that has stayed with both of us, and we often talk of it and smile.

II Radio Tay

I had by this time started to work for Radio Tay. We worry now about how much spying on our activities goes on but we tend to forget just how heavy handed the State could be in Thatcher's Britain. I am sure most of you remember Sarah Tisdell, the civil servant who leaked details to the *Guardian* of the arrival of Cruise Missiles in the UK. *The Guardian* gave the photocopies back to the authorities, enabling her to be identified and she was jailed for six months. I have not bought the *Guardian* since but if the editor gets jailed over the Snowden affair I will.

The Independent Broadcasting Authority was a bunch of Nervous Nellies and we were forever getting directives on what we could and could not play. The IRA was suddenly banned from being on the airwaves, their words having to be read by an actor. Its main usefulness was to give a number of Irish actors quite a good income for quite a few years! The week it was announced, we had a memo telling us to be careful when playing Irish songs so, of course, I started my programme with 'The Wearing of the Green'!

> Oh, Paddy dear, and did you hear the news that's
> going round
> The shamrock is by law forbid to grow on Irish
> ground.[10]

A fair number of my listeners enjoyed that little joke, but the station's Board members missed it.

'Victor Jara of Chile' is a lovely song with words by Adrian Mitchell, set to a tune by Arlo Guthrie. One evening I played it, dedicating it to the memory of Victor Jara, and it caused no

---

[10] Dion Boucicault, 'The Wearing of the Green' (1864), in his play *Arragh na Pogue*, London: Methuen, 2010.

comment from the Board. A couple of weeks later I played an Inti Illimani track and remarked that luckily they had been out of the country touring in Europe when the coup happened in Chile, otherwise they probably would have suffered the fate of Victor Jara who was murdered by the Junta. All hell broke loose! A Board member had complained about my political stance and I was severely reprimanded.

I met Hamish at an event shortly after and told him about it. 'It's never wrong to tell the truth, Sheena!' – Them's my sentiments, too!

Peter Wright, and the Spycatcher business, also caused a stir. This exposal of MI5 dirty tricks by a former operative was published in Australia. An injunction was taken out, banning publication in England, but they forgot to try to get an interim interdict to ban it in Scotland. I went into Radio Tay clutching the single of Leon Rosselson's wonderful 'Ballad of a Spycatcher'[11] which had arrived that morning to find a notice in my pigeonhole saying it was absolutely forbidden to play the song. No problem, I flipped it over, played the other side – I remember it was 'I Heard It On The Radio' (but it was actually called 'Song of the Free Press') – and said that I could not play 'Ballad of a Spycatcher' which was on the other side.[12] Next morning I had a phone call from Allan MacKenzie, Radio Tay manager and real radio man, who told me that he had just had a visit from a couple of IBA representatives, and an unidentified man in a suit, telling him that by mentioning 'Ballad of a Spycatcher' I had acted in contempt of court. Allan pointed out to them how stupid they would look if they charged me, especially as the book was on open sale in the town. I heard no more about it, but the story tickled Hamish enormously.

III The Spirit of Scotland

When I was asked in 1999 to sing at the Opening of the Scottish Parliament I was delighted and honoured. Hamish was delighted for me, but I was outraged that he, one of our greatest living cultural figures, was among the

[11] First published in the *New Statesman* on 7 August 1987.

[12] Upside Down Records UPDO 007 (single, UK, 1987). Leon Rosselson was backed by Billy Bragg and the Oyster Band, and the record was sponsored by the Campaign for Press and Broadcasting Freedom.

distinguished citizens not invited when several half-baked celebs and people who were disparaging of the whole idea were. I did seriously consider withdrawing from the event in protest, and it was Hamish himself who persuaded me to sing. 'Sheena, I don't matter in this. I'll be watching you on the television and be with you. I just want you to remember that you are representing something that's greater than me and greater than you. You are singing for the spirit of Scotland!'

So many memories, such a wealth of knowledge so generously shared. Hamish was, in every sense of the word, that larger than life character. Thank you for asking me to share my thoughts on Hamish Henderson – let's give him the last word:

The 51st Highland Division's Farewell To Sicily

The pipie is dozie, the pipie is fey,
He winna come roon' for his vino the day,
The sky ow'r Messina is unco an' grey,
  An' a' the bricht chaulmers are eerie.

Then fare weel ye banks o Sicily,
Fare ye weel ye valley and shaw.
There's nae Jock will mourn the kyles o' ye,
  Puir bliddy swaddies are wearie

Fare weel, ye banks o' Sicily,
Fare ye weel, ye valley and shaw
There's nae hame can smoor the wiles o' ye,
  Puir bliddy swaddies are wearie

Then doon the stair and line the waterside,
Wait your turn, the ferry's awa',
Then doon the stair and line the waterside,
  A' the bricht chaulmers are eerie

The drummie is polisht, the drummie is braw
He cannae be seen for his webbin' ava.
He's beezed himsel' up for a photy an a'
  Tae leave wi' his Lola, his dearie.

Sae fare weel, ye dives o' Sicily
(Fare ye weel, ye shieling an' ha'),
We'll a' mind shebeens and bothies
  Whaur kind signorinas were cheerie.

Fare weel, ye banks o' Sicily
(Fare ye weel, ye shieling an' ha'),
We'll a' mind shebeens and bothies
  Whaur Jock made a date wi' his dearie.

Then tune the pipes and drub the tenor drum
(Leave your kit this side o' the wa'),
Then tune the pipes and drub the tenor drum
  A' the bricht chaulmers are eerie[13]

[13] *Collected Poems and Songs*, pp.84-85.

Hamish – Ma Big Pal

Dolina Maclennan

Meeting Hamish

It all happened in 1958.[1] I had come to Edinburgh in 1957 to start occupational therapy. In April, I was invited to a dance outside Edinburgh by a second-year medical student. My sister had bought me an amazing frock, and I was looking forward to the ball. But then the castle actually turned out to be a ruin – Rosslyn Castle. There I was in my white frock and my flowers. Everyone wore casual trousers and sat around on bales of straw or hay. I felt like a real twit. The medic had never told me. I left him there, never to be seen again, and just jumped on a bus back into town.

That same evening, my friend Christine Fletcher from Stornaway had been invited to a party in Leamington Terrace in the posh West End of Edinburgh, in the house of Robin Scott-Moffat, a well-known man about town and part of the Edinburgh social scene. And there was everybody. It was wonderful.

We had not been there long when a dental student came into the kitchen and asked if anyone could sing. Christine said 'Doli sings,' and the lad said 'Come on – and sing!' I did, and he cried 'Stop! Don't do anything more till I get MacGregor.' Shortly after, this guy Stuart MacGregor came into the kitchen, hair hanging over his eye as usual. I sang again, and this time I got a few verses out, before he said 'For God's sake, don't let Henderson get a hold of her!' Promptly, another big fellow came in. 'Who is she?,' he inquired and gave me a big hug. That's how I first met Hamish

---

[1] This is a revised version of Dolina Maclennan's Hamish Henderson Memorial Lecture, delivered during the 13th Carrying Stream Festival at the Edinburgh City Chambers on 8 November 2014. Her memoir, *Dolina: An Island Girl's Journey* (Islands Book Trust), based on conversations with Stuart Eydman and Jim Gilchrist, was also launched during Carrying Stream 2014.

Henderson. Within a week I was in the School of Scottish Studies recording everything I knew.

I became the sort of *pet* of the new folk music scene in Edinburgh, largely because of my youth, my innocence and because I may have represented something authentic and of another world. Hamish Henderson told his biographer that he recalled me arriving 'like a shepherdess, trailing these songs of gold from ancient times.'[2]

Edinburgh University Folk Song Society

That very night of our first meeting, Stuart MacGregor and Hamish had inaugurated the Edinburgh University Folk Song Society. It was soon to become a riot of hectic activity. A year later it had over a hundred members, and I was singing along with the likes of Robin Gray and Ella Ward. When Stuart was called up on National Service, I succeeded him as President and was looking to generate further interest. I remember scouring the Common Room in the University's Old College and finding out what country the students came from. I got them all together for an evening and they sang their own countries' songs. That was the first ever international folksong concert in Edinburgh, a forerunner of similar concerts which would become quite common later.

That was back in 1959. Then one night a new girl turned up and sang. In my notebook of those days, which I recently re-discovered, I recorded 'New girl, Jean Redpath ... sounds promising.' Patronising bitch that I was! Jean was very shy, having just come over from Leven in Fife. Those were the days, when Robin Gray and I became the first pub-singers in Edinburgh, upstairs in the Waverley Bar. At the same time, Roy Guest ran the Howff folk club at 369 High Street. Bert Jansch had started playing there as a fourteen-year old.

Hamish was so supportive of the Folk Song Society, attending every meeting and introducing and encouraging new members, even some of dubious talent – but that was his way.

Also in 1959, Hamish and I were involved bringing folk to the Edinburgh Festival Fringe, featuring Jeannie Robertson and a

---

[2] Timothy Neat, *Hamish Henderson: A Biography vol. 2 Poetry Becomes People (1952-2002)*, Edinburgh: Polygon/Birlinn, 2009, p.127.

very young Robin Hall (who would later go on to form the widely renowned duo with Jimmie Macgregor).

In 1963 Hamish and I took part in the award-winning documentary *Songs for Scotland*, made for Films of Scotland by directors Laurence Henson and Edward McConnell, in which we sang 'Bonnie Lassie I'll Lie Near Ye' in Scots. It was filmed in the bar of the old Habbie's Howe at Nine Mile Burn at the foot of the Pentlands, with a lively audience joining in the chorus. Hamish and I also appeared in Robert Peter Hertwig's *Die Armee des Duke*, a German film, along with Jeannie Robertson, Jimmy McBeath, Andy Hunter and the Royal Scottish Country Dance Society.

Hamish's Letters

Over the years, I received many letters from Hamish Henderson, on all sorts of subjects. On 28 December 1959 I received a missive addressed to Birniestrasse in Lochgelly:

> Liebe Dolina!
>
> As you see, Kätzel and I are spending the Festive Season in Germany – Christmas here is very nice (it ought to be, as the Germans practically invented it!)
>
> Many thanks for the notes on the songs – when I get back to Auld Reekie, I'll play-back, edit (if nec.), annotate and dispatch the whole clanjamfrie. Meanwhile I've written to Alan Mills, telling him to get ready to receive a direct hit from the Lewis secret weapon... I've also told him to get good terms for you from Mo Asch of "FOLKways". So keep your fingers crossed.
>
> It's very nice of you to say that the Deilidh Caly was 'a good night! Personally I find it rather wearing ... Luckily, the real ceilidh in Lawrence's house later (which went on till about 5 a. m.) was the exact opposite – the thing really began to warm up. There was plenty of booze, and both Kätzel and the Irish cailin not only began to thaw perceptibly, but were shortly singing like linties – of one thing I'm 100% certain, and that is that no 'ceilidh' which bears the remotest relation to the real thing can ever be held in a hall where TV has reared its ugly head, and opened its blotchy eye! ... We'll know better the next time.

Two nights ago a bull-calf was born on the farm – as his mother's name is Hedwig, and it's the practice to give the calf a name with the same initial, I've a shrewd idea that my name is being taken in vain across in the stable every now and then.... Sssh! I think I hear an indignant juvenile bellow!

Love, Dolly,
and all best wishes for 1960!
Slàinte Mhor
Hamish (and Kätzel)

There were great celebrations earlier in 1959 when Hamish and Kätzel came back from their wedding in Germany – and their home in Melville Terrace was welcoming and hospitable to all. I once spent Christmas with them. It was on Christmas Eve that they exchanged presents, and we had raw herring and beetroot, which was a traditional German dish. The neighbour came in on Christmas Day, and that was another new experience for me, never having really celebrated Christmas at home apart from hanging up your stockings.

When, after a sojourn in Fife, I came back to Edinburgh I stayed with Hamish and Kätzel for a few weeks (where I was first introduced to the concept of 'Federbetten'). Through Hamish I had met an American called Bobby Botsford who was part of the scene and a great friend of Hamish's. He had a flat at 19 Bristo Place, above Napier's the herbalist. I was gong to have the use of the flat. But I stayed with Hamish because Roy Guest (of Howff fame) was still staying there.

Hamish and Kätzel were keen for me to stay with them as long as possible but I wanted to get into my own flat – Bobby's flat. After all, I paid the rent for it, not to Bobby, but to an agency he had looking after it – all above board.

I went over one lunchtime and there was a fire engine there outside and lots of burning rubbish. It wasn't the first fire-raising incident. Everybody thought that someone with a grievance at Roy Guest must have been behind it. But it eventually transpired that it wasn't that at all. Hamish recalled the tale more than a decade later in the *Sandy Bell's Broadsheet* of 16 March 1974:

After lunch Dolly and I decided to go and have a clear look at the ruin and (fortifying ourselves with a drink or two on the way) we returned to Bristo Place, passed the smouldering wreckage on the pavement and started to climb the stair.

On the way up we met Donny MacDonald, a policeman from near Oban, who was coming down. Dolly said, 'So they've got it at last,' and the bold Donny replied, 'It's not yours this time!'

And right enough, we found upstairs that Dolly's flat was untouched – the smoking ruin was the flat opposite!

The door was wide open, and inside we could see two policemen taking a statement from the inmate, an old woman. And then it all came out.

The fire-raiser, in all cases, had been this same old screwball who lived across the way. Hopelessly behind with the rent, she had got the idea into her head that she might be able to move into Roy's flat when it was empty, and seeing it occupied by what she took to be a tribe of hirsute, glazed-eyed hippies, she hit on the idea of scaring them out by fire-raising.

Finally, realising that the new inmate was resolved to hold the fort, she had made the best of a bad job and set fire to her own flat – the interior looked like something out of the blitz: hundreds of old jam jars, opened tins, empty milk bottles and miscellaneous hoarded paraphernalia of every description. In the middle of the floor of the living room lay four partly burned car tyres.

In a later issue of *Sandy Bell's Broadsheet*, Hamish would describe these and other goings-on at the Bristo Place flat as 'a mixture of Grand Guignol, the Marx Brothers and Edgar Allan Poe.'

Other shenanigans were going on in the early 1960s, sparking some verbal fireworks. The letter-pages of the *Scotsman* were full of the folk-song flyting between Hamish Henderson and Hugh MacDiarmid. The letters have been published in *The Armstrong Nose* but, just to give you a flavour, here are a few samples. MacDiarmid called folksong 'doggerel and mediocre versifying' and moaned: 'I for one have been bored to death listening to [folksong], including the renderings of Jeannie Robertson, Jimmy MacBeath, and others…' Hamish countered that he had no doubt 'that we are again in a period when folksong and art-poetry can interact fruitfully' and accused MacDiarmid of being 'ignorant'. MacDiarmid insists that folksong amounts to not much more than 'the simple outpourings of illiterate and backward peasants.' Hamish sees MacDiarmid's attacks on 'the people of his country's past' as representing an 'anti-humanist strain' in the poet's thinking.[3]

The whole thing came to a climax at the Traverse Theatre on 13 April 1964. The arena was set – Hugh MacDiarmid and Norman MacCaig on one side, and Hamish and the Marxist critic David Craig on the other. I was of course on Hamish's side. But don't ask me who won – I cannot remember. Craig gave this account to Tim Neat:

> MacDiarmid was a good debater, and McCaig had any amount of *savoir-faire* – tall, handsome, speaking slowly with great poise and clarity of expression. They thought on their feet. Hamish did well enough but, even with Jeannie Robertson there, to sing for our side, we landed no *coup de grâce*. As soon as the debate was over, a newspaper man came up to me and said, 'You boys had the best ideas, but they had the best speakers.' As far as speaking went, they won – on points – and I did feel crestfallen afterwards.[4]

The Dead, The Innocent

After having been expelled from Italy by the right-wing government in October 1950, Hamish had not been back in Italy until the BBC's Keith Alexander (Head of Arts programmes) invited Hamish to get involved into a major film about himself and his war experience. In January 1979, Hamish flew to Rome, and from there onwards to Egypt. From the Shepheard's Hotel in Cairo he wrote to me and my husband George on 16 January 1979:

> Dear George and Dolly,
>
> I've been having a marvellous time – the filming went very well in Rome and Sicily, and tomorrow we're going into the Western Desert to 'do' the Elegies. It's all a kind of a dream!
>
> I couldn't resist sending you this on Shepheard's note-paper because of the Latin inscription which says 'He who

[3] Hamish Henderson, *The Armstrong Nose: Selected Letters of Hamish Hendrson*, edited by Alec Finlay, Edinburgh: Polygon, 1996, pp.117-139.

[4] Tim Neat, vol.2, pp.152-153.

شركة الفنادق المصرية
THE EGYPTIAN HOTELS Co.

فندق شبرد
SHEPHEARD'S HOTEL

CAIRO 16. Jan. 79 القاهرة

Dear George and Dolly,

I've been having a marvellous time – the filming went very well in Rome and Sicily, and tomorrow we're going into the Western Desert to 'do' the Elegies. It's all a kind of dream!

I couldn't resist sending you this on Shepheard's note-paper because of the Latin inscription which says "He who drinks the water of the Nile will drink it again"!

In Sicily we found the little Highland Div war memorial which overlooks the battlefields of Sferro and Gerbini, with Etna towering up in the distance. A fantastic site! I doubt if many [illegible] people have seen it since it was erected in 1943.

Love to all

See you soon Hamish

ADDRESS : CORNISH EL NIL CAIRO - EGYPT - TELEX. 379 SHEPOT UN - CABLE : SHEPHEARD'S' CAIRO TELEPHONE : 33800 - 33900

Letter by Hamish Henderson to Dolina Maclennan and George Brown from Egypt, 16 January 1979

drinks the water of the Nile will drink it again'!

In Sicily we found the little Highland Div war memorial which overlooks the battlefields on Sferro and Gerbini, with Etna towering up in the distance. A fantastic site! I doubt if many other people have seen it since it was erected in 1943.

Love to all
See you soon
Hamish

But what had started as a dream soured somewhat in post-production. The main disagreement seemed to be about the title of the film. Keith Alexander wanted 'Keep Listening for Reveille' – similar to the last line in the Ninth Elegy. Hamish had set his heart and mind on 'The Dead, The Innocent' – the final words of the First Elegy. He sent me a copy of this pretty exasperated, terse letter which he sent to Keith Alexander on 25 February 1980:

Dear Keith,

This is just to let you know, in writing, that 'Keep Waiting for Revelle' is a totally absurd and unacceptable title for the film we have worked on together. Since you have attempted, in telephone conversations, to defend this crass nonsense, I see I have no alternative but to spell it out to you.

Soldiers in barracks or on active service do not <u>listen</u> for reveille. It bomb-blasts them into wakefulness. In my poem 'Fort Capuzzo', the line

Keep waiting for the angels. Keep listening for reveille has poignancy and irony precisely because it is spoken by a living soldier to one who is dead. The line foreshadows

o for ever
not sleeping but dead

in the 10th Elegy (The Frontier). It is part of an intricate palimpsest of allusions which I worked – and re-worked – many times.

There are other reasons why this title can only be regarded as an egregious lapse of taste. However, this one is enough and will do for the time being. Sufficient to say that if you used 'Keep Listening for Reveille' as the title for a programme which subsumes the Fosse Ardeatine, the victims of Auschwitz, the self-sacrifice of the partisans, and all the annihilated of 'history's great rains', you would without any doubt expose yourselves, the programme and me to ridicule.

Ten days ago I heard, more or less by accident, of this 'new' title (first mooted, as you now tell me, before Christmas); since then, not unnaturally, I have had more than one sleepless night. – Last night I had a troubled sleep and then a ghastly dream, in which I was mocked by the dead. – I doubt if all this is doing me any good.

At the beginning of last week I sent Jim Hunter a telegram requesting a time and place for discussion, and pre-paid his reply. A week later I have still heard nothing from him. This is not only a breach of common courtesy – it is also a breach of trust.

There is no way this programme can go out called 'Keep Listening for Reveille'. And if by any remote chance – and against all possible measures taken against it – it does so, I give you my word of honour that I shall use every means of publicity in my power, here and abroad, to make known the incredible way – the disgraceful and scandalous way – you and Hunter are treating a writer who has given you a fair amount of assistance in putting together a programme which is maybe not without a certain intrinsic interest.

Hamish Henderson

Hamish won the battle, and when the film was broadcast, he was widely congratulated on his and the film's achievement. Tim Neat quotes the Marxist critic Arnold Kettle ('... marvellous television programme. I found your evocation and testimony so moving...'), David Hammond from Belfast ('a marvellous occasion'), the Traveller Betsy White ('I could almost feel with you the deep emotions and nostalgia you felt on seeing those places again...'),[5] and Robert Garioch (who had himself experienced

[5] Tim Neat, vol.2, p.259.

desert warfare) wrote to Hamish praising 'a remarkably fine and unusual television programme.'[6]

Ninth Elegy

Fort Capuzzo

For there will come a day
when the Lord will say
– Close Order!

One evening, breaking a jeep journey at Capuzzo
I noticed a soldier as he entered the cemetery
and stood looking at the grave of a fallen enemy.
Then I understood the meaning of the hard word 'pietas'
(a word unfamiliar to the newsreel commentator
as well as to the pimp, the informer and the traitor).

His thought was like this. – Here's another 'Good Jerry'!
Poor mucker. Just eighteen. Must be hard-up for man-power.
Or else he volunteered, silly bastard. That's the fatal
the – fatal – mistake. Never volunteer for nothing.
I wonder how he died? Just as well it was him, though,
and not one of our chaps... Yes, the only good Jerry,
as they say, is your sort, chum.
        Cheerio, you poor bastard.
Don't be late on parade when the Lord calls 'Close Order'.
Keep waiting for the angels. Keep listening for Reveille.[7]

Sandy Bell's

Sandy Bell's was very important to us. The School of Scottish Studies and the Medical School were near, and Hamish and Stuart would be there. I had spent a convivial afternoon with Violet Williamson, the wife of Roy Williamson, in Sandy's, and

---

[6] Garioch letter to Hamish Henderson, dated 9 November 1980. *The Armstrong Nose*, p.236.

[7] Hamish Henderson, *Elegies for the Dead in Cyrenaica* (1948), Edinburgh: Polygon/Birlinn, 2008, p.47.

we stepped out into Forrest Road just before five o'clock. There were no cars around, and very few buses. In fact, at that moment the street was empty and in eerie silence. And there were Hamish and John MacInnes coming toward us, deep in conversation, both carrying their briefcases. 'Edinburgh is herself tonight,' Violet said. Isn't that beautiful? The two academics with their briefcases in an empty street...

Hamish took great interest in John McGrath's 7:84 theatre company, whose first Scottish work was *The Cheviot, the Stag, and the Black Black Oil* in 1973. We premiered the play at an Edinburgh conference on the future of Scotland, in which Hamish took part, and then took it on tour, playing in twenty-eight village and small town venues in the north of Scotland, the Hebrides, and in Orkney. Joyce McMillan would later call it a 'brilliant ceilidh of rage and laughter against the exploitation of land and people'.[8] Later that year we returned for a second Highland tour, before travelling to Ireland. We took it to the Abbey Theatre in Dublin. It was a riot. There was an old guy doing the curtains who said, 'There hasn't been a night like this in here since O'Casey.' Hamish just loved this story when I later related it to him. The play was subsequently broadcast on the BBC 'Play for today' programme in 1974, and again in 1975.

Hamish had been very supportive during the writing and rehearsal period. But his support and encouragement was even more pronounced for *The Game's a Bogey*. This 7:84 production about John Maclean, the Red Clydesider, was designed to balance out the Highland focus of *The Cheviot*, by aiming at working-class audiences in industrial Scotland. Hamish gave us plenty of information on John Maclean and the Red Clydesiders, and of course he had already written his 'John Maclean March'.

From the early 1980s I lived in Blair Atholl running a bed and breakfast. Woodlands Guest House acquired a very fine reputation – even if it's me who says so. And lots of pals would stop by. One day when Lindsay Porteous paid me a visit, I must have mentioned that I'd like to have the words of one of Hamish's favourite songs – 'Tail Toddle'.

On 5 July 1988, I received another letter from Hamish:

---

[8] Joyce McMillan, 'The axeman cometh', *Scotland on Sunday*, 11 August 1996.

Dear Dolly,

Lindsay Porteous has asked me to send you the words of 'Tail Toddle'. Here it is (the way I usually sing it):

(Chorus) O tail toddle, tail toddle
Tammy gars my tail toddle.
But an' ben, wi' diddle doddle
Tammy gars my tail toddle

Jessie Jack she gied a plack;
Helen Wallace gied a boddle.
Quo the bride, it's ower little
For to mend a broken doddle.

When I'm deid, I'm oot o' date
When I'm seik I'm fu' o' trouble.
When I'm wed, I stap aboot.
And Tammy hars my tail toddle.

Our gudewife held o'er to Fife,
For to buy a coal-riddle.
Lang or she cam back again
Tammy gart my tail toddle.

Sheila Douglas has included it in her *Come Gie's A Sang* and explains that 'Hamish has, on more than one occasion, sung this for dancers to do a reel.'[9] Hamish can be heard singing 'Tail Toddle' on Alan Lomax' 'Scotland' recording.[10] The sleeve note says that Hamish learned the song from an old gentleman named Ramsay, who lived in Glenshee, and recorded the song in 1951. Lomax, the distinguished American collector, refers to this as a diddling song, with verses made up of nonsense words, but these words had perhaps more meaning than he knew. Ah, the blessed innocent!

---

[9] Sheila Douglas, *Come Gie's a Sang: 73 Traditional Scottish Songs*, Prestonpans: The Hardie Press, 1995.

[10] World Library of Folk and Primitive Music, vol.3.

SCOIL EOLAIS NA H-ALBA
27 CEARNAG SHEORUIS
DUN-EIDEANN EH8 9LD

Fear-stiùiridh agus Ceann-roinne
AN T-OLLAMH IAIN MacCUINN
Fòn: 031-667 1011

Oilthaigh Dhun-Eideann

Telex: 727442 (UNIVED G)

SCHOOL OF SCOTTISH STUDIES
27 GEORGE SQUARE
EDINBURGH EH8 9LD

Director and Head of Department
PROFESSOR JOHN MacQUEEN
~~Tel: 031-667 1011~~

5 July 1988

Dear Dolly,

Lindsay Porteous has asked me to send you the words of "Tail Toddle." Here it is (the way I usually sing it)

(Chorus) O tail toddle tail toddle
Tammy gars my tail toddle.
But an' ben, wi' diddle doddle
Tammy gars my tail toddle

Jessie Jack she gied a plack:
Helen Wallace ~~gied~~ gied a boddle.
Quo the bride, it's ower little
For to mend a broken doddle.

When I'm deid, I'm oot o' date;
When I'm seik I'm fu' o' trouble.
When I'm weel, I stap aboot,
And Tammy gars my tail toddle.

Oor gudewife held o'er to Fife,
For to buy a coal-riddle.
Lang or she cam back again
Tammy gart my tail toddle.

Letter by Hamish Henderson to Dolina Maclennan with lyrics of 'Tail Toddle', 5 July 1988.

Bidding Farewell

Towards the end of his days, Hamish came to stay with me at my guest house in Blair Atholl for a while. When Kätzel phoned me asking whether I could accommodate Hamish for a week, my response was *Cha be ruith ach leum!* – I didn't run, I jumped!

By that time, Hamish had difficulty getting in and out of his bath, and the family had decided to install a shower for convenience. Hamish had to be got out of the way for that little business. Delighted, I put the 'No Vacancies' sign out. It was the most remarkable time of all the years we had known each other.

It was the most wonderful week. Beautiful weather. Hamish was in a big bed in the blue room looking out on the hills. He was in his element. I'd bring him up a cup of tea about half past eight in the morning and he'd be sitting up reading one of the many books I kept, which were of interest to him. His favourite was the story

Hamish Henderson, Dolina Maclennan and Kätzel Henderson – off to Blair Atholl

of Evelyn Murray, the eighth Duke of Atholl's sister. 'Ah, Dolinka (that's what he called me), I couldn't ask for anything better than to be lying here in this great big brass bed, gazing at Ben Vrackie and reading my auntie's biography.' There had been rumours about his origins, but I did not pry. He always had an affinity with the Murrays of Atholl, and indeed with the village of Blair Atholl. His mother had been a nurse at Blair Castle when it was a hospital during the First World War.

I told Hamish in midweek that I would have a party for him on Saturday. Each morning he would ask me 'Is this my party day?' 'No, it's another two days.' I had to teach him some of the songs that he had taught me – among them the dirtiest song I've ever heard. 'Sing it again, Dolinka.'

Come five o'clock every evening, Martin Stuart, the local chef, would take Hamish to the Roundhouse at the Tilt Hotel for a nip and a half pint, before walking him back to the house where I would have his tea ready for him. Martin had a bad leg at the time, and was using a stick – just like Hamish. It was a picture seeing them two hirpling through the gate and down the path towards the pub...

On Saturday afternoon, the party commenced. I had invited everybody furth of the Forth. The St Andrews crowd was there, Jimmy Hutchison, Arthur Watson, Jock Duncan and Pete Shepheard were there, and so many others. Tea and scones and beer were laid out, and the party lasted from two to seven. It was an amazing afternoon, so full of memories, songs and stories. We shared so much that day. Though the place was packed, you could hear the proverbial pin drop throughout a ballad, even if it lasted for twenty minutes.

Hamish was at home wherever he went. It is well known that he spent a lot of time with the travellers and collected their songs and stories. It was through him that I met Jeannie Robertson, the Stewarts of Blair and many other travelling people.

I still miss Hamish, ma big pal.

Charles Hamilton Sorley (1895-1915) – from Arthur St. John Adcock, *For Remembrance: Soldier Poets Who Have Fallen in the War*, London: Hodder and Stoughton, 1918.

Charles Hamilton Sorley and Hamish Henderson: Two Voices From The Battlefield

Lesley Duncan

War poets of both World Wars have been much in the public mind since the hundredth anniversary of the outbreak of the 1914-1918 conflict. Two young writers of great talent and potential are the theme of the following paper, given at the 2014 StAnza Poetry Festival in St Andrews. Both were Scots, though schooled south of the Border; both experienced the realities of war, one in the trenches of Flanders, the other in the Libyan desert of the North African Campaign in the early 1940s; both wrote with an admirable combination of humanity, eloquence, and indignation.

There, however, their life stories diverged. The first was killed at Loos in 1915 when barely out of his teens. The latter survived to have a long and distinguished literary and cultural career. Their names were Charles Hamilton Sorley and Hamish Henderson.

'When you see millions of the mouthless dead': Charles Hamilton Sorley

SONNET, 1915

When you see millions of the mouthless dead
Across your dreams in pale battalions go,
Say not soft things as other men have said,
That you'll remember. For you need not so.
Give them not praise. For, deaf, how should they know
It is not curses heaped on each gashed head?
Nor tears. Their blind eyes see not your tears flow.
Nor honour. It is easy to be dead.
Say only this, 'They are dead.' Then add thereto,

Officer Hamish Henderson (Jan Miller, 2015)

'Yet many a better one has died before.'
Then, scanning all the o'ercrowded mass, should you
Perceive one face that you loved heretofore,
It is a spook. None wears the face you knew.
Great death has made all his for evermore.[1]

This most bleak and nihilistic of sonnets, written from the Trenches in 1915, does not belong to any of the more celebrated poets of the First World War such as Wilfred Owen, Siegfried Sassoon, or Rupert Brooke. Its writer was a young ex-public (we Scots would say private) schoolboy, barely out of his teens, but with a wisdom beyond his years; and a creative promise which led John Masefield to claim that he was potentially the greatest poet lost in the war.

His name was Charles Hamilton Sorley. He was a Scot, born in 1895, the son of William Ritchie Sorley, Professor of Moral Philosophy at Aberdeen University. The family moved south when Charles was five, on his father's appointment to a professorship at Cambridge. The young Sorley was sent to Marlborough College, where he spent six years. He shone there, but, perhaps reflecting his staunchly individualist Scottish roots, was critical of the hierarchical structure that made the senior boys 'tin gods'.

He was writing poetry while still a precocious schoolboy. Here is the young non-conformist musing in June 1913:

WHAT YOU WILL

O come and see, it's such a sight,
So many boys all doing right:
To see them underneath the yoke,
Blindfolded by the elder folk,
Move at a most impressive rate
Along the way that is called straight.
O, it is comforting to know
They're in the way they ought to go.
But don't you think it's far more gay
To see them slowly leave the way
And limp and loose themselves and fall?
O, that's the nicest thing of all.

---

[1] Charles Hamilton Sorley, *Marlborough and other poems*, Cambridge: Cambridge University Press, 1916, XXVII, p.69.

I love to see this sight, for then
I know they are becoming men,
And they are tiring of the shrine
Where things are really not divine.[2]

The young Sorley loved cross-country running on the downs around Marlborough, doubtless the inspiration for his poem 'The Song of the Ungirt Runners', with its terse, rhyming lines and vivid images. The ungirtness of the title, one guesses, refers as much to the spirits as the bodies of the runners!

THE SONG OF THE UNGIRT RUNNERS

We swing ungirded hips,
And lightened are our eyes,
The rain is on our lips,
We do not run for prize.
We know not whom we trust
Nor witherward we fare,
But we run because we must
Through the great wide air.

The rain is on our lips,
We do not run for prize.
But the storm the water whips
And the wave howls to the skies.
The winds arise and strike it
And scatter it like sand,
And we run because we like it
Through the broad bright land.[3]

With a place at Oxford to read Classics already guaranteed, Sorley left Marlborough two terms early, in December 1913, to go to Germany to study, as his father had done. His months there are described in numerous lively and engaging letters to his family and to friends still at Marlborough. He spent the first three months in the provincial town of Schwerin, in northern Germany, with a typical bourgeois family, headed by a stout Herr Doktor whose

---

[2] *Ibid.*, III, p.9.

[3] *Ibid.*, XIII, p.40

wife gave him German lessons. Sorley viewed his new environment with a keen eye, commenting on a goose-stepping parade on the Kaiser's birthday: 'German soldiers have an unfortunate way of marching as if there were something in front whom they had to kick!'[4] But he was soon caught up in local life, playing hockey, 'looking quite Byronic,' though disconcerting his companions by wearing shorts rather than breeches; going to see productions of Ibsen at the fine local theatre; immersing himself in Goethe's *Faust*, Heine, and Schiller; enthusing about Thomas Hardy.

Was he aware, wrapped in his intellectual and literary concerns, what was happening in the real world of international politics? In a letter to the headmaster of Marlborough he describes passing a couple of military companies returning from a field day: 'Were they singing? They were roaring – something glorious and senseless about the Fatherland (in England it would have been contemptible Jingo: it wasn't in Deutschland)...' He adds, 'It's the first time I have had the vaguest idea what patriotism meant – and that in a strange land.'[5]

After three months in North Germany, he moved to the university town of Jena, near Weimar, for the summer semester and again immersed himself in gregarious student life. He felt so at ease that, as late as June 1914, he was writing to a friend that he wanted to have another term at Jena, move on to Berlin, and not go to Oxford at all. As the Continent moved inexorably to war, he and a companion set off on a carefree exploration of the Moselle Valley. Reality caught up with the two on 1 August and they were imprisoned briefly before allowed to return to England, just before the declaration of war with Germany.

In spite of his mainly positive, and indeed affectionate, view of Germany and Germans and total absence of thoughtless chauvinism, Sorley quickly enlisted after his return from the Continent. This may seem paradoxical, but of course the free-thinking teenager was, after all, a child of his time and circumstances. Besides, it put off the business of studying Classics at Oxford about which he was at least ambivalent. He would never turn Hun-hater, as this sonnet, entitled 'To Germany', demonstrates:

---

[4] *The Collected Letters of Charles Hamilton Sorley*, edited by Jean Moorcroft Wilson, London: Cecil Woolf, 1990, p.63.

[5] *ibid.*, p.81.

TO GERMANY

You are blind like us. Your hurt no man designed,
And no man claimed the conquest of your land.
But gropers both through fields of thought confined
We stumble and we do not understand.
You only saw your future bigly planned,
And we, the tapering paths of our own mind,
And in each other's dearest ways we stand,
And hiss and hate. And the blind fight the blind.

When it is peace, then we may view again
With new-won eyes each other's truer form
And wonder. Grown more loving-kind and warm
We'll grasp firm hands and laugh at the old pain,
When it is peace. But until peace, the storm
The darkness and the thunder and the rain.[6]

Sorley spent many months training – at which he fretted – before he was finally deployed in the battlefield in May 1915. His free spirit and independent attitudes continued to be manifest in his letters to friends and family over the period. He wrote to his mother in March 1915: 'I do wish also that people would not deceive themselves by talk of a just war. There is no such thing as a just war. What we are doing is casting out Satan by Satan.'[7] And commenting to her, the following month, on the death of Rupert Brooke, now lionised in the popular press, he made the harsh judgment on his fellow poet: that he was 'Far too obsessed with his own sacrifice.'[8]

His letters from the Trenches are marked by stoicism and humanity – more than once he asks his family to send him Woodbine cigarettes for his men – and there are his usual irrepressible moments of humour. But underlying all is the nightmare reality. In one terrible passage in a letter to his friend Arthur Watts in August 1915, he describes:

---

6 *Marlborough and other poems*, XXI, p.56.

7 *Collected Letters*, p.217.

8 *ibid.*, p.218.

> the wail of the exploded bomb and the animal cries of wounded men. Then death and the horrible thankfulness when one sees that the next man is dead: 'We won't have to *carry* him in under fire, thank God; dragging will do': hauling in of the great resistless body in the dark, the smashed head rattling: the relief, the relief that the thing has ceased to groan: that the bullet or bomb that made the man an animal has now made the animal a corpse. One is hardened by now; purged of all false pity: perhaps more selfish than before.[9]

This is the background to Sorley's black fatalism that reached its poetic climax in the sonnet quoted at the start, 'When you see millions of the mouthless dead.'

There were other creative flowerings from that final year, including a companion-piece double sonnet. But here is an extract from the poem that follows 'To Germany' in the collection of his work published by Cambridge University Press in 1916. The 'Ungirt Runners' of Marlborough had morphed into the doomed marchers of 'All the Hills and Vales Along':

ALL THE HILLS AND VALES ALONG

All the hills and vales along
Earth is bursting into song,
And the singers are the chaps
Who are going to die perhaps.
    O sing, marching men,
    Till the valleys ring again.
    Give your gladness to earth's keeping,
    So be glad, when you are sleeping.

Cast away regret and rue,
Think what you are marching to.
Little live, great pass.
Jesus Christ and Barabbas
Were found the same day.
This died, that went his way

---

[9] *Ibid.*, p.254.

So sing with joyful breath.
For why, you are going to death.
Teeming earth will surely store
All the gladness that you pour.

Earth that never doubts not fears,
Earth that knows of death, not tears,
Earth that bore with joyful ease
Hemlock for Socrates,
Earth that blossomed and was glad
'Neath the cross that Christ had,
Shall rejoice and blossom too
When the bullet reaches you.
Wherefore, men marching
On the road to death, sing!
Pour your gladness on earth's head,
So be merry, so be dead.[10]

On 13 October 1915 Sorley, who had by then been promoted captain and was acting that day as temporary company commander of the 7th Suffolks, was killed by a sniper's bullet north of Loos. He was barely twenty. A late photograph shows his thoughtful, handsome face, with just the down of a first moustache. One individual tragedy amongst countless, but what humanity and creative potential was snuffed out.

'There were our own, there were the others': Hamish Henderson

My second poet, Hamish Henderson, born in 1919, was caught up in the Second World War but survived it to lead a long and distinguished life, dying as recently as 2002. He was particularly notable for his work with the School of Scottish Studies in Edinburgh and as an influential collector of folk material.

I recall him in Edinburgh's Assembly Rooms in the 1980s at a celebration for his fellow poet Norman MacCaig. When his turn to perform came, he burst into song. Was it his anti-apartheid

[10] *Marlborough and other poems*, XXII, p.57.

anthem 'Rivonia', with its hypnotic refrain 'Rumbala rumbala rumba- la... Free Mandela Free Mandela', or 'The Freedom Come-All-Ye'? Memory is unclear. Whichever, he was a flamboyant figure.

Among his varied, energetic, writing, much of it in Scots and displaying his radical credentials, there is one particularly impressive text, 'The Flyting o' Life and Daith' – which recalls the work of the great sixteenth-century Makars. 'The 51st Highland Division's Farewell to Sicily' has an engaging zest and immediacy. However, the aspect of his writing I want to consider is his acknowledged masterpiece, his *Elegies for the Dead in Cyrenaica*, inspired by his experiences, as a young officer, in his early twenties, in the North African Campaign, though not published until the late 1940s.

There are ten of them and together they offer the most sustained evocation-cum-indictment of modern warfare – war waged in this case over a large geographical area, rather than the nightmare stalemate of the Trenches.

As a radical young scholar-turned-soldier, Henderson weaves all sorts of European, classical, and Scottish cultural references into the sequence. If there is sometimes a whiff of youthful intellectual arrogance about this aspect of his writing, he does also manage to include a reference to Rangers-Celtic rivalry, obviously unabated by war!

Like Sorley, Henderson was a Scot (he came from Blairgowrie). He also had a southern education (at Dulwich College) before studying modern languages at Cambridge. Mirroring Sorley's time in pre-First-World-War Germany, Henderson had been a visiting student there before the Second.

In an echo of Sorley's preoccupation with Goethe, he prefaces his 'Prologue' to the *Elegies* with a quatrain from the poet, often apparently included in little anthologies German soldiers took to the Front. Henderson's translation reads: 'The gods, the unending, give all things without stint to their beloved: all pleasures, the unending – and all pains, the unending, without stint.'[11] Henderson sets out his literary intentions in this short 'Prologue':

---

[11] 'Prologue', Hamish Henderson, *Elegies for the Dead in Cyrenaica* (1948), in *Collected Poems and Songs*, edited by Raymond Ross, Edinburgh: Curly Snake Publishing, 2000, p.51.

PROLOGUE

Obliterating face and hands
The dumb-bell guns of violence
Show up our godhead for a sham.
Against the armour of the storm
I'll hold my human barrier,
Maintain my fragile irony.

I've walked this brazen clanging path
In flesh's brittle arrogance
To chance the simple hazard, death.
Regretting only this, my rash
Ambitious wish in verse to write
A true and valued testament.

Let my words knit what now we lack
The demon and the heritage
And fancy strapped to logic's rock.
A chastened wantonness, a bit
That sets on song a discipline,
A sensuous austerity.

His ambition to write 'a true and valued testament' includes an aesthetic dimension (the 'bit that sets on song a discipline'), though the elegies do not have the metre or rhyme of traditional poetic convention. Here is the opening of the 'First Elegy' (subtitled 'End of a Campaign'):

There are many dead in the brutish desert,
    who lie uneasy
among the scrub in this landscape of half-wit
stunted ill-will. For the dead land in insatiate
and necrophilous. The sand is blowing about still.
Many who for various reasons, or because
    of mere unanswerable compulsion, came here
and fought among the clutching gravestones,
    shivered and sweated,
cried out, suffered thirst, were stoically silent, cursed
the spittering machine-guns, were homesick for Europe
and fast embedded in quicksand of Africa

agonized and died.
And sleep now. Sleep here the sleep of the dust.

The bitter wordplay on the biblical 'sleep of the just' shows the poet craftsman as well as the reporter of events. The second section introduces some homely images of life back in Britain amid the harshness, but ends with a brutal stab:

There were our own, there were the others.
Their deaths were like their lives, human and animal.
There were no gods and precious few heroes.
What they regretted when they died had nothing to do
with
race and leader, realm indivisible,
laboured Augustan speeches or vague imperial heritage.
(They saw through that guff before the axe fell.)
Their longing turned to
the lost world glimpsed in the memory of letters:
an evening at the pictures in the friendly dark,
two knowing conspirators smiling and whispering secrets;
or else
a family gathering in the homely kitchen
with Mum so proud of her boys in uniform:
their thoughts trembled
between moments of estrangement, and ecstatic moments
of reconciliation: and their desire
crucified itself against the unutterable shadow of someone
whose photo was in their wallets.
Then death made his incision.[12]

The 'First Elegy''s final lines reiterate the wider issues of shared humanity, beyond revenge or patriotism:

There were our own, there were the others.
Therefore, minding the great word of Glencoe's
son, that we should not disfigure ourselves
with villainy of hatred: and seeing that all
have gone down like curs into anonymous silence,
I will bear witness for I knew the others.

---

[12] *Ibid*, p.52.

Seeing that littoral and interior are alike indifferent
and the birds are drawn again to our welcoming north
why should I not sing them, the dead, the innocent?

The ten elegies are broken by an 'Interlude', entitled 'Opening of an Offensive'. Its subsection, 'The Jocks', vividly describes the impact of bagpipes in battle and reminds readers of the poet's strong attachment to his Scottish heritage:

They move forward into no man's land, a vibrant sounding
board.
As they advance
the guns push further murderous music.
Is this all they will hear, this raucous apocalypse?
The spheres knocking in the night of Heaven?
The drummeling of overwhelming niagara?
No! For I hear it! Or is it?. . . tell
me that I can hear it! Now - listen!

Yes, hill and shieling
sea-loch and island, hear it, the yell
of your war-pipes, scaling sound's mountains
guns thunder drowning in their soaring swell! . . .
Now again! The shrill war-song: it flaunts
aggression to the sullen desert. It mounts. Its scream
tops the valkyrie, tops the colossal
artillery.[13]

It is a wonderfully vivid evocation of the din of battle ('this raucous apocalypse') with the exhilarating counterpoint of the pipes.

[There may be echoes in this 'Interlude' of the American John Greenleaf Whittier's poem about the Siege of Lucknow in the Indian Mutiny of 1857-58, a schoolroom favourite which Henderson must surely have known. 'Pipes of the misty moorlands, / Voice of the glens and hills, / The droning of the torrents, / The treble of the rills,' the poem starts, before describing the despair and desperation of the besieged garrison and civilians. The tension is suddenly broken by a Scots girl with her ear to the ground: 'Dinna

[13] *Ibid*, pp.60-61.

ye hear it?- dinna ye hear it? she cries, The pipes of Havelock sound!']

After the tour de force of Henderson's battle description, there is almost bathos in the moral that he then draws:

> Meaning that many
> German Fascists will not be going home
> meaning that many
> will die, doomed in their false dream...

If that sentiment sounds strangely bellicose for Henderson, the 'Ninth Elegy', subtitled 'Fort Capuzzo', shows him at his most compassionate, though cynical, not just sharing the thoughts but the vernacular of his fellow soldiers.

NINTH ELEGY

> *For there will come a day*
> *when the Lord will say*
> *- Close Order!*
>
> One evening, breaking a jeep journey at Capuzzo
> I noticed a soldier as he entered the cemetery
> and stood looking at the grave of a fallen enemy.
> Then I understood the meaning of the hard word 'pietas'
> (a word unfamiliar to the newsreel commentator
> as well as the pimp, the informer, and the traitor).
>
> His thought was like this. – Here's another 'Good Jerry'!
> Poor mucker. [a euphemism here!] Just eighteen. Must be
> hard-up for man-power.
> Or else he volunteered, silly bastard. That's the fatal,
> the-fatal mistake. Never volunteer for nothing.
> I wonder how he died? Just as well it was him, though,
> And not one of our chaps . . . Yes, the only good Jerry,
> as they say, is your sort, chum.
> Cheerio, you poor bastard.
> Don't be late on parade when the Lord calls 'Close Order'.
> Keep waiting for the angels. Keep listening for Reveille.[14]

[14] *Ibid.*, p.70.

Hamish Henderson, 'Song of the Banffies' (Jan Miller, 2015)

The crofters' sons o' Banffshire
The cooper frae the glen,
The weaver frae Strathisla,
Aye, and shepherd frae the ben;
The fisher lads alang the coast
They made up their min'
Tae fecht an' save their country
In nineteen thirty nine

Henderson's use of the demotic is joltingly effective. There are also moments of sheer linguistic bravura in the *Elegies*. At one point, for example, he describes how 'the limitless shabby lion-pelt of the desert completes and rounds' a sentry's ennui. And he peppers his text with memorable abstract concepts such as 'death's proletariat.' This particular phrase is reiterated to powerful effect in the 'Third Elegy', in which, at the end, the British forces see the advancing Germans as 'the others, the brothers in death's proletariat.'

The 'Sixth Elegy' considers the impossibility of justifying the 'sacrifice' of those killed in war, putting the issue, beyond the 'dope of reportage' or the 'anodyne of statistics.' 'O, to right them/ what requiem can I sing in the ears of the living?' Henderson agonises. 'No blah about their sacrifice: rather tears or reviling/ of the time that took them, than an insult so outrageous.' The last lines of this 'Sixth Elegy' come perhaps as close to a moral resolution as Henderson can go:

> So the words that I have looked for and must go on
> looking for,
> are worlds of whole love, which can slowly gain the power
> to reconcile and heal. Other words would be pointless.[15]

These two young Scottish war poets, Charles Hamilton Sorley and Hamish Henderson, though so different in character and their fates, both offer, I believe, a message of magnanimity, an acknowledgement of shared humanity, in the most extreme and dreadful circumstances of war.

A message still worth pondering.

---

[15] *Ibid.* pp.62-63.

No Gods and Precious Few Heroes

John Lucas

I

The title of this chapter[1] is taken from one of the most interesting, accomplished, and least celebrated poems to have come out of WWII. Quite why Hamish Henderson's book-length *Elegies for the Dead in Cyrenaica* should have been so disregarded is something of a mystery. Written between 1942 and 1947, it was published by John Lehmann in 1948, and since then has been three times re-printed, by EUSPB in 1977, by Polygon, in 1990, and again by Polygon/Birlinn in 2008; and it can be found in Henderson's *Collected Poems and Songs*, edited by Raymond Ross and published by Curly Snake Publishing in 2000. (Though Polygon was acquired by Birlinn in 2002, a company with an international reputation.) That he entrusted his work to independent publishers may help to explain the virtual disappearance of Henderson's work from public awareness south of the border. Few of the major anthologies of WWII poetry include him, and those which offer bits of the *Elegies* do so without bothering top identify the source from which they come. Ian Hamilton, the editor of *The Poetry of War, 1939-1945* (New English Library, 1972), prints a poem he calls 'Seven Good Germans', which is in fact the subtitle for the Seventh Elegy; in Brian Gardner's *The Terrible Rain: The War Poets, 1939-45* (Methuen, new ed., 1987) Henderson is represented by 'Fort Capuzzo', the subtitle for the Ninth Elegy; and Desmond Graham's *Poetry of the Second World War: An International Anthology* (Pimlico, new ed., 1998) has the 'Second Elegy: Halfaya'. And that is about it.

---

[1] This chapter is a slightly revised extract from the eponymous chapter 7 in John Lucas, *Second World War Poetry in English*, London: Greenwich Exchange, 2013 – here published with the kind permission of the author.

Perhaps Henderson's enthusiastic support not merely of Marxism but of Stalin allowed editors to assume that they could treat him with a disregard bordering on contempt. In addition, English editors, for whom British and English are often interchangeable concepts, may have taken Henderson's passionate Scottish nationalism as sufficient reason for thinking of him as a kind of wild man, beyond the pale of serious consideration, rather as they think of MacDiarmid. But Henderson needs to be distinguished from what he himself calls MacDiarmid's 'Scotchiness', which he attacks in a letter-poem to his great contemporary. There, he claims that for all MacDiarmid's declared Anglo-phobia, it's not so much England as Scotland that has driven him to

> ruination,
> Why not admit it? The meanness, the rancour,
> The philistine baseness, he divisive canker,
> The sly Susanna's elder-ism, McGundyish muck-raking
> Are maladies of Scottish, not of English making.
> If we think all our ills come from 'ower the Border'
> We'll never, but never march ahead in 'guid order'.[2]

As these few lines indicate, Henderson was an enthusiastic and adroit argufier in verse. More importantly, although his radical politics sometimes led him into a simplistic hero-worshipping of Stalin – there is for example a dire 'Ballad of the Taxi Driver's Cap' (O Hitler's a non-smoker / and Churchill smokes cigars / and they're both as keen as mustard / on imperialistic wars. / But your uncle Joe's a worker / and a very decent chap / *because he smokes a pipe and wears / a taxi-driver's cap.*)[3] – politics are at the core of his concern with the experiences of ordinary soldiers fighting and dying in a war not of their choosing but in which they can, perhaps, assert themselves as part of a movement to bring about a transformed world.

To put it tis way is, however, to turn to propaganda, to sloganise, a poem whose great virtue lies in its attention not merely to the actuality of the fighting but to the many defeats this involves and perhaps requires. Such defeats, while never definitive, include

2 Hamish Henderson, 'To Hugh MacDiarmid', in *Collected Poems and Songs*, edited by Raymond Ross, Edinburgh: Curly Snake, 2000, p.119.

3 *Ibid.*, p.96.

not merely those of the battlefield, but of decency, of vision, of communality. Yet there are also victories of the spirit and, yes, hope. This is a war over which, *pace* F. T. Prince, the Gods do not preside and one where heroism isn't to be thought of in Romantic terms, as the achievement of larger-than-life individuals.

There will be much more to say about this, but for the moment I want to touch on the poem's first epigraph, from Goethe. In an end note Henderson says that the quatrain he reproduces 'was frequently included in small anthologies "for the Front" carried by German soldiers in the field – and indeed its thought lies very near the mood of many of them. One might translate it as follows: "The Gods, the unending, give all things without stint to their beloved: all pleasures, the unending – and all pains, the unending, without stint."' There is also an epigraph to the second part of the ten poems that make up the *Elegies*, its two parts separated by an 'Interlude'. Again, I quote Henderson's own words:

> Set against [Goethe's quatrain]... is the sceptical ironic spirit of a Gaelic poet who fought in the desert and was wounded at El Alamein. Sorley Maclean translates his own poem thus: 'Sitting dead in "Death Valley" below the Ruweisat Ridge, a by with his forelock down his cheek and his face slate-grey. I thought of the right and joy he had from his Fuehrer, of falling in the field of slaughter to rise no more... Whatever his desire or mishap, his innocence or malignance, he showed no pleasure in his death below the Ruweisat Ridge.'[4]

Cyrenaica, the setting of Henderson's *Elegies*, is part of Libya, desert land which was settled by the Greeks about 630 BC and then ruled successively by the Egyptians, Romans, Arabs and Turks. It is inhospitable territory, steeped in history, mostly of conflict, a good deal of which Henderson skilfully alludes to in the course of his poem. Fighting in the desert, such as soldiers encountered in the Second World War in far larger numbers than in the first, came to provide not merely a testing, exhausting, experience, but also a troubling metaphor of war's outcome. 'They make a desolation and they call it peace,' Tacitus had written almost twenty centuries earlier of the triumphs of war. Soldiers not familiar with those words would as schoolboys almost certainly have read

[4] *Ibid.*, p.158

'Ozymandias' (it's in Palgrave). With its powerful sense of the wreckage of imperial might, where 'Nothing beside remains' but 'The lone and level sands [which] stretch far away'.

You can feel the presence of this almost existential emptiness in Patrick Anderson's 'Desert'. 'Hereabouts is desert,' the poem begins, 'it's a bad country, / grows nothing, nothing to show for'. In desert land a man can die, 'a khaki / hero with his life blood blotting entirely and quickly / into the khaki sand'. Nothing beside remains. 'There's no purpose here, / nothing but a blanket warming a blanket, or a sum / multiplying and dividing itself forever.'[5] In this vast, featureless landscape, soldiers must surely have wondered what on earth they were fighting for, must have felt that the desert's uniform indifference called into question any of the purposes for which they had been set into battle.

Anderson's poem broods over generalities. His solder is any soldier. But Henderson's gaze, though it begins with a kind of panoptic sweep of the terrain, focuses on specific experiences. These are opening lines of the First Elegy, subtitled 'End of a Campaign':

> There are many dead in the brutish desert,
> Who lie uneasy
> among the scrub in this landscape of half-wit
> stunted ill-will. For the dead land is insatiate
> and necrophilous. The sand is blowing about still.
> many who for various reason, or because
> of mere unanswerable compulsion, came here
> and fought among the clutching gravestones,
> shivered and sweated,
> cried out, suffered thirst, were stoically silent, cursed
> the splittering machine-guns, were homesick for Europe
> and fast embedded in quicksand of Africa
> agonised and died.
> And sleep now. Sleep here the sleep of the dust.[6]

The 'sleep of the dust' is not cheap cynicism. At the end of the first Elegy, Henderson asks rhetorically, 'Why should I not sing *them*, the dead, the innocent?'

---

[5] in *Poetry of the Forties*, introduced and edited by Robin Skelton, Harmondsworth: Penguin, 1968, p.140.

[6] *Collected Poems and Songs*, p.52.

Nevertheless, many of those who died in the desert, perhaps all, could not claim to be dying for a just cause. German soldiers couldn't do so, nor could allied soldiers who died for the sake of Empire. The sands of North Africa cover ruckled strata of historical complexity. Besides, as Henderson adds, 'Their deaths were like their lives, human and animal', and

> What they regretted when they died had nothing to do with
> race and leader, realm indivisible,
> laboured Augustan speeches or vague imperial heritage.
> (They saw through that guff before the axe fell.)[7]

The anti-imperialism accords with Roy Fuller's line about the ridiculous empires breaking like biscuits, and it connects, too, with other poets who were openly contemptuous of the imperial claims for which they were supposed – partly – to be fighting. The dead in Cyrenaica died, not in the contented knowledge that they were vindicating the words of leaders, but regretting

> a family gathering in a homely kitchen
> with Mum so proud of her boys in uniform
> ...
> ... and their desire
> crucified itself against the unutterable shadow of someone
> whose photo was in their wallets.[8]

II

Elegies for the Dead in Cyrenaica is in two parts of five sections each, with, between them, an Interlude. There is also a Prologue to the entire poem and, as conclusion, 'Heroic Song for the Runners of Cyrene'. This is followed by an end note which says simply:

> *Cyrene*, 1942 –
> *Carradale, Argyll*, 1947.

---

[7] *Ibid.*, p.52

[8] *Ibid.*

I set this out as it is given in Henderson's *Collected Poems and Songs* because from the names and dates we are surely invited to conclude that he wants his reader to understand the length of time he took over composing this ambitious work. Not, I am sure, in order to solicit our admiration for his effort but to indicate that it was written both *in media res* and later: in other words, the sequence is at once an immediate response to a bloody battle and an attempt to meditate upon conflict in history, conflict *through* history, conflict *as* history.

William Scammell doesn't approve of this. 'The elegies contain some interesting and vivid detail, and a moving compassion for the dead,' he says, but then comes the put-down. The poems are

> seriously weakened by inflation and Eliotesque ambition, as the symptomatic reference to the 'North African wasteland' implies. MacDiarmid too is a discernable influence, but unfortunately it is the posturing Marxist 'intellectual' side of that fine poet that Henderson chooses to imitate, abandoning particulars for portentous historical juxtaposition.[9]

Scammell is unwilling to conceive of poetry as attempting to align its vision with long perspectives. This seems unduly prescriptive. I grant that there are moments in the poem where Henderson seems himself prescriptive, trying to shoehorn the desert war into History; but there are others where his allusive method allows us to consider the possibility that as a recurring phenomenon war not only creates what he calls 'the proletariat of the dead' but is expressive of the desert we make out of all that life offers. This is not so much posturing as awareness – now laconic, now grim, now wry, now tragic – of history's repetitions. It also makes possible a refusal to demonise 'the other'. We are all – past and present, friend and enemy – in this together. *And we always have been*. So, yes, the *Elegies* may provide historical juxtaposition. But I don't see anything especially portentous about this, unless we take the word in its meaning of 'presaging an ominous event', in which case Henderson need be held guilty of doing no more than refusing to believe that this war will end all wars. Breaking eggs doesn't guarantee an omelette, let alone the omelette to end all omelettes. And having said this, I want to provide a more detailed

[9] William Scammell, *Keith Douglas: A Study*, London: Faber & Faber, 1988, p.162.

account of Henderson's remarkable poem.

The first five elegies are set before a particular battle, though one that has been preceded by other battles. 'First Elegy', entitled 'End of a Campaign' is about the dead from earlier desert battles who now 'Sleep [...] the sleep of the dust.' The second elegy 'Halfaya' locates a precise spot where the new battle will be fought. It begins:

> At dawn, under the concise razor-edge
> of the escarpment, the laager sleeps. No petrol fires yet
> blow flame for brew-up. Up on the pass a sentry
> inhales his Nazionale. Horse-shoe curve of the bay
> grows visible beneath him. He smokes and yawns.
> Ooo-augh,
> and the limitless
> shabby lion-pelt of the desert completes and rounds
> his limitless ennui.[10]

The rhythmic assurance of these loosely five-stress lines recalls, if distantly, Chorus's description of the setting for battle in *Henry V*; 'through the foul womb of night, / The hum of either army still sounds ... Fire answers fire.' And behind that are Homer's accounts of the Greek army stirring itself on the plain before Troy. The elegy ends:

> the sleepers toss
> and turn before waking: they feel through their blankets
> the cold of the malevolent bomb-thumped desert,
> impartial
> hostile to both.
>
> The laager is one.
> Friends and enemies, haters and lovers
> both sleep and dream.[11]

But in the Third Elegy, 'Leaving the City', this panoptic vision is exchanged for the bustle of activity that is the prelude to battle. The elegy commences with the two italicised lines, '*Morning after.*

[10] *Collected Poems and Songs*, p.53.

[11] *Ibid.*, p.54.

Get moving. Cheerio. Be seeing you / when this party's over. Right, driver, get weaving.'[12] The army slang, the clipped jocularities, humanise the immensity of the impeding battle, emphasise the alienation of the soldiers from the township in which, as they travel out into the desert, they leave behind 'the scrofulous sellers of obscenity, / the garries, the girls and the preposterous skyline', and head for the moment when 'stripes are shed and ranks levelled / in death's proletariat.'

The Fourth Elegy, 'El Adem', brings the soldiers nearer to battle, in a desert where 'we're uneasy, knowing ourselves to be nomads, / impermanent guests on this black moon-surface / of dents and ridges, craters and depressions'. Prisoners in cages are guarded by 'fearful oppressors' who tomorrow may be the defeated. In his account of Keith Douglas's war diary, *Alamein to Zem Zem*, Scammell alludes to Douglas's account of the desert landscape, its ridges and hollows, the uncertainties of a front line that shifts so fast that pursuer can on an instant become the pursued. What to do in such hostile corcumstances? 'Endure, endure,' Henderson says.

The Fifth Elegy, 'Highland Jebel', offers a connection between the awfulness of the desert landscape and the repeated bloody Anglo-Scottish wars, including, no doubt, Culloden and the Highland clearances.

> In our ears a murmur
> of wind-born battle. Herons stalk
> over the blood-stained flats. Burning byres
> come to my mind...
>
> ...
>
>   Aye, in spite of
> the houses lying cold, and the hatred that engendered
> the vileness that you know, we'll keep our assignation
> with the Grecian Gael. (And those others). Then foregather
> in a gorge of the cloudy jebel
> older than Agamemnon.[13]

---

[12] *Ibid.*, p.55.

[13] *Ibid.*, p.59.

A jebel is a hill or a mountain in Arab country, and for the life of me I can't see that Henderson's effort here to ghost various tragic clashes between civilisations is portentous. Anyone wanting to arraign him on this charge should at the very least recognise that modern Scottish history is more tragic than England's and that Henderson, fighting in the desert, had good reason to understand something of the historic and legendary histories of North Africa and the Middle Eastern desert, from the fate of Araby the Blest to what befell Carthage. The *Elegies* do, however, form an insistently modernist poem in their speculative, suggestive and wide-ranging view of history, of the local and the world-wide, the present and the past.

Interlude is entitled 'Opening of an Offensive', and is divided into a) the waiting, and b) the barrage. The latter repeatedly invokes the Scottish phrase 'mak siccar', which in his own end-notes to the poem Henderson tells us means make sure and is 'one of the famous phrases of mediaeval Scottish history.' He refers his readers to the moment when Robert the Bruce stabbed the Red Comyn in Dumfries Kirk 'and was found outside the building by Lindsay and Kirkpatrick. Lindsay asked if Comyn were dead. Bruce replied that he didn't know. "Aweel," said Lindsay, "I'll mak siccar."'[14] Making sure in the battle in the Libyan desert means guaranteeing that 'many / German fascists will not be going home / meaning that many / will die, doomed in their false dream.'[15]

The focus of the second part of the poem differs from the first. Where the first five poems had closed in on battle, the view now widens. Consideration is given to history in a manner that chastens and implicitly rebukes the perhaps intense, if excusable, eagerness for battle of the poem's first half. Here, then, the act and consequence of killing come under intense scrutiny. Elegy Six, 'Acroma', begins a process of meditations on the deaths of those who have been fighting. It is a particularly impressive, if awkward elegy, shifting from grieving through questioning to anger about these deaths.

> To justify them, what byways must I follow? ...
> Neither by dope of reportage, nor by anodyne of statistics
> is *their* lot made easier: laughing couples at the tea-dance
> ignore their memory, the memoirs almost slight them

---

[14] *Ibid.*, p.159.

[15] *Ibid.*, p.61.

and the queue forming up to see Rangers play Celtic
forms up without thought of those dead – O, to right them
what requiem can I sing in the ears of the living?

No blah about their sacrifice: rather tears of reviling
Of the time that took them, than an insult so outrageous.[16]

The awkwardness is essential to the elegy's meaning. Henderson doesn't have the words to communicate the dire disjunction between those who fight and are killed and the people at home who are, perhaps understandably, so remote from the action that they can't be expected to grieve for innumerable deaths. But at least let them not wrap up such deaths in the muffling language of 'sacrifice.' (I think of politicians who today mouth not merely that word but speak of how their 'hearts and minds go out' to those who have suffered loss, especially in war.)

More questionably, perhaps, Henderson tries to notionalise the deaths in battle as caused by 'history's great rains', its 'destructive transitions.' And yet, he may be right, who can know? He can't, surely, be criticised for trying to make sense of the war. Nor for saying that he must go on looking for 'worlds of whole love, which can slowly gain the power / to reconcile and heal.'[17]

Herein lies the importance of the seventh elegy, 'Seven Good Germans', which records the deaths of some enemy soldiers whose corpses Henderson presumably saw after the battle was done. The elegy humanises enemies that the rhetoric of war demonises, rather as Douglas in 'Vergissmeinnicht' and Sorley Maclean do.

Seven poor bastards
dead in an African deadland
(tawny tousled hair under the issue blanket)
wie einst Lili
dead in an African deadland
einst Lili Marlene[18]

---

[16] *Ibid.*, p.63.

[17] *Ibid.*

[18] *Ibid.*, p.66

The seventh corpse in particular takes Henderson's attention because 'he had written three verses in appeal against his sentence / which soften for an hour the anger of Lenin'. I take this to mean that the young German squaddie had been trying to write a poem – make an assertion of life against death – which merits Lenin's imagined display of magnanimity even though the soldier was on the wrong side of history. If so, I have to cede Scammell a point. Lenin's intrusion into the poem is gratuitous, a bit of forelock tugging. I would also say, though, that it feels at odds with the typical procedures of the *Elegies*, which don't at all try to shape the events with which they are concerned into a History-according-to-Marxism – beyond, that is, imagining 'destructive transitions' as the prelude to (re)construction. And as a combatant you didn't have to be a Marxist to believe, or anyway, hope, that WWII might prove to be such a prelude. It wasn't Stalin who spoke of the bright uplands of futurity that waited beyond the sacrifices of the present.

The Eighth Elegy, 'Karnak', is a prolonged meditation on the rises and falls of civilisations. Now a village on the upper Nile near Luxor, Karnak possesses some of he most famous ruins in the world, including the great temple of Amun-Ra. 'The shambles of Karnak,' Henderson calls the place which once boasted a civilisation supreme not merely in its insolence but in its confident belief of assured immortality. Karnak is imagined as playing reluctant host to 'the trampling migrations of peoples, / the horsemen of Amr, the "barbarians" of Cavafy / and Rommel before the gates of Alexandria.'[19] Henderson brilliantly figures 'masters of the chisel' working on the colossi of the temple, before asking 'Are Bedouin herds moving up from the South?' Confident assumptions of permanence are challenged by movement, transition, destruction. History shows the folly of any belief in such permanence. Change is the only constant.

Henderson doesn't allude to Hitler's claim that the Reich he had built would last a thousand years, but I don't see how you can read this particular elegy without the claim coming to mind. And what of Churchill's counter claim that if the British Empire should last as long, people would say that the Battle of Britain was its finest hour? 'O unheeding / the long ambiguous shadow / thrown on the overweening temple / by the Other…' The Other here is any oppositional force, and though we may not want to think of it

---

[19] *Ibid.*, p.68

in terms of the dialectic of history, as Henderson assuredly does, we have surely to acknowledge that others have seen to it that neither Hitler's Reich nor the British Empire has endured.

But people, endless, altered, do indeed endure. The short Ninth Elegy, 'Fort Capuzzo', records Henderson looking on as a soldier enters a cemetery to peer at the grave of a fallen enemy. Seeing this, he says, he understands 'the meaning of he hard word "*pietas*" / (a word unfamiliar to the newsreel commentator / as well as to the pimp, the informer and the traitor.)' In his end-notes Henderson remarks that in his reference to the newsreel commentator he was thinking of 'one whose mike-side manner when referring to the area targets of Bomber Command or when delivering ignoble gibes at the expense of enemy front-line soldiers filled me (and plenty of others) with shame and fury.'[20] I wish he had quoted some words of this commentator, had perhaps named him. As it is, the line feels almost vacuous, especially when compared to the soldier's internal communing: 'Cheerio, you poor bastard. / Keep waiting for he angels. Keep listening for Reveille.'[21] No matter how clumsy, the humour here feels appropriate and in no sense condescending, the fragmentary moment of '*pietas*' a plausible attempt to reconcile and heal. We are now a long way from the dumb-bell guns of violence of the *Elegies*' opening lines.

As a result, when in the tenth and final elegy, 'The Frontier', we revisit the panoptic vision of the first elegy, we see the battlefield through the eyes of casually curious air passengers imagined to be overflying it at some future date. 'The outposts / lay here: there ran the supply route. / Forgotten.'[22] The full-stop after 'route', he line break and then the bleak one-word sentence 'Forgotten', snapped-off from what went before, between them heart-achingly tell how history will in all likelihood shrink to near insignificance events that seemed cataclysmically important to those engaged in the battle. 'Still, how should this interest the airborne travellers, / being less real to them than the Trojan defence-works / and touching them as little as the Achaean strategies?'[23] The war in the desert will become as mythic and unreal as that which Homer recounts.

---

[20] *Ibid.*, p.160.

[21] *Ibid.*, p.70.

[22] *Ibid.*, p.71

[23] *Ibid.*

Against the vast indifference of history it will therefore be the responsibility of those who were engaged in the battle – including Henderson himself – to

> carry to the living
> blood, fire, and red flambeaux of death's proletariat.
> Take iron in your arms! At last, spanning this history's
> Apollyon chasm, proclaim them the reconciled.[24]

The destructive power of Apollyon, the devil of Revelations, can't be undone.

But a bridge from past to future can be built over the hell Apollyon created. It doesn't at first seem very satisfactory, this closing image, not only because the 'iron in your arms' sounds – misleadingly but suspiciously – like further warfare, but because to reconcile death's proletariat to the future can look emptily pious. But against this we have to acknowledge that it isn't only the defeated whom history can neither help nor pardon. The victors – or anyway, the survivors – have to *make* history, shape it to their needs. 'We must face reality,' the pessimists, the fatalists say. No, we make the reality, has to be the answer; reality wears the face we give it. Henderson's sense of history is not merely shaped by his Marxism, it is nourished by hopes for the future men struggle to create. Why else did he and countless others fight? Read this way, the elegy's closing lines can be seen as an urgent invitation to take up the challenge of transforming, or at least, reshaping society, to realise hopes which had been denied after 1918. And after all, the election of the Labour government in 1945 *did* for a while allow many to hope that Apollyon's chasm might be spanned, though they wouldn't have put it in such terms. I don't see Henderson is to be blamed for voicing the hope; nor can he be indicted because he hope wasn't fully realised.

But anyway, this is not the end point for the *Elegies*. That comes with the 'Heroic Song for the Runners of Cyrene' which pointedly is not called an Epilogue. (History has no end.) Instead, the poem is another opening out. It is prefaced by a quotation from Denis Saurat's *Death and the Dreamer*:

> Without suffering and death one learns nothing.
> We should know the difference between the visions

[24] *Ibid.*, p.72.

> of the intellect and the facts.
> Only those ideas are acceptable that hold through suffering and death....
> Life is that which leaps.[25]

Sadly, the poem that follows is Henderson at his most didactic. (Another round to Scammell.) The warriors of a much earlier conflict are imagined as running freely 'to the chosen assignation; / ineluctable role, / and they're ready to accept it.'[26] And later,

> The goal is in sight. Simultaneous the onrush,
> The clash close at hand, o incarnate dialectic!
> The runners gain speed. As they hail their opponents
> They can hear in the ear the strum of loud arrows
> Which predestined sing to their point of intersection.[27]

Life may indeed be that which leaps, but running at death in these lines feels an altogether inadequate not to say leaden way to end a major poem. I prefer what seems to be an afternote. 'So Long', which begins 'To the war in Africa that's over – goodnight' and concludes fewer than twenty lines later with the imprecation:

> To the sodding desert – you know what you
> can do with yourself.
>
> To the African deadland – God help you –
> And goodnight.[28]

Too personal, perhaps, too casually dismissive, to bring so ambitious a poem to an appropriate conclusion? But Henderson handles this caustic swaddie lingo with great brio, not merely here but in a number of ballads – particularly in the 'The Ballad of the D-Day Dodgers'. If Henderson had written nothing else, that ballad alone ought to ensure him his place in the history of the poetry of WWII. As to his big poem, for all its flaws, *Elegies for the Dead in Cyrenaica* remains one of the most important

---

[25] *Ibid.*, p.73.
[26] *Ibid.*, p.74.
[27] *Ibid.*, p.75.
[28] *Ibid.*, p.77.

poems to have come out of the Second World War. The failure of commentators to make much of it – even sometimes to mention it – is quite simply inexcusable.

‘Mak siccar!’: A Reading and Critical Commentary of Hamish Henderson’s *Elegies for the Dead in Cyrenaica*

Richie McCaffery

Hamish Henderson’s war poetry expresses his profound commitment to enacting, witnessing and recording the defeat of fascism ‘on the field of battle’ in North Africa and Italy as well as looking towards the post-war virtues of peace, in poems such as ‘Karnak’, with its desire to see the end of death-cults and drives of previous civilisations.[1] After the war, Henderson’s poetry began to move away from the desolate ‘landscape of half-wit / stunted ill-will’ of World War Two to a post-War Scotland that was both politically reformist, egalitarian and forward-looking but also a culture that reclaimed its rich oral heritage. The celebration, recording and dissemination of song, from pubs to the School of Scottish Studies in Edinburgh where Hamish worked for most of his life, was the particular strand of the ‘assets of peace’ pursued by Henderson, that is to say the vision of a better post-war Scotland that informs his activities and poetry and motivates his later life. The ideas of wholeness and ‘reconciliation’[2] are recurring terms in Henderson’s work and letters and highlight his commitment to facilitating ‘the constant fruitful interaction of folk-song and art literature in our tradition.’[3]

---

[1] Joy Hendry, ‘The Scottish Accent of the Mind: Introduction to the Sympathetic Imagination: Scottish Poets of the Second World War’, in Eberhard Bort (ed.), *Borne on the Carrying Stream: The Legacy of Hamish Henderson*. Ochtertyre: Grace Note Publications, 2010, pp. 195-227; 216.

[2] Alec Finlay, ‘Afterword’, Hamish Henderson, *The Armstrong Nose: Selected Letters of Hamish Henderson*, edited by Alec Finlay, Edinburgh: Polygon, 1996, pp.299-356; 304.

[3] Hamish Henderson, ‘Review: *The Uncanny Scot: A Selection of Prose* by Hugh MacDiarmid’, in *Alias MacAlias: The Collected Essays of Hamish Henderson*, edited by Alec Finlay, Edinburgh: Polygon, 1992, pp.304-307; 305.

Elegies for the Dead in Cyrenaica represents Henderson's move away from the hieratic Modernist tones celebrated in the Cambridge circles he moved in before the war towards a 'poetry which must become the people.' Tessa Ransford reminds us that poetry for Henderson was synonymous with life and with people,[4] and this statement reworks Heine's 'freedom must become the people.'[5] Written in the 1830s, Heine also qualifies his statement with another which claims that when 'books are burnt, people will be burned too.' However, the parallels remain between the threats Heine saw towards artistic freedom and the burning of books and that witnessed by Henderson and the great Nazi conflagration of books in Berlin in the 1930s. Heine's dictum was used by Henderson to help to precipitate cultural renewal in Scotland, a freedom that is manifested in people but a freedom that has been achieved in such a way as to suit ('become') those who practice it.

This essay will examine Henderson's poetry sequence *Elegies for the Dead in Cyrenaica* (1948), offering a sustained critical commentary. Due to the scale of this work, it has often been only passingly mentioned by critics and academics alike, although Mario Relich and Tessa Ransford have both written deeply and insightfully on the poem. *Elegies for the Dead in Cyrenaica* contains both a steely resolve to defeat fascism but also the search for an adequate register in which to document the many voices of the war. Their composition coincides with the break-down in Henderson's faith in one overarching *ex cathedra* poetic singular voice and his movement towards anonymous and fluid folk-song. Beyond Henderson's growing interest in the medium of folk-song is the search for a polyphonic sequence that would not only speak for and encapsulate the 'wronged dead' but also suggest, as Angus Calder has noted, that 'history' and the historical verse of war is 'not cyclical but progressively dialectical.'[6]

---

4 Tessa Ransford, 'Hamish Henderson and Scotland: A Crucible of Experiment', *Scottish Review*, no. 539 (19 April 2012), <www.scottishreview.net/TessaRansford257.shtml>.

5 Hamish Henderson, 'Freedom Becomes People', in *Chapman*, no.42 (1985), p.1.

6 Angus Calder and Beth Junor, 'Introduction', in A. Calder and B. Junor, (eds), *The Souls of the Dead Are Taking the Best Seats*, Edinburgh: Luath Press, 2004, pp. 11-14; 12.

Raymond Ross refers to the *Elegies for the Dead in Cyrenaica* as 'a cairn built to the memory of the dead, the innocent but also a cairn to the living – they (the poems) symbolise our human house and they prefigure a life-long dedication to the clear imperative of action – to build our new Alexandria in the aftermath of the fascists' final solution.'[7] For Henderson, the point of the war was to defeat fascism and this mind-set could be transferred back home to Scotland where work could be undertaken with 'no other solution than to acknowledge with pride the clear imperative of action.'[8] Henderson brought to the cultural life of Scotland in the immediate aftermath of the war his 'human steel' and 'revolutionary humanism' to embark on what Corey Gibson describes as 'the next cycle, another revival which sought to expand the awareness of folk-song's existence and breathe life back into its rebel veins.'[9]

In interview, Henderson revealed the small collection of poetry books he carried with him during the desert campaign, Robert Garioch and Sorley Maclean's *17 Poems for 6d* (1939), MacDiarmid's *A Drunk Man Looks at the Thistle* (1926) and both Yeats's *Last Poems* and the poetry of Wilfred Owen: 'without any doubt as far as the *Elegies* are concerned, Wilfred Owen influenced me greatly.'[10] In an essay, G. S. Fraser (1915-1980), a poet who met and befriended Henderson while on service in Cairo, writes that the poet has a responsibility to the future generations in his work, as they may be in some way 'affected' by his ideas. While it is perhaps unlikely that any of G. S. Fraser's work will be carried in a young soldier's kit-bag these days, he does note that 'if that generation has to go through the same intense and complicated suffering that I have, I shall feel my own suffering has been a little futile.'[11] With Henderson there is never any suggestion of the ownership

---

7 Raymond Ross, 'Hamish Henderson In the Midst of Things', in *Chapman*, no.42 (1985), pp.11-18; 12.

8 *Ibid.*, p.11.

9 Corey Gibson, 'Hamish Henderson's conception of the Scottish Folksong Revival and its place in literary Scotland', in *The Drouth*, no.32 (2011), pp.48-59; 52.

10 Hamish Henderson, 'The Poet Speaks', in *Alias MacAlias*, pp.321-325; 322.

11 G. S. Fraser, 'Recent Verse: London and Cairo', in *Poetry London*, X (1944), pp.215-219; 219.

of suffering. Suffering belongs to the 'wronged proletariat of levelling death' and all those left behind to sing for them, but that singing is in itself a form of salvation.

Throughout his life, Henderson received many letters from servicemen expressing praise for *Elegies for the Dead in Cyrenaica*, such as that of Brigadier Lorne Maclean Campbell who wrote 'I find your poems give a voice to all the queer and, for me, quite inarticulate feelings one had in the desert'.[12] The poem, however, was not sufficiently grappled with or appreciated at the time in London or Cairo. In a *New Statesman* review of 1949, Giles Romily clearly missed the overarching theme of safeguarding 'our human house' and the poem's countless tributes to the dead on both sides when all he could see was 'a capacity for almost barbaric physical feeling, possibly helped by the fact that he is a Scot.'[13] This comment compounds bad literary criticism with tacit racial disdain. Timothy Neat's biography of Henderson reminds us that we need to look 'seriously at the *Elegies*' as today's 'academic silence' towards them 'is deafening', which is where this essay begins.

The Prologue and Foreword

The major function of the 'Prologue' is to highlight some of the seeming paradoxes of the coming sequence, such as its call for a 'unified sensibility' and its use of a 'sympathetic imagination.'[14] We are plunged into violence with the 'dumb-bells' and the 'brazen clanging path' but in this we see the poet's aim to salvage meaning, understanding and 'a true and valued testament' in a godless wasteland or desert. Here 'our godhead' is 'a sham' and only the 'brittle arrogance' of a 'rash' poet remains to hold a 'human barrier' against the man-made 'storm.'[15] By letting his words 'knit what now we lack / the demon and the heritage' we realise that he is devoted to not only chronicling

---

[12] Hamish Henderson, 'Letter to Marian Sugden (1949)', in *The Armstrong Nose*, pp.31.

[13] Raymond Ross (1985), p.12.

[14] Joy Hendry (2010), p.212.

[15] Hamish Henderson, 'Prologue', in *Elegies for the Dead in Cyrenaica*, Edinburgh: Edinburgh University Student Publishing Board (EUSPB), 1977, p.7.

the horror of the immediate conflict but a history that calls for 'a chastened wantonness' which 'sets on song a discipline / a sensuous austerity.'[16] While these closing lines appear at first glance to be oxymoronic, they in fact give the first idea of one of the central themes of reconciliation and wholeness. They allude to the ability of the sequence to plough a furrow between 'an eccentric lament for the German dead' and 'mere propaganda for his (Henderson's) beloved Highlanders' to deliver a 'sublimely equal-handed treatment of men and nations at war.'[17]

The prose 'Foreword', coming after the poetic 'Prologue', is significant because it introduces motifs and concepts that are unique to the sequence and its setting. Here Henderson establishes his compassion for the enemy via a fruitful dialogue with a captured German soldier who observes that 'Africa changes everything. In reality we are all allies and the desert is our common enemy.'[18] In the turbidity of desert sand storms, boundaries are crossed and obscured and vision is blurred or deceived. This is precisely what Henderson refers to as the curious 'doppelgänger effect' where each side is forced to live off each other against the 'geological scale of opposition.' Added to this is the bewildering effect of mirage which 'became for me a symbol of our human civil war, in which the roles seem constantly to shift and vary.' The conflict becomes for Henderson something much more than a moral struggle between right and wrong and a need to defeat fascism. It is also a desperate drive to secure 'peace and well-being' in a terrible ontological war between 'the dead, the innocent – that eternally wronged proletariat of levelling death' and 'ourselves, the living, who cannot hope to expiate our survival but by spanning history's apollyon chasm.' The grave task is to span the chasm and not fall into its historical traps but to acclaim 'the runners' of peace 'who have not flinched before their ineluctable exploit.'

The implication here is that World War Two calls for something revolutionary and not merely elegiac. Against this backdrop we see the dying breed of the Highland soldier cast against 'a universal predicament' with only 'the heroic tradition of gaisge'

---

[16] *Ibid.*

[17] Timothy Neat, *Hamish Henderson: A Biography. Volume 1: The Making of the Poet 1919-1953*, Edinburgh: Birlinn/Polygon, 2007, p.98.

[18] Hamish Henderson, 'Foreword', in *Elegies for the Dead in Cyrenaica*, pp.59-60; 59.

to 'sustain them in the high places of the field.' Henderson sides with this disappearing and oppressed people, characterised by the legacy of the Clearances but, as a result, he feels and sings for the fallen on either side.

'First Elegy: End of a Campaign'

Preceding the first elegy is a quatrain from Goethe, drawing attention to the great corpus of literature in German and looking towards intellectual and cultural reconciliation. Henderson explains in his notes that it translates as: 'The gods, the unending, give all things without stint to their beloved: all pleasures, the unending – and all pains, the unending, without stint,' and was frequently used in small anthologies carried in the field of battle by German troops.[19] Given the secular overtones of the poem set in a desert where there are 'no gods and precious few heroes' ('First Elegy') this can be taken as bitterly ironic and shows the layers of disillusionment with World War Two already at work, the repudiation of God and the grand illusion of war. The gods present in the Goethe quatrain show themselves to be arbitrary in their unstinting supply of pleasure and pain and this neatly predicts the poem's juggling of both 'Eros and Thanatos' locked in what Tessa Ransford terms an 'eternal flyting.'[20] Henderson claimed that 'poetry is one aspect of human love. As such it is hugely valuable and sets itself against the religious and legal attitudes to life that are frequently not just stupid and cruel but practically obscene.'[21]

Tessa Ransford has written that the main stimuli behind Henderson's poetry are 'pilgrimage, love-energy, integration and companionship'[22] and these are quickly established in the first poem. In interview Henderson claimed that each elegy 'has an

---

[19] Hamish Henderson, 'Notes', in *Elegies for the Dead in Cyrenaica*, pp.53-56; 53.

[20] Tessa Ransford, 'Encompass the Cross-sword Blades: Hamish Henderson's Poetry', in Eberhard Bort, (ed.) *Borne on the Carrying Stream: The Legacy of Hamish Henderson*. Ochtertyre: Grace Note Publications, 2010, pp.137-160; 138.

[21] Timothy Neat (2007), p.357.

[22] Tessa Ransford (2010), p.138.

aim'[23] and the aim here is to set out the overarching themes in the aftermath of a battle, set against a landscape:

> (...) of half-wit
> stunted ill-will. For the dead land is insatiate
> and necrophilous.[24]

The poem begins in a highly rhetorical and sweeping, almost panoramic, fashion. It has distinct emotive shifts from the grand surveying of the destruction of the scene to the cost in lives of a campaign where the disembodied poet speaks for the fallen to 'sleep now. Sleep here the sleep of the dust.' Relich has noted that this sounds uncomfortably close to 'the sleep of the just' and 'makes for a muted, yet powerful irony about the waste of war.'[25] From this 'necrophilous' and 'insatiate dead land' the poet's gaze moves closer to home, beyond the 'laboured Augustan speeches or vague imperial heritage' to a poignant vignette of the damage caused to domestic life at home with 'a family gathering in the homely kitchen' and a 'lost world glimpsed in the memory of letters.' From this microscopic gaze at one bereaved soldier's family, the poetic scope is exploded in the final stanza where the poet looks back upon his Scotland's war-ravaged history to salvage one dictum that 'we should not disfigure ourselves with the villainy of hatred.' It is the sight of those who go down 'like curs into anonymous silence' that spurs the poet into his task of remembrance and espousal of peace. He 'will bear witness for I knew the others' and, considering the indifferent birdsong of the battlefields, he asks 'why should I not sing them, the dead, the innocent?', leaving the following poem as his coronach.

---

[23] Joy Hendry (2010), p.212.

[24] Hamish Henderson, 'First Elegy: The End of a Campaign', in *Elegies for the Dead in Cyrenaica*, pp.17-18; 17.

[25] Mario Relich, 'Apollyon's Chasm: The Poetry of Hamish Henderson', in Eberhard Bort (ed.), *Borne on the Carrying Stream: The Legacy of Hamish Henderson*, pp.123-136; 125.

'Second Elegy: Halfaya'

The 'Second Elegy' is set in a cantonment in Halfaya, Egypt and carries a dedication to 'Luigi Castigliano', the Milanese Classics student attached to the Eighth Army whom Henderson met during the war. Peter Mackay has said that the number of epitaphs and dedications throughout the book make each encounter or poem read in a 'programmatic' way.[26] Not only is Henderson trying to depict a series of scenes of warfare and its effects systematically but he is also intending that each poem should touch upon and therefore represent the lives and experiences of others. In contrast to the 'First Elegy', this is more terse, elliptical and almost note-book like in its swift setting of the scene, the laager where not only do the ally units sleep but the enemies also, for the:

> (…) laager is one.
> Friends and enemies, haters and lovers
> both sleep and dream.[27]

Henderson is writing here from a disembodied, omnipresent perspective where he observes both sides temporarily relieved from 'the shabby lion-pelt of the desert' and their 'limitless ennui' and unified in their dreams of Arcadian idylls such as 'a landscape / associated with warmth and veils and pantomime / but never focused exactly.' Here where 'companionable death / has lent them his ease for a moment' the sleepers dream:

> Eros, grant forgiveness and release
> and return – against which they erect it,
> the cairn of patience. *No dear, won't be long now*
> *keep fingers crossed, chin up, keep smiling darling*
> *be seeing you soon.*

The cairn is a reminder of Scotland in the centre of the existential turmoil and conflict. The sleepers are haunted too by the voices

---

[26] Peter Mackay, 'Scottish and Irish Second World War Poetry', in *UCD Scholarcast Series*, 4 (2010), pp.2-19; 14.

[27] Hamish Henderson, 'Second Elegy: Halfaya' in *Elegies for the Dead in Cyrenaica*, pp.19-20; 20.

of their loved ones and read in letters such advice as 'chin up, keep smiling darling.' The sleep of the soldier is both a blessing and a curse – it is a welcome escape but also tinged with bitterness in the fact that eros, or the hopes and dreams of the sleeping laager, are trapped in the teeth of God, or 'Yahveh and his tight-lipped sect / confound the deniers of their youth.'

Despite the clipped nature of the 'Second Elegy', it ends on a high rhetorical note, reminding the reader of the similarities of both sides, humanising both sides once again, and reiterating that the true enemy is a topographical and ontological one bearing striking parallels with the God of Calvinism:

> (...) they feel through their blankets
> the cold of the malevolent bomb-thumped desert,
> impartial
> hostile to both.

'Third Elegy: Leaving the City'

The 'Third Elegy' is a touchstone poem in the sequence and deals with the mobilisation of troops from Cairo out to the desert to fight and 'rejoin the proletariat / of levelling death' where 'stripes are shed and ranks levelled.' This poem is one of the most linguistically fluid and varied, encompassing not only droll radio commands: 'be seeing you when this party's over', but also dated soldier parlance: 'the wogs.'[28] This is a pithy and action-filled narrative with allusions to Cavafy whose 'The God Leaves Anthony' also posits 'Alexandria' as 'a symbol of life itself.' It is in the final two stanzas, beyond the setting of the scene, leaving a lush and teeming city to venture out to egalitarian sacrifice where 'the Colonel of Hussars' crouches 'with Jock and Jane in their holes like helots' and where the poet asserts that 'we are the agents / of a dialectic that can destroy us.' This poem, after the Eros of the 'Second Elegy', presents the necessary thanatic and adamantine drive of the soldier who grasps the idea of the deadly dialectic and thus sacrifices his own life for a greater cause. Like Cavafy, Henderson feels himself a man 'worthy of such a city,' and it is for this reason that he must:

---

[28] Hamish Henderson, 'Third Elegy: Leaving the City', in *Elegies for the Dead in Cyrenaica*, pp.21-22; 21.

be glad that the case admits no other solution,
acknowledge with pride the clear imperative of
action
and bid farewell to her, to Alexandria, whom you are
losing.[29]

The final stanza of the 'Third Elegy' presents most powerfully Henderson's deep-seated humanist dilemma. As the enemies approach almost like mirages, Henderson sees his own soldiers in the mirror of his truck, but he avoids personal pronouns and instead uses the collective and possessive 'ours.' The enemy is an ideology and a dialectic, not the men who advance 'in tropical kit' who are 'brothers / in death's proletariat, they are our victims and betrayers' so 'we send them our greeting out of the mirror.' The preternatural idea that the greeting comes 'out of the mirror' not only implies that there is something horrific unfolding but that the poetic gaze sees itself returned in the form of not the enemy, but the ally, another human being who will be slain for the sake of an ideology.

'Fourth Elegy: El Adem'

In interview with Joy Hendry in the mid-1980s, Henderson was to recite his 'Fourth Elegy' and explain that there was little to distinguish 'El Adem' from 'the miles and miles of sweet FA in the desert.'[30] It was here he philosophically considered the 'plight of soldiers on both sides, and because I'm thinking of the Germans as well as our own troops, I interweave, in this poem, echoes of German soldiers' slang as well as British slang.' We need to add to this the underlying existence of Scots words which bring the poem to a close with the memorable image of a cairn built from bravery and perseverance.

The final stanza is perhaps one of the key passages in the whole sequence, where Henderson orders the soldier to 'endure, endure' for 'there is as yet no solution / and no short cut, no escape and no remedy / but our human iron.'[31] Timothy Neat has described this

---

[29] *Ibid.*, p.22.

[30] Joy Hendry, (2010), p.212.

[31] Hamish Henderson, 'Fourth Elegy: El Adem', in *Elegies for the Dead in Cyrenaica*, pp.23-24; 24.

poem's unique aim as the search for 'lyric perfection in exchange for the sacrifice of the creator'[32] and Alec Finlay has gone further to say that 'from the crucible of war Henderson brought home a new understanding of the Scottish psyche and of Scottish history.'[33] However, this poem is attempting to convey much more than both of these quotations suggest. In it Henderson speaks for a great many of the oppressed voices of the desert, opening with the translation of a German slang word for cold – the wind of the desert is 'sow-cold' or 'saukalt.'

Henderson captures the desolation of the desert and the limitless cafard of the fighters whose minds 'are as slack and as rootless / as the tent-pegs driven into cracks of limestone.' They are abject and transitory creatures knowing themselves 'to be nomads, / impermanent guests on this bleak moon-surface.' These are the 'sons of man' who have grown to 'go down in pain' and accept their burden but cannot even hear the cries of Europe 'through the nilhilist windvoice.' Out of this spiritual nadir comes a clear voice that urges the troops 'to use / our rebellious anger for breaking / the vicious fetters that bind us.' Therefore, the only solution is to endure the hellish conditions of the desert and fight a way out of the dead land where a cairn will be built for the fallen.

'Fifth Elegy: Highland Jebel'

The 'Fifth Elegy' is not only historically but, to an exceptional extent, topographically engaged. The fusion of Scots and the desert terrain continues and is expanded upon with the vision moving beyond and leaving behind the 'instant camp', 'imbecile wasteland' and 'black sierras' for a 'well-known house' in the 'treeless machair' with 'kirkyard and valley.' Here the landscape is morphing into that of the blackhouses and crofts of the Clearances where 'burning byres come to my mind.' History has blurred the 'motive and aim' of this massacre and the 'dark moorland' is 'bleeding for wrong or right.'[34]

---

[32] Timothy Neat, *Hamish Henderson: A Biography. Volume 2: Poetry Becomes People* 1952-2002. Edinburgh: Polygon, 2009, p.308.

[33] Alec Finlay (1996), 'Afterword', p.303.

[34] Hamish Henderson, 'Fifth Elegy: Highland Jebel', in *Elegies for the Dead in Cyrenaica*, pp.25-26.

The milieu constantly shifts to encompass not only the immediate terrain but that of the Clearances, the Trojan War and the mythological 'Kythiaron', a place of punishment, violence and bloody sport. Henderson's 'cloudy jebel' is a massif on which people re-live all of these grisly events simultaneously. We see the brutal oppression of the 'highlander' reflected in the regiment in which Henderson is fighting and whose ghostly memories are exerting themselves on the modern soldier's consciousness and sense of identity. Henderson has written that this is particularly a layered poem of 'multiple betrayals'[35] and the caverns 'will number / our momentary cries among the sounds and echoes / of this highland's millennial conflict.' This poem is a ruminative lull before the storm and salvoes of the 'Interlude.' Henderson is musing upon Scotland's place in this global war and considering, as he does in his foreword, the dying tradition of gaisge. The imminent battle is framed as one of mytho-historical and actual clan skirmishes taking place vividly upon a meta-battle-field in a place almost timeless. 'The Grecian Gael' heads towards the site of conflict, weighted with the duty to fight but also haunted on many levels by the 'multiple betrayals' of his people and of 'those others.' The epigraph by Hölderlin talks about a land so captivating that the poet loves it more than his own native land. This can be read as a mordant irony, but it is much more plausible that with Henderson's fusion of different battle-torn lands he is implicitly looking for that elusive coastal land where peace might flourish and prevail once more.

'Interlude: Opening of an Offensive'

The 'Interlude' is broken into three discrete sections – 'the waiting', 'the barrage' and 'the Jocks.' Few poems of World War Two have gone so far to vigorously capture a sense of involvement and action in one of these major offensives with specific narrative description akin to that of a documentary or filmic depiction. Henderson has stated that he is here re-living the battle of El Alamein (1942), one of the most decisive and significant of the desert war. The 'waiting' section is muted and tersely conversational, giving little clue as to the impending onslaught. It is again ironic that Henderson has chosen a full-scale

[35] Timothy Neat, (2009), p.205.

artillery attack for an 'interlude' – traditionally the juncture in an opus reserved for refreshment and quiet reflection. The 'barrage' section is appropriately a manic short burst of energy which contains some of the most convincing 'murderous music' of the war. It is a fulmination of sound and a conflagration of words with lines such as:

> Dithering darkness, we'll wake you! Hells bells
> blind you. Be broken, bleed
> deathshead blackness!
>   The thongs of the livid
> firelights lick you
>   jagg'd splinters rend you
>   underground
> we'll bomb you, doom you, tomb you into grave's
>   mound[36]

These terrifying lines are addressed not to the German troops but seem to be the voice of Hell itself, which has been blasted open by both Allied and Axis forces during this offensive. It is only in the third section, 'Jocks', that we get a sense of 'the heroic tradition of gaisge' with the 'fast vanishing race' in the midst of a 'raucous apocalypse.' The sound of the battle is so ear-shattering that it knocks in 'the night of Heaven' and is a 'drummeling, overwhelming Niagara.' Yet beyond this deadly cacophony comes the sound of the 'war-pipes' and the big music which transcends everything. The war threatens to strike the pipes dumb 'in the blunderbuss black' but they come again and flaunt 'aggression to the sullen desert' where 'its scream tops the valkyrie' and the 'colossal artillery.' This sound if of the adamantine resolve of the Highlanders to see not only the fascist threat to freedom removed but that of religion, of 'tyrannous myth.' The fact that they hear this stirring strident and prideful music means:

> (...) that many
> German Fascists will not be going home
> meaning that many
> will die, doomed in their false dream

---

[36] Hamish Henderson, 'Interlude: Opening of an Offensive', in *Elegies for the Dead in Cyrenaica*, pp.27-29: 27-28.

Such is the might and determination of the Highlanders they are committed to quelling anything that might be deemed a threat to peace and freedom. In this they will 'mak siccar' that they destroy 'the leaching lies' and 'the worked out systems of sick perversion.' The rallying cry 'mak siccar' recollects the episode in Scottish history when, in 1306, Robert the Bruce stabbed John Comyn, one of the claimants for the Scots throne, and his aid Roger de Kirkpatrick, sensing that Robert the Bruce was in doubt, vowed to 'mak siccar' he was dead. This reminds the reader of the martial and blood-soaked history of Scotland but also shows a deep desire to simultaneously observe and move away from that mentality once and for all. If this war is intended to end fascism, Henderson seems to be saying, we need to make absolutely certain that we get the job done.

Of all the poems in the sequence, the bellicosity of this passage is the most difficult to read from a humanist angle, as it does relish the task of defeating the enemy and finds great pride in doing so. Henderson's 'Interlude' serves to show the ugly side of fighting in the heat of battle, and the 'sabre-rattling' nature of the poem shows the problematic links between Scottish poetry, battles and nationhood and also evokes the Gaelic tradition of poetic incitement. The poems leading up to this onslaught have evoked the history of oppression of the Highlands and this could be seen as the last eruption of bloody revolution to ensure peace was secured. What is especially novel about this section is that it makes clear that the Highlanders are murderers as well as liberators. Henderson has said that he felt on the level of the ordinary soldier that both sides were as 'guilty or as innocent' as each other.[37]

Part Two

We are beginning to see how the poem tackles the conflict from a different focal point or stage in the campaign. The intensity and energy of the 'Interlude' is sustained in the 'Sixth Elegy – Acroma', as we shall see, but Part Two begins with a quotation from Sorley MacLean's 'Death Valley.'[38] The extract deployed by Henderson is that of the closing lines of the poem, where MacLean reflects upon the sight of a dead German 'boy' soldier and sees through all of the centuries'

[37] Joy Hendry (2010), p.212.

[38] Hamish Henderson, 'Part Two', in *Elegies for the Dead in Cyrenaica*, p.31.

worth of militaristic mummery to the intrinsic lie of 'honourable death' in battle:

> Whatever his desire or mishap,
> his innocence or malignance,
> he showed no pleasure in his death
> below the Ruweisat Ridge.[39]

After the violence of the 'Interlude', this extract re-introduces the great problematic humanist dilemma that underpins the sequence. There is no vaunting or gloating at the death of a fascist here, but the grave moral ambivalence of seeing a dead boy on the battlefield. The poem is quoted in Gaelic and this shows not only the great range of cultures affected by the war but also makes a point about the exclusions and oppressions of language in the long history of war. The fact that Gaelic was a language in decline, that readers might not be able to understand, is exactly the point.

'Sixth Elegy: Acroma'

Acroma is a turning-point in the sequence where, after the violence of the 'Interlude', the poet is forced to re-assess his position within the desert war and to question the purpose of his poem recounting and memorialising the events because 'the lying films / contain greater truth than most of our memories.' The poem vacillates between the previous carnage and the antithetical idea that this vast 'sacrifice' was 'on the whole "necessary".' Henderson laments that he too has:

> (...) acquiesced
> in this evasion: that the unlucky
> or the destined must inevitably fall
> and be impaled on the basalt pinnacles of
> darkness.[40]

[39] Sorley MacLean, 'Death Valley/ Glac a' Bhàis', in *Caoir Gheal Leumraich: White Leaping Flame: Collected Poems*, Edinburgh: Polygon, 2011, pp.206-207.

[40] Hamish Henderson, 'Sixth Elegy: Acroma', in *Elegies for the Dead in Cyrenaica*, pp.33-34; 33.

It is a Tartarean image but the 'evasion' to which Henderson refers is also a linguistic one, that it is simply too easy to say that death on such a vast scale is 'necessary.' On the other hand, to expose the dignified language that surrounds and attempts to euphemise war as a manifest lie would cast 'shame' on the dead or to lazily say 'that it was expedient / a generation should die for the people?' Here, Henderson is articulating the purpose of *Elegies for the Dead in Cyrenaica* as a work that must find its own 'adequate exclamation' against the cruelty of killing.[41] It is Henderson's conviction that only poetry can take the war to 'inaccessible sierras / of naked acceptance, where mere reason cannot live.' Henderson doubts that he is the poet to 'attain it' even as he knows that something is needed beyond the inadequacies of 'reportage' or the 'anodyne of statistics.' With only these means of seeing the war, people will ignore the memory of the dead. Henderson visualises a time where such sacrifice will be forgotten and eventually marred by the sectarian animosities of football:

> (...) laughing couples at the tea-dance
> ignore their memory, the memoirs almost slight
> them
> and the queue forming up to see Rangers play
> Celtic
> forms up without thought to those dead.

Against this, Henderson sees the words that his poem has looked for and 'must go on looking for' are: 'words of whole love, which can slowly gain the power / to reconcile and heal. Other words would be pointless.' In the 'Sixth Elegy' the idea of polyphony versus the lyric ego is left to one side as the poet takes upon himself the weight of singing about 'the whole love.' Henderson's friend, the Marxist historian E. P. Thompson, believed that this first person voice twinned with the 'egotistical sublime' of the imagery of 'inaccessible sierras' 'becomes self-conscious; the focus of attention is shifted from the men and their actions to the poet and his words.'[42] Alec Finlay disagrees and sees the difference between the voices of the men on the battlefield and the higher poetic reveries of the poet as 'essential to the cause he fought

---

[41] Donald Wesling, *Internal Resistances: The Poetry of Edward Dorn*, Oakland, California: University of California Press, 1985, p.226.

[42] *Ibid.*, p.312.

for.' They mark the movement towards a reconciliation which synthesises 'emotion and intellectual argument.'[43] If anything, the 'Sixth Elegy' shows us the intensity of Henderson's 'yearning for the shared human values of love and solidarity' and expounds a 'new understanding of the Scottish psyche and history'[44] as one that is self-referential enough to see its historical pitfalls and can learn from them to 'slowly gain the power / to reconcile and heal.'

'Seventh Elegy: Seven Good Germans'

In sharp contrast with the singular bardic persona of the previous poem, 'Seven Good Germans' is a series of small cameos of fallen German soldiers, interweaving the idiolects and parlances of each dead soldier as the poem progresses. The opening explains that the land where these men were to die, and lie in anonymous quiet, is 'a kind of no-man's land' in Libya called 'El Eleba.' This terse opening stamps upon the poem a feeling of spiritual and existential desolation where it falls upon the folkloric collector of voices to stitch together utterances to invest the dead with last words or snippets of written confessions found on their persons. In naming the place, Henderson seems to be providing topographical exactness, the precisions of the map-reader, but the very act of finding 'El Eleba' in itself seems uncanny:

> to get there, you drive into the blue take a bearing
> and head for damn all. Then you're there. And
> where are you?[45]

True to the poem's overall assertion that all the fallen in the conflict are 'death's proletariat' the first encounter is with a dead 'Lieutenant' – the highest ranking officer within the 'Seventh Elegy' – and he is accorded only the briefest and most cursory of epitaphs, that he wished to remain 'steadfast / there is only decision and the will / the rest has no importance.' In fact as the poem interviews each of the dead, they lower in military rank and the ghostly voices become more demotic and open. The second

---

43 *Ibid.*

44 *Ibid.*, p.303.

45 Hamish Henderson, 'Seventh Elegy: Seven Good Germans', in *Elegies for the Dead in Cyrenaica*, pp.35-37; 35.

is 'a Corporal', and he is much more vociferous in his opinions towards a Dutch Nazi conscript, or an 'old Afrikaner' who moans about his lack of rations. The inference is that if he can 'dodge the column, pass the buck / and scrounge' then he should have no problem becoming a turncoat and going over to 'Tommy' who has 'all the eats.' This fragment reveals the racial divisions at play and this emphasises Henderson's attempt to illuminate them and heal such schism.

Perhaps more poignant is the plight of the 'third' who was truly a 'helot' being a 'farm-hand' sent to the desert as nothing more than 'fresh-fodder for machine-guns.' The clinical, mortuary sound of the language that 'his dates are inscribed on the files, and on the cross-piece' not only hammers home the notion that millions died in this way with only dates and not even rudimentary crosses to commemorate them, but it also reminds the reader of the oft-quoted gnome of Stalin that 'one death is a tragedy, a million deaths is just a statistic.' All of the German soldiers who perished in the desert are described as 'good', and the purpose here is to aim for reconciliation by showing their deaths and their domestic pre-war lives. It is an expansive attempt to re-humanise the ordinary deaths of mass statistics. In a sense it resembles the collecting of ballads and folk-songs to prevent them from falling into obscurity.

'The fourth was a lance jack' and he seems to have died, as the 'Interlude' claims, 'in his false dream' for trusting in 'Adolf / while working as a chemist in the suburb of Spandau.' A fuller and more genteel picture emerges of this soldier as 'his loves were his cello, and the woman who had borne him / two daughters and a son.' Here we see one of the many who lived and died by the credo of the Third Reich as 'he had faith in the Endsieg / THAT THE NEW REICH MAY LIVE prayed the flyleaf of his Bible.' Henderson acknowledges the zeal of his ideology while simultaneously seeing the need to end it and its murderously 'false dream.'

Pathos builds up throughout so that with 'the fifth – a mechanic' we see that abstract values of 'honour and glory' in battle mean nothing. This trooper is not under the thrall of any Nazi ideology, all he cares about is 'how to get back to his sweetheart,' and the defeatism in his voice is apparent when he states that 'Tommy' could 'put our whole Corps in the bag.' Each of the dead has a motive, and a singular perspective on the desert war, and the poem reveals a gamut of human reactions, such as the difficult status of the sixth, 'a Pole' 'who had put off his nation to serve in the Wehrmacht.' Despite this act of tergiversation, the speaker insists that 'he was not a bad bloke,' although 'his mates' thought he was 'just a polnischer Schweinhund.' The 'seventh' and final dead soldier is 'a young swaddy' who had died 'cramped in a lorry' on the road to 'El Eleba' which, the poem tells us, is no-where but the destination of the dead. What marks his end out is that he was a poet who 'had written three verses in appeal against his sentence / which soften for an hour the anger of Lenin.'

'Eighth Elegy: Karnak'

In 'Karnak', Henderson is largely concerned with making the Ancient Egyptian resonances of the battlefield vividly present. As such, this elegy is an historically, linguistically and mythologically complex poem about a modern soldier's attempt to salvage meaning and answers from the Ancients, whose ruinous temple complexes at Thebes form part of the backdrop of this mechanised, mobile war. The 'masters of war' that preside over this poem are that of Osiris, Mohammed and Ra. In Henderson's war notebooks he noted that the Ancient Egyptian civilisation of Karnak was filled 'with a profound death-longing.' In 'the shambles' of the crumbling temples and tombs, Henderson sees a thanatic land and people of a perverse kind of 'Vollendung' or achievement, those devoted to reaching the fields of Aaru in the afterlife. In all of this spent magnificence it is clear that the 'triumphal barque of civilisation / was weighed down with a heavy ballast / of magnetic death.'[46] This knowledge forms a stark historical antithesis between the dead and fallen age and those of the vivid present, the living combatants.

As a caveat, Henderson reminds us that those who go 'a-whoring after death / will assuredly find it' and 'will be sealed in, confined / to their waste palaces' much like Antigone, whose mythology is also deeply steeped in warfare. Henderson is acutely aware of a generation either willingly or reluctantly going down with the 'horsemen' into 'craved annihilation' and we already know that the desert's history of bloodshed and death-lust makes it 'necrophilous.' Beyond the macabre architecture, this poem carries a surprisingly clear, optimistic and life-affirming message

[46] Hamish Henderson, 'Eighth Elegy: Karnak', in *Elegies for the Dead in Cyrenaica*, pp.38-41; 38.

which is hinted at by the nod towards Cavafy's 'barbarians.' Cavafy's grand realisation, as channelled through Henderson, is that the 'barbarians' are 'a kind of solution' and that 'all of us, from Hellenes to Gaelic outlanders of the western world, are in a sense beside Thebes' half-civilised clod-hoppers.' In his notes, Henderson says that even in the modern day the barbarian persists, despite all of the time that has lapsed between the past of the desert and the present, and it is this war-like atavism that Henderson seeks to put to an end.

The modern soldiers in the desert are the 'standard bearers of the superb blasphemy, / felling gods, levelling cities', they are even 'severing the umbilical cord of history.' In their deathly pursuits they are like these barbarians, they are 'trampling migrations' or 'fellaheen' to 'death's proletariat', but Henderson also sees the potential to harness their dedication to seeking death as a power that could be used for seeking and securing life. As Henderson writes: 'if we of the modern west devote a tenth of the time to life that Karnak devoted to death, we'll bring a tangible hope.' Henderson recognises this as a synthesis implicit in his human condition, to take the best from a fallen civilisation and evolve, but he also painfully accepts that his great vision of 'vaunted reconciliation' belongs to that of 'Rilke's single column' or 'Vollendung' which is intellectually mountainous and solitary. Henderson is calling for a movement towards a more life-centred civilisation and not one reflexively turning to war or theatres of global conflict. After making this haunting comparison, the poem moves on to imagine the day as one of feast or celebration in some Arcadian afterlife where the ordinary workers must still do their bit which invariably involves drudgery for a higher power such as working the 'shadouf.'

The final passages try to imagine the afterlife expected by the previous inhabitants of this desert. It is a place of vibrant and pullulating activity and diversity but the poet recognises that this is all part of another great illusion from another time and that 'prisoners of the war' will be left to 'drive the shaft for a tomb.' While Oedipus is seen in aristocratic ostentation 'in his state chariot', to his 'fellaheen' or 'helots' of 'wronged death' he is a sham 'flower-strewn godhead / the scourge and the crook, under the sycamore leaves of life.'

'Ninth Elegy: Fort Capuzzo'

Fort Capuzzo is set in the Italian colonies of Libya at the time of World War Two and deals with a soldier visiting the makeshift graveyard where he meditates upon the death of an enemy. As Mario Relich claims, it is 'the most straightforward of the Elegies' and 'most directly encapsulates the liminal aspects of life and death experienced in desert warfare.'[47] The perimeters of the 'desert warfare' can be expanded upon as this poem tries to speak for a type of 'hard pietas' that outreaches that of simply the desert conflict. It is something that exists throughout modern warfare and harks back to the virtues of Ancient Rome and that of Aeneas. If we are to take the Ciceronian definition of 'pietas' as that of a virtue 'which admonishes us to do our duty to our country or our parents or other blood relations'[48] then we find it wanting, along with Henderson who observes the soldier's pang of duty and loyalty mixed with that of 'survivor's guilt' and pathos for 'another "Good Jerry" just eighteen' to die so far from home. Indeed, the 'real enemies' of this war turn out to be the finagling bureaucrats and propagandists such as the 'newsreel commentator' whose language has no scope or capacity for such emotion as that of one soldier's 'pietas' for a fallen enemy.[49]

The 'pietas' in this case is not Ciceronian but the informal speech of an ordinary soldier who calls him 'a poor mucker' and a 'poor bastard.' This colloquial soliloquy at the graveside not only encapsulates guilt and contrition but a sense of waste for he was 'only eighteen' but this outpouring of visceral grief is kept in check by the bonds of military bonds. There is a hint of gallow's humour to the soldier's claims that it was:

> just as well it was him, though,
> and not one of our chaps.
> Yes, the only good Jerry,
> as they say, is your sort, chum.[50]

---

[47] Mario Relich (2010), p.125.

[48] Hendrik Wagenvoort, *Pietas: Selected Studies in Roman Religion*, Leiden, Netherlands: E. J. Brill, 1980, p.7.

[49] Mario Relich (2010), p.129.

[50] Hamish Henderson, 'Ninth Elegy: Fort Capuzzo', in *Elegies for the Dead in Cyrenaica*, p.42.

This, however, can be interpreted as lines that have been drummed into the soldier, feelings he is expected to experience, and it therefore can be read ironically. The sonnet-like form seems to bring a sense of canonical or classical discipline to the soldier's 'pietas.' It closes with an image of a regiment united in death, waiting for the 'reveille' of the Rapture where they mistakenly believe, or died believing, they would be elected to heaven for their acts of bravery and self-sacrifice.

'Tenth Elegy: The Frontier'

Tessa Ransford has said that the 'Tenth Elegy' of the sequence has a 'particular overview' to it.[51] This comes from the positioning of the dead and the 'remembrancer' poet in the desert while affluent and carefree people travel overhead in aeroplanes, barely taking account the meaning of the wars that raged below, 'idly' inspecting from the windows 'the lunar qattaras, the wadis like family trees.' This bird's-eye view, is not an attempt to close the poem as a summation of its main argument and themes, as it is only the beginning of a long movement towards peace. The 'remembrancer' is prognosticating a time when all of this bomb-thumped desert with its 'dried blood in the sangars' will be of as much interest to the 'airborne travellers' as the 'Trojan defence-works' and will touch them 'as little as the Achean strategies.'[52]

The epigraph from the later poems of Rilke which reads 'one must die because one knows them' brings the reader back to the impossibility of Rilkean reconciliation and takes a step towards a more unified understanding between nations who all bear the grim bequeathal of the dead whose 'sleep is our unrest, we lie bound in their inferno.' The final conflict is between the wronged dead and the indifferent living inheritors who have lost touch with them.

The task of the poet, then, is to defy the traditional modes of grief and remembrance in the aftermath of such a cataclysmic war. As Edwin Morgan has noted:

---

[51] Tessa Ransford (2010), p.142.

[52] Hamish Henderson, 'Tenth Elegy: The Frontier', in *Elegies for the Dead in Cyrenaica*, pp.43-45: 44.

> his duty as an elegist must include something more than remembrance, there must be something more active if the dead are to be appeased, more active even than Wilfred Owen's warnings. The dead will hold us in contempt if we fail to change society, reform government, make freedom and justice efficacious.[53]

Morgan's view is one of the most accurate distillations of the poem's implicit purpose. Henderson's intention is that this poem should go beyond the poetry of World War One and break free from the cyclical idea of wars in history as necessary events that will recur, leaving poets to mourn in the aftermath.

Henderson demands that we must 'either build for the living love, patience and power to absolve the tormented, / or else choke in the folds of their black-edged vendetta' and this is a radical form of poetic manifesto for war poetry. As Angus Calder has noted, the poem is active and progressive. It is about breaking away from the usual bonds of what war poetry should do towards something aggressively life-affirming and dedicated to pursuing the 'assets of peace' whilst also remembering and honouring the dead.

'Heroic Song for the Runners of Cyrene'

Edwin Morgan detects in 'Heroic Song for the Runners of Cyrene' something of a break in mood and tenor from the present-day and forward-looking zeal of the Tenth Elegy and the 'extreme stoicism and heroic individualism' of the epilogue which seems 'at odds with much that had been foregrounded in the Tenth Elegy.'[54] The dedication is to the Spanish painter and friend of Lorca, Gregorio Prieto, whose work was inspired by ancient civilisations and their architectures. This is apposite as on a surface reading it concerns the rivalry between athletes from Cyrene and Carthage, running from each other's cities to decide

---

[53] Edwin Morgan, 'The Sea, the Desert, the City: Environment and Language in W. S. Graham, Hamish Henderson, and Tom Leonard', in *The Year-Book of English Studies* (1987), pp.31-45; 38.

[54] *Ibid.*, p.39.

upon a frontier, the exact point where the runners meet, fight and die. In the notes, Henderson makes it clear that he sides with Cyrene, as a 'symbol of civilised humanity, of our "human house".' This is difficult to reconcile with the poem's treatment of the futility of their contest, that each runs 'to achieve, without pause or evasion / his instant of nothing.'[55]

However, the intertextual layering shows that Henderson is not merely re-enacting a legendary bloody pageant like 'the jousts of the Toppo' from Dante but is attempting to depict the layers of history one must grasp and learn from in order to be part of a better 'civilisation.' As the epigraph from Denis Saurat suggests, these are salutary examples of clan and tribal warfare for 'without suffering and death one learns nothing' and that 'only those ideas are acceptable that hold through suffering and death (...) Life is that which leaps.'[56] In the three sections of this poem, Henderson shows a race of tremendous achievement and vitality but ultimately doomed to 'history the doppelgänger', the same deathless force at work in the same desert thousands of years in the past. In the third, final section, all of the Cyrenians' athletic prowess is wasted as they lock 'in a fatal embrace which solves nothing for the rival cultures.'[57]

It is the book's closing image of the rival runners falling locked 'like lovers / down the thunderous cataract of day' that gives a stark image of beauty darkened by the utter nihilism of their final emptily heroic act. The abruptness of the ending led Edwin Morgan to ask if the poem is about 'heroism' not being 'enough.' This seems a valid assumption, as heroism without any programmatic idea of the assets of peace, is an empty and exhibitionist act, no matter how laudable. The fault-lines of previous battles and wars underscore any poetic treatment of modern conflict and the poet must come to terms with them in order to see and move beyond them. In the midst of all of this 'suffering and death' only ideas that 'hold through' are 'acceptable.' 'Heroic Song for the Runners of Cyrene' shows a culture nullified by territorial dispute leading to bloodshed, one of many fallen cultures whose ghostly presence enriches the sequence and gives the poems their resonance. It

[55] Hamish Henderson, 'Notes', in *Elegies for the Dead in Cyrenaica*, pp.53-56; 55.

[56] Hamish Henderson, 'Heroic Song for the Runners of Cyrene', in *Elegies for the Dead in Cyrenaica*, pp.47-51; 47.

[57] Edwin Morgan (1987), p.39.

must be noted that this poem prefigures the shadow cast by the Cold War, and implies that the battle is never completely over. Nevertheless, the sequence sets a way of thinking that might actively shape the future.

Conclusion

Tessa Ransford observes that *Elegies for the Dead in Cyrenaica* and the songs are a form of literature that 'constitutes life' rather than being an 'idea of it', that is, they are not commentaries so much as active engagements and represent some of the most vigorous of post-war poetry.[58] Timothy Neat has written that Henderson was devoted to 'artistic love' as a force 'in modern societies' to 'address and embrace the collective', a 'democratic wish to raise the bar of our understanding of what human beings are capable of.'[59] Taken as part of a cohesive and reconciliatory oeuvre, Henderson's poems look towards the death of the lonely soldier poet, or the singular lyric voice for the sake of democratic polyphony.

More than this, Henderson as a cultural figure in Scotland is proactively devoted to the assets of peace fought for in the war, shown by his dedication to folk-song, art and culture and his belief, dramatised in 'The Flyting o' Life and Daith', that in the dialectical struggle between life and death he would strive to ensure that life could always claim 'the warld is mine'.[60]

---

[58] Tessa Ransford (2010), p.142.

[59] Timothy Neat, (2007), p.360.

[60] Hamish Henderson, 'The Flyting o' Life and Daith', in Hamish Henderson, *Collected Poems and Songs*, edited by Raymond Ross, Edinburgh: Curly Snake Publishing, 2000, pp.144-145.

I Heard Scotland Singing

Ewan McVicar

My title comes from one of the 1950s BBC radio programmes written and presented by renowned American folklorist Alan Lomax, sharing his field recordings in Scotland. In 2011 I wrote a piece for the book *'Tis Sixty Years Since* about Lomax collecting in North East Scotland in 1951. In the same book Margaret Bennett investigated the 1951 Lomax recordings of Gaels in Edinburgh and the Gaeltacht, and I also contributed there my detailed CD notes and transcriptions for the Rounder CD *The 1951 People's Festival Ceilidh*.

Some of the singers I wrote about in that piece were recorded by Lomax in the 1950s with the assistance of Hamish Henderson and the MacLeans of Raasay, and soon became well known in the Folk Revival – Jimmy MacBeath, Flora MacNeil, Jessie Murray, John Strachan, Jeannie Robertson and Davie Stewart. At the time of the book there were only 30 second snippets of each of his 1950s Scottish recordings available to listen to online. Although the Kist o' Riches website has thousands of hours of recordings from the School of Scottish Studies, the twenty hours of recordings by Lomax that are the foundation of the Association For Cultural Equity (ACE) Archive are, for copyright reasons, omitted there. However, everything Lomax recorded in Scotland or from Scots singers is now online in full.[1]

The site also has the dates and the places of recording, allowing me to consider here in detail the 54 items of songs and tunes and interviews about the material recorded from Hamish Henderson in London in early 1951, several items from Morris Blythman in Glasgow *re* the initial development of his political songs, and some of the other North East Scots riches. The ACE Archive has also enabled the issue in the USA by Rounder Records of several more CDs of Lomax's Scottish recordings, including an album of Gaelic women that Margaret Bennett edited, *Portrait* albums of the key source singers Jeannie Robertson, Jimmy MacBeath

[1] http://research.culturalequity.org/audio-guide.jsp

and Davie Stewart, an album of children's songs and games, and a double album of MacBeath and Stewart titled *Two Gentlemen Of The Road*. In the Archive still lurk many less celebrated gems, but, like the Kist o' Riches, the site can be dived into from several different launch points, which each give a varying view of the prizes that swim past.

To Begin Before The Beginning

The online material can be ordered in various ways to be viewed, searched and listened to – by country location, then by track title, by tape reference number, or by session/town, and each can throw up illuminating information on Lomax's work and approach. For example, choosing 'Scotland recordings', then ordering by the reference numbers of Lomax's tapes, results in, first of all, three tracks recorded in Glasgow in August 1951 from Scots singer and actress Isla Cameron, whom Lomax had already recorded in London in February. In August she sings 'Pu'in Bracken' and 'Can Ye Sew Cushions'. Cameron is described on the site as a 'Scottish revival singer', and Lomax on the tape box notes that she learned the latter song 'from old lady at a party in Edinburgh'.

Then, on the website list, come eight tracks copied from BBC discs, all dated Glasgow 1951. (These would have been made either in June or August 1951.) The Archive notes that

> 1. These dubs from disc were made by Lomax from the Permanent Record Library of the BBC in Glasgow, presumably with the forthcoming Columbia World Library albums in mind. Original recordists, dates, locations, and accession numbers when known, are listed in specific tracks' notes. [Source: Editor]
>
> 2 - The tape box credits for T3397 and T3398 are very jumbled, or the contents of these tapes were later cut into different combinations and kept stored in their original tape boxes. We have tried to identify the performers and performances to the best of our ability. [Source: Editor]

These BBC tracks are followed by tracks sung by children of Norton Park School, Edinburgh. I included some of these in the

Singing In The Streets album I edited for Rounder Records. Now I learn to my modified chagrin that none of these were recorded by Lomax himself in 1951 as I had previously understood and asserted in the sleeve notes. All are in fact 1949 recordings made in the BBC studios for the film *The Singing Street*.

Searching the Archive seeking to resolve a long-standing puzzle reveals that a suspicion of mine is justified. In two radio programmes for the BBC, Lomax gives very attractive romanticised and contradictory accounts of encountering and recording Edinburgh busker Joe Cadona playing on panpipes and drum the tunes 'Orange and the Blue' and 'Mrs MacLeod Of Raasay'. This has been one of my very favourite Lomax recordings, and I have included it in several educational publication recordings for Scottish children, but it is in fact a copy from a BBC disc. Though the Lomax organisation the Association for Cultural Equity in previous years had told me the artist's name, in the move to the current online format this name has been mislaid, and the track is now labelled as 'pipe tunes' by an 'unidentified artist'. Let us move swiftly on to calmer ground.

Alan Lomax met singer and playwright Ewan MacColl in London in 1951, and on 12 February recorded an astonishing 79 tracks from him, mostly of Scots song, but also some child lore from his home town of Salford, and a few tracks of what a caustic note in the School of Scottish Studies labels 'cod Gaelic'. MacColl on 16 February wrote to Hamish Henderson urging him to write to Lomax c/o BBC, London, and the exciting results of Lomax's resultant seminal 1951 recording trip around Scotland, assisted by Henderson and others, have been very widely documented in print and commercial recordings. However, much less investigated is the product of their initial meeting, now fully available to listen to online.

Hamish Henderson and Alan Lomax in London

This is surely the point, in March 1951, where Henderson, a song enthusiast and informant, begins to observe the value of being a recording collector. On 6 March, in Hotel Meurice, 36 Lancaster Gate, London, Hamish starts to give Lomax a crash course in Scots song culture. The 30 items recorded that day begin with the bothy ballad 'The Muckin O Geordie's Byre', sung with great spirit. Hamish repeats each chorus, and as he does so, when he reaches the final word of the chorus first line, 'The graip wis tint, the besom wis deen', he pushes *deen* with a fine flourishing pause.

This song is not the eighteenth-century lyric given by David Herd, nor the mid twentieth-century pastiche recorded by Andy Stewart, but substantially an early twentieth-century composition by G S Morris. Henderson later detailed its complex ancestry in Scottish Tradition booklet 1, *Bothy Ballads: Music from the North-East*. Although the 'Barnyards o Delgaty' recording is relegated as a 'fragment' to the very end of the ACE listing, it must have been recorded next. Henderson sings it in much more sedate style, one verse and chorus, as the 'Barnyards of Delgadee', a fine example of oral mis-transmission in action. He proceeds to tell Lomax about Bothy Ballads, and the bothies.

As he begins his next topic, he suggests rather coyly that "with another rum or whisky" his singing voice would improve. Then he gives a lecture-style introduction. 'Here is a little collection of reel tune, tunes for the reel, one of the liveliest of the Highland dances. It's mouth music, when the people haven't got a pipe or the fiddle, well then somebody of the company would sing. And this is the sort of effect it made.' Hamish launches into two short songs he was to use as key performance pieces throughout his life, 'Tail Toddle' followed by 'Wap An Row'. An interesting discussion ensues, Henderson as always politely informative.

> 'Would they be able to dance to that, eh, just the way you sing it?'
>
> 'Well, yes, very nearly, maybe I was, seeing as there's nobody dancing here I don't have the impetus to sing it exactly the way a man would like to dance to it.'

Lomax as always has a keen interest in any song or story with a sexual element.

> 'Would that song be sung eh with any group of people? Or is it I mean slightly improper. So could anybody be singing it, would it be sung in any kind of group?'
>
> 'Well, in the old Scots society anyone would sing it. There wasn't so much prudishness among the old Scots people. Nowadays of course ...'
>
> 'What do you mean by that? How, how far back?'

'Well, about a hundred years in some parts. But uh, in a lot of parts of Scotland today, to tell you the honest truth, in which they would sing it in company now, without any trouble.'

'What places? What kind of company?'

'Well, if you had for example a farm gathering in Perthshire or in Angus, or in Aberdeenshire or Kincardine, there are all the people together there and after about and hour or two of singing and drinking you would get that sort of stuff without any trouble.'

'Women sing it as well as men, eh?'

'Well, they mightn't sing it but they'd be there and they'd relish it.'

Lomax then asks for and gets a translation of 'Wap An Row'. Hamish sounds as though he is experiencing a mixture of slight embarrassment and amusement, but immediately sings a frankly bawdy song that recommends rape – 'Gie The Lass her Fairin'.

> Coup her o'er among the creels,
> The more ye bang the less she squeels.

Lomax in an awed tone says, 'Gosh. Translate that.' Henderson replies 'Well, that's a tall order, actually', then gives a clear account, ending with 'So hey for hochmagandy – and so, [pauses then laughs] good luck to it.'

Next Hamish lilts 'the Bloody Fields of Flanders' and the 'Reel of Tulloch', using canntaireachd-style vocables, and explains 'Well now, that's a type of mouth music that hasn't actually got words on it, either in Gaelic, the old Celtic language of Scotland, or in lowland Scots. It's just "hederam haderam", a type of singing which incorporates words that are just gibberish, nonsense, but it's very fine for dancing, for the mouth music, for it seems you can lift peoples' heels to it even more than you can with words, for it corresponds more to the rhythm of the dance.' Now comes an 'Unidentified Gaelic mouth music piece'. This is a popular puirt a beul called 'Cairistìona Chaimbeul (Christina Cambell)'. Hamish now sings his own song, then entitled 'Highlander's Farewell To Sicily', in fine march tempo. Lomax wrote on the tape box 'A song Hamish made himself, and was sung by a hundred other soldiers'. Hamish explains.

> Well, that song is a ballad about the departure of the Highland Division from Sicily after the campaign in which it took part, which ended in the withdrawal of the Gerries from Sicily. And the Highland Division was needed to take part in the Western offensive, the assault against the Vestvaal in France, and so it wasn't able to go on through Italy as it looked as if it would like to do at that time. And so it was withdrawn from Messina down to Catania and Augusta, and gradually all the battalions and the units of the Highland Division were embarked to go home to Scotland. And just about that time when I saw everything packing up I got into my head that I would write a ballad about it. And hearing the old pipe tune 'Farewell To The Creeks', [composed during World War 1 by Pipe Major James Robertson of Banff, and referring to the creeks of the Banff coast] which is the tune of this song, it was played one day by the massed bands of the 153 Brigade of the Highland Division, I started putting words to it, and this is the song as it eventually turned out.

His next song is also his own lyric, the 'John Maclean March'. Hamish's tune for the song is 'The Bloody Fields of Flanders', composed by John (Jock) McLellan who served in World War One, and became Pipe Major of the 8th Argyllshire Battalion, the HLI. This is, as Henderson pointed out in a letter to me, a pipe march version of an old Perthshire song tune, sometimes called 'Busk Busk Bonnie Lassie', sometimes called 'Bonny Glenshee'. The pipe march was made during the First World War. Hamish also used the same march tune for his famous song 'The Freedom Come-All-Ye'. And another Scottish writer, Cliff Hanley, used a different setting of the same march tune for his music hall song 'Scotland the Brave'.

Hamish now moves to a different topic, Scots children's song, beginning by talking about 'Saw'd Ye The Cotton Spinners', which he says is 'A song of the 1848 [Workers'] Rising.' Hamish emphasises that the tune derives from the Jacobite song 'Wha Wouldny Fight For Charlie?', of which he sings two lines. Then he talks about the strength of the People's Chart movement in 1840s Scotland, particularly among the spinners and the Lanarkshire coalminers. He says the song of the cotton spinners 'marchin doon the Broomielaw' 'describes the march of the cotton spinners into Glasgow to take part in the Rising, a rising incidentally which kept the city in the hands of the people for three days.' However, particularly since the lyric talks of the spinners 'gaun awa', it seems to me rather to belong to the 1837 strike by Glasgow cotton spinners, for which union leaders were sentenced to seven years of transportation, though they got only as far as the hulks at Woolwich in London, and were pardoned in 1840.

Hamish proceeds in passing to remind us again of his precise military knowledge. 'A little later in the nineteenth century, at the time of the Boer War, new words were put on this same tune, when the 42nd Regiment, which is the Black Watch, the Royal Highland Regiment was being sent out to South Africa to take part in the war.

> Wha saw the 42nd, wha saw them gaun awa,
> Wha saw the 42nd sailin doon the Broomielaw.
> Some o them had tartan troosers, some of them had nane ava
> Some o them had tartan troosers, sailin doon the Broomielaw.'

He continues, 'And in the First World War, at the time when Scottish regiments were being sent out to fight in the trenches in France, new words again were put on this, which are not maybe singable in some companies, but here they are.

> Ya ya, ya Heilan bastard, ya ya ye big Scotch hoor,
> Ya ya kilted bugger, muckin through the shithoose door.'

Hamish chuckles heartily. Lomax noted on the tape box 'Unsuitable words'.

Next, Hamish delves further into his stock of bawdy song, and his North African wartime experiences.

> When the allied armies got to Egypt, and they went to the cinema, at the end of the show they saw on the screen the face of King Farouk, and the orchestra, or a recording, started playing [he lilts the then Egyptian National Anthem]. Well it was more or less inevitable that sooner or later words would be put on that particular tune... Well anyway, Australian soldiers, in a cinema somewhere in Cairo, began

> singing 'King Farouk, King Farouk, hang yer bollocks on a hook.'
>
> That was I think the start of King Farouk. Well, I came out to Egypt myself round about the beginning of 1942, and I heard a few scattered fragments of this, and eh seeing that I was going to sing for various people at the time in my own unit at a concert, I wrote five or six stanzas, and sang them, and they were a considerable success. So a little later on I cyclostyled them and handed them out to various friends. Well, that was during the war in Africa. And I went on collecting variants of my own verses, and new verses added to the tune of King Farouk, right the way through Egypt, Libya, Tunisia, Sicily, and right the way up Italy as far as the Alps...
>
> Finally, when the war finished, I put together a complete version of the ballad, based to a certain extent upon the original words of the Aussies, to a certain extent on my own intermediate version, but chiefly on the various versions and alterations and new stanzas that I got between Cairo and Italy. So here at any rate is a selection of some of the King Farouk stanzas as the ballad eventually came.

The song starts with

> Oh, we're all black bastards, but we do love our king.
> Every night at the flicks you can hear us fucking sing
> Quais ketir King Farouk, quais ketir King Farouk.
> Oh you can't fuck Farida [Farouk's queen] if you don't pay Farouk.

And continues for nine more scurrilous and libellous verses, which eventually complain that Farouk is a Nazi sympathizer. The website editor has added the following helpful note.

> The story of the song of 'King Farouk,' Hamish's collection, its stanzas, and his singing of the 'complete' version. An Arabic glossary for the song: Quais ketir: plenty good; bint: woman; tarboosh: fez; gamel: camel; gamoos: water buffalo; filoos: money; mafeesh: 'there ain't none'; Babel-

> Louk: Cairene railway terminus; stanna shwaya: 'take it easy' (Lit. stay a little). [Source: Editor]

In a letter to me of 7 May 1992 giving permission to quote his version of the song 'The D-Day Dodgers', Hamish wrote that that song 'was first printed in *Ballads Of World War II*, edited by me for the Lili Marlene Club of Glasgow, and printed by the Caledonian Press, 793 Argyle St, in 1947. (At the instigation of Hugh MacDairmid, believe it or not!)' He adds, 'The Lili Marlene Club, needless to say, was just a device to sell the book: we printed leaflets advertising it, and order came by post. It couldn't be sold openly, because the version of 'King Farouk' and the other songs were unbowdlerised.'

Next in 1951 London he gives another canntaireachd-style lilting of the march 'The 79th Farewell to Gibraltar'. This perhaps puts him in mind of another pipe march, 'The Barren Rocks Of Aden', since that tune is the basis of his next song, a Boer War version of 'Auntie Mary Had A Canary', with the classic child spelling error of 'J for General French', and follows immediately with 'Wee O'Hara's Barra'. Then he shifts gear, into the lullaby 'Dum a dee a daddy o, there's a babby in the hoose', and finishes the recording session with another Gaelic puirt a beul which Lomax notes as 'Pot a hen a hero' – the correct title is 'Bodachan A' Mhirein', and Henderson explains the lyric's meaning.

On 2 April at 4 Downshire Hill, Hampstead, London, Henderson records anothers 24 items. He begins with narrative songs, first the comic lament for spinsterhood 'Auld Maid In A Garret', followed by 'As I Came O'er the Kearney Mount', about a sexual encounter, 'The Highland laddie threw his dirk, and sheathed it in my wanton leather.' Robert Burns made a rather sickly polite version of this song, including the line 'Now Phoebus blinkit on the bent'. Hamish's next song is 'Tramps and Hawkers', titled by Lomax 'The Galway Tinker', and the attractive text differs substantially from the version that Lomax recorded later in the year in Turriff from Jimmy MacBeath that became the standard text for Revival singers.

> Oh, come all ye darlin tinker lads, come gaither in yer blaw.
> Come on noo, aa ye tinker lads, come gaither yin

an aa,
An ah'll sing till yeez o my exploits, an the things
that I hae seen
When ah'm marchin up the snowy north, or sooth
by Gretna Green.

Oh, ah've seen the great Ben Nevis, aye, it's toorin
tae the mune.
Ah've been by Crieff an Callander, an roon by bonny
Doune.
Ah'm no thinkin whaur ah'm comin frae, nor whaur
ah'm gaun tae gang.

Oh, it's fine ah like the simmer time, when dodgin
on the run,
Wi lumps o tattie scone an cheese and plenty jeelie
scran.
Ah'm no thinkin whaur ah'm comin frae, nor whaur
ah'm gaun tae gang.

Oh, ah think ah'll go tae Paddy's Land, ah'm makin
up ma mind,
For Scotland's getting gummy noo, ah can hairdly
raise the wind.
Ah think ah'll go tae Paddy's Land, ah'll cross the
rollin main,
An ah'll sing tae yeez o Erin's Isle when I come back
again.

Now comes a substantial series of Jacobite songs, with lecture style introductions. 'Blue Bonnets Over The Border' in two versions, the second one a 'Royalist parody'. One of the various songs about 'The Battle of Sheriffmuir', then 'Up An Waur Them Aa, Willie', and 'Aiken Drum'. Lomax titled the next one 'Away Tae Aa The Whigs O Fyffe'– it is of course more correctly spelt 'Awa Wi Aa The Whigs O Fife'. The puzzling track title of the next item, 'The Galloway Countryside' proves to be 'Kenmure's Up An Awa' which Hamish has introduced as 'one of the Jacobite songs of the Border, the Galloway countryside.'

Next, Henderson couples a Robert Burns verse and chorus titled by Lomax 'A Highland Lad My Love Was Born' with a track in the Archive titled 'My Love Was Born'. Both are versions of 'The White Cockade'. The next title is 'The Bonniest Lad I E'er Saw', not with the text Burns worked over as 'The Hielan Laddie', and the last Jacobite song is 'Wha Wouldna Fecht For Chairlie'. Then Hamish lilts in sweet canntaireachd style the tune 'The Gillie Callum', saying it is 'the Sword Dance, it's a very old tune, indeed it's suppposed to be about a thousand years old, and it's believed to have been composed some time after the accession of King Malcolm Canmore.' Then he introduces and sings the well known Gaelic song 'Oh Hi Ri Ri, Tha E Tighinn (O Hi Ri Ri, He Is Coming)', followed by what is labelled as an 'unidentified lullaby', but is the Gaelic waulking song that welcomes Prince Charles Edward Stewart, 'Òran Eile don Phrionnsa (Another Song to the Prince)'. This waulking song is by Alexander MacDonald, who also composed 'O Hi Ri Ri, Tha E Tighinn'. He finishes with two more Jacobite songs, 'Come O'er The Stream Chairlie' and 'Falkirk Muir'. The latter addresses the English general Hawley.

> I hae but juist a word tae say, an ye maun hear it aa,
> Hawley ,
> We're come tae charge wi sword an targe, an nae
> tae hunt ava, Hawley.
>
> Up an rin awa, Hawley, up an rin awa, Hawley,
> The Heiland dirk is at yer dowp and that's the
> Hieland law.

Recording Around Scotland

The website information allows us to reconstruct the Scottish sequence of Lomax's 1951 recording work. He came up to Edinburgh in June, and on the 14th he was recording piper John Burgess, and on the 16th Morris Blythman in Glasgow. Lomax's guides in Lowland and North East Scotland were Henderson and William Montgomerie, and for the Gaeltacht the McLeans of Raasay – Calum and Sorley. Calum Maclean became, along with Hamish Henderson, one of the first collectors for the School of Scottish Studies. The MacLeans took Lomax to the Gaeltacht, where he recorded from 17 to 30 June. Onich on the 17th, Uig on the 18th, back to Onich the next day, on to Daliburgh from the 20th to the 22nd, that same day to Garrynamonie, next day to Snishival, the following to Lochdar and Balvanich. Then on the 25th to 'Near Loch Bee' and to Daliburgh again, 25th at Garrynamonie, 26th and 27th at Garrygall, 27th to 30th at Earsary. Some Garrynamonie recordings are dated 25 to 30 June.

Lomax was back recording in Edinburgh on July 12th and 13th. On the 12th he got duets from Gaels Kitty and Marietta Macleod, and a remarkable fiddle pibroch from poet Norman McCaig. The same day he recorded children's songs and game descriptions from collector Dr James T. R. Ritchie and 15 year old informant Peggie MacGillivray. On the 13th in the Edinburgh BBC studios he recorded Pipe Major William Ross, and a pair of sets from John Burgess. That same day he went to Gael Calum Johnston's home to record him and his sister Annie, and also Flora MacNeil.

On the 15th Lomax was in Aberdeen, in the house of bothy singer John Mearns and his family, 5 Cedar Place, where he recorded fiddler Hector McAndrew, then John Mearns and his wife, then out into the street to record their son Jack and his pals. Lomax stayed with the Lennox family, and on the 16th recorded Archie Lennox, grandfather of the singer Annie Lennox, plus Dave Dowman and Bob Cooney. That same day he went on to Crichie near Fyvie where he recorded John Strachan, and further on to Turriff to record Lordie Hay. On the 17th in the Commercial Hotel, Turiff, he recorded Jimmy MacBeath, Willie Mathieson and others. Then he dashed on to Portnockie for Jessie Murray and Blanche Wood plus a wonderful Codlins song from James Wiseman. Lomax was in Inverness on the 23rd where he recorded Pipe Major John MacDonald playing and singing canntaireachd, then in Dundee on the 26th for tunes from Jimmy Shand and Sydney Chalmers. On a return visit to Garrygall on 1 August Lomax got vigorous group waulking songs and port a beul.

Some tracks on the website are undated. Lomax got two songs from Isla Cameron at some time in August, and pieces from Josh MacRae, Enoch Kent [who gets soloist credit for tracks where he is one of several singers] and 'unidentified' others. The last 1951 recordings were in Edinburgh on 30 August, of the People's Festival Ceilidh.

At some point during his visit he was in the BBC's Glasgow HQ copying recordings from their archives. But he was not in Edinburgh's Old College recording the hazing of an Edinburgh University rectoral candidate. On the website, and on the cover of *'Tis Sixty Years Since*, is a photograph of Lomax doing this with a high-held microphone, while Hamish Henderson lifts a slim recording machine and poet Tom Scott looks on. The image has been dated either to 1951 or 1958, but neither date can be correct. The elections were and are held in February every third year. They were in 1951, and Lomax was in London then, plus the recording machine he was using was much heavier then. According to Hamish Henderson it was "a colossal uncouth beast of a thing. It came in two huge halves". So it is not the machine Henderson holds at arm's length in the graph. 1954 or 1957 are both possible, probably the latter since there is a pencilled date of 1958 on the back of the Lomax Archive copy. It has not so far proved possible to identify any sound recording of the event in the Lomax or School of Scottish Studies archives.

Morris Blythman and Sangs o The Stane

In the recording session on 16 June in Glasgow, Lomax catches the moment that Morris Blythman, another of the key instigators and enablers of the 1960s Scottish Folk Revival, was moving from writing as a poet to become a maker of songs. Morris Blythman, Hamish Henderson and Norman Buchan were the three key architects and educating figures of the early days of the Revival in Scotland, with Ewan MacColl fuelling and enriching the young Scots singers' repertoire with his commercial recordings on the Topic label and occasional visits to perform in Scotland. Buchan was not an informant, but he was inspired by the singers at the 1951 Edinburgh People's Festival Ceilidh to eventually publish and disseminate songs, to teach them to his school pupils who became stalwarts of the Revival, and with his wife Janie to promote and support local and visiting singers through concerts and recordings.

Blythman was a well-known Lallans poet under his pen name Thurso Berwick, and already active in promoting traditional Scots song, particularly in his strong support for the combinations of ceilidh, political meeting and dance run regularly in Bo'ness from the 1940s to the 1960s by The Bo'ness Rebels Literary Society. Blythman eventually edited and published several booklets of highly influential traditional and new Scots song, and wrote and inspired others to write and sing protest and political campaign songs for anti-nuclear protests at the Holy Loch, and songs supporting Scottish Republicanism. But when recorded by Lomax, Blythman had recently gathered in songs for and edited the little booklet *Sangs o' The Stane*, to which he and seven other Scottish poets anonymously contributed fifteen lyrics, to traditional Scots tunes, on the topic of the lifting and returning to Scotland of the Stane o' Scone from Westminster Abbey on Christmas Eve, 1950.

The local Bo'ness newspaper reported a few days later that

> The atmosphere at the Rebels' Hogmanay ceilidh of the 29th December 1950 was supercharged. ... The ceilidh was dominated by one topic – the Stone of Destiny and where was it? The ceilidh moved to its climax when the chairman called on Thurso Berwick, the well known Lallans poet, to do his piece in 'Poets Corner'. This recitation of the humorous poem 'The Muckle Stane o Scone' was the highlight of the whole evening, and was of a highly amusing nature.

Though a poem initially, Blythman afterwards converted 'The Muckle Stane' into a song, set to the tune of 'The Ball Of Kirriemuir', and he recorded it for Lomax. Here is his own orthography in the *Sangs o' The Stane* booklet, published by the Scottish National Congress, Elmbank Crescent, Glasgow, price 6d.

The Stane, the Stane, the muckle Stane.
The Stane worth half a croun;
Whit's aa the steer aboot the Stane
This affa Stane-o-Scone
Singan:
Fa's taen it this time? Fa's taen it nou?
The Dean thit hed it yon time hesna got it nou.

Was Reid-nose Rudolph Reindeer there
Sae fou o Christmas cheer,
He taen the Keeper o the Stane
Oot for a gless o beer?

Others who appear on the way include Santie Claus or King Wenceslas as the possible thief with a sideswipe at King George's stammer, or Lang-neb Nell, Tousie-heidit Tam, Solomon, or Mao-tze-Tung. Has Hugh MacDairmid taken it 'Tae croun hissel'? Blythman ends with the assertion that the Stane is 'oot in Timbuktou'. Morris tells in clear interesting detail the background to the making of this and his other songs, and dismantles the topical references he used for his two pieces about Superintendant Thomas Barratt of Scotland Yard, who came up to search in Scotland for only four unproductive days.

> O, Sherlock Holmes is deid lang syne
> In some forgotten garret
> Bit aa o youse hae heard the news
> O Superintendant Barrat.
>
> Fur aa he got whin he cam North
> Wis: 'Here!' an 'There!' an 'Yonder!'
> He fleed aboot in a high-speed caur
> But his clues wad only daunder.
> (To the tune 'Barbara Allen)
>
> There wis a wee Super o Scotland Yaird
> Barraty-parraty, cocatou!
> He cam up tai Glesca – He wisna feared!
> Barraty-parraty
> Gie him ti Charity!
> Niver fund clarity,
> Niver a clue![2]

In his last song, in praise of Johnny Destiny-o, 'Scotland's hero' who 'taen the Stane', he is supported in the chorus by his wife Marion and another female voice. This song was not in the *Sangs o' The Stane* booklet, nor in the larger booklet of traditional and new songs, *The Rebels Ceilidh Song Book*. It eventually appeared in the next booklet of lyrics Blythman edited, and published as the Glasgow Song Guild, *Patriot Songs for Camp & Ceilidh*.

Recording in the North East

First to be recorded in Aberdeen was Hector McAndrew, 'possibly the greatest exponent of the Scots fiddle tradition of his generation.' Then there are fifteen tracks of John Mearns, one of the best kent solo performers and recorders of

[2] To the tune of 'The Wee Cooper o' Fife'.

bothy ballads, sometimes solo and sometimes with his wife. Their son Jack and a group of his Aberdeen school pals then sing street and play songs and game lyrics. Jack Mearns gave me a vivid account of Lomax's visit.

> After all the recording was over, and in response to my constant pleading, my father eventually asked Alan if he would be willing to play for us. Alan immediately agreed and retrieved his guitar. He sat down on the piano stool and started singing an up-tempo American country song. While he was singing he stamped loudly on the floor with his foot. My brother and I were mortified because, as we stayed in an upstairs flat, we were never allowed to make a noise with our feet. My father always reminded us that 'it was Mrs Brown's roof'. Our horror quickly changed to sheer delight to see that Alan was being allowed to do what we children were forbidden to do.

Next day Lomax recorded Archie Lennox, singing 'Come up an see ma garret, it's aa furnished new' and two other songs; Dave Dowman singing 'Auld Maid In A Garret'; and Hamish Henderson gave 'The Muckin O Geordie's Byre'. The other singer that night was Bob Cooney.

An online search for 'Bob Cooney Aberdeen' finds much detail about his remarkably rich life as a singer, political activist and song maker. For Alan Lomax he recorded three well known songs, and one that is perhaps his own composition, telling of his working and political life. 'I Have Never Ever Blacklegged In My Life' has vigorous chorus singing.

That same day Lomax went on to Crichie near Fyvie where he recorded John Strachan, a highly knowledgeable champion of the songs of farm life and old ballads. John Strachan's *Portrait* CD shows the richness of his versions of songs, which led the American collector James Madison Carpenter in 1930 to invite John to visit Harvard College, but to his regret John did not go. 'I wis pretty busy, I'd a lot o' farmin to do.'[3]

Later on that day Lomax proceeded on to Turriff, to record 'Lordie' Hay, who gave 'The Bonny Lass o Fyvie', 'Jock Hawk's Adventures in Glasgow', and 'The Tarves Rant', and also told Lomax and Henderson that they should find and record Jimmy MacBeath.

---

[3] Henderson, *Alias MacAlias*, p.200.

The lead that carried us to Jimmy came from 'Lordie' Hay, a veteran bothy singer whom I had met on an earlier tour. We recorded a number of songs from 'Lordie' Hay in the Commercial Hotel in Turriff; in addition, he provided a graphic account of the career and personality of Jimmy MacBeath and obligingly told us where we would probably find him; this turned out to be the North Lodge, a model lodging-house in Elgin.

The following day we drove west from Turriff, via Banff and Buckie. Alan dropped me off at Jessie Murray's house in Buckie and drove on alone to Elgin to pick up Jimmy. Jessie Murray, a great ballad singer, was in rare fettle and I hardly noticed the two hours go by, when suddenly I heard Alan's car draw up in front of the house. A moment or two later, Jessie and I had a simultaneous first vision of Jimmy's beaming, rubicund, booze-blotched face as he walked into the kitchen, followed by Alan. There was a moment of silence. Then Alan said: 'Hamish, Jessie – I want you to meet Jimmy MacBeath.'

Half an hour later we were en route for Turriff, and Jimmy was singing in the back of the car. To start the ball rolling, I had sung him a short four-verse variant of 'Come Aa Ye Tramps and Hawkers' which I had learned from a Dundee-born farm servant, Tam MacGregor, when I was a student. Jimmy at once sang his own version, now world-famous, and we were away.

When he learned that we were heading for 'Turra Toon', Jimmy was none too confident of his reception. The last time he had been there, he had been slung out of the town by the local police, who had told him never to set foot in Turriff again. However, Alan assured him that this was a 'special case' – as indeed it was – and Jimmy rode back into Turriff in triumph. He was shortly taking his ease, and royal dram, in the best hotel in the town.'[4]

For most of his life, Jimmy had footslogged the roads of Scotland and beyond, earning pennies from street singing and shillings from casual labour, living in 'model' public lodging houses.

In the 1960s he began to be recorded commercially and to

[4] Hamish Henderson, from *Tocher*, 12, 1973.

sing in folk clubs and festivals. Alan Lomax described Jimmy as 'a quick-footed, sporty little character, with the gravel voice and the urbane assurance that would make him right at home on Skid Row anywhere in the world.' In November 1953 Lomax recorded several hours of Jimmy singing and talking. Much of this has been issued on the albums *Jimmy MacBeath: Tramps & Hawkers* [Rounder CD 1834] and *Two Gentlemen Of The Road* [Rounder CD 1793] with Davie Stewart. That same day Lomax recorded retired farm servant Willie Mathieson, getting him to sing only one verse of each of 21 ballads, and two all through, 'Died For Love' and 'The Death of Harry Bradford', a song from North America aka 'True Born Lumbering Rocks' or 'The Jam On Gerry's Rocks' or 'The Foreman Young Munro'.

Henderson felt that Lomax was pressuring Mathieson by seeking only single ballad stanzas from the three large ledgers of lyrics that Mathieson had filled with songs, and complained on his behalf. It would have been at a calmer pace that Henderson himself eventually recorded for the School of Scottish Studies Mathieson's entire repertoire.

And I speculate that it was in the evening several singers were gathered in to sing and support in fine chorus – Jimmy McBeath, John Strachan, George Chalmers, Bill Finney, Andy Dey – and John Steven, who is listed as only supporting MacBeath on 'Ma Big Kilmarnock Bunnet', but is clearly the lead singer.

On the same day, Lomax had in Portnockie recorded Jessie Murray and Blanche Wood. Murray, said by her niece Blanche Wood not to be known as a singer in her own community, had superb versions of old ballads. She was a fisherman's widow who trudged from door to door, 'a little lady' dressed all in black wearing a black shawl, a basket of fish or shellfish on her back. When she lived in a home for the elderly in the 1950s a carer told a visitor that Jessie was failing mentally, because she thought she was to be on the radio that evening. The caller was able to explain that Lomax was indeed to feature Jessie's singing in a programme that night. 18 year old Blanche Wood sang for Lomax local Portnockie songs her aunt had taught her. In the 1960s she and her sister formed a singing double act which toured working men's clubs in Scotland and England, singing 'more modern songs.'

Also on that Portnockie tape is a fine 'Codlins' (cod lines rather than young cod, I think) song from James Wiseman, mislabelled for obvious reasons as 'a Jacobite song'. Indeed, the first verse works off 'Hey Johnnie Cope', the Adam Skirling song of the 1745

Prestonpans fight, but it is to a different tune, 'Niel Gow's Farewell to Whisky'. There are not many Scots songs of the sea, and this for me is among the best of them.

Hey Johnnie Cope, are ye waakint yet, or es yer
drums abeatin yet?
If ee be waakint we will wite, an we'll gyang tae the
codlins in the morning.

As we were on the mussel scaubs, jist as hungry as
ony haauks,
We'd nithin tae ait bit a biled head ran, comin hame
fae the codlins in the morning.

Weel geaar the foresail, the mainsail an aa, an the
face o the dracht sheet's taut like a baa,
An ah'm weel sure she'll beat them aa, comin hame
fae the codlins in the morning.

As we wis sailin sow wast en, wi twa three rhines o
the foresail in,
She wis gaun sae spritely merrily in, comin hame
fae the cod lins in the morning.

Strachan, MacBeath, Murray, Wood and John Burgess were all performers at the first People's Festival Ceilidh in Edinburgh's Oddfellows Hall on 30 August, along with Flora MacNeil and Calum Johnston, with Hamish Henderson as magisterial MC. Alan Lomax's recording of the ceilidh was a fitting finale to his 1951 stravaiging.

After the End

Under the 'Scotland' listing in the Alan Lomax Archive are various later recording sessions. In December 1953 Lomax visited the Newtongrange home of the Cosgroves to record Annie Cosgrove, her brother Bob Holland and her husband's aunt Mary Cosgrove, singing and telling about Scots songs of coalmining. This led to Annie and Bob going to London to take part in a BBC TV series about Lomax's work that was directed by a youthful David Attenborough.[5]

On separate occasions in 1953 Lomax brought both Jeannie Robertson and Davie Stewart to London to record them over several days, and did the same with Davie Stewart in 1957. In 1956 he recorded three songs from popular Scots revival singers Rory and Alex McEwan. And in 1957/1958 Lomax recorded another 37 tracks from Ewan MacColl, most of them traditional pieces, but a few of them MacColl's own compositions.

Lomax had come to Britain in 1951 to record and edit an LP for his record series, a 'World Library of Folk and Primitive Music', and had thought his LP of English folk music should include a corner of Scottish material. His encounters with MacColl, Henderson and the MacLeans led him to discover and record some of the riches of Scotland's song and music. Lomax made several BBC radio broadcasts about his Scottish collecting, and he edited two LPs that collected together selected gems. Over the succeeding years, the copies of his collecting work that he made for the School of Scottish Studies were ransacked by young revival singers for their emerging repertoire. Now all his Scottish recording work is available to us at a couple of clicks of a computer mouse.

---

[5] I have written in detail about the Newtongrange visit in my book *Bonny Collier Lads and Lasses*, Linlithgow: Gallus, 2014.

In Tune with the 'Underground of Song'

Alison McMorland and Geordie McIntyre

Geordie: We are dealing here with the 'Underground of Song'.[1] It has a double meaning – 'underground' as something subversive, radical, anti-establishment, and then there's the fact that songs have been driven underground, out of sight. Many songs, and particularly the muckle ballads, were kept alive by the Travellers, and they were totally marginalised.

This is based on an article written by Hamish Henderson in *The Scots Magazine* of 1963.[2] But he didn't have a chance in the article to develop the idea that all the songs were underground because they were not readily available. They were held within family traditions, which kept them alive. There's always been different views in the last two centuries when folk song whichever way defined was declared moribund, if not actually dead. And that has most obviously not been the case. So what we want to try here is to illustrate some of these points, highlighting the fundamental importance of song and singing. If Hamish was about anything it was about getting people to express themselves in, broadly speaking, the folk song idiom.

It might surprise that we start with an example from the American tradition – the American song-writing tradition. Because the balladeer Woody Guthrie was not only a collector of songs who roamed the country collecting from the dustbowls of Oklahoma to California, he also wrote some wonderful songs which are still in the global repertoire. 'Pastures of Plenty' is interesting because it was commissioned under the umbrella of

---

[1] This conversation recreates a song-filled presentation, 'The Underground of Song', given by Alison and Geordie at the Scottish Storytelling Centre as part of Tradfest Edinburgh Dùn Èideann on 6 May 2014.

[2] Hamish Henderson, 'The Underground of Song', *The Scots Magazine*, May 1963, reprinted in Hamish Henderson, *Alias MacAlias: Writings on Songs, Folk and Literature*, edited by Alec Finlay, Edinburgh: Polygon, 1992, pp. 31-36.

Roosevelt's New Deal, and it is just a wonderful song written to the slightly re-worked traditional tune of the murder ballad 'Pretty Polly', an example of the well-established practice of setting new songs to old 'service' or 'carrying' tunes.

Pastures of Plenty

[Words and Music by Woody Guthrie]

It's a mighty hard row that my poor hands have hoed
My poor feet have traveled a hot dusty road
Out of your Dust Bowl and Westward we rolled
And your deserts were hot and your mountains were cold

I worked in your orchards of peaches and prunes
I slept on the ground in the light of the moon
On the edge of the city you'll see us and then
We come with the dust and we go with the wind

California, Arizona, I harvest your crops
Well its North up to Oregon to gather your hops
Dig the beets from your ground, cut the grapes from your vine
To set on your table your light sparkling wine

Green pastures of plenty from dry desert ground
From the Grand Coulee Dam where the waters run down
Every state in the Union us migrants have been
We'll work in this fight and we'll fight till we win

It's always we rambled, that river and I
All along your green valley, I will work till I die
My land I'll defend with my life if it be
Cause my pastures of plenty must always be free[3]

It is worth pointing out that the roots of the modern British revival, including the Scottish revival, reach back to the United States. The late Alistair Cook – whose famous 'Letter from America' is very much part of the broadcasting tradition – was alerted to a repertoire of songs from America – chain gang songs, songs from the Southern cottonfields, field recordings made by John Lomax and his son Allan in the 1930s. Some of these songs

---

[3] Judy Bell and Nora Guthrie (eds), *Woody Guthrie Classics Songbook*, Milwaukee: Hal Leonard Publishing Corporation, 2000.

winged their way to London and ended up on a programme called 'I Heard America Sing'. These had a profound influence on Alistair Cook. Here was a body of song that was creative, dynamic, and with something to say. He was immensely attracted by them. So, the American influence is there, built in right from the beginning.

Fast forward, and we find some of the young, inspired revival singers like Hamish Imlach modelling themselves on American singers. In the case of Hamish, who developed his own individual style, the major influence came from a New York based singer called Dave van Ronk. And there were countless others – like that New Yorker who had never been out in the prairies, but suddenly became Ramblin' Jack Elliott – rather than just Jack Elliott. And that, too, would be replicated here, when young, urban singers would turn up in rural sweaters and tweed, maybe to creatively underline their claim of authenticity.

Alison: But if we go back to the immediate post-war era when Hamish Henderson returns from the Second World War – just before leaving Italy he stays with the Olivetti family who introduce him to a tape recording machine. Its possibilities fire him up with ideas which he wants to try and put into practice on returning to Scotland. And, when meeting up with Alan Lomax, this gives his activities a direction that would take to him to becoming the leading researcher and fieldworker for the School of Scottish Studies after its foundation in 1951. In that very year, he had been heavily involved in creating the first Edinburgh People's Festival, organising the Festival Ceilidh, which was recorded by Alan Lomax.[4] It ran for three years, and the audiences may not have, numerically, been huge, but there were people in the audience like Thurso Berwick (Morris Blythman) and Norman Buchan, exposed to singers whom Hamish brought 'out of the woodwork' – out of the underground. Like Flora MacNeil from Barra (who was working in Edinburgh at the time as a telephonist), Jessie Murray, the fishwife from Buckie, Jimmy MacBeath from Portsoy and, of course, Jeannie Robertson, the settled Traveller from Aberdeenshire, and the wonderful piper John Burgess. Hamish took them out of their local, family context – 'You people deserve to be heard,' was his message. Now, there are views that say traditional song is a private matter and it should stay within the family, that it inevitably

[4] See Eberhard Bort (ed.), *'Tis Sixty Years Since: The 1951 Edinburgh People's Festival Ceilidh and the Scottish Folk Revival*, Ochtertyre: Grace Note Publication, 2011.

changes in character when performed on a stage. Hamish encouraged public performance, and Jessie Murray sang a beautiful song at the first People's Festival Ceilidh:

Skippin' Barfit Through the Heather

As I was walkin' doon yon hill,
'Twas on a summer evenin',
There I spied a bonny lass
Skippin' barfit through the heather.

Oh but she was neatly dressed,
She neither needed cap nor feather;
She was the queen among them a,
Skippin' barfit through the heather.

Her gown it was a bonnie blue,
Her petticoat of pheasant colour,
And in between the stripes was seen
Shinin' bells o' bloomin' heather.

'Oh lassie, lassie, will ye come with me?
Will ye come wi' me and leave the heather?
It's silks an' satins you shall have
If ye come wi' me and leave the heather.'

'Well kind sir, your offer's good,
But it's well I ken you'll deceive me.
Gin I gie my heart awa
Better though I'd never seen you.'[5]

The way I first heard of that song illustrates very well how songs are being transmitted: within family settings, groups of friends, communities, both working and living communities, and of course the radio and TV programmes of the day.

In the 1960s I was living in Helston, Cornwall, home of the *Furry Dance* May custom, and also the *Hal an Tow*, a song which later became very famous through the Watersons' recording of it. I

---

[5] Alison McMorland learned her version of this song from Jessie Murray and recorded it in 1977 for her album *Belt wi' Colours Three.* It is also on her Tradition Bearers CD *Cloudberry Day* (2000).

found myself at the heart of living traditions, surrounded by a folk culture that was very much alive and no more so than the ancient *Padstow Obby Oss on May Day* – an annual favourite of Hamish's which he visited over many years. I was asked to be a resident of a folk club just opening. This became my weekly night out for 5 years, and in the course of it I came in touch with a huge amount of songs and singers from Cornwall's folk community. Traditional singers like Charlie Bates of St Issey, fisherman Tommy Morrisey of Padstow's Peace Oss, to name but two. Oh, and Cyril Tawney, of course, was very active in the South West, as well as the visiting guests in the summer on the folk circuit.

In 1964 I managed to buy myself a reel-to-reel tape recorder and the first thing I did was record the regular Sunday morning radio programme 'As I Roved Out'. This was showcasing really the field recordings Séamus Ennis and Peter Kennedy made in the 1950s, and these BBC Home programmes popularised Irish and British folksongs. So this is how I first heard Jessie Murray singing 'Skippin' Barfit Through the Heather'. She made a huge impression on me. I think there is nothing like being away from your birth-home to strengthen your sense of identity. So, although I felt very much at home in Cornwall, with all its Celtic connections, in listening to Jessie Murray I realised also the depth of my own Scottish roots – which before I had not thought about much. When I heard 'Skippin' Barfit Through the Heather', that did it for me. I immediately learned it. Her singing was so direct, so pure, and the song – a gem! So, that is a good example: you learn from other people's singing, directly, but also via the radio and recordings, although I had no records at the time while my father had albums by the brothers Rory and Alex McEwan and by Mary O'Hara.

And, linking in with what Geordie has said, there were two Americans who came over in the late 1950s and early '60s, and both proved to be influential in the two-way passage of Scotland's music. One was Kenneth Goldstein and the other the graphic artist and calligrapher Howard Glasser. I have treasured the meetings with Howard and our correspondence, having received letters and copies of his publications. In one letter he describes visiting Edinburgh at the beginning of his three-month sojourn to Scotland when, at Hamish Henderson's invitation, he attends a pre-concert meeting with the singers of the 1963 Festival Fringe. Around a table were Jeannie Robertson, Jimmy

MacBeath, Davy Stewart and others. He was fascinated by the Ceilidh – the happening itself of singers and musicians informally meeting at home or in the community to make music, tell stories and the news of the day. And when he went back to America, over the following forty years – wherever he worked at universities as professor of graphic arts – he organised informal gatherings and concerts which were titled Ceilidhs. These then grew into a famous folk festival, the Eisteddfod, which ran for many, many years, starting in 1971. He would design wonderful posters and flyers, showing the invited guests and featuring many Scottish artists. These are now considered collector's items.

Geordie: In the decade following the People's Festival Ceilidh a great deal happened. There was a mushrooming of folksong clubs, particularly from the end of the 1950s onwards. While music halls closed down, folk song clubs were springing up all across Scotland. Songbooks were printed; the most significant, for me, being Ewan MacColl's compilation *Scotland Sings*[6] – a wonderful collection with music, and a big input from Hamish Henderson, which ought to be reprinted.

There was a lot of experimentation going on among young singers – some excellent, some perhaps lamentable, but all in a way inevitable. There was such an excitement of learning in the air. We were lucky to be caught up in this. Some singers would come from Skiffle, others from traditional song. My background was quite different from Alison's – I was inspired by black American gospel singers and the likes of Paul Robeson – not just by the calibre of his vocal technique, but also by the contents of his songs. Young people were looking for songs of substance, something that said something for them, dealing with social issues.

Now, my luck was in, on one particular day. In the early '60s I was a radio and TV technician and was called out to do a repair job – and the man in the house was Andrew Tannahill, a direct descendant of the weaver poet Robert Tannahill's youngest brother. He was a bibliophile, his knowledge about Scottish poetry an tradition was encyclopaedic, and he could not have done more for me. He gave me books, he gave me advice, he introduced me to George Douglas Brown's *The House with Green Shutters Minstrelsy* and Lewis Grassic Gibbon's *Cloud Howe*, to Doric books, books like William Alexander's *Johnny Gibb of Gushetneuk*. I had not even been aware of Doric – having been

[6] Ewan McColl, *Scotland Sings*, London: Workers' Music Association, 1953.

Howard Glasser with his recording machine in Scotland, 1963 [Howard Glasser forwarded this photo to Alison McMorland for inclusion in the book *Up Yon Wide and Lonely Glen*; it is here reprinted with her kind permission.]

Cover of Ewan McColl's seminal Songbook (Workers' Music Association, 1953)

brought up in Glasgow. And he introduced me to a friend of his, Arthur Lochead who had a magnificent repertoire of songs which he had learnt from his aunt – who, by the way, had supped tea with William Motherwell of Motherwell's Minstrelsy. And I recorded these – ballads like 'Lamkin', 'Braes o' Yarrow' and 'The Douglas Tragedy', or 'The Croppy Boy', an Irish rebel song, and many more.[7] That is an example of the opportunity that existed to actually field-record, from singers who were not performers. Arthur Lochead described them as 'family songs'. He had them written out in his beautiful copperplate writing. They may have found their way into the family tradition by way of chapbooks,

[7] 'Lamkin' and 'Braes o' Yarrow' are recorded on the Tradition Bearers' CD *Ballad Tree* (LTCD1051, 2003) – by Alison McMorland, Geordie McIntyre with Kirsty Potts.

broadsides or direct oral tradition.

Lamkin

It's Lamkin was as guid a mason
As ever hewed wi' stane,
He built Lord Louden's House
But payment he got nane.

The lord said to the Leddy,
E'er he gaed abroad,
Beware of the Lamkin
That lives in the wood.

Then Lamkin he rockit,
And the fauce nurce she sang
Till the tores o' the cradle
Wi' red bluid doon ran.

Now, increasingly, songbooks and records were being published: the fantastic *Bo'ness Rebel Ceilidh Songbooks*, with songs by Hamish Henderson, Morris Blythman, Norman Buchan and Roddy Macmillan; and then Norman Buchan's *101 Scottish Songs*[8] and, eventually, *The Scottish Folksinger*.[9] And on telly, of course there were the shows with Jimmie Macgregor and Robin Hall and Rory and Alex McEwen. Archie and Rae Fisher were appearing on the Hootenanny show.

Alison: I think one of the songs that was very popular and that everybody sang was 'The Plooman Laddies' from the singing of Lucy Stewart. It was Arthur Argo, the grandson of Gavin Greig, who knew the Stewart family up in Fetterangus. They were neighbours. And when Howard Glasser came over, it was Arthur who took him to meet Lucy Stewart. Arthur himself went over to America, too, and he produced *A Wee Thread o' Blue* – an LP with extensive notes.[10] He was invited by Kenny Goldstein.

---

[8] Norman Buchan, *101 Scottish Songs*, Glasgow: Collins, 1962.

[9] Norman Buchan and Peter Hall, *The Scottish Folksinger*, Glasgow: Collins, 1973.

[10] Prestige 13048 (1962).

The Lamkin.
Frag No. 3. ment.

The Lamkin was as guid a mason,
As ever hewed stane,
He builded Lord Loudens House
And payment gat nane.

The Lord said to the Leddy,
e'er he gaed abroad,
Beware o' the Lamkin,
that lives in the wood.
. . . . . .

The Lamkin he rockit,
And the fauce nurce she sang
Till the tores o' the cradle
wi' rid bluid doon ran

Oh please my babie nurcie

'The Lamkin' in Arthur Lochead's copperplate writing (Letter to Geordie McIntyre)

lamkin (CHILD 93) As sung by ARTHUR LOCHEAD

Lamkin was as guid a mason
As ever hewed wi' stane,
He builded Lord Louden's hoose,
And payment got nane.

The Lord said to the Lady
E're he gaed abroad:
"Beware o' the Lamkin
That lies in the wood."

"How can I come doon
On a cauld winter night?
There's neither coal not candle
To show me doon licht."

"There's two globes in your chamber
As bright as the sun,
Take one of them with you
And show you light down."

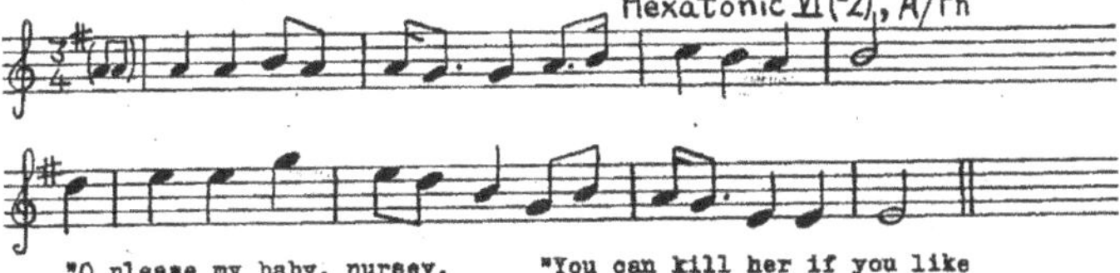

"O please my baby, nursey,
O please him wi' the bell."
"He'll no' be pleased, madam,
Till you come doon yoursel'."

"You can kill her if you like
As she's ne'er been guid to me;
And ye'll be laird o' the castle,
And I'll be leady."

'Lamkin' - *Chapbook*, vol.3, no.2 (1966), p.23

Kenny, too, when he was over in 1959-60, was taken up to meet the Stewarts, by Hamish and Kätzel Henderson. The influence in the North-East of this settled Traveller family cannot be overestimated. There were ten brothers – military pipers, singers, whistle players and accordion players. The youngest daughter of the fourteen children was Elizabeth Stewart's mother Jean, who had taken piano lessons and formed her own family dance band when still a teenager. She went on to broadcast regularly from Aberdeen for many years, becoming a household name.[11]

So, Arthur Argo sang the 'Plooman Laddies', picked up from the Stewarts, and spread it round on his travels. This bothy ballad about a young female farm worker admiring the handsome young ploughman from afar became a firm favourite of folk singers, and it introduced a distinctive North-Eastern flavour to their song repertoire:

Plooman Laddies

Doon yonder den there's a plooboy lad,
And some simmer's day he'll be aa my ain.

Chorus:
An sing laddie aye, and sing laddie o,
The plooboy laddies are aa the go.

Doon yonder den I could hae gotten a miller,
But the smell o stour would hae deen me ill

Doon yonder den I could hae gotten a merchant,
But aa his riches wereny worth a groat

I love his teeth and I love his skin,
I love the very cairt he hurls in

---

[11] See Elizabeth Stewart, *Up Yon Wide and Lonely Glen: Travellers' Songs, Stories and Tunes of the Fetterangus Stewarts*, compiled and edited by Alison McMorland, Jackson, MS: University Press of Mississippi, in association with the Elphinstone Institute, University of Aberdeen, 2012. See also Alison McMorland, 'Challenge and Response: Elizabeth Stewart and the Fetterangus Stewarts', in Eberhard Bort (ed.), *At Hame Wi' Freedom: Essays on Hamish Henderson and the Scottish Folk Revival*, Ochtertyre: Grace Note Publicatons, 2012, pp.43-52.

Plooman Laddies

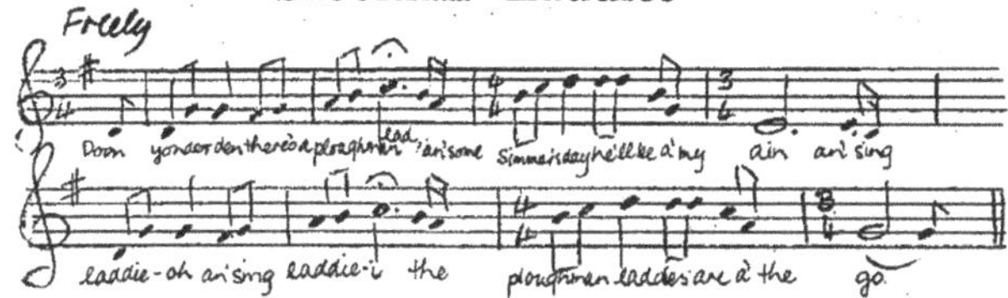

I love his teeth and I love his skin --
I love the verra cairt he hurls in: Cho.

Doon yonder den I coulda gotten a merchant,
Bit a' his stuff wisna worth a groat: Cho.

Doon yonder den I coulda gotten a mullart,
Bit the smell o' dust widda deen me ill: Cho.

It's ilka time I gyang tae the stack,
I hear his wheep gie the ither crack: Cho.

I see him comin' fae yonder toon,
Wi' a' his ribbons hingin' roo an' roon: Cho.

An' noo she's gotten her plooman lad,
As bare as ever he left the ploo: Cho.

Doon yonder den there's a plooman lad,
An' some simmer's day he'll be a' my ain: Cho.

Lucy Stewart, one of the most magnificent of Scotland's traditional singers, has an equally magnificent repertoire. When I first taped Lucy singing this haunting love-song, I considered it one of the musical highlights of my life...A.A.

‘Plooman Laddies’, with a note by Arthur Argo, *Chapbook*, vol.2, no.1 (1965), p.3.

I see him comin fae yond the toon,
Wi aa his ribbons hingin roon an roon

And noo she's gotten her plooboy lad,
As bare as ever he's left the ploo.

Geordie: What Hamish Henderson was concerned about was people expressing themselves. We had the good fortune to be able and meet genuine tradition bearers like Jeannie Robertson, Jimmy MacBeath, Willie Scott and Lucy Stewart – it was possible to meet them and to learn from them. They were both self-effacing and confident – this is what we do, and we believe in the quality of what we're doing – and that had a big influence on us.

Alison: I very much see the 'Plooman Laddies' as a song that came into the folk revival. And it was Hamish who sent me up to Fetterangus in the early 1970s to meet Lucy, after I had listened to recordings of her in the School of Scottish Studies. She was an extraordinary singer, like a beacon of light for me. As singers ourselves, both Geordie and I were inspired to meet and learn from the older singers, it was important not just for the songs but also the background and to be in touch with them as people within the living tradition.

Geordie: One of he important things we picked up from those older singers in the 1960s and '70s was the importance to acknowledge where a song came from, how it was created, who sang it, whether there were different versions, was it composed or traditional. Some would say that if a song was composed, it would disqualify it in terms of folksong – which is total nonsense. I am reminded of Alan Lomax's *Folk Songs of North America* way back in 1960 – a great collection of songs, with the music transcribed by Peggy Seeger. There are on two consecutive pages two songs: the first one is 'Dark as a Dungeon' and the second one is 'Sixteen Tons', both written by Merle Travis. According to Lomax, these songs tick all the boxes – tune, narrative style, use of language – and they qualify as folk songs, as far as he is concerned. Being too rigid about these definitions simply does not wash. And that liberates young people's creativity. Songs are made and remade, written and re-written; it is an organic, creative process.

All these people, the movers and shakers in England and Scotland, Bert Lloyd, Ewan McColl, Norman Buchan, Morris Blythman, Hamish Henderson, they were not antiquarians – they all were, after all, songwriters.

Alison: Ewan MacColl and Peggy Seeger had a missionary zeal in all they did, and Peggy, when speaking of Ewan's songs very recently at the Charles Parker Day 2015, was emphatic as to their always having a political thrust. To both of us Ewan and Peggy were very positive and supportive. They encouraged the singing of old songs but, importantly, also added new songs to the tradition.

Geordie: A very interesting ballad is 'The Twa Corbies', first published by Walter Scott in the *Minstrelsy of the Scottish Border*. It was known as a poem, until Morris Blythman married it to a Breton tune. The ballad in print was a bird in the cage – it had to be released from its cage to let it sing and fly. Another example how songs entered the revival.

The Twa Corbies

As I was walking all alane,
I heard twa corbies makin a mane;
The tane unto the ither say,
'Whar sall we gang and dine the-day?'

'In ahint yon auld fail dyke,
I wot there lies a new slain knight;
And nane do ken that he lies there,
But his hawk, his hound an his lady fair.'

'His hound is tae the huntin gane,
His hawk tae fetch the wild-fowl hame,
His lady's tain anither mate,
So we may mak oor dinner swate.'

'Ye'll sit on his white hause-bane,
And I'll pike oot his bonny blue een;
Wi ae lock o his gowden hair
We'll theek oor nest whan it grows bare.'

'Mony a one for him makes mane,
But nane sall ken whar he is gane;
Oer his white banes, when they are bare,
The wind sall blaw for evermair.'[12]

---

[12] Norman Buchan, *101 Scottish Songs*.

Alison: Francis Collinson, a member of the newly formed School of Scottish Studies, first met and recorded Willie Scott in 1951. He had thought 'the flood of song of Walter Scott's day had dwindled to a trickle' until he was tipped off about a singing Liddesdale shepherd. This was the start of several recording sessions when on one occasion, moving to Bonchester Bridge where there was electricity for the recording machine, his brothers Jock and Tom and son Sandy joined Will. You can hear on this early recording how the men come in out of the pouring rain, shaking it off their coats before sitting down and launching into 'The Kielder Hunt'.

> Hark hark I hear Lang Will's clear voice sound through the Kielder Glen,
> Where the raven flaps her glossy wing and the fell fox has his den,
> There the shepherds they are gathering up wi' monie a guid yauld grew,
> An' wiry terrier game an' keen an' fox-hound fleet and true.
>
> *Chorus*:
> Hark away! Hark away!
> O'er the bonnie hills o' Kielder, hark away.

A wonderful rendition from this family of big men with hearty voices finishing off with Willie hollering 'Whup, Whup, Whup!'

From then on Willie, who had been a shepherd in Liddesdale, Yarrow, Ettrick and in the Lothians, moved up to the Cleishhills above Keltie in Fife after the death of his wife. One day a young joiner lad, Sandy Scott, was doing a job in the house of John Watt, all the time whistling tunes and singing a particular song. John Watt asked him, 'What's that song?' 'Oh, that's one o' ma faither's.' 'Who's your faither?' 'Oh. He just bides near here.' Word got to Hamish, and he wrote to Willie that there was a seat for him in the front row of the newly opened Dunfermline Howff Folk Club. But Willie was not at all sure about going, because he thought it would be, as he said, 'full of hippies'. But Hamish's invitation did the trick.

Now, Liddesdale is a very remote area. And Willie Scott had all the local memory. He was a very important figure, as he was a link with the very old world. His mother was born in the mid-nineteenth century, and James Hogg, whom Willie identified with – the Ettrick Shepherd – and Walter Scott and Robert Burns would have been within people's living memory. Willie was aware of this literary tradition. Although he sang only one Burns song. But then, Burns was rarely heard in the early folk revival – the nineteenth and early twentieth centuries had 'elevated' him to the salon, and it was only in the course of the folk revival that he was rediscovered as a fellow folk singer and songwriter. The older traditional singers seemed not sing much Burns.

It was a great privilege for me to have known him closely in the final ten years of his life. From the days of 1963, singing in the Dunfermline Howff, his 'career' had taken off, both in Scotland and in England. He would be repeatedly invited down to sing at the Whitby Folk Festival. He sang in Arnold Wesker's Centre 42, he sang at the Singer's Club in London, and in many English folk clubs. He was taken out to America by Jean Redpath; he went to Australia, where his son Sandy was working and living. If he was asked – he would go. If people could get him there, he would go. He acquired a huge following, but remained a very down-to-earth person.

He would stay with me *en route* to or from Whitby, and eventually I had the privilege of putting together his book with him. On one visit, he was sitting there writing out the words of a song with a pencil, licking it every now and then. 'Ah, I should have a book.' He muttered. And I asked him did he really mean it. 'If you really want to do it, I'll be your scribe,' I said, not realising what I let myself in for, of course.[13]

Hamish Henderson and Francis Collinson had recorded his work songs – the songs of the shepherd. I was particularly interested in his early childhood memories, the songs he learned in the family. He had not wanted to become a shepherd. He wanted to be a gamekeeper, so at the age of 11-12 he would go to a shooting club, where after the practice, they would 'aye hae a sang'. That was where he first sang outside the family.

He was particularly known for singing 'The Shepherd's Song', but since his death and from my recording of it, 'Time Wears Awa', a song by the nineteenth-century Fermanagh born Thomas Elliot, who was of Border descent, has been taken up by many, many singers.

---

[13] Willie Scott, *Herd Laddie o the Glen: Songs of a Border Shepherd: Willie Scott, Liddesdale Shepherd and Singer*, compiled by Alison McMorland [1988], new and expanded ed., with an introduction by Hamish Henderson, Newtown St Boswells: Scottish Borders Council, 2006.

Willie Scott singing in the Dunfermline Howff Folk Club, 1961 [The photo appeared in the book *Willie Scott, Herd Laddie o the Glen: Songs of a Border Shepherd* and is here reproduced with the kind permission of Alison McMorland – Willie had it in his box of photos for the book.]

Time Wears Awa

Oh but the oors rin fast awa
Like the Kelvin tae the Clyde,
Sin' on its bonnie gowan banks
I wooed thee for my bride

My ain dear love sae sweet and young
Sae artless and sae fair,
Then love was a' the grief we kent
And you my only care

Chorus:
Time wears awa, time wears awa,
And winna let us be,
It stole the wild rose frae my cheek
And the blyth blink frae your ee

When woods were green and flooers fair
While you were a' my ain,
I little reckoned what years would bring
O poortith, toil and pain

Some waefu oors hae flapped their wings
Dark shadows ower oor lot,
Sin like twa cushats o the glen
We strayed in this dear spot

The voices o these happy days
Steal on oor dreams by night,
And cherished mem'ries rise and glow
Wi their depairted light

But still the birds and burnies sing
Their 'wildered melodies,
As in the gowden dawn o life
When we were young and free[14]

That was a song he rarely sang in public, but the family asked me to sing it at his funeral. That was one of his mother's sangs. When

[14] Alison McMorland and Geordie McIntyre, *White Wings*, Edinburgh: Greentrax, CDTRAX 306, 2007.

he was very ill and had only about a year to live, and I asked him what needed to be in the book and what could perhaps be left out, he said his mother's sangs needed to be there. It is a very personal song, but it is also collective, universal. And that is why it has been taken up by so many singers. It simply resonates.

Geordie: As Alison says, his mother was a huge influence on Willie Scott. And so was James Hogg's mother for him, and Walter Scott's, and Burns's and Hamish's – so that gives you a glimpse of women as the most important tradition bearers.

Alison: Mothers have always been the emotional heart of the home. And they would sing while they saw to their work, they would sing lullabies for their babies and play and sing with the bairns. And you might add grannies and nannies into the mix

Geordie: Another very interesting character was Willie Mathieson whom Hamish called a 'ploughman folklorist'. There are over 600 items of his recorded in the School of Scottish Studies. One of his songs was 'My Last Farewell to Stirling', a transportation ballad. Caught poaching the Laird's hare and pheasant, twenty years in Tasmania beckon:

My Last Farewell to Stirling

Nae lark in transport mounts the sky
Or leaves wi early plaintive cry
But I will bid a last goodbye
My last fareweel tae Stirling, oh

Chorus:
Though far awa, my heart's wi you
Our youthful oors upon wings they flew
But I will bid a last adieu
A last fareweel tae Stirling, oh

Nae mair I'll meet ye in the dark
Or gang wi you tae the King's Park
Or raise the hare from oot their flap
When I gang far fae Stirling, oh

Nae mair I'll wander through the glen
Disturb the roost o the pheasant hen

Or chase the rabbits tae their den
When I gang far fae Stirling, oh

There's one request before I go
And this is to my comrades all
My dog and gun I leave tae you
When I gang far fae Stirling oh

So fare thee weel, my Jeannie dear
For you I'll shed a bitter tear
I'll hope you'll find another dear
When I go far fae Stirling, oh

So fare thee well, for I am bound
For twenty years to Van Dieman's Land
But think of me and what I've done
When I gang far fae Stirling, oh.[15]

We have already mentioned the American influence on the Scottish revival. 'King Orfeo' was collected by Patrick Shuldham Shaw, the Englishman who was the founder-editor of the Greig Duncan collection. The English influence on the Scottish tradition has been absolutely positive. Shuldham Shaw is a prime example of that. We have re-energised and revitalised and reinvigorated our own patterns of expression through that cross-border interaction.

Way back in 1967 I was introduced to Duncan Williamson. I recorded him in Argyll where he came from. It was all facilitated by the wonderful Helen Fullerton who had 'discovered' the Williamson family while she was working as cook in the Shira dam hydro scheme and recorded them extensively. Duncan was one of our finest sources. Gems like 'Tam Lin' were big finds. We loved those great narrative songs – 'muckle' ballads like 'Sir Patrick Spens', 'Hind Horn' or 'Tam Lin', wonderful narrative songs with great tunes!

The original tune for 'The Great Selkie of Sule Skerrie' was nearly lost, but was noted down in 1938 by Dr. Otto Anderson, who heard it sung by John Sinclair on the island of Flotta, Orkney. The tune was then matched to a text found in the *Shetland Times*. Sule Skerry is a small uninhabited rocky island in the west of Orkney. A seal from there has a liaison with a maiden in Norway. She has a son by him, but he mysteriously disappears. After seven years he returns to claim his son, and they both return to the sea.

---

[15] *Ibid.*

The woman then marries a hunter who unknowingly kills two seals, his wife's former lover and her child.

The Great Silkie of Sule Skerry

In Norway land there liv'd a maid, 'hush ba loo lil-lie' this maid began,
'I know not where my bairn's father is, whether land or sea he travels in.'

It happened on a certain day, when this fair lady fell fast asleep,
That in there came a grey Silkie and set him down at her bed's feet.

'Awak', awak', my pretty fair maid, for oh how soundly thou dost sleep
I'll tell thee where thy bairn's father is, he's a-sitting close at thy bed's feet.'

'I am a man upon the land; I am a Silkie in the sea,
And when I'm far from ev'ry strand, my dwelling is in Sule Skerry.

'Alas, alas, this woeful fate, that weary fate that's been laid on me,
That a man should come from the Wast o' Hoy and that he should have a bairn with me.'

'O thou wilt nurse my little wee son for seven long years upon thy knee,
And at the end of seven long years I'll come back and pay thy nursing fee.'

'I'll put a gold chain around his neck, and a gay good gold chain it will be,
That if e'er he comes to the Norway lands thou may have a gay good guess on he.'

'And thou wilt get a gunner good, and a gay good gunner it will be,

And he shall gae out on a May morning and shoot thy son
and the grey Silkie.'

Oh she has got a gunner good, and a guy good gunner
it was he,
And he gae'd out on a May morning and he shot the son
and the grey Silkie.

'Alas, alas, this woeful fate, this weary fate that's been
laid on me!'
And once or twice she sobb'd and sigh'd, and her tender
heart did break in three.[16]

Alison: We have a wonderful song and ballad tradition in Scotland. And the supernatural songs are a significant part of that tradition. In the 1970s, Pat Shuldham Shaw was funded by the English Folksong and Dance Society to come up to the School of Scottish Studies to work on the Greig-Duncan collection, and he was very helpful, providing me with photocopies of songs. The whole interplay between the singers, the collectors and the tradition bearers constitutes a wonderful milieu of people that make up our folk world.

The 1970s also saw a re-evaluation, a re-discovery of regional voices and dialects, not just here, but across Europe, which helped in the acknowledgement of the diversity and richness of our cultural heritage. But it cannot be said often enough that our traditions need to be supported. Without recognition for the people involved, and the songs, these remain submerged in the underground. But they need to be known and recognised. Hamish wrote in a letter to the *Scotsman* in 1953: 'It would be a great irony if your readers assumed that I did not want my recordings of Scots folksongs to be broadcast. On the contrary, I believe that the broadcasting of them would be an event of great cultural significance in Scotland.'[17]

So we have American, English and Scandinavian influences. Add to that the huge Irish input, from the 1950s ballad boom,

---

[16] Alison McMorland and Geordie McIntyre with Kirsty Potts, *Rowan in the Rock: Songs of Love, Land and Nature*, The Tradition Bearers (LTCD302201, 2001).

[17] Hamish Henderson, 'Letter to the *Scotsman*', in *The Armstrong Nose: Selected Letters of Hamish Henderson*, edited by Alec Finlay, Edinburgh: Polygon, 1996, pp.62-63.

featuring the Clancys and, a little later, the Dubliners, and the Travellers and seasonal workers crossing frequently between Ireland and Scotland, we realise how interwoven the tapestry of the folk revival is. Davy Stewart's wife Molly was Irish. Lucy Stewart had a lot of Irish songs in her repertoire. Delia Murphy's broadcast recordings were immensely popular!

New songs find their way into the tradition when songwriters are in tune with the tradition. Sometimes that can be demonstrated when bits and pieces, wee phrases of other songs are incorporated into a new song. Adam McNaughtan shows that brilliantly in the case of Hamish's 'The Freedom Come-All-Ye'.[18] It's a doffing of your cap, a sign of real recognition and respect. Now, we are making no claims for Geordie's 'From Gulabeinn' to be on par with Hamish's song, but here, too, echoes and allusions can be found in every verse. The memory of sound is everywhere.

Geordie: The song relates to the scattering of Hamish's ashes on Ben Gulabeinn, the Curlew Hill, in the shadow of which he had grown up, and to which he had wished to return after death. In the first verse

From Gulabeinn's bell-heathered slopes
His dust was scattered to the sky
Particles of song unite
With trilling curlew cry.

The 'particles of song' are clearly meant to be Hamish's songs but, in a wider sense, also the songs of the tradition, and the way songs carry echoes from older songs, or even phrases and expressions from older songs. It celebrates song, the idea of putting something out into the ether. Songs are so important, they are the expression of the people's muse. When Ailie Munro was looking for a title for the second edition of her book, I suggested 'The Democratic Muse'.

---

[18] Adam McNaughtan in *Chapman*, 42 (1985). He describes the language as 'a tight-packed literary Scots with folksong phrases embedded in it: "heelster-gowdie" from "McGinty's Meal-and Ale"; the rottans that McFarlane flegged frae the toon; the most appropriate "Afore I wad work I wad rather sport and play"; the "crouse crawin" from "Willie MacIntosh"; the repeated "Nae mair" recalling the "No more" of Jeannie Robertson's "MacCrimmon's Lament"; the "pentit room" of "King Fareweel".'

Alison: Folk is about people – it is not just a genre term. It is all about what people put into songs, how they breathe life into them. People are at the heart of the tradition.

Geordie: Appropriately, the last two verses of 'From Gulabeinn' are directly related to the 'Underground of Song': they reflect on the radical roots, the progressive pedigree, if you like, of the revival:

Rabbie Burns and Thomas Paine
Gramsci, Lorca, John Maclean
Listen to the clarion call
Let peace and freedom reign.

All the sacrifices made
Do not let them be betrayed
Raise your voices, stand as one
Is the song – from Gulabeinn.[19]

Raising their voices, the singers of the on-going Scottish folk revival have come a long way in making traditional songs less 'underground' – having them heard in public spaces, in tune with a living tradition. But that other aspect of 'underground', the anti-establishment, subaltern tradition, the tradition of Robert Burns, James Hogg, Hugh MacDiarmid, Mary Brooksbank, Helen Fullerton, Matt McGinn, of course, Hamish Henderson, and right up to Michael Marra, Dick Gaughan, Karine Polwart, Alasdair Roberts and Penny Stone, needs to remain a focus of folk singers, as an indispensable counterweight to the daily feed of bland, manufactured commercial pop.

---

[19] The full song lyrics of 'From Gulabeinn' can be found in Eberhard Bort (ed.), *Borne on the Carrying Stream: The Legacy of Hamish Henderson*, Ochtertyre: Grace Note Publications, 2010, pp.23-24. It is recorded on Alison McMorland and Geordie McIntyre, *Where Ravens Reel*, Rowan Records CD, 2010.

Ewan McVicar (photo: Allan McMillan)

Alison McMorland and Geordie McIntyre at the Scottish Storytelling Centre, TradFest 2014 (photo: Allan McMillan)

Visions and Voices: The Flyting of Hamish Henderson and Hugh MacDiarmid

Raymond Ross

> I do not believe that a nation can be regenerated by arguments based on statistics or improved business techniques. The true saying is that without a vision the people perish. I underline the word vision... I am not denying the importance of practical affairs. But all the Scottish issues one can think of – emigration, rural depopulation, housing, and all the rest – cannot add up to Scottish nationalism.

So wrote Hugh MacDiarmid in 1967 in an article entitled 'The Upsurge of Scottish Nationalism'.[1] I think by and large Hamish Henderson would have agreed with these sentiments. Like MacDiarmid he certainly believed and wished that Scotland could be 'regenerated' though the word 'nationalism' was not always a positive in Henderson's lexicon; and although a Home Ruler, nationalism was certainly not something which he embraced uncritically or unequivocally.

I think we could safely say that MacDiarmid was fundamentally 'nationalist'; but also very much on his own terms:

> Is Scotland big enough to be
> A symbol o' that force in me,
> In wha's divine inebriety

[1] This chapter is a slightly amended version of a lecture, 'Clash of the Titans: Revival and Renaissance', delivered at the National Library of Scotland on 6 May 2014 as part of TradFest Edinburgh Dùn Èideann 2014. Hugh MacDiarmid, 'The Upsurge of Scottish Nationalism' (1967), in *Selected Essays of Hugh MacDiarmid*, ed. Duncan Glen, London: Jonathan Cape, 1969 pp. 228-232.

A sicht abune contempt I'll see?
For a' that's Scottish is in me...[2]

Note that the question here (*A Drunk Man Looks at the Thistle*, 1926) is not whether the poet is big enough to be a symbol of things Scottish but rather it is a question of whether Scotland is up to the job of grasping the poet's vision and taking a trip with him into 'divine inebriety'.

He does not say (ignoring for the moment matters of rhythm and rhyme) 'For a' that's in me is Scottish' but rather, and rather typically, 'For a' that's Scottish is in me'. Perhaps no other poet could have written that line – *and meant it*. Certainly, Hamish Henderson could not have in all sincerity and would not have in all temerity.

The important word, or at least the term I want to focus on from the above 1967 MacDiarmid quotation, is not 'nationalism' which is actually secondary to the (in)famous Henderson-MacDiarmid flyting in the late 1950s / early 1960s in the letters page of *The Scotsman*, but the word 'vision'. If they did both agree that without a vision the people perish, does that mean that they both shared a single 'vision' of things Scottish?

The short answer is, of course, an emphatic 'No'. But how far their 'visions' of Scotland, of Scottish culture, of Scotland's future and its place in the world were (in) compatible is a far more vexed and complex question.

Let us return for the moment to MacDiarmid's Romantic Egoism, his claim to embody all things (truly) Scottish. In his poetry and other writings, in his aesthetic (his 'political aesthetic' if we can use such a term) this is a *given*; and it re-appears throughout his work with a remarkable consistency.

In *Lucky Poet*, his autobiography of 1943, he writes:

> I always like to feel... that my principal personal characteristics exhibit clearly the great historical directives of my people...

Again:

---

[2] All poetry extracts from Hugh MacDiarmid, *Complete Poems, 1920-1976*, London: Martin Brian & O'Keefe, 1978.

> My ambition was to be the creator of a new people, a real bard who 'sang' things till they became, yet, as an individual, the incarnation of an immemorial culture.[3]

Now, how do you debate culture, immemorial or otherwise, with a man whose unashamed 'bardic' claim is not only to embody 'his' people, but to be the creator of 'a new people' – and wherever the debate is going to go he is never, but never, going to shift from this 'divine inebriety'?

Now, again, let us pause for a moment. Whatever we make of MacDiarmid's 'bardic' claim in the cold light of day, we have to remember that this Romantic Egoism infuses some of the greatest poetry Scotland has ever produced. We can gainsay it in rational debate, perhaps, but we cannot discard the poetry it inspired, particularly his epic *A Drunk Man Looks at The Thistle*.

MacDiarmid's tendency to swallow up Scotland undoubtedly relates to his own psychological solipsism: the feeling or belief that the self is the only knowable or existent thing. I say 'psychological' because, although it comes at times close to a philosophical position and permeates the poetry, it grew out of his personal, mental (or spiritual) experience as a young man and it always came to bear when he felt at the peak of his creative powers.

Writing to his old teacher and mentor George Ogilvie in 1920 he says of moments of creative intensity:

> I am mobilised to the last fraction... My 'temptation' lies simply in the fact that when I reach a certain pitch everything outside me ceases to exist.[4]

The solipsism, then, is not an affectation. It is not evidence of a literary *poseur*. The subject mind of his early prose writings, *The Annals of the Five Senses* (1923), as of the early correspondence with Ogilvie, shows a constitutional predisposition, borne out in the poetry, towards this solipsism.

---

[3] Hugh MacDiarmid, *Lucky Poet* (1943), Oakland: University of California Press, 1972, pp. 36, 81.

[4] The Ogilvie correspondence is held by the National Library of Scotland: NLS Acc. 4540.

In early poems not only is the universe dependent on the poet's subjective vision, so is God:

> And God Himsel' sall only be
> As far's a man can tell,
> In this or ony ither life
> A way o' lookin' at himsel'.
> ('Ballad of the Five Senses')

In *To Circumjack Cencrastus* (1930), he writes:

> Man's the reality that mak's
> A' things possible, even himsel'.

Perhaps his most notorious solipsistic, super-bardic incarnation occurs in the closing couplet of 'At the Cenotaph' (*Second Hymn* 1935):

> Keep going to your wars, you fools, as of yore;
> I'm the civilisation you're fighting for.

That's MacDiarmid, isn't it? It's never Henderson. But if we could separate or divide the public bard Hugh MacDiarmid from the private citizen Chris Grieve we could maybe debate different approaches to Scotland, to Scottish culture, to the way forward. But the solipsism is not just a mask; 'MacDiarmid' is not just a *nom de plume* or a *nom de guerre* as Henderson well knew; and the solipsism is a motive force in almost everything MacDiarmid writes. It is inherent in his world view. It informs his ontology. It infuses his epistemology. It is part of who he is.

Coupled with this sometimes cosmic egoism is a profound elitism. In *A Drunk Man* where he writes 'A Scottish poet maun assume / The burden o' his people's doom / And dee to brak' their livin' tomb' he will only address with any respect those who are on his cultural, historic or spiritual level: figures like Christ, Nietzsche, Dostoevsky or Spengler. Later, of course, Lenin comes into the fold.

Did Hamish Henderson ever come into that fold? I think not: not from MacDiarmid's perspective and not from Henderson's either, though Timothy Neat tries to make a case for Henderson being

MacDiarmid's filial inheritor in his biography; a point to which I will return later.

Now, this vision without which the people perish (derived from the Old Testament Proverbs) involves, for both makars, some form of socialism and/or communism. Did they see eye to eye on this? Did they share a political philosophy of the left? Again, the short answer is an emphatic 'No'.

This may be partly to do with MacDiarmid's pronounced elitism which will come into play in the *Scotsman* flyting. But the division of itself is too simple.

To begin with, classical Marxism (to say nothing of Leninism) is riddled with elitism. The very concept of communists being 'the vanguard of the proletariat' is *au fond* elitist. And when you couple that with historic determinism, with the belief that the dialectic of history is on your side, making communism inevitable, then, all is justified in the name of that determinism.

As MacDiarmid was to put it in 'First Hymn to Lenin' (1931):

> As necessary, and insignificant, as death
> W' a' its agonies in the cosmos still
> The Cheka's horrors are in their degree;
> And'll end suner! What maitters't wha we kill
> To lessen that foulest murder that deprives
>   Maist men o' real lives?

But it is not really a case of Stalinist MacDiarmid versus socialist Saint Hamish. In an early poem, 'Sitzkrieg Fantasy', Henderson clearly embraces historical determinism while (following MacDiarmid's example) he hymns Lenin in religiose terms:

> And Lenin had *luck* – luck, faith and reason,
>   The holy three,
> When he opened wide an historical door with
>   History's key...[5]

In the later post-war and aptly entitled 'Hate Poem' Henderson satirises an anti-red British diplomat who had hobnobbed around pre-War Nazi Germany, concluding:

---

[5] All poetry extracts from Hamish Henderson, *Collected Poems and Songs*, ed. Raymond Ross, Edinburgh: Curly Snake Publishing, 2000.

> But long enough he's had his fun,
> This dodo of a die-hard race.
> When Seumas finds a tommy-gun
> He'll find, or his vile course is run
> That liquidation meets his case.

This is not the voice of the ordinary soldier, of one of the 'Puir bliddy swaddies' in Henderson's famous 'The 51st Highland Division's Farewell to Sicily'. This is not war-time combat. This is political murder – sanitised in communist speak as 'liquidation'. And note that the implicit dialectic of historical determinism has already overtaken the diplomat who is but a 'dodo.[6] And note, too, the man holding the gun is one Seumas (Hamish).

Now, while no one is accusing Henderson of wishing to join the ranks of the Cheka or the NKVD, it is apparent that we are not a million marching steps from MacDiarmid's bloodier pronouncement. My primary point here may be that we cannot simply colour the contrasts and antagonisms between Henderson and MacDiarmid as humanist socialism versus dictatorial communism; but there is a secondary point also: while MacDiarmid has been consistently lambasted for his Stalinism, Henderson's has largely been overlooked.

In the post-war 'Brosnachadh' (Incitement to Rise), a complex poem with both Christian and communist overtones, Henderson seems to address both contemporaries and a new generation, asking them in conclusion to 'Prove / That with us is no "villainy of hatred", / and history will uphold us – / justify and forgive.'

This poem is dedicated to the Partisans of Peace who were (and I quote from *The Great Soviet Encyclopaedia* of 1979):

> an international mass movement against war and militarism, whose members are willing to fight for a stable and indestructible peace, regardless of the differences in their nationality and political and religious beliefs. The peace movement arose in response to the profound changes in the international situation after World War II (1939–45), when

[6] The detailed portrait of this figure and the personal tone of the poem suggests that the subject was (at least based on) a real-life character whom Henderson met or knew. If memory serves, Hamish confirmed this while we were working on his *Collected Poems and Songs* but he either refused to say who it was; or said he had 'forgotten'.

> the forces of peace increased their activities, supported by the countries of the world socialist system, other peace-loving states, and the international working class and its vanguard—the Communist and workers' parties—as well as by the national liberation movement and the popular masses in all countries.
>
> The First World Congress of the Partisans of Peace was held from Apr. 20 to Apr. 25, 1949, a few days after the Western powers signed the aggressive North Atlantic Treaty.

Given the dedication, what is it the poet is asking to be justified and forgiven? It cannot be for waging war against Nazi Germany. For Henderson that war was entirely justified; nothing there to be forgiven. And what are we to make of the reference to (or invocation of) 'history'? If history is determined, what is there to 'justify'? Historical determinism provides all the justification necessary and 'forgiveness' is a moral concept quite alien to communism.

Given the dedication to what was in effect a Soviet front organisation, is Henderson trying to bridge a chasm here between Christian morality and communist necessity? I quote again: 'Prove / That with us is no "villainy of hatred", / and history will uphold us – / justify and forgive.'

Henderson has certainly shifted post-war to a more complex and sensitive appraisal of his own 'position' which now seems far removed from the simplicity and naïve portrayal of Stalin in his humorous war-time 'Ballad of the Taxi Driver's Cap':

> O Hitler's a non-smoker
> and Churchill smokes cigars
> and they're both as keen as mustard
> on imperialistic wars.
> But your uncle Joe's a worker
> and a very decent chap
> *because he smokes a pipe and wears*
> *a taxi-driver's cap.*

Stalin, of course, was never a worker. He was a henchman and bank robber for a gang of opportunist, political thugs led by one Vladimir Ilyich Ulyanov. The latter, an extremely thuggish intellectual, was to become known as Lenin, the gang as the Bolshevik Party.

It is, of course, easy to judge in retrospect. The ballad is of its day; and it was popular among some allied soldiers in its day. It is certainly ironic, however, that while Hitler and Churchill are lambasted for 'imperialistic wars', Stalin ('a very decent chap') was to become the imperialist writ large; expanding a terrifying dictatorship into a huge semi-criminal empire which only crumbled (if indeed it has entirely) in the early 1990s.

If MacDiarmid was Stalin's dupe, was Hamish Henderson? To a degree and to a lesser extent and for a shorter period, maybe. There was certainly no way Henderson was going to join (or rejoin) the Communist Party of Great Britain (CPGB) after Hungary 1956, as MacDiarmid so notoriously did.

But then, as with nationalism,[7] MacDiarmid's approach to communism was very much his own. For MacDiarmid the function of poetry, the function of all art was what he often called 'the extension of human consciousness' which he also took as the ultimate aim (or ideal) of communism.

Writing about 'Problems of Poetry Today' in 1933, he says:

> The interests of the masses and the real highbrow, the creative artist, are identical, for the function of the latter is the extension of human consciousness. The interests of poetry are diametrically opposed to whatever may be making for any robotisation or standardisation of humanity or any short-circuiting of the human consciousness.[8]

This argument is one he will use against Henderson in *The Scotsman* flyting. The question to bear in mind here is: where will the Folk Revival fit in to this pre-determined *schema*? The question MacDiarmid will ask himself and others is: does it extend human consciousness?

---

[7] It should also be noted that Henderson's poetry is not entirely free of a more fundamental nationalism as in 'Here's to the Maiden' which, although comic in tone, nevertheless relishes the idea of beheading 'oor Scots Quislings' while stating 'The heids o' a score o' Vichy Scots / Wad suit these partisan days.'

[8] Hugh MacDiarmid, 'Problems of Poetry Today', *New English Weekly* (21 September 1933).

Again, in *The Company I've Kept* (1966) he writes:

> There must be an enormous mutation of the human species, and that mutation can only be towards higher intellectuality.[9]

The question is begging. Can folk music or song be said to promote a 'higher intellectuality'? We can already intuit what MacDiarmid's answer will be, I think, and the clash between him and Henderson is beginning to take on something of the nature of an historical inevitability itself. And here MacDiarmid will bring into play one of his biggest guns.

In 1943 in *Lucky Poet*, his autobiography, he quotes Lenin to the effect that:

> It would be a very serious mistake to suppose that one can become a Communist without making one's own the treasures of human knowledge... Communism becomes an empty phrase, a mere façade, and the Communist a mere bluffer, if he has not worked over in his consciousness the whole inheritance of human knowledge – made his own and worked over anew all that was of value in the more than two thousand years of development of human thought.[10]

And this is a quotation he will also throw Henderson's way in the 1950s/60s flytings. But its use is in no way gratuitous. It is an attitude that goes to the heart of MacDiarmid's own political aesthetic.

In *Second Hymn to Lenin* (1932), a poem which is to feature quite prominently in the later flyting, MacDiarmid writes of wanting:

> Nae simple rhymes for silly folk
> But the haill art, as Lenin gied
> Nae Marx-without-tears to workin' men
> But the fu' course insteed.

'Nae simple rhymes for silly folk / But the haill art'. We know where he is coming from and we can recognise a consistency in his elitist

---

[9] Hugh MacDiarmid, *The Company I've Kept* (London 1966), p. 55.

[10] *Lucky Poet op. cit.* pp. xxxi-ii, 152-53.

approach. Whether or not *we* wish to characterise folk song and/or poetry as 'simple rhymes for silly folk', we can see it would have been entirely surprising were MacDiarmid *not* to have attacked what we might call 'folk culture'.

But, as he swallowed Scotland whole and all things Scottish, so he sees all politics as subservient to his poetic intent:

> Sae here, twixt poetry and politics,
> There's nae doot in the en'.
> Poetry includes that and s'ud be
> The greatest poo'er amang men.

And so, in closing his second 'Hymn' to Lenin, he turns the tables on the Bolshevik leader in a dramatic, if not indeed comic and satirical reversal. If poetry is not just simple rhymes for silly folk, what else can it be?

> The core o' a' activity,
> Changin't in accordance wi'
> Its inward necessity
> And mede o' integrity.
>
> Unremittin', relentless,
> Organized to the last degree,
> Ah, Lenin, politics is bairns' play
> To what this maun be!

So, that puts Lenin in *his* place! If MacDiarmid swallowed up Scotland whole for his own poetic purposes, he does so with communism itself. What we also have to bear in mind – and this is my final contextual point before we visit the flyting itself – is that we cannot simply characterise MacDiarmid as an elitist, authoritarian Leninist or Stalinist any more than we can Henderson as a soft-soap, sentimental socialist. For, there is also a strong libertarian and anarchist element to MacDiarmid. After all, this is the man who wrote (in 'Talking with Five Thousand People in Edinburgh'):

> For I am like Zamyatin. I must be a Bolshevik
> Before the Revolution, but I'll cease to be one quick
> When Communism comes to rule the roost,

> For real literature can exist only where it's produced
> By madmen, hermits, heretics,
> Dreamers, rebels, sceptics,
> – And such a door of utterance has been given to me
> As none may close whosoever they may be.

The flyting itself, which was to go on intermittently between 1959 and 1964, does not begin with the Folksong Flyting but with what has become known as The Honor'd Shade Flyting and in many ways they are two blood-boltered battles in the same guerrilla war.

What they share are principled arguments, combative alliances, vituperations, ideological onslaughts, gratuitous side-swipes, denigrations and below-the-belt punches over matters at once personal, political and cultural, concerning questions of spiritual, moral and intellectual integrity; questions of cronyism and elitism, avant-gardism and conservatism, authoritarianism and libertarianism. Welcome to 1960s Scotland; and welcome to a guid goin' rammy!

Now, 'flyting' is traditionally a 'war of words' between two contesting poets as in *The Flyting of William Dunbar and Walter Kennedy* before the court of James IV. In flyting anything really goes, from caricature to character assassination, from high-principled point-scoring to a thorough, metaphorical groin-kicking. It must be one of the few intellectual or aesthetic pursuits in which the *argumentum ad hominem* is applauded almost as a philosophical virtue.

The debate, quickly taking on the tones of a full-blown flyting, has already begun about a recently published poetry collection *Honor'd Shade: An Anthology of New Scottish Poetry to Mark the Bicentenary of the Birth of Robert Burns* (1959) edited by Norman McCaig, poet and friend of MacDiarmid. The anonymous *Scotsman* reviewer says, among other things, the book 'might perhaps almost' have been called *The Muse in Rose Street*, implying that McCaig's choice of contributors merely reflected the work of the so-called Rose Street group, satellite poets who revolved around planet MacDiarmid, who met and drank regularly together (with or without MacDiarmid) in The Abbotsford and Café Royal: poets and writers like Sydney Goodsir Smith, Tom Scott, Fionn MacColla and McCaig himself.

The implicit accusation is that this is a self-serving *clique* which regards itself as the literary establishment of Scotland. Indeed, a group of younger poets, including Ian Hamilton Finlay, Stewart Conn and Tom Buchan, go on to produce an audio-tape the following year entitled *Dishonour'd Shade: Seven non-Abbotsford Poets*. So, along with attendant arguments about Scots or Lallans poetry which draw in Douglas Young, things are festering rather nicely when Henderson enters the fray.

Indeed, *The Scotsman* reviewer has already drawn attention to the fact that among others Henderson and Alan Riddell were not included in the volume. The use of his name certainly allows Henderson the right of reply.

But the boy isna blate and it seems to me that his first contribution sets out quite consciously to rile the Old Man of Letters, to draw him out into the field of battle; or, better still, to sucker him into the narrow pass between the Braes o' Killicrankie with a couple of well-aimed pistol shots. Here, the Perthshire callant lies in wait, with a stout targe, a ready claymore and, for the close-quarter fighting which he bloody well knows will ensue, a wee sharpened *sgian dubh*.

Henderson does not, for example, open his account by saying that he was in fact invited to contribute but did not submit a poem until it was too late. This comes later in the letter. Rather, he opens with MacDiarmid clear in his sights.

> Sir,
>
> Returning to Scotland after a short absence, I am amused to find the Rose Street tattoo going great guns in your columns.
>
> Hugh MacDiarmid defends the 'right of association' of like-minded men of letters... in the main his contention is perfectly justified. It is also true, of course, that sometimes such groups can make life difficult for the lone wolves of literature, but probably no poet of the Western world needs less reminding of this than Mr MacDiarmid.[11]

On the face of it this might seem an innocent enough reference to the young MacDiarmid who had, practically single-handedly, forged the Scottish Literary Renaissance of the 1920s in the face

[11] All *The Scotsman* correspondence quoted or referred to can be found in *The Armstrong Nose: Selected Letters of Hamish Henderson*, ed. Alec Findlay, Edinburgh: Polygon, 1996.

of Scotch philistinism and Anglo-Scottish indifference. But the wolf image is at least ambiguous and the implication is clear: the lone wolf now leads a pack making life difficult for new or younger poets.

Henderson continues:

> Mutual admiration can be helpful and well-merited, but it has obvious drawbacks. The trouble is that half the clique is sometimes nothing more than a claque.

To extend the military metaphor, that 'claque' echoes like another pistol shot aimed to draw his opponent further into the defile; a 'claque' being a group of persons hired to applaud an act or performer, with the secondary meaning of a group of sycophants. Henderson also concludes the letter by mentioning 'culture vultures' who cannot, in the context of the letter, be other than this alleged MacDiarmidian 'claque'.

But also, in explaining that 'it was nobody's fault but my own that I did not submit [a poem] till it was too late,' Henderson widens the debate by saying:

> In any case, I have come to set greater store by my songs 'in the idiom of the people' than by other kinds of poetry I have tried to write. By working in the Folksong Revival, therefore, I am paying what is probably congenial tribute to the 'honour'd shade'...

It is a fair point, given Burns was a great collector and adaptor of Scottish songs. But, is Henderson implying that the Folk Revival is in some ways equivalent to the Literary Renaissance? Or a continuation of it? Or another side to it? And, therefore, as the by now acknowledged Father of the Folk Revival, is he implicitly putting himself on a par with Grrreat Man? Whatever, it would seem to me that he is leading his opponent onto boggy ground to leave him swinging his claymore at thin air or, to use a metaphor of MacDiarmid's own, trying to stab malaria with a bayonet.

Interestingly, on the same day, MacDiarmid has also fired off a letter to *The Scotsman* (meaning he cannot have read Henderson's missive), stating:

> ... your reviewer says I have persistently claimed that Mr Hamish Henderson is an 'inferior' poet. I challenge him to cite any comments I have ever published on Mr Henderson's poems. 'Silence gives consent', perhaps, and I will not deny that Mr Henderson's work is hardly 'my cup of tea'... I am unaware – and do not believe – that any critic of international repute has praised Mr Henderson's poetry... Anyhow, whatever may be said about Messrs Riddell and Henderson, I do not think they are poets of such consequence that it matters one way or another whether they appear or do not appear in any selection.

The battle lines have then, indeed, already been drawn. And while Henderson's award-winning *Elegies for the Dead in Cyrenaica* (1948), his poems of World War II, were widely and positively reviewed, MacDiarmid would not have known of E.P. Thompson's letter to Henderson (which I do not think became public until the first re-publication of *The Elegies* in 1977) to the effect that 'you are that rare man, a poet. You have achieved poems out of our dead century... And you must not forget that your songs and ballads... are quite as important as the Elegies.' Mind you, had MacDiarmid known of this, he would probably have replied that while Thompson was an eminent historian, that would hardly qualify him as a literary critic (while possibly adding an acerbic comment about Thompson having left the CPGB in 1956 in protest over Hungary) ...

Henderson replies to MacDiarmid, reminding him that he had actually reviewed the *Elegies* in 1949 and had said:

> It is, in fact, one of the few books – and the only volume of poems in English which has come my way – that expresses an adult attitude to the whole appalling business [of the war], and thoroughly deserves the honour of securing the first award of the Somerset Maugham prize.

He adds that MacDiarmid had also described his song 'The John MacLean March' as a 'splendid song'. However, in a flyting, there's no point in simply defending yourself or simply trying to embarrass your opponent with irony. It's time to get personal:

> What does disturb me, whiles, is the whole tenor of Mr MacDiarmid's approach to argument, which positively reeks of that very same self-centred provincialism which he is forever and a day claiming to combat.

MacDiarmid responds that he sticks by his positive review of the *Elegies* ten years earlier (which rather contradicts his previous letter) but opines that as a poet Henderson seems 'to have petered out, unfortunately,' while his praise for the 'John MacLean March' was about its merits 'as a song... the question of its quality as poetry' being a 'very different' matter. So, he tries to parry the first point by ignoring it, but the second is a neat thrust. But, whether from Parnassian disdain or personal *sang froid*, the poetic genius of European sensibility and world renown chooses to ignore the direct accusation of 'provincialism'.

Henderson's assault has failed to draw him out fully from his redoubt. So Henderson replies, keeping to theme, thus ensuring his letter will be published, talking about philistinism 'even of the Rose Street pub' with the neat aphorism that 'Every country gets the "culture vultures" it deserves'. But this is a feint. The real attack comes now and it comes from the Left.

> On the political side, since Mr MacDiarmid has mentioned it, I hope you will allow me space to make one brief point.

The 'brief point', some three paragraphs long, concerns 'a new school of Socialist thinking' which has grown up around, among others, 'Raymond Williams's *Culture and Society*, a school which is not afraid of sociological revaluations, and goes out into the streets to hear... the voice and song of the people.'

He then delivers his *coup de grace*:

> It is strange to find the author of 'A Seamless Garment' and Second Hymn, to Lenin officially enrolled not among the sponsors of New Left Review but among the British representatives of what is now, in the Western world, a withered and archaic political spent force.

Three years earlier the CPGB had bled most of its intellectual, academic and 'forward-thinking' membership over the Soviet invasion of Hungary. It was at this point MacDiarmid had chosen to rejoin the withered, archaic and spent political party. The CPGB has to follow Moscow's dictates and there's an end of it. As a Stalinist cadre, MacDiarmid will have to reply. Moscow will expect. The CPGB will insist. Henderson has him now. He has to come out and fight like a good 'tankie' should.

It is in this reply that MacDiarmid makes use of Lenin's statement that the communist should embody 'the whole inheritance of human knowledge,' contrasting this to the 'illiterate doggerel' of folk song, and describing the Folk Revival as 'a fresh wallowing in the mud-bath of ignorance.' He characterises Henderson as 'of the teddy boy type,' placing him on a par with 'the hordes of football enthusiasts, readers of the big circulation press, patrons of rock 'n' roll and all the rest.'

On the personal side, this characterisation seems a silly enough diatribe, though the image of Teddy Boy Henderson rocking round the clock in drain-pipe trews and winkle-picker brogues is wonderfully ludicrous.

However, here MacDiarmid's main frontal assault is on the 'hordes' that together represent the 'rising tide of subhumanity' who are threatening to swamp 'literature and the arts'.

Now, talk of 'subhumanity' is positively Nietzschean, and MacDiarmid, like many writers and intellectuals of his time, has long been immersed in the cult of the *übermensch*, the 'superman' (or 'overman') and that, indeed, is how he characterises the Bolshevik leader in his Hymns to Lenin.

Nietzsche is, of course, often associated with Hitler, with Nazism and Fascism. But Bolshevism too was deeply entangled with Russian Messianism and with the creation of the 'New Man'. Nietzschean Marxists who often envisioned the 'New Man' as the 'Man God' which communism was setting out to create would include many figures well-known to MacDiarmid. Numbered among them, in various ways and to differing degrees, are Maxim Gorky, Anatole Lunacharsky, Vladimir Mayakovsky, M.A. Reisner and N.A. Rozhkov – and MacDiarmid's poetry is peppered throughout with allusions to 'Him, whom nocht in man or Deity, / Or Daith or Dreid or Laneliness can touch, / Wha's deed owre often and has seen owre much' (*A Drunk Man*).

So, we can see both consistency and inevitability in MacDiarmid's communistic 'superhumanity' attack on things Folkie. He concludes by dismissing the revisionist New Left thinkers as 'sucklings of that mother [the CPGB] they are now seeking to devour, an ambition which has done and is likely to do no more than change them from sucklings into suckers.'

It is now (in his next response) that Henderson turns the poet's Hymns upon him, arguing that while MacDiarmid 'affects to despise the folksong revival,' yet he had written in *Second Hymn*:

> Are my poems spoken in the factories and fields,
> In the streets 'o the toon?
> Gin they're no', then I'm failin' to dae
> What I ocht to ha' done.

Henderson comments:

> The problem implicit in these lines do not admit of easy solutions, but I have no doubt that in the long run it is the folksong revival which offers the best hope for a genuine popular poetry...

It is a fair point, well made, but it is not one MacDiarmid could agree with, unless he were to shift ground radically and perhaps undermine his whole life's work and his entire world view. Henderson then sticks it into MacDiarmid quite personally, describing him as being 'like some feudal Balkan grandee who continues to exercise his *droit de seigneur*, oblivious to the fact that a revolution is building up all round him.' He finishes by imaging MacDiarmid and what he stands for as outmoded and outdated:

> The CPGB is a shrivelled limb on the tree of British Socialism, and Hugh MacDiarmid is out on it.

Now, we know what MacDiarmid's 'ideal man' is. He soars Icarus-like somewhere between (another God-Builder) George Bernard Shaw's socialist superman and the full-blown Man God of the Bolshevik intellectuals.

In reply to Henderson, MacDiarmid quotes from his own poetry to the effect that he has always envisioned a Scotland where the 'ruling passion' of 'our people' would be 'the attainment of higher consciousness' while:

> Mr Henderson... seems to find his ideal man in the 'muckle sumph', and to wish to scrap all learning and all literature as hitherto defined in favour of the boring doggerel of analphabetic and ineducable farm-labourers, tinkers, and the like... unlettered ballad singers yowling like so many cats on the tiles in moonlight.

We can see that MacDiarmid is deliberately missing the point here. He is sticking to written literature and ignoring the oral tradition holus bolus. And if we accept, for example, Edwin Muir's observation in relation to the Border Ballads that the greatest of all Scottish poets is, in fact, 'Anon', we can see further that MacDiarmid is well adrift.

The mention of 'tinkers' is, of course, a sly dig at Jeannie Robertson and the other tradition bearers whom Henderson has discovered among the Travellers. The first round of the flyting is now coming to a close, probably through editorial control, but not before MacDiarmid gets one more stab into the flesh of the Folk Revival:

> ... the present folksong cult plays into the hands of the great number of people who are hostile to all intellectual distinction and to experimental and avant-garde work generally, and I regard their attitude as a menace to the arts not less serious than, and closely connected with, the pressure to reduce all the arts to the level of mere entertainment.

And this letter is dated, ironically enough, 25th January (Burns Day) 1960.

The Marxist literary critic David Craig hoists the folk flag for the next battle in March 1964 with a letter attacking MacDiarmid and McCaig for a 'decidedly ignorant depreciation of folksong' in a BBC Third Programme survey of Scottish culture compiled by Professor David Daiches.

We are on familiar ground now when MacDiarmid replies he has 'been bored to death listening to... the renderings of Jeannie Robertson, Jimmy MacBeath and others' while declaring:

> The demand everywhere today is for higher and higher intellectual levels. Why should we be concerned then with songs which reflect the educational limitations, the narrow

> lives, the poor literary abilities, of a peasantry we have happily outgrown?

Henderson enters the field quoting MacDiarmid's *bête noire*, the poet Edwin Muir, on Robertson's renderings being 'extremely noble' and having 'wonderful dignity'. He quotes the English folklorist A.L. Lloyd calling her 'a singer sweet and heroic' and the American collector Alan Lomax naming her 'the greatest ballad singer in the world.'

Since MacDiarmid has mentioned (alongside Shakespeare, Dante, Goethe, Rimbaud, Rilke and Pasternak) the poet Eugenio Montale among his canon of the literary greats, the Italophile Henderson points out, with delicious irony, that it was he who introduced MacDiarmid to Montale in 1947 and acted as interpreter during their conversation.

> I well remember how keen Mr MacDiarmid was to stress the fruitful interaction from which folksong and art-poetry have always benefited in the Scots literary tradition.

He then pierces the heart of the matter as he sees it:

> There can be no doubt that by denigrating Scots popular poetry now, Mr MacDiarmid is trying to kick away from under his feet one of the ladders on which he rose to greatness.

Now on his back foot, MacDiarmid responds:

> I cannot deny that in Scottish literary history there have been fruitful interactions between folksong and art-poetry, and that this happened in some of my own early lyrics. But that was nearly forty years ago.

Again, he talks of the 'menacing form' of the 'folksong movement', no doubt meaning it is an expression of the 'subhuman' or *untermenschen* mentality, while pointing out:

> ... as a poet I have had to abandon many of my early ideas and during the past thirty years I have been writing kinds of poetry quite unindebted to any folksong source and for the

> most part utterly opposed to anything of the kind... I do not believe that folksong sources can now supply springboards for significant work.

Many, of course, have argued and will continue to argue that a lot of MacDiarmid's best work is actually in his early Scots lyrics and *A Drunk Man* where there was fruitful interaction between folk-song and art-poetry; and that the later highly and self-consciously intellectualised English poetry is just not as good and sometimes descends into 'chopped-up prose'. But neither Craig nor Henderson are drawn into this defile which would put them very much on MacDiarmid's territory and where he could easily snipe them down for a perceived anti-intellectualism and perhaps even proletcultism.

Instead, both of them cast up once more the *Second Hymn* with Henderson quoting back at MacDiarmid his own words:

> Gin I canna win through to the man in the street,
>   The wife by the hearth,
> A' the cleverness on earth'll no' mak up
>   For the damnable dearth.
>
> Haud on, haud on; What poet's done that?
>   Is Shakespeare read,
> Or Dante or Milton or Goethe or Burns?
>   – You heard what I said.

In preface to this, Henderson has already pointed out that while fighting alongside the *Partigiani d'Italia* in 1944, one partisan had quoted to him some fifteen to twenty lines from Dante's *Purgatorio* in relation to the death of a comrade while another had explained his reason for fighting the Fascists and Nazis by quoting Dante's words: 'Freedom he is seeking which is so precious – as they know who give up their lives for it.'

In other words, Mr MacDiarmid (Henderson is implying), Dante has succeeded where it seems you might be failing. This is close-quarter fighting and that is the sound of a *sgian dubh* slicing in.

MacDiarmid's *riposte* concerns Henderson and Craig 'basing their "case" on fragments of my work torn out of context' while he still maintains 'the same position.' He re-iterates his position on 'the extension of human consciousness,' rattling on that 'The art of Communism will present us with ever more edifying, artistic alloys, superior forms of Lenin's "monumental propaganda",' while Craig and Henderson are so questionably concerned with 'inferior stuff and so indifferent to the peaks of human achievement in the arts,' while stating 'the multiplication of mediocre writers is no contribution to literature.'

Henderson's reply neatly quotes Lomax describing Jeannie Robertson as 'a monumental figure of the world's folksong' while pointing out that the 'unresolved contradictions in Mr MacDiarmid's approach to the problems of language and folk arts... represent no new development, but are the logical outcome of a train of thought... observable in his writings for twenty years and more...'

He now goes for the jugular, and here I think it would be fair to say there is a distinct element of the Highland Episcopalian cavalier setting about the doun-hame Presbyterian Calvinist:

> Mr MacDiarmid has come to despise and reject the 'people of his country's past' with all the ardour of a seventeenth century 'saint' outlawing the folk-singing and dancing damned to outer-darkness.

In other words (Henderson implies), for all his intellectual highbrowism, artistic avant-gardism and communistic posturing, is the ultra-modernist MacDiarmid not, *au fond*, just a secular re-invention (or re-incarnation) of the self-appointed Calvinist Elect?

It cannot get more personal than that. Or can it? Henderson now begins to twist the knife.

> He has been, in fact, for years – in one of his personae, at least – the apostle of a kind of spiritual apartheid, and an anti-humanist flavour in some of his writings is readily documentable.

And, to hoist MacDiarmid properly on his own petard, he quotes him perfectly (1946):

> I... would sacrifice a million people any day for one immortal lyric. I am a scientific socialist. I have no use whatever for emotional humanism.

Now, the idea that Chris Grieve would sacrifice even a poodle for a poem is a bit of a nonsense. But MacDiarmid is a hot-air balloonist of the first degree. He is the man to start a fight in an empty hoose and argue a black craw white even before his breakfast porridge has cooled. And Henderson has him by the short and curlies – and you can almost hear the squeak in his voice:

> How silly can Mr Hamish Henderson get? Everybody in some degree practises what he calls 'spiritual apartheid' if he or she likes one thing and dislikes another, prefers to associate with certain people and not with others, and so forth. I dislike folksong and as far as folksong concerts go simply ask, 'Include me out.'

That *is* a gem. It is not often you hear MacDiarmid so obviously on the defensive. Henderson has struck home. But MacDiarmid recovers his breath towards the end of his letter.

> It is all too easy to bandy words like 'human' – they are the common stock of all demagogues and can mean anything or nothing. So far as Mr Henderson's attempts to prove me or my work 'anti-human' goes, the significance of the term is nil.

This is sleight-of-hand, of course, and Henderson won't let him struggle free.

> ...what on earth is one to say of Mr MacDiarmid's charge that because I drew attention to the anti-humanist flavour of certain of his writings, I was calling him and his work 'anti-human'? A person who can argue like this... would never find any difficulty earning a living as a professional contortionist.

In this reply Henderson also nails his final thesis firmly to MacDiarmid's 'Auld Licht' Auld Kirk (Cauld Kirk) door:

> Mr MacDiarmid's comments on the phrase 'spiritual apartheid' are transparently disingenuous. To me, it signifies a great deal more than just preferring one pub to another, or one companion to another. It is a malady which used to be

> very rife among the 'justified sinners' of old-style Calvinism, and it still bedevils some of their descendants. It never did us, or the world, any good.

There was, of course, a further flyting over the 1320 Club in 1968 which covers a lot of similar ground, with Henderson arguing 'Groups of "self-elected Elect" have always been the bane of Scottish Home Rule politics,' and MacDiarmid replying 'It is natural that Mr Henderson should inveigh against intellectuals and dub them "self-elected"'; arguments centring around elitism and democracy, digging up the younger MacDiarmid's occasional Fascist utterances and much to-ing and fro-ing over the work and thought of Antonio Gramsci.

Yet, throughout all this, both men stayed on pretty good terms; sometimes cool, sometimes cold but also warm-hearted and well-met. And Henderson never tired of championing the best of MacDiarmid's work, never tired of recognising him as *il miglior fabbro*, and helped spearhead the campaign to have the MacDiarmid Memorial erected outside Langholm where MacDiarmid was born.

But was he, in any kind of sense, the inheritor of MacDiarmid's kingdom? The spiritual son whom MacDiarmid blessed to carry on the good fight for Scotland, its culture and its people? The short answer is 'No'. The long answer is doubly 'No'. And yet this is the case proposed by Timothy Neat in his two-volume biography of Hamish Henderson.

Neat points out that in a 1947 poem, 'Glasgow' MacDiarmid makes reference to one 'Scott' as 'The only other "whole and seldom man" I know here,' arguing that the Scott referred to is one 'James Scott (Henderson);'[12] that is, Hamish Henderson. Yet the context of the poem which talks of 'compositions' and 'arrangements', along with MacDiarmid's own footnote to the poem, makes it quite clear that MacDiarmid is referring to the composer Francis George Scott who had set MacDiarmid's early Scots lyrics to ('art') music. Henderson is patently not 'The only other "whole and seldom man"' MacDiarmid is referring to.

Neat then goes on to argue that MacDiarmid wrote three poems 'that can be read as discursive evaluations of Hamish's art,

---

[12] Timothy Neat, *Hamish Henderson: A Biography; Volume 1: The Making of the Poet*, Edinburgh: Birlinn, 2007, p.206.

persona and ideas.'[13] The first, 'A New Scots Poet' (1952) reads, says Neat, 'as though it were a "critical review" of Hamish's *Elegies*.' Although there is, in fact, in MacDiarmid's poem, no mention of the war, the desert or the soldiers which form the main subjects of the *Elegies*. Indeed, the poem seems taken up with the classical music of Mahler and, in conclusion, with *Piobaireachd*, the classical music of the Great Highland Bagpipe. Now, while Henderson knew his pipe tunes and composed songs to them, he was not himself a piper, far less an exponent of *Ceol Mor*. In any case, lines such as 'Bringing Scotland alive in people's blood again... Making them vividly aware / Of every element in the Scottish scene' suggest this 'ideal' new Scots poet is but another extension of MacDiarmid's own consciousness.

The same is true of the 1953 poem 'The Poet as Prophet – The Man for whom Gaeldom is waiting'. It is not about any 'skills, qualities and experience... Hamish Henderson embodied,' as Neat claims; he is much nearer the mark when he says 'It is just possible that MacDiarmid has conjured a composite, metaphorical "bard" into being.' And this bard is easily recognised through his solipsism, cosmic egoism and his embodiment of all things Scottish:

> He was the wind, the sea, the tempest, the hurricane.
> He was the marvellous embodiment
> Of the complete identification
> Of the Celtic mind with all nature and with all life ...

In fact, the poem is a rather prosaic rendering of the same ideas which infused the best of MacDiarmid's earlier poetry. Again:

> Scotland felt at that moment
> That no man ever personified her,
> Ever would represent her,
> As he did,
> And she grew in glory
> And was transfigured with pride.
> It was not a Scottish moment;
> It was a universal moment.

[13] *Ibid*, pp.343-346.

Aye, and one can say it was also very much a MacDiarmid moment, too; or, at least, another extension of his own particular consciousness.

The same pattern emerges in Neat's third chosen poem, 'King Over Himself' (1956). This idealised character, Neat suggests, hopefully, might be 'substantially Hamish'; yet it is but another instance of the same kind of MacDiarmid persona 'summing up in himself / The whole range of Gaelic wisdom…'

Regarding the relationship between these two makars I think we come much nearer the mark through Henderson's unpublished notebooks, which Neat makes good use of in his biography. Henderson writes:

> MacDiarmid fears his sons will kill him.
> Wants to write prefaces to give birth to them.
>
> *MacDiarmid: the Old Testament, vengeful God.*
> *Jonathan and David syndrome –*
> *The Greek myths tell the story:*
> *The political 'King' emerges as the dominant autocrat*
> *Out of the mythological line.*

And, finally, Henderson's own private reflection on the flyting:

> MacDiarmid interpreted my wish to elevate Jeannie and the song tradition as an attempt to bring him down! I thought of Ferrey's description of Voltaire, 'What a pity that such a great genius should have a heart so mean!' By the late Fifties MacDiarmid, obtusely, began to regard the Folksong Revival as the New Kailyard and a threat to his Renaissance. I think it probable he intervened to stop the BBC using traditional singers at this time. George Bruce was his ally… Back pocket: re MacDiarmid 'I let the great captive albatross quiver for a minute in my hand.'[14]

[14] Timothy Neat, *Hamish Henderson: A Biography; Volume 2: Poetry Becomes People*, Edinburgh: Birlinn, 2009, pp.145, 148.

may 14th

the last ceilidh of the season
for informal music making
featuring special guest, from
Scotland, **archie fisher**
in a free concert promptly at
8:00 pm to be followed by
the usual ceilidh come-all-yea
north lounge group one

traditional music & crafts festival
smu · north dartmouth · ma · 02747

Howard Glasser, The Last Ceilidh of the Season

Hamish Henderson and Martyn Bennett: Conversations and Collaborations

Margaret Bennett

Most folk musicians would agree that compiling a set-list is an important consideration for any gig. There are two basic points to pin down: How should we open, and how should we close? (We can fill in the rest.) There may be no folk club in Scotland where the night hasn't ended with Hamish Henderson's the 'Freedom Come-All-Ye'. It may not have been what the 1997 Celtic Connections late-night Festival Club expected, however, as most of the punters had just been to a sell-out gig at the Fruitmarket. The 'traddies' may have given it a miss (is that folk music?) but the audience (or clubbers) had been wildly dancing for hours to the music of Martyn Bennett. Rumour had it that 'the boy himself' was headed to the Festival Club, but few may have anticipated that he would arrive on stage with a tall, grandfather-like figure. If the late-nighters had hoped for a second helping of the Fruitmarket, they may have been surprised. A quiet, unassuming young man stood there, small-pipes at the ready, and a broad smile that reflected admiration and affection. The audience had to hush to hear what was being said, as Martyn brought Hamish centre-stage, while blowing up the bellows and saying something about 'the real man of the night'. On cue, with characteristic closed fist in gear, Hamish began: 'Roch the wind in the clear day's dawnin....' At the end of the song, to a resounding applause, both left the stage, smiling and waving to the audience.

BBC Scotland captured the gig for television, and in March 1997 telecast an hour-long programme compiled of edits, with clips of musicians who appeared at the festival. As time passes, the programme has become a record of the evolution of Celtic Connections, as well as one of the few pieces that illuminate the friendship between Hamish Henderson and Martyn Bennett. Television aside, it had been their own decision to appear together at the Festival Club, as this was (and still is) the place where performers and audiences unwind. That session, may, however, have given the TV producer the idea of an interview the following day. More of that anon, but before we switch on the TV, a brief background sketch may be useful:

In 1995 Martyn recorded his first album, simply titled 'Martyn Bennett', which included one of Hamish's poems. Despite all tracks being rooted in Scottish and Irish tradition, the CD did not exactly fit any given category, and it soon became apparent that record-shops found it difficult to classify. Before long, it settled into the World Music section, and young musicians on both sides of the Atlantic began to create their own versions of 'anything goes'. (Some even sent Martyn cassette tapes.) This was one response from Martyn:

> The unfortunate term 'World Music' has given rise to many so-called alchemists who, I believe, do not actually understand the music they borrow, and unfortunately they tend to tout their works as being authentic, with no upbringing in any tradition whatsoever.[1]

Though the CD sleeve notes gave details about the voices (sampled or recorded) there was no room to explain the music. To some listeners and friends, it seemed clear that Martyn's choice of samples was not based on a liking for the musical extracts, or even for the performers. Sometimes it was quite the reverse, being more a statement of his response to how Scots at home and abroad regard Scottish music. He deliberately re-used a Harry Lauder sample for his third CD, and later rewrote the 'Martyn Bennett' CD notes (published online), hoping that more detail might make the point. There could hardly have been more of a contrast between tracks 5 and 7:

> ***Deoch an Dorus:*** A title of a song by 1930s Scottish Megastar, Sir Harry Lauder. Although I can't say I particularly 'like' what Lauder did, he was as big in his day as Michael Jackson - and he was Scottish. I did a remix of this track on 'Hardland' called 'Harry's in Heaven'. Up yours, Sir Harry!

---

[1] Martyn Bennett, 1996, now on <www.martynbennett.co.uk>

Colin Ross and Martyn Bennett / Hamish Henderson and Martyn Bennett at Celtic Connections, 1997 / Martyn Bennett reciting 'Floret Silva Undique' by Hamish Henderson

> ***Floret Silva Undique*** [All around the flowers are in bloom]: This lovely poem was written by Hamish Henderson. This exceptionally gifted man is, for many, the most important figure of the twentieth century in terms of Scottish culture. He has collected a wealth of Scottish folklore and written volumes on its heritage. He is also a great poet and song-smith, and has written such great songs as the 'Freedom Come-All-Ye' and 'John MacLean's March'. The poem I chose to arrange is concerned with procreation and the spring season, the same 'spring' that I hope we all see with traditional music in Scotland.

No matter what he wrote, it was evident that the music world was divided. Time and time again he could be heard to say, 'Folk just don't get it!' Though the album was top of the USA world-music chart for nearly a year, at home, some older 'folkies' who had heard him play in his early teens seemed disappointed he hadn't lived up to expectations. As Brian McNeill later suggested, however, the best way to understand his music, or find out what he was about, would be to talk to Martyn about his views on Scottish music:

> I first met Martyn in the early nineties at the Tønder festival in Denmark ... He wanted to know what made *me* tick, musically, and he proceeded to grill me. I don't remember much about my replies, but I do remember knowing – immediately – that my answers mattered, that I had to be honest with this wise old man of half my age. ... We agreed that the old fogeys weren't the problem, it was the young ones you had to watch out for ... The next time I met him was at Danny Kyle's funeral in Paisley. By then he was a recognised force ... I congratulated him on the CDs and told him that I couldn't understand all of his music. He didn't even pause to think. 'Could I react to it?' When I said I could, he assured me that was more important, even if my reaction was negative.[2]

---

[2] In 2005, when Brian was Director of Scottish Music at the RSAMD, he included this anecdote in a speech at the graduation ceremony, when a posthumous Doctrate of Music was conferred on Martyn. A fuller version has been published in *It's Not the Time You Have...: Notes and Memories of Music Making with Martyn Bennett.* (2006): Grace Note Publications.

The same year as the CD was released (1995), BBC Schools Broadcasting was recording a new series for students and teachers of 'Standard Grade Music', still a relatively new subject on the Scottish education curriculum. Several producers were already familiar with Martyn's work as, from the age of fifteen, he had collaborated on a variety of media productions. The aim of this new series was to trace music in Scotland through the centuries, and Martyn's music would take the time-line to the end of the twentieth century. The last in the series of six 19-minute programmes, his programme title was 'Sampled Tradition'. The remit was to select one of his own compositions and explain why, and how, it had been composed, giving as much detail as possible while demonstrating at each stage.[3] The piece he chose was 'Floret Silva Undique', which, by that time, had already been released. As the entire programme had to fit the 19-minute slot, the basics are distilled to give the essentials and there is no time to go into the sort of detail that truly gives the inside story. And so, at the risk of giving a background to the background, it may interest Hamish's readers to discover how this poet got involved with a maverick young musician.

Though their first meeting was at a Traditional Music and Song Association (TMSA) festival in the late 1970s, the friendship between Hamish and Martyn began in 1984. Martyn was thirteen and we had moved to Edinburgh when I was appointed lecturer at the School of Scottish Studies. He had played at several TMSA festivals, and showed considerable promise on bagpipes, while at school he studied classical violin, viola and piano and all areas of musical theory. Often on his way home from school he would stop in at the School of Scottish Studies, to 'see the techy guys' (the late Fred Kent, ex-BBC sound-recordist, and Neil MacQueen, who was up to speed with the world of audio-technology), or the photographer and photographic archivist (the late Ian MacKenzie, who shared his love of mountains). He got to know others too, and it was in that setting that Hamish invited both of us to our first Edinburgh poetry-reading. It was to be one of many for, in the eighties and nineties, Edinburgh seemed abuzz with poets and folk musicians. Some gatherings were to celebrate 'milestone birthdays', which seemed to be regular events – in

[3] Thanks to Dr Jonathan Kemp of the Music Department of St Andrews University, who advises students to study this piece, it is now available on Youtube: <www.youtube.com/watch?v=B6QQVRoFW90>

1984 William Montgomerie turned 80 and George Bruce 75; the following year Norman McCaig was 75; 1986 marked Sorley MacLean's 75th birthday; and in 1989 Hamish turned 70. Thanks to Joy Hendry and fellow-poet and editor, Raymond Ross, from the age of fourteen Martyn spent a significant time with elder statesmen of the poetry world.[4] Both Joy and Raymond, as well as Hamish, regularly invited him to contribute music to these gatherings. Thus he got to know William Montgomerie (1904–1994), George Bruce (1909 – 2002), Norman McCaig (1910–1996), Sorley Maclean (1911–1996), Iain Crichton Smith (1928–1998), Edwin Morgan (1920–2010) and Duncan Glen (1938–2008), not to mention the 'younger generation', Liz Lochhead, Aonghas Dubh MacNeacail, George Gunn, and others. The circle became wider as prose writers were also part of the scene, adding to inspiration and discussion – Owen Dudley Edwards, Alan Spence, Angus Calder and John MacInnes were among the regulars. As Aonghas Dubh remarked one night in the Queen's Hall, 'If the roof were to cave in, God forbid, it'll completely wipe out Scotland's twentieth-century literary scene, not to mention a few singers and musicians, including Flora MacNeil and a very young musician, Martyn Bennett.'[5]

It was at a poetry reading that Martyn first heard Hamish recite 'Floret Silva Undique'. He was about fourteen, and though he made no mention of it, something must have impressed him, as he spent time browsing through poetry books. I have a vivid recollection of the sound of youthful, wild enthusiasm,

---

[4] Some became his friends, and he got to know them in a way that few might imagine: for example, he liked to visit William and Norah Montgomerie, as he was also drawn to their work with children's rhymes and stories, as well as Norah's drawings. When William died, and Norah was in a care-home, he would bring her recordings, or (as the staff told me) he would arrive with his fiddle or whistle, and play by Norah's bedside. He visited Sorley and Rene in Skye, returning home with amusing anecdotes about conversations (told in a Sorley voice). In 1998, Martyn was clearly affected by the news that Iain Crichton Smith had been taken to hospital in Oban, so visited him there not long before Iain passed away. Flora talks of conversations with Martyn, as do Raymond, Joy, George, and Liz.

[5] These gatherings also date Martyn's association with Sorley MacLean, Ian Crichton Smith and many of the younger poets. It also marks the beginning of a long friendship between Flora and Martyn, which later inspired one of the final pieces he composed, 'Grit', with samples of Flora's voice.

bursting though the kitchen door: 'I've found it! Listen to this! This is fantastic!' Whatever he had been looking for had been anybody's guess, though it was not unusual for Martyn to be so preoccupied. Book in hand he began, 'Floret silva undique ...' and reading on in measured pace, with intonation echoing Hamish's voice. I have no recollection of ensuing discussion, and perhaps there was none. The reading had given pleasure to both of us, and that, as far as I understood, was the point of searching for the poem.

Largely due to these poetry-readings and to Hamish, Martyn developed a great love of the spoken word, and, perhaps not surprisingly, several of his compositions were inspired by the voices of poets. And so to the TV documentary that aimed to explain to young musicians how, and why, a composer uses sampled sound-recordings. There is no script, and Martyn speaks directly to the camera, conversational style:

> Folk music is important. All music is important, but especially folk music because it's indigenous. It's not affected by anything artificial, it's all completely natural. In the kind of thing that I write (in this idiom), I tend to use a cross-over: ethnic musics and indigenous cultures then, for example, hip-hop... The composition I've chosen has two melodies that I've written for a friend of mine, Hamish Henderson, who's a poet. The piece was written after hearing his poem, 'Floret Silva Undique', meaning, more or less, 'all around the flora is in bloom'. Basically it's about springtime in Edinburgh, with everything coming alive in the Meadows, right next to where Hamish lived....
>
> The piece has three musical sections, played on flute, fiddle and pipes, reflecting Hamish's life. What I do is, I listen to how the piece goes, Hamish recites the first verse [21 seconds]:

Floret Silva Undique
The lily, the rose, the rose I lay.
Floret silva undique
Sweet on the air till dark of day.
The bonniest pair ye iver seen
Play chasie on the Meedies green.
Floret silva undique
The Lily, the rose, the rose I lay.

I improvise while listening and add 'voices', so, we have the introduction, the ambient section on the flute, setting the atmosphere, with occasional sounds of bells ... a gong... a tabla ... voices that don't sound Scottish, like a Muslim chant – Hamish spent time in North Africa. Then over this I recite:

Floret Silva Undique
The lily, the rose, the rose I lay.
Floret silva undique
Sweet on the air till dark of day.
The bonniest pair ye iver seen
Play chasie on the Meedies green.
Floret silva undique
The Lily, the rose, the rose I lay.

Then the next section is a fiddle tune, which has an Irish feel to it, because Hamish spent a lot of time in Ireland. It goes like this [he plays the tune, explaining]: The rhythm is fairly laid-back, it's got a swing to it... So that establishes the rhythm [of the piece and also the pace of the recitation]. And I use a break-beat and add that to establish a beat[6], then come the percussion instruments the tabla, which suits ...and I wanted a 'sparkly' sound, so we have tiny cymbals, and then I've added a gong, (for occasional, distant, dull sound). So that's the second section and [he demonstrates]. At that point I bring in the poem, the first verse of Floret Silva Undique ... 16 bars reciting the poem:

I come out of that to the middle section of Hamish's poem, where I whisper the poem... [and here there are elaborate descriptions in musical terms that weave in and out of the whispered verse]

Flora is the queen of lusty may
The Lily, the rose, the rose I lay.

[6] As this programme was directed at senior school pupils, he did not explain that he used a break beat so that their generation, and his generation, would listen to Hamish's poem, or Sheila Stewart, and the real voices of Scottish tradition. 'This might be the only way they'll ever hear it,' and, as he once said to Sheila, 'I want people all over the world to hear you singing – they're not going to come to a wee folk festival.'

> Floret silva undique
> Sweet on the air till dark of day.
> The bonniest pair ye iver seen
> Play chasie on the Meedies green.
> Floret silva undique
> The Lily, the rose, the rose I lay.
>
> Then, because Hamish is quite a lad, I'm going to shout the poem, as loud as I can [as if I'm in the Meadows, where all this is going on].
>
> Tell-tale leaves on the elm-tree bole;
> Reekie's oot for a sabbath stroll.
> Sma' back pipes and they dance a spring.
> Over the grave all creatures sing.
> The sun gangs doon under yon hill
> Jenny and Jake are at it still.
> Reekie, tell me my true love's name.
> Floret silva undique.
>
> I'll change the mood and bring in sounds we haven't heard, some pipe-drums, a base line in fifths – I like fifths.... The poem is spoken over the pipes. And a new section for one final verse of the poem, and there you have it.
>
> Floret silva undique
> The lily, the rose, the rose I lay.
> Floret silva undique
> The rocker, the ring and the gowans gay
> Floret silva undique
> Sweet on the air till dark of day
> Flora is queen of lusty May,
> The lily, the rose, the rose I lay.

As Martyn put it, 'And there you have it.' Listening again to the original track, which opens with Hamish's solo voice (recorded, not sampled), may not, however, prove that he collaborated with Martyn. Might that verse not have been recorded at a poetry reading and used with permission? Anyone searching for the evidence will easily find it, as the verse is not exactly from the original poem but is an adaptation of Hamish's 70-line poem.

In Martyn's piece, we hear four 8-line verses, but anyone who presumes that it was simply a matter of lifting those out of the original will have missed the point that, as poet and musician, they worked closely together. They discussed the text at length, producing a seamless re-creation that pleased both artists.[7] The following is the sequence on the CD:

Verse 1, recited by Hamish: line(s) 1, 2, 11, 48, 13, 14, 19, 2
Verse 2, recited quietly by Martyn: same as verse 1
Verse 3, recited by Martyn: line(s) 69, 46, 29, 48, 65, 14, 64, 2
Verse 4: shouted by Martyn: line(s), 3, 4, 49, 50, 51, 52, 60, 68

Two years later, the Celtic Connections Festival Club was a memorable gig for both of them. We return now to the interview that was televised the following morning. The meeting place was the bar, which was entirely empty, apart from Hamish and Martyn who were seated by a table with a couple of glasses of whisky – the absence of people suggested it was a television set for an impromptu conversation about the previous night: the Fruitmarket gig and the Festival Club. Verbatim transcriptions convey their discussion, though the printed page can only give a pale reflection of the dynamics of the interaction between Hamish and Martyn.

The camera turns to Martyn who is responding to a question about the Fruitmarket gig:

> We have to be mindful that, with all this technology we could lose the culture, and the things that are organic ... Celtic Connections has fused these things together so that, yes, we can do this, but let's not forget what happened by the fireside.

Martyn picks up his small-pipes and turns to Hamish, and, facing each other, they smile and begin to play and sing the 'Freedom Come-All-Ye'. The song fades (BBC style) and while the tune continues and Hamish speaks: 'The Freedom Come-All-Ye

[7] See *Hamish Henderson: Collected Poems and Songs*, edited by Raymond Ross, (Curly Snake Publishing, Edinburgh), 2000, pp. 140-141. For this paper (as Martyn used to say) I had to 'listen and listen and spend a lot of time working it out for myself!' I had not, however, fully appreciated how much had gone into these discussions between poet and musician.

expresses that human beings everywhere should be united ...' The camera picks up the expression between them, at ease in each other's company, reflecting that this is no studio interview, but the spontaneous conversation between long-time friends and an opportunity to speak to a wider audience. Hamish continues:

> It seems to me that, from the times of the early People's Festival, just after the war, when the Labour Movement got together, they decided that, whatever the high heid yins decided, with respect to the big festivals, we were going to create something else, the People's Festival Ceilidh. And I think you can trace one line from the early period to right on to now [Celtic Connections]. If I give it a Scottish flavour, it's because Scotland has a long history in it, right from the 18th century, through Robert Burns, to the present.

As he finishes his statement the camera shifts to Martyn, and Hamish picks up his whisky glass. A quiet sip, and he nods, inviting Martyn's response:

> This is where it came from... You have to know where music comes from, before you can develop it. Yes, you can do a lot with the expensive technology we have today, but then that's not what happened by the fireside. We mustn't forget that. There is a lot of discussion going on about classical, jazz and rock. It's not all about hip-hop, or Islamic dub or [Hamish nods again while taking another sip, but soon has to suppress a cough that catches him by surprise. Martyn realises what happens and breaks into a smile, completing his statement over Hamish's attempt to recover]: It's not about all that beat stuff, it's about – coughing and spluttering in your whisky!

They both burst out laughing, like old friends. The camera cuts to the previous night's session to the point where Martyn had been asked to play. On stage in front of a packed house, he brings Hamish up to centre stage, the small pipes strike up, and Hamish sings the 'Freedom Come-All-Ye'. When the song ends, the audience is ecstatic, which is exactly what Martyn had hoped might happen. 'Let's not forget where it all came from...'

Margaret Bennett at Edinburgh Folk Club (photo: Allan McMillan)

Eberhard 'Paddy' Bort at Edinburgh Folk Club (photo: Allan McMillan)

‘The Shamrock and the Thistle’: Hamish Henderson’s Ireland

Eberhard Bort

I

It is early 1949, in Belfast. The young Robin Morton hears of a strange fellow who apparently regularly sings Scots folk songs in the Duke of York (a pub in what is now the Cathedral Quarter). He goes there one night to explore – and finds this ‘wild-haired’ man standing at the bar belting out a Spanish Civil War song:

Los Cuatro Generales

Los cuatro generales
Los cuatro generales
Los cuatro generales
Mamita mia
Que se han alzado
Que se han alzado

The four insurgent generals…
Mamita mia
They tried to betray us…

At Christmas, holy evening…
Mamita mia
They’ll all be hanging…

Madrid, you wondrous city…
Mamita mia
They wanted to take you…

> But your courageous children...
> Mamita mia
> They did not disgrace you...

That was Robin's first encounter of Hamish Henderson. Soon after, he had disappeared. Years later – in the mid-sixties when Morton, Tommy Gunn and Cathal McConnell – the nucleus of the Boys of the Lough – did a gig for the Edinburgh University Folk Society at the Chaplaincy Centre, they met up again. Either there, or perhaps in Sandy Bell's afterwards, Robin asked Hamish why he had left Belfast. Apparently, one night a guy in a trench coat had turned up in the Duke of York and accosted him: 'Are you Hamish Henderson?' Hamish said 'aye', whereupon the guy opened his coat and pointed at his revolver: 'You're leaving Belfast!' And, knowing when to follow sound advice, Hamish vamoosed.

So far, so good – or is it? Well, actually Robin Morton would have been just 9 years old in early 1949, so the encounter must have happened about ten years later. Robin had a good laugh when I pointed that out to him. That's folk memory for you.

Hamish was, of course, in Belfast in 1949. He had arrived in September of 1948 to work for he WEA – the Workers Education Association (from 1 Oct '48). That he left in the spring of 1949 had maybe more to do with his receiving the Somerset Maugham Prize for poetry for his *Elegies of the Dead in Cyrenaica* – which was announced in March 1949 and came with a stipulation to use he prize money of £300 for research abroad. And that he won at the races! He decided to return to Italy where the Partisans had introduced him to the work of Antonio Gramsci, whose *Prison Letters* he now set about to translate. It was that I guess he referred to when he called his Belfast time 'a turning point in my life.'[1]

There can be little doubt that Hamish in Belfast, talking about setting up a Scottish Republican Army, and making no secret of his anti-sectarian stance, was not necessarily welcome by everyone. So there may well be a kernel of truth in the 'Shadow of a Gunman' story. But the Robin Morton anecdote also points towards an engagement with Ireland that was not confined to the months spent working for the WEA – Hamish's 'Irish sojourn'.[2]

[1] Quoted in Timothy Neat, *Hamish Henderson: A Biography*, vol.1 *The Making of the Poet*, Edinburgh: Polygon/Birlinn, 2007, p.222.

[2] *Ibid.*, p.219.

II

In fact, Hamish visited Ireland with great regularity for most of his life. In an interview in 1998 with Paul Nolan, which is quoted in Tim Neat's biography of Hamish Henderson, he reflects: 'My familiarity with Ireland went back to my childhood, my mother knew a good number of Irish songs and I had a good store of Irish jokes when I was nine years old!'[3]

Kätzel Henderson thinks that Hamish was in Ireland as a child with his mother. In an interview with Andrew Means, Hamish recollects: 'I was first in Ireland when I was quite a small bairn, and always have liked and loved Ireland.'[4] In 1936, as a teenager (Hamish was born in 1919), Hamish visited Dublin. Neat gives this vignette:

> Knowing that W B Yeats often visited Oliver St John Gogarty at the Shelbourne Hotel, he decided to hang about and, late one night, introduced himself to the great poet and joined the small band that strolled with him down O'Connell Street. In 1974 Hamish told me the only thing he remembered clearly was 'Yeats coming to a tree and pausing – he was at that time a distinguished senator of the Free State – pausing to pish against a tree! It was only a small thing, but it meant a great deal to me.' And he roared with laughter.[5]

Yeats's poetry would accompany him through the Italian campaign. In a letter to a friend in Dublin, Hamish mentions how the Cuala Press edition of the Irish poet's *Last Poems* 'bring back memories of the Anzio Beach Head, where the book landed and helped me face the Huns; and of Easter Sunday years ago when I marched as a Glaswegian behind the Finton Lodge Pipe Band – down Baggot Street in the spring of 1939,'[6] In 1948, Hamish had just settled in with the poet John Hewitt at the beginning of his

---

[3] *Ibid.*, p.224.

[4] Andrew Means, 'Scottish Studies', *Melody Maker*, 17 March 1973 – reprinted in this volume.

[5] *Ibid.*, pp.24-25.

[6] Quoted in Timothy Neat, Hamish Henderson: A Biography, vol.2, Poetry Becomes People, Edinburgh: Polygon/Birlinn, 2009, p.83.

WEA employment when he offered him a ride over to Sligo to attend Yeats's funeral. Yeats had died in 1939 in France, but now was his 'homecoming'. Hamish distilled his impressions into a poem first published in Tim Neat's biography:

The distant pipes cried faintly their lament,
The drum-beats dropped their clods on coffin lid
As the town band stepped bravely into view;
Slow, slow, as if to stop, yet never stopping;
Then the procession, square black-coated men,
The glinting chain, the coloured Galway hords,
The straight clenched faces, then the droning motors,
The pitch-pine coffin bright in the large hearse.
So without banners into Sligotown
The poet came, impressive as his verse.[7]

The gravestone would carry the last lines of one of Yeats's final poems – 'Under Ben Bulben' (1939):

Under bare Ben Bulben's head
In Drumcliff churchyard Yeats is laid.
An ancestor was rector there
Long years ago, a church stands near,
By the road an ancient cross.
No marble, no conventional phrase;
On limestone quarried near the spot
By his command these words are cut:

Cast a cold eye
On life, on death.
Horseman, pass by![8]

That experience would have been heightened by the awareness that Ben Bulben is, in Irish, *Binn Ghulbain*, the same as Ben Gulabeinn in Perthshire, the mountain under which Hamish grew up – and where his ashes would be scattered, as thrillingly evoked in Geordie McIntyre's poem 'Fom Gulabeinn':

---

[7] *Quoted in Timothy Neat, Vol. 1, p 220.*

[8] William Butler Yeats, *W. B. Yeats: Selected Poetry*, ed. by A. Norman Jeffares, London: Macmillan, 1968, pp.205-208.

From Gulabeinn's bell-heathered slopes
His dust was scattered to the sky
Particles of song unite
With trilling curlew cry.

This mystic hill 'of youth and age'
Towers o'er the Fairy Glen
Banner-bright in May morn light
To welcome Hamish home.[9]

After his return from Germany in 1939, Hamish lodged with the Armstrong family in Cambridge. The Reverend Allan Armstrong, an Anglo-Irishman ordained in the Church of Ireland, 'had been driven out by the IRA'[10] and was now the Rector in the village of Dry Drayton. It was the beginning of a life-long friendship. Dry Drayton would become a home from home for Hamish: 'From Dry Drayton he went out to fight fascism, and to Dry Drayton he would return until he was too old to travel.'[11] At Cambridge, Hamish met Irishmen like Maurice Craig, who recalled in a letter to Timothy Neat in 2003 how he wrote the first stanza of the 'Ballad of a Taxi Driver's Cap', the song he calls 'a good-humoured salute to Stalin [which] Hamish expanded ... into a popular army song.'[12]

Hamish also contributed a play for the Cambridge Mummers, *The Humpy Cromm*, set at Speaker's Corner in Hyde Park:

> Its subject is IRA terrorism, English Imperialism, the clash between communism and fascism, and the play gives voice to a radical Irish nationalism rarely heard in England at that time.[13]

At the beginning of the war, Hamish was also in touch with the poet Paul Potts, an Irish Canadian Londoner who published a

---

[9] The full poem was fist published in the 2009 Carrying Stream Festival programme, and then in Eberhard Bort (ed.), *Borne on the Carrying Stream: The Legacy of Hamish Henderson*, Ochtertyre: Grace Note Publications, 2010, pp.23-24.

[10] Neat, vol.1, p.37.

[11] *Ibid.*, p.38.

[12] *Ibid.*, p.36.

[13] *Ibid.*

poem about Hamish in the summer edition 1940 of *Cambridge Front* – 'The Poet and the Harvester' casts, according to Tim Neat, Hamish as the poet and Potts as the harvester.[14] Shortly after, Hamish was alerted by a Cambridge friend to the new poetry of W R Rodgers, whom, as Hamish writes back, Stephen Spender had called a 'hairy man from the Irish bogs'. Hamish was not fully convinced of the poet's diction – 'his literary language would do well to dip down to common Irish folk speech again for a lyrical impulse,' but he was 'still overcome with admiration at the power of our Irish poet... '[15]

During the war, a young Classics student from Milan, who had deserted from Mussolini's army and joined the British army as a camp follower, had become an assistant, student and, eventually, intellectual friend of Hamish's.[16] After the war, working as a translator in Milan, he applied to the University of Milan as he wanted to embark on a PhD thesis. On the advice of Hamish, this was to be about 'The Relationship between James Joyce's "Ulysses" and Homer's "Odyssey"' – Hamish would, over the next four years, act as 'Luigi's long-distance and very unofficial thesis supervisor.'[17]

Shortly after Yeats's funeral, Hamish was helping to organise the quarter-century meeting in memory of the death of Red Clydesider John Maclean. By the end of July '48, he had completed 'The John Maclean March'. But he was not only to-ing and fro-ing between Ulster and Scotland, he also used his time to get acquainted with his new environs: within the first few weeks he had visited, on his Rudge motorbike, Carrickfergus, Derry, Warrenpoint, Ballymena, Newtownards, Omagh, Ballycastle, Banbridge, Ballymoney, Ballycloy and Lisburn – 'and been bought drinks in every town!'[18] No wonder would he sum up his time in the North with the words: 'Ulster has many happy memories for me.'[19]

---

[14] Timothy Neat, 'Hamish Henderson: As the Poets Saw Him (1940-2004)', in Eberhard Bort (ed.), *Borne on the Carrying Stream: The Legacy of Hamish Henderson*, pp.161-194.

[15] Neat, vol.1, pp.72-73.

[16] *Ibid.*, p.155.

[17] *Ibid.*, pp.183-184.

[18] *Ibid.*, p.223.

[19] *Ibid.*, p.225.

As Tim Neat notes, his being a decorated British army officer brought him instant cudos with the Unionists, but his Celtic nationalism opened doors within the republican and Catholic community. Belfast was good to Hamish – he had a great time there – 'life was a pleasure. I had time to write. I had enough money to buy a round – I was meeting all these fine folk and my memory is of a bright and eager period,' he said to Paul Nolan, and added: 'I was close to both the Orange and the Green...' In retrospect he saw 'the years 1945-1955 as a surprising, golden period in the history of Northern Ireland: if not idyllic, it was a peaceful, pleasant and human society – and full of song.'[20] He met not only John Hewitt, with whom he stayed initially, but also Louis MacNeice (whom he had already known from his Cambridge days); Andy Boyd – a journalist, communist, Protestant republican – became a good friend. And he met Sam Hanna Bell, a BBC producer and writer, 'fascinated by the historical and cultural links between past and present and between Ulster and Scotland.'[21] He would publish his novel *December Bride* two years after Hamish left Belfast.

From Belfast, Hamish continued planning for the Macean celebrations in Glasgow. These culminated on 28 November with William Noble's singing of 'The John Maclean March' – with the famous lines

> Hullo Pat Malone, sure I knew you'd be here son:
> The red and the green, lad, we'll wear side by side[22]

which bridge the sectarian divide between the Catholic Irish workers and the Protestant Scots which has 'caused so much division and bloodshed in Glasgow.'[23]

Another of Hamish's great songs dates from that Belfast period: the 'Ballad of the Men of Knoydart', about the 'Seven Men of Knoydart' (who had all, like Hamish, served in the War) and who, led by the local parish priest, Father Colin Macpherson,

---

[20] Paul Nolan interview, quoted in Neat, vol.1, pp.224-225.

[21] Neat, vol.1, p.237.

[22] Hamish Henderson, *Collected Poems and Songs*, ed. by Raymond Ross, Edinburgh: Curly Snake, 2000, p.126.

[23] Jack Mitchell, 'Hamish Henderson and the Scottish Tradition', *Calgacus*, 3 (Spring 1976), pp.26-31; p.29.

had occupied a piece of land on Lord Brocket's estate and begun turning it into crofts. Brocket had been a Nazi-supporter and absentee landlord. After the war, as Dick Gaughan notes, 'hundreds of local people all over the Highlands – most of whom had just fought a war for "freedom" – applied for crofting land, land which had been stolen from their ancestors, but were informed by the Department of Agriculture that no land was available. Yet vast estates all over the Highlands were lying waste under the hands of private landlords.'[24]

Hamish's landlady, Jean Connor, at one of their 'hoolies' in 43 Fitzwilliam Street (off University Road), sang a spirited version of the Irish rebel song 'Johnston's Motor Car' –

> the tune kept dancing in my memory. A few weeks later, when I was returning from a short holiday in Scotland aboard one of the Burns-Laird steamers, I composed 'The Men of Knoydart' to that same air. The song began while we were lying at the Broomielaw, and was complete before the Clyde coast faded from sight. It had its premiere in Kelly's Cellars in Belfast the following lunch-time.'[25]

In March 1949, Hamish introduced Paul Robeson, the legendary American singer, socialist and supporter of black people's civil rights – he would be blacklisted as 'un-American' in the McCarthy era – when he gave is 1949 concert in the Ulster Hall: 'My task in introducing Paul Robeson to Belfast is to commend the way in which he is exploiting his magnificent voice to the full – for the good of the citizens of this city and working people of the world... '[26]

In 1952, Hamish was back in Dublin, meeting up with the Behans, whom he had first encountered on a visit in 1946. And then again at Easter 1949, when he had also seen Sean O'Casey's 'The Plough and the Stars' at the Abbey with Peadar O'Donnell (the founder of literary magazine *The Bell*). The Behans, Kearneys and Bourkes (or de Burcas) – a triangular, intertwined family – Peader Kearney wrote 'The Soldier's Song – the Irish national

---

[24] Dick Gaughan, Lyrics and Song Notes to 'The Men of Knoydart', <www.dickgaughan.co.uk/songs/texts/knoydart.html>.

[25] Hamish Henderson, 'William McGonagall and the Folk Scene', *Chapbook*, vol.2, no.5, pp.3-10 and 23-34; p.27.

[26] Neat, vol.1, p.232.

anthem; his nephew Seamus de Burca was a playwright, costumier and publisher, whose father had been the playwright P J Bourke, supplying patriotic melodramas for the Queen's Theatre in Pearse Street, of which he was managing director; Brendan Behan, who would become a famous playwright – after borstal (for a botched juvenile IRA mission) in England, Dominic Behan, a famous songwriter ('The Patriot Game'), Brian – a writer and biographer. But first and foremost, Kathleen, the Mother of All the Behans.[27] 'They were magnificent company and Hamish had not felt so much at home since his fireside nights with the Partisans above San Lorenzo.'[28] In 1946, shortly after he had first encountered this remarkable family, he had watched, back in Cambridge, a group of Irish Travellers singing Peader Kearney's 'The Bold Fenian Boys' – Tim Neat gets slightly carried away when he adds that Hamish had been drinking with 'his friend'... 'just a few weeks earlier' – Peader Kearney had died in 1942.

Now, in 1952, Brendan Behan showed Hamish the script of his play *The Quare Fellow*. Hamish tipped him off in the direction of Joan Littlewood who was running the Theatre Workshop at Stratford East in London's East End[29] – a fact, he adds, which was omitted in Howard Goorney's history of the theatre.[30] While mentioning that Littlewood had heard of Behan through Hamish, Michael O'Sullivan's biography of Brendan Behan states that Brendan acted upon spotting a notice in the *Daily Worker* inviting playwrights to submit scripts to the Theatre Workshop.[31] Anyway, *The Quare Fellow* and Brendan's later play, *The Hostage*, would become landmark successes of the Theatre Workshop. For the next decade, Hamish and Brendan kept in touch, and visited each

---

[27] Brian Behan, *Mother of all the Behans: The Story of Kathleen Behan*, London: Hutchinson, 1984. It was adapted for the stage by Peter Sheridan and premiered at the Abbey Theatre in Dublin in 1987, featuring Rosaleen Linehan; in 1989, that production won a Fringe First in Edinburgh.

[28] *Ibid.*, p.183.

[29] Hamish Henderson, 'Letter to Ewan McColl 10 March 1986', in *The Armstrong Nose: Selected Letters of Hamish Henderson*, edited by Alec Finlay, Edinburgh: Polygon, 1992, p.261.

[30] Howard Goorney, *The Theatre Workshop Story*, London: Eyre Methuen, 1981.

[31] Michael O'Sullivan, *Brendan Behan: A Life*, Dublin: Blackwater Press, 1997, pp.203-204.

other – with major drinking sessions in McDaid's in Dublin and Sandy Bell's in Edinburgh. But Neat may go a tad too far when he stylises Hamish into a literary role model for Brendan Behan.

As John Hewitt noted, reminiscing about Hamish dropping by 'unexpectedly', 'on his way to Dublin to call with the Behans,' it was initially not Brendan in whom Hamish was interested. 'Brendan, we supposed; but no; he had just heard of him. It was the old father and mother whom he sought, fountains of balladry, and the most important of the clan.'[32]

Hamish collected 20 songs from Kathleen Behan in 1956, and – three years later – arranged for BBC sessions with her in Dublin. He had been shocked that these urban tradition bearers, fiercely nationalist, republican and communist, had been ignored by RTÉ and by the folklore commission. Among the recorded songs was 'My Bonny Brown Boy', a version, as Hamish notes, of Child 12, 'Lord Randal':

The Bonny Brown Boy

'Where have you been to, my bonny brown boy?
Where have you been to, my heart's love and joy?'
'To the fair o Ballytober. Mother, make my bed soon,
For I'm tired to the heart and I long to lie down.'

'What's for your dinner, my bonny brown boy?
What's for your dinner, my heart's love and joy?'
'Cabbage and thump. Mother, make my bed soon,
For I'm tired in the heat and I log to lie down.'

'What's for your father, my bonny brown boy?
What's for your father, my heart's love and joy?
'A coach and six horses. Mother, make my bed soon,
For I'm tired in the heart and I long to lie down.'

'What's for your childher, my bonny brown boy?
What's for your childher, my heart's love and joy?'
'Good school and education. Mother, make my bed soon,
For I'm tired in the heart and I long to lie down.'

---

[32] John Hewitt, *A North Light: Twenty-five years in a municipal art gallery*, Dublin: Four Courts Press, 2013, p.239.

'Now, where will we bury you, my bonny brown boy?
Where will we bury you, my heat's love and joy?
'Put a stone at me head and a stone at me feet,
And place me in Glasnevin for to take a long sleep.'[33]

In *Tocher*, not only the song is printed, but also a snippet of the collector's conversation with Kathleen Behan:

HH: Tell me, Kathleen, when did you first hear that song?
KB: Oh, whin I was a child.
HH: And who sang it?
KB: My own mother.
HH: Did she? Where was she from?
KB: County Meath.
HH: And what was the place that she heard it first sung at?
KB: Slane, in County Meath, Slane.
HH: And tell me, did she have a different way on it to the last verse?
KB: Oh yes. She sung ... place ... on the Hill of Slane.
HH: Ah but sing it! Sing it the way she sang it.

'And where will we bury you, my bonny brown boy?
Where will we bury you, my heart's love and joy?'
'Put a stone at my head an' a stone at my feet,
Place me on the Hill o Slane for to take a long sleep.'

HH: Tell me, Kathleen, you were devoted to the cause of Irish freedom from the word go, weren't you?
KB: Oh, all the time, yes.
HH: And now tell me, your brother [Peadar Kearney], he began composing songs. Where did he get the idea of those songs from?
KB: His own father ... our own father ... yes.
HH: Where was he from?
KB: County Louth, Ardee... ... I t'ink he [Peadar] composed 'The Soldier's Song' ... he must've composed 'The Soldier's Song' about nineteen hundert an' twelve. Must have. He used to sing it round the

[33] *Tocher*, no. 43 (1991), pp.14-16

Irish class in the Barns, the Ulva Barns (?) Irish class we attended.[34]

HH: Now tell me, Kathleen, you used to talk about the Gaels goin' out to the Village. What did you mean? Where was the Village and who were he Gaels?

KB: Oh the *Village*! A public house was the *Village*. Phil Shanahan's.[35]

HH: And who used to go down there, now tell us?

KB: Oh, Phil Shanahan, and Peadar, and Sean MacDermott, I suppose, and all the lads, all the '16 lads. Went out in '16 after. They all gathered in the *Village*, in… eh, Phil Shanahan's.

HH: Yes. And they'd sing?

KB: Oh they'd sing! They'd pull the rafters down! They'd pull the house down. And we used to sing over in Kearney's too, in Peadar's. His wife was a nice singer, too, Eva (?). She was, a very lovely singer…[36]

KB: Now tell us, Kathleen, what were the most popular songs when these lads were singing in that place?

KB: Well, we would song … oh, we used to sing all the Irish … every Irish song. 'Fineen the Rover' was one. We'd sing that.[37]

---

[34] 'The queried names may need to be corrected by a reader who knows the background,' says the note accompanying the tape in the School of Scottish Studies. I think Kathleen Behan refers to the Irish class in Dolphin's Barn, a Southside inner city suburb of Dublin where Peadar Kearney was brought up; the Behans lived there before moving out to Crumlin. Kearney wrote the original English lyrics of 'The Soldier's Song' in 1907 and his friend and musical collaborator Patrick Heeney composed the music. The lyrics were published by Bulmer Hobson in *Irish Freedom* in 1912, and the music in 1916. In 1926, four years after the formation of the Irish Free State, the Irish translation, 'Amhrán na bhFian', was adopted as the Irish national anthem. See Seamus de Burca, *The Soldier's Song: The Story of Peadar Ó Cearnaigh*, Dublin: P.J. Bourke, 1957.

[35] Phil Shanahan's pub in Foley Street was situated in a rough part of Dublin called the 'Monto' which was a hive of IRA activity around the time of the war of independence, with several safe houses including Phil Shanahan's public house. Shanahan was originally from Co Tipperary, a noted hurler; he took part in the Easter Rising of 1916, and was elected a Sinn Féin MP in 1918.

[36] Peadar Kearney's wife was indeed Eva, née Flanagan.

[37] It can be heard on Dominic Behan's album *Ireland Sings* (Pye, 1965).

In 1955, the wealthy American divorcee Diane Hamilton, heiress to the Guggenheim dynasty and ardent lover of Irish music (and of Liam Clancy), toured Ireland and Scotland, recording folk singers. She had met Liam's older brothers on the Greenwich Village folk music scene and when they heard she was going to Ireland they insisted she visit their mother, a renowned singer, in Carrick-on-Suir.

> Once there, she became smitten with Liam's powerful singing voice and good looks and invited him to pack in his job as an insurance salesman and join her and Scottish poet Hamish Henderson on a visit to the Aran Islands, then Armagh and on to Scotland.
>
> The wickedly flamboyant Henderson had also taken a shine to Liam, and both he and Diane spent the trip mooning over the teenager.
>
> (...)
>
> Liam managed to rebuff advances from both, but the wealthy American, undeterred, invited him to follow her to New York. She paid for his ticket and in 1956 he set off on the long sea voyage.[38]

Next thing, and – to Diane's delight – The Clancy Brothers and Tommy Makem, as they became known, began to conquer America from their base in New York, celebrating their breakthrough when they appeared nationwide on the Ed Sullivan Show in 1961.

III

Song collecting clearly was Hamish's main interest after the founding of the School of Scottish Studies at Edinburgh University in 1951. He had, of course, already experienced the work of the Irish Folklore Commission. His colleague at the School, Calum Maclean (the brother of the poet Sorley) was in the employ of the Commission – set up under Séamus Delargy in 1935. In 1946, Calum and Hamish and Séamus Ennis were on Canna, on the invitation of John Lorne Campbell, and he could see the principles of collecting as set out by Delargy and Seán

[38] Donal Lynch, 'A boy in a bainin sweater', *Irish Independent*, 5 March 2006.

Ó Suilleabhainn at first hand. He always had a great respect for these two – 'my first folklore mentors'.[39] While others came to prefer ethnographer and anthropologist as descriptions of their profession, Hamish, like his mentors (and like his disciple Margaret Bennett) always took pride in calling himself a folklorist. As Adam McNaughtan noted, working with John Lorne Campbell, Séamus Ennis and Calum Maclean 'fired his own ambition to work in the field of collecting.'[40] Where Hamish differed from the Irish Folklore Commission was in his rejection, particularly as the folk revival took root, of its 'cultural pessimism' – after all, had not Máirtín Ó Cadhain, the Irish storyteller, 'admired [Lady] Gregory and Yeats for their imaginative use of folklore'?[41]

Encouraged by Alan Lomax, the BBC, in conjunction with the English Folk Dance and Song Society, launched a project to 'mop up' what was left of the British and Irish song and musical tradition. Peter Kennedy was appointed director, and his team included Séamus Ennis, Sean O'Boyle, Bob Copper, along with Hamish Henderson. Thus, backed by the British taxpayer, the largest and most important collection of British and Irish field recordings was put together and sets of these recordings were, subsequently, held at the BBC library and the Vaughan Williams Memorial Library, both in London.[42]

As Tom Munnelly, Ireland's leading folklorist and close friend of Hamish's, reflected on collecting in Ireland, including his great discovery, the Roscommon Traveller John Reilly, it

> has made it obvious that the well springs of folksong among them is as deep as that already demonstrated by Scots travellers as a result of the work of Hamish Henderson. Of course Irish travellers travelled in Britain and vice versa

---

39 Hamish Henderson, 'Letter to Ewan McColl, 7 October 1986', in The Armstrong Nose, p.270.

40 Adam McNaughtan, 'Hamsh Henderson', *Tocher*, no.43, pp.2-5; p.3.

41 Diarmuid Ó Giolláin, 'Folk Culture', in Joe Cleary and Claire Connolly (eds), The Cambridge Companion to Modern Irish Culture, Cambridge: Cambridge University Press, 2005, pp.225-244; p.233.

42 A small number of those recordings were used for a series of programmes in the 1950s entitled 'As I Roved Out', and a magnificent series of programmes 'The Song Carriers' also made use of them to discuss the song tradition. A selection of the songs, in some cases heavily edited, was released in a record series 'Folk Songs Of Britain'.

> and the importance of this musical cross fertilization is just coming to light.[43]

It was Munnelly who had 'given' Reilly's 'The Maid and the Palmer' to Christy Moore and Planxty. 'And as "The Well Below the Valley" [on the eponymous Planxty album of 1973], it went forth and multiplied again for the benefit of a new generation.'[44] Munnelly was 'a world authority on his homeland's folkways' who gathered 'the largest collection of Ireland's traditional song amassed by one individual.'[45]

Another good example of cross fertlisation is 'The Lakes o' Shillin', as recorded by Cathie Stewart on *The Stewarts of Blair*. 'Irish songs have enjoyed tremendous popularity in Scots bothies and farm kitchens,' Hamish Henderson commented in the album notes: 'Most of them were probably brought over by harvesters and itinerant labourers, though Greig thought that some at least may have been learned by Scots soldiers from Irish comrades-in-arms at camp-fire ceilidhs during the Napoleonic wars.' In P W Joyce's collection, Hamish adds, 'it is called *The Lakes of Coolfin* but it has been popular in Aberdeenshire for many years.'[46]

Hamish was well-versed in Irish folklore, from the *Táin Bó Cúailnge* [the *Great Cattle Raid of Cooley]* to Finn MacCool – particularly folk myths and tales shared between Ireland and Scotland as, for example, the story of Diarmuid and Gráinne. He was interested in gender issues in these tales, from the homo-erotic practices between Ferdia and Cú Chulainn to the role of women in Celtic mythology. He quotes Dillon and Chadwick: 'In Irish and Welsh stories of Celtic Britain the great heroes are taught not only wisdom but also feats of arms by women.'[47] Like Rudolf Pörtner in Germany and the Irish historian Kenneth Nicholls he was convinced that Celtic folkways had survived into the middle ages and beyond in their Irish '*Naturschutzgebiete*' [protected

---

[43] Tom Munnelly, *Planxty Olympia Theatre Concert Programme*, Dublin, August 1980.

[44] Frank McNally, 'In search of lost rhyme – An Irishman's Diary on the song collecting of Tom Munnelly', *The Irish Times*, 5 February 2015.

[45] Martin Ryan, 'Tom Munnelly obit', *The Times*, 30 August 2007.

[46] *The Stewarts of Blair* (Topic Records, 1965).

[47] Myles Dillon and Nora Chadwick, *The Celtic Realms*, London: Weidenfeld, 1967, p.194.

nature reserves], as in Scotland's Highlands and islands.[48]

Hamish saw the performances of the Irish Festival Players in the early days of the Edinburgh Fringe, where they performed works by Yeats, among them his Cu Chulainn plays. One of the actors was Denis Tuohy, a Belfast Catholic, who struck up a friendship with Hamish, as Owen Dudley Edwards – another colleage and friend of Hamish's – remembers.[49]

In an interview with Radio Ulster Hamish said in 1956 that 'South-west Scotland and North-east Ireland may be said (from the point of folklore) to form a single cultural area,'[50] anticipating Seamus Heaney's observations, made when he came to Edinburgh in 1996 for the bi-centennial commemorations of Burns's death. Heaney spoke of the sensation of turning the book in his school class in Bellaghy and finding 'To a Mouse, On turning her up in her Nest, with the Plough, November, 1785' – and how it immediately spoke to him, as it would to all 'who hailed from somewhere north of a line drawn between Berwick and Bundoran.'[51]

> The way Burns sounded, his choice of words, his rhymes and metaphors, all that collapsed the distance I expected to feel between myself and the schoolbook poetry I encountered first at Anahorish Elementary School.[52]

Heaney put it in verse, in his contribution, 'A Birl for Burns', for a selection of Burns's poems by Andrew O'Hagan:

---

[48] Hamish Henderson, 'Women of the Glen', in Robert O'Driscoll (ed.), *The Celtic Consciousness*, Edinburgh: Canongate, 1982, pp.255-264. See also Rudolf Pörtner, *Bevor die Römer kamen*, Berlin: Econ, 1961; Kenneth Nicholls, *Gaelic and Gaelicized Ireland in the Middle Ages*, Dublin: Gill and Macmillan, 1972.

[49] Owen Dudley Edwards, 'Sectarian Songs: The Hamish Henderson Lecture 2011', in E. Bort (ed.) *At Hame wi' Freedom: Essays on Hamish Henderson and the Scottish Folk Revival*, Ochtertyre: Grace Note Publications, 2012, pp.151-196; pp.151-152.

[50] Timothy Neat, vol.2, p.226.

[51] Seamus Heaney, 'Burns's Art Speech', in Robert Crawford (ed.), *Robert Burns and Cultural Authority*, Edinburgh: Edinburgh University Press, 1997, pp.216-234; pp.217-218.

[52] 'Heaney's tribute to the Scottish bard', *BBC News*, 25 January 2008, <http://news.bbc.co.uk/1/hi/northern_ireland/7209402.stm>.

From the start, Burns' birl and rhythm,
That tongue the Ulster Scots brought wi' them
And stick to still in County Antrim
  Was in my ear.
From east of Bann it westered in
  On the Derry air.[53]

Hamish visited the Folklore Commission frequently, and he recorded with Ciarán MacMathúna for his Radio Éireann programme in 1956 and 1958. MacMathúna was, as Sam Smith remarked, 'on a mission to collect songs and stories, music, poetry and dance before they were buried under the coming tsunami of pop music.'[54] That connection would last well into the 1990s when he visited Ireland in the company of Margaret and Martyn Bennett[55]. In 1958 he also paid a visit to the Blasket Islands and Peig Sayers who was, as he noted at that time, 'lying blind and bedridden in a hospital above Dingle, but her mind is as alert as ever.'[56]

IV

Back in Scotland he recorded Jeannie Robertson singing for the famous Irish street balladeer Margaret Barry's step-dancing, as she did not have a store of lilting Irish tunes to accompany herself. 'Margaret was surprised that Jeannie knew so many Irish songs.'[57]

Hamish also collaborated with Dominic Behan, whom the Belfast-born singer and storyteller Maggi Peirce recalls at the

---

[53] in Andrew O'Hagan (ed.), *A Night Out with Robert Burns: The Greatest Poems*, Edinburgh: Canongate, 2009, pp.viii-ix.

[54] Sam Smith, 'Tributes flood in for veteran RTE broadcaster', Irish Independent, 12 December 2009.

[55] 'The Pure Drop' on RTÉ, March 1993.

[56] Quoted in Neat, vol.2, p.227.

[57] 'Jeannie Robertson sings for Margaret Barry's step-dancing', Tobair an Dulchais/Kist o Riches, 1960, <www.tobarandualchais.co.uk/en/fullrecord/23506/3;jsessionid=E68166B8B8D822D8617887FBB086E8FF>. There are about 80 songs and tunes from Ireland (some in various different versions) among the 3,607 items Hamish recorded for the School of Scottish Studies – all available through Tobar an Dulchais/Kist o Riches.

Howff folk club 'as a very pleasant person and a good singer.'[58] A planned tour of them both through the GDR in 1960 did, alas, not materialise. Kätzel had looked forward to that return to Germany. She had perhaps more mixed feelings about being dragged, on a holiday to Ireland in 1961, into McDaid's, where Paddy Kavanagh and Brendan Behan were holding court (together when they were on speaking terms, separately more often, when they were not). Soon they were downing pints at the bar with Hamish. 'In McDaid's pub, Hamish was always greeted like a hero, and never allowed to buy a round himself – a great week unfolded,' as Tim Neat puts it. [59] I somehow doubt that Kätzel was quite so enthusiastic about the prospect.

Kätzel and Hamish also visited Belfast that year and stayed with David Hammond, singer, collector, teacher, broadcaster and film maker – for whom Seamus Heaney would later write 'The Singer's House', and who would, together with Heaney, Brian Friel and Stephen Rea become a founder member of Field Day Theatre Company.

> When I came here first you were always singing,
> a hint of the clip of the pick
> in you winnowing climb and attack.
> Raise it again, man. We still believe what we hear.[60]

The poem is, as Heaney said in an interview, 'about the poet's and the poem's right to a tune in spite of the tunelessness of the world around them.' In the same interview, he called Hammond 'a good friend [who] had been a kind of lord of misrule in our early days around Belfast.'[61]

In Armagh, Hamish and Kätzel stayed with another friend, the folk-collector Sean O'Boyle. Hamish had been invited by BBC Northern Ireland in 1956 to contribute to its 'Folksong Forum'. He reported that year:

---

[58] Maggi Peirce in an email to the author, 11 March 2015.

[59] *Ibid.*, p.85.

[60] Seamus Heaney, 'The Singer's House', in Seamus Heaney, *Field Work*, London, Faber & Faber, 1979, p. 27.

[61] Henri Cole, 'Seamus Heaney: The Art of Poetry No.75', *The Paris Review*, no.144 (Fall 1997).

> I made contact with the distinguished Irish collector Sean O'Boyle, and spent a week with him in Armagh listening to his vast collection of Ulster folksong, and comparing notes with him on songs of mutual interest. He showed me his catalogue of the contents of the Sam Henry collection in Belfast, which stands comparison, both as regards quantity and quality, with the Gavin Greig collection housed in King's College Library, Aberdeen. Interesting Scottish material, which has not so far turned up here, has survived in Ireland.[62]

Apart from praising Sean O'Boyle's hospitality, Hamish Henderson puts on the record In the same piece how he made contact in Dublin with Ciarán MacMathúna of RTÉ's folk-music section, recorded Kathleen Behan, 'exchanged notes on songs and singers with Seán MacRéamoinn' and 'had a long discussion on the various points raised by my Irish tour with Professor Séamus Delargy.'[63] MacRéamoinn had been attached to RTÉ's outside broadcast unit and worked with the distinguished uilleann piper, Séamus Ennis, travelling the country to record the music and folklore of rural Ireland. On one occasion, as P J Gillan mentioned in his *Guardian* obituary, 'a farmer took a break from haymaking to explain what made one poem better than another: "Better words, better placed."'[64]

Also in 1956, Sean O'Boyle came to Scotland, on a recording trip with Hamish to Perthshire and the Western Isles. In a letter to Herschel Gower, Hamish gives a flavour of it:

> Sean's trip to Scotland went off very well indeed – first of all, he came to Blairgowrie, met Jeannie (who was down for the picking season), and had one or two great ceilidhs in Bella Higgins's house. Needless to say, he was a 'success fou' with the tinkers – and 'fou', now I come to think of it, is the 'mot juste.' (...)
>
> After Perthshire, we made tracks for the Western Isles, and there Sean was in his glory – especially on Barra,

---

[62] Hamish Henderson, 'Progress Report, School of Scottish Studies', 'Appendix B' in James Porter, *Jeannie Robertson: Emergent Singer, Transformative Voice*, East Linton: Tuckwell Press, 1995, p.313.

[63] *Ibid.*, p.314.

[64] P J Gillan, 'Seán MacRéamoinn: Obituray', *The Guardian*, 16 February 2007.

> which completely captured his allegiance. It was great fun being with him; in fact, there was never a dull moment, his sympathy and wit are so lively, keen and kindly. Everything in the islands, from the priests to the pagans, came in for an appreciative lick of his tongue.[65]

V

In 1965, Hamish meets the poet and reviewer Hayden Murphy in McDaid's in Dublin, who was then a Trinity College student and member of the music group that was perhaps the closest the Irish music scene got to match the Incredible String Band, Dr Strangely Strange. After Murphy's move to Edinburgh in 1966, Hamish was invited by him to become a contributor to *Broadsheet*, a magazine Murphy edited between 1967 and 1978.[66]

At the Edinburgh Festival Hamish first encountered Brian Trevaskis, an Irishman right after Hamish's taste. He was a budding writer, and got a scholarship for Trinity College, where he seemed to have modelled himself on colourful characters like Oliver St John Gogarty and John Pentland Mahaffy, attacking, as he wrote in a letter to Hamish, 'the moral hypocrisy of the Irish Catholic Curch, "personified", he declared, "by Archbishop John Charles McQuaid of Dublin!" In 1966 he reported 'mission accomplished – he had called the Bishop of Galway 'a moron, on television!'[67]

Another important encounter in the 1960s was with Paddy Moloney and Garech Browne, the Guinness millionaire and owner of Claddagh Records – which, eventually, led to the production of Hamish's LP 'Freedom Come All-Ye – the Poems and Songs of Hamish Henderson', released by Claddagh in 1977. Back in 1971, Garech had asked Hamish (alongside Sean MacRéamoinn and Susanna York) to provide liner notes for *Chieftains 3*. Hamish

---

65 Hamish Henderson, 'Letter to Herschel Gower, 1956', in James Porter and Herschel Gower, *Jeannie Robertson: Emergent Singer, Transformative Voice*, 'Appendix C', pp.317-321; p.318.

66 Hayden Murphy, 'Hamish Henderson and *Broadsheet*: Putting the Teeth in Context', in Eberhard Bort, *At Hame Wi' Freedom: Essays on Hamish Henderson and the Scottish Folk Revival*, Ochtertyre: Grace Note Publications, 2012, pp.142-150.

67 Trevaskis letter to Hamish, quoted in Neat, vol.2, p.230.

obliged and called the album 'something of an event for the aficionado'.[68]

Hayden Murphy recalls a visit with Hamish to the Haymarket Ice Rink to see the Irish playwright Sean McCarthy's *The Fantastical Feats of Finn McCool*, for which Planxty was providing the music.[69] That was in 1974.[70] Christy Moore, who was with Planxty, would remember Hamish as 'a tall kind man very interested in the songs and their singers,' whom he met in Sandy Bell's, 'at Blairgowrie Festival and in various Folk Clubs.'[71] Christy remembers how he 'sipped whiskey [*sic*] with Hamish Henderson' at Blargowrie in 1967.[72] In 1974, Luke Kelly of the Dubliners, who had just appeared at Dublin's Abbey Theatre in Brendan Behan's *Richard's Cork Leg*, had a memorable session in Bell's with Hayden Murphy and Hamish.[73]

The Ulster-born poet and editor of *Aquarius*, Eddie Linden, was, according to Tim Neat, 'of Glasgow's many writers, the one who owes the biggest personal debt to Hamish.'[74] Having moved from Glasgow, where he had been brought up after adoption, to London, he frequently turned up in Edinburgh on visits to Hamish. He recalled in a communication with Tim how he met Hamish:

> I remember my first meeting with Hamish. It was a beautiful summer's day, midday: Sandy Bell's was packed and the musicians were there in the corner. I saw this tall-legged man wearing a sport's [*sic*] jacket and a white open-necked shirt, as he always did – entertaining in a very generous way. He

---

68 John Glatt, *The Chieftains: The Authorized Biography*, New York: St Martin's Press, 1997, p.82.

69 See also Dolina Maclennan, *Dolina: An Island Girl's Journey*, Laxey: Islands Book Trust, 2014, p.110. Dolina, as most of the cast of 7:84's *The Cheviot, the Stag, and the Black Black Oil* (1973), appeared in it, as well as Hamish Imlach.

70 See the account given in Leagues O'Toole, *The Humours of Planxty*, Dublin: Hachette (Ireland), new ed., 2007.

71 Letter from Christy Moore to Hayden Murphy, 2012, quoted in Hayden Murphy, p.146.

72 Christy Moore, *One Voice: My Life in Song*, London: Hodder and Stoughton, 2000, p.30.

73 Hayden Murphy, p.144.

74 Timothy Neat, vol. 2, 180-189

> approached me as if he'd known me all his life. He handed me a glass of whisky, and I handed him a copy of Aquarius, issue number one – and I read him one of my poems, 'City of Razors'.[75]

That day ended jovially in an Italian restaurant. But not all visits went so smoothly. 'One night,' Linden's recollection continues:

> I shared Hamish's flat with an entertaining old shepherd from the Hogg country – Willie Scott. It was the time of the terrible tragic war that was going on in Ireland and me, with my Irish background, I was wearing a big sash round my waist, hanging down. We polished off a bottle of Glenmorangie; then Hamish took me down to the bus station to catch the overnight coach to London. Having climbed aboard, I declared myself an Irish Republican! I was taken off the bus and put in a police cell and questioned about a bomb that had gone off near the castle. It was said to have been planted by a Glasgow Irishman with a strong Scottish accent and red hair. That was me! So I got them to phone up and ask Hamish where I'd been that night, and next morning he came down and paid the fine for my drunkenness…[76]

In 1967, Hamish published 'The Ballad of the Speaking Heart'.[77] Even there was an Irish connection. The origins of that ballad, Hamish explains, go back to a nineteenth-century 'chanson populaire' by Jean Richepin, 'a buccaneering Villonesque bohemian figure in the Paris of Verlaine and Rimbaud.' But the first translation 'was made by the Anglo-Irish poet Herbert Trench, who was born in Co Cork' and 'was a member of Yeats's circle at the "Cheshire Cheese" pub in Fleet Street.'[78]

Around the same time, The Boys of the Lough started touring in Britain, originally consisting of Robin Morton, Tommy Gunn and Cathal McConnell – later joined by Aly Bain. They were a

---

[75] Quoted in Neat, vol.2, p.181.

[76] *Ibid.*, pp. 181-182.

[77] Recently recorded by Lucy Pringle and Chris Wright on their album *The Speaking Heart* (Mondegreen Music, 2010).

[78] Hamish Henderson, 'The Ballad of the Speaking Heart', *Chapbook*, vol.4, no.2 (1967), pp.15-16.

'unique combination of traditional musicians ..., highlighting both the similarities and the differences in the various traditions of Britain and Ireland.'[79] Based in Edinburgh, Cathal has been, for the best part of half a century, a fixture of the Celtic music scene. Whenever Hamish Henderson met up with Cathal, he requested two songs from him: 'The Bonny Blue-eyed Girl' and 'The Banks of the Bann'.[80] In 1976, the band allowed Hamish to use their version of 'Lochaber No More' for the pearl-fisher sequence in Tim Neat's film *The Summer Walkers*.[81]

One of their haunts was the Girvan Festival, which celebrated its fortieth anniversary in 2014. Hamish, too, attended in the early days. It has always been a prime meeting place between Irish and Scottish musicians and singers. 'Altan, Dervish, Croabh Rua, Arcady, Liam O'Flynn, The Voice Squad, Mary Black and many other Irish performers spread their wings and made connections through Girvan.'[82]

Hamish championed the Glasgow-based, Irish-born poet and playwright Freddy Anderson, pal and comrade of Matt McGinn and Dominic Behan, whose play *Krassivy* was shown at the Edinburgh Festival in 1979 to mark the centenary of John Maclean's birth and whom he had first met through the 'Clyde Group of left-wing poets in the late 1940s. In 1987, he wrote the 'Foreword' for Anderson's At *Glasgow Cross and Other Poems*, comparing him to one of his favourite poets, Patrick Kavanagh, likewise Monaghan-born. He loved the 'oral' quality of Freddy's poems:

> Freddy had mastered the 'feel' and the rhythms of Scots traditional ballad-poetry; this means that he had effectively bridged the idiomatic divide between his Ulster poetry and the kindred but separate literary tradition of his adopted country.[83]

---

79 Pete Heywood, 'Cathal McConnell: The Hand of Cathal', *Living Tradition*, issue 31 (1999).

80 Cathal McConnell in conversation with the author at The Royal Oak, Edinburgh, 27 March 2015.

81 Tim Neat, vol.2, p.134.

82 [Pete Heywood], 'The Girvan festival... An Incomplete History', programme of 'Girvan's 40th' (2014), pp.5-11; p.8. <www.girvanfestival.trad.org.uk/wp-content/uploads/GirvanFestival_2014.pdf>.

83 Hamish Henderson 'Foreword' (At *Glasgow Cross and Other Poems*, Glasgow: Fat Cat, 1987), reprinted in *Alias McAlias*, pp.447-448.

In 1989, Hamish attended the Cork Film Festival, and holidayed afterwards in Co Clare where he appeared on Clare FM – which triggered a letter from Mark Wringe, then at University College Galway, now a senior lecturer at Sabhal Mòr Ostaig UHI and presenter on BBC Radio nan Gaidheal:

> I felt I ought to let you know not only how pleased I was that the people of Clare heard the very fabric of Scotland so warmly represented ... It is amazing how that fundamental bond between Scotland and Ireland shows through when you least expect it.[84]

And when Martyn Bennett in the 1995 used Hamish Henderson's 'Floret Silva Undique' for a complex composition and arrangement on his first album,[85] he chose an Irish tune for one of the parts of it, as 'Hamish spent a lot of time in Ireland.'[86]

VI

Two more Scottish-Irish connections need to be briefly explored: William McGonagall and James Connolly – both intricately linked with Edinburgh's 'Little Ireland'.[87] Hamish himself gives the geographical context:

> ... the Coogate of Edinburgh had a big Irish population (still has, in fact); the birthplaces of McGonagall and of James Connolly, the hero of Easter 1916, are not far apart. Also, the Coogate lies 'contagious' to the Burke-and-Hare axis, which runs from the West Port, through the Grassmarket and up Candlemaker Row, in the direction of Surgeon's Hall.[88]

---

84 Quoted in Neat, vol.2, p.236.

85 See Margaret Bennet's piece on Martyn Bennet and Hamish Henderson, and Archie Fisher's interview with Hamish, both in this volume.

86 See BBC Scotland Standard Grade Music, "Sampled Tradition", BBC Scotland, 1995 <www.youtube.com/watch?v=B6QQVRoFW90>.

87 Kevin Toolis, in *Rebel Hearts: Journeys within the IRA's soul*, London: Picador, 1995, reflects in the opening chapter about growing up in Edinburgh's 'Little Ireland'; see also Samuel Levenson, *James Connolly: A Biography*, London: Martin Brian and O'Keeffe, 1973, p.28.

88 Hamish Henderson, 'William McGonagall and the Folk Scene', p.3.

Indeed, the 'great Edinburgh socialist James Connolly'[89] was born in the Cowgate in 1868, and in 1986 Hamish writes repeatedly to the *Scotsman* in response to an article on Connolly by Ian Bell. He hails him as 'a genuinely proletarian Socialist' but also notes that 'it must be admitted Connolly's 1914 vision of a rising in Ireland, igniting world revolution has in the long run more in common with he millennarian visions of earlier centuries than with the steely route that led Lenin to the Finland Station.'[90]

He cites Seán O'Casey – who back in 1949 had heaped praise on Hamish's *Elegies* ('Good man. Grand book'[91]) – and his sharp criticism of Connolly's decision to throw his and the Irish Citizen Army's lot in with Patrick Pearse's nationalists in 1916. O'Casey accused Connolly of having sold out the cause of Labour at the Easter Rising of 1916. Connolly, he argued, had followed ideas 'which were, in many instances, directly contrary to his life-long teaching of Socialism': the siren call of Irish nationalism had, ultimately, proved 'in his ears a louder cry than the appeal of the Internationale.'[92] Hamish concedes that O'Casey may 'have overstated his case' and quotes Connolly's belief, as expressed in the *Irish Worker*, that

> Ireland may yet set the torch to a European conflagration that will not burn out until the last throne and the last capitalist bond and debenture will be shrivelled on the funeral pyre of the last warlord.'[93]

And he added that Connolly 'maintained this position with heroic fortitude, and gave his life for it on 12 May 1916. The wisdom of his decision, from a Socialist point of view, is still, alas, a debatable issue.'[94]

---

[89] Hamish Henderson, *The Armstrong* Nose, p.261.

[90] *Ibid.*, p.264.

[91] *Ibid.*, p.33.

[92] Seán Ó Cathasaigh [Seán O'Casey], *The Story of the Irish Citizen Army*, Dublin: Maunsel, 1919, p.55. For a discussion of the complex relationship between O'Casey and Connolly and their respective involvement and dramatic output, see James Moran, 'Conflicting Counter-Hegemonies? The Dramaturgy of James Connolly and Sean O'Casey', *Kritika Kultura*, 21/22 (2013/2014), pp.516-532.

[93] *Hamish Henderson, The Armstrong Nose*, p.263.

[94] *Ibid.*

Hamish praised Bell for having highlighted Connolly's Edinburgh background, showing that 'Little Ireland' was formative for his life. As it was, Hamish argued, for somebody completely different. In 1965, he published an extended essay in *Chapbook* on William McGonagall – the world's worst poet: the bard of the Silvery Tay.... 'poet and tragedian, and unchallenged prince of bad verse writers.'[95]

Now, McGonagall may of course not have been born in Edinburgh at all. Hamish seemed to take McGonagall's autobiographical jottings at face value, but as Norman Watson in his biography documented,[96] the poet's origins are far from clear. That he was born of Irish parentage seems agreed upon – Edinburgh was there, as was Paisley, and then, of course, Dundee. Watson's biography is a great document of McGonagall's life and times, social history as well as the comic-tragic account of the poet's life and work. What he makes very little of, by largely ignoring Henderson's reading of McGonagall, is his Irish background. Though he initially mentions the *Chapbook* piece, he never refers to it when it comes to assessing McGonagall's writings.

While McGonagall regarded himself an art-poet rather than a folk poet, seen in the context and tradition of ballads and traditional songs, in particular Irish 'Come all-yes', the poetry of McGonagall may not markedly improve, but we may realise some method in his badness. Hamish Henderson mentions among the few songs that McGonagall wrote 'The Rattling Boy from Dublin' – 'apparently one of his most popular items.'[97]

> I'm a rattling boy from Dublin town,
> I courted a girl called Biddy Brown,
>
> Her eyes they were as black as sloes,
> She had black hair and an aquiline nose.
>
> *Chorus* – Whack fal de da, fal de darelido,

---

[95] Hamish Henderson, 'William McGonagall and the Folk Scene', p.3.

[96] Norman Watson, *Poet McGonagall: the Biography of William McGonagall*, Edinburgh, Birlinn 2010.

[97] 'William McGonagall and the Folk Scene', p.5.

Whack fal de da, fal de darelay,
Whack fal de da, fal de darelido,
Whack fal de da, fal de darelay.[98]

Take Robert Tannahill's 'The Braes of Balquhidder', which the McPeakes in Ireland turned into 'Wild Mountain Thyme' (or 'Will You Go Lassie Go').

Let us go, lassie, go
Tae the braes o' Balquhidder
Whar the blueberries grow
'mang the bonnie Hielan' heather
Whar the deer and the rae
Lichtly bounding thegither
Sport the lang summer day
On the braes o' Balquhidder

John MacDonald (the Molecatcher) sang *The Braes o' Balquhidder* on his 1975 album. Hamish Henderson supplied the sleeve notes:

> A song by the Paisley weaver-poet Robert Tannahill (1774-1810), to an old air *The Three Carles o' Buchanan*. This exquisite song became very popular in the 19th century throughout Scotland and Ireland. It was in the repertoire of the celebrated ballad-singer Mrs Elizabeth Cronin of Macroom, Co. Cork, and the version recorded by the McPeake family of Belfast – now known throughout the modern folk revival as *The Wild Mountain Thyme* – continues to enjoy widespread popularity. It belongs to a well-known class of courtship songs in which the lover appeals to his girl to leave the city and enjoy the pleasures of country life. These songs gained added pathos in the period of the Industrial Revolution, when so many of the Lowland towns turned into smokey hell-holes.[99]

---

[98] William McGonagall, *Poetic Gems, selected from the works of William McGonagall, poet and tragedian, with biographical sketch and reminiscences by the* author, London: Winter, Duckworth, 1934, p.47.

[99] John MacDonald, *The Singing Molecatcher of Morayshire: Scots Ballads, Bothy Songs & Melodeon Tunes* (Topic, 1975), reissued on CD by Greentrax in 2000.

William and Francis McPeake's version begins like this:

The summer time is coming
And the trees are sweetly blooming,
And the wild mountain thyme
All around the blooming heather
Will you go, lassie, go?

And we'll all go together
To pull wild mountain thyme
All around the blooming heather,
Will you go, lassie, go?

In McGonagall's inspired hand it turns into something like this:

Bonnie Clara, will you go to the bonnie Sidlaw hills
And pu' the blooming heather, and drink from their rills?
There the cranberries among the heather grow,
Believe me, dear Clara, as black as the crow.

Then Bonnie Clara, will you go
And wander with me to and fro?
And with joy our hearts will o'erflow
When we go to the bonnie Sidlaws O.[100]

And he has another bite at the cherry:

Bonnie Helen, will you go to Callander with me
And gaze upon its beauties and romantic scenery?
Dear Helen, it will help to drive all sorrow away;
Therefore come, sweet Helen, and let's have a holiday.[101]

Seeing echoes of ballads and songs in McGonagall's work makes us, Hamish seems to suggest, understand McGonagall better.[102]

---

[100] William McGonagall, *More Poetic Gems, selected from the works of William McGonagall with biographical sketch and reminiscences by the author*, London: Winter, Duckworth, 1962, p.72.

[101] *Ibid.*, p.73.

[102] See also 'Opening Up the Lore of the Travelling People' – A *Textualities* Interview with Hamish Henderson (1987), reproduced in this volume.

As does a better comprehension of the social and cultural, Irish and Scottish context, which Hamish provides, by alluding to Dion Boucicault's 'Silly Jack heroes', on which McGonagall may have modelled himself 'as a sort of licensed buffoon', and by reminding us of the Scots bourgeoisie's attitude towards art and poetry which was one of 'amused contempt, not unmixed with hostility.'

> Victorian Scotland was horrifyingly Philistine, and the mental attitudes of those days are still very much alive in the country today. When one comes across a portrait of McGonagall, and contemplates his sensitive histrionic features, which so strikingly recall Henry Irving and Oscar Wilde, one can't help feeling that when that monstrous money-glutted Victorian society was laughing at McGonagall, it was to a certain extent laughing at poetry itself.[103]

But Hamish leaves no doubt: 'The hard truth is that folk-song becomes poetry – or has a chance of becoming poetry – as and when it gets rid of McGonagall.'[104] And he profoundly disliked McGonagall's politics: 'Apart from one poem in which he expresses admiration for Parnell, his flag-waving jingoism was outrageous enough to scunner even an Empire Loyalist.'[105] To the Parnell poem one could add the one on 'Women's Suffrage', where the sentiment is right, even if the poetry is not:

> Fellow men! Why should the lords try to despise
> And prohibit women from having the benefit
> of the parliamentary franchise?
> When they pay the same taxes as you and me,
> I consider they ought to have the same liberty.[106]

---

[103] Hamish Henderson, 'William McGonagall and the Folk Scene', p.10.

[104] *Ibid.*, p.28.

[105] *Ibid.*

[106] William McGonagall, *Last Poetic Gems, selected from the Works of William McGonagall*, London: Winter, 1968, p.157.

– but, otherwise, McGonagall's *oevre* is indeed littered with imperial grandieur.[107]

As the 'Troubles' in the North of Ireland shattered the hopes of the 1960s of a peaceful and more equal development in Ireland, Hamish lashed out against sectarian loyalist marches, 'Orange bowsies sing[ing] the sash',[108] and the historical and political role of the Orange Order.

> It is farcical to compare an orange parade with, say, the Civil Rights march from Belfast to Derry which was ambushed in Burntollet. The Orange Order, for all, its public prancings, is a secret society which has much more in common with the Ku Klux Klan than with a normal political organization or pressure group.[109]

And he adds: 'I have no sympathy with political gangsterism on either side of the religious fence. A plague on both your bowseys!' This was a far cry from his more 'idyllic' days in Belfast in the late 1940s. But even now he could separate the 'sectarian' quality of songs like 'The Old Orange Flute'[110] – not 'just an anti-Catholic song,' but one 'that gave expression to myths and forces going back thousands of years – to Orpheus, the world of Apollo and Marsyas…'[111] That, Owen Dudley Edwards recollects, was amply demonstrated when Hamish 'lectured' his daughter Leila in Sandy Bell's, greeting her – 'You are a Papist. I will therefore sing "The Ould Orange Flute".'[112]

---

[107] For Hamish Henderson and William McGonagall, see also Ian Spring, 'Hamish Henderson: Man and Myth', in I. Spring, *Hamish Henderson and Scottish Folk Song*, Edinburgh: Hog's Back Press, 2014, pp.142-175.

[108] Hamish Henderson, 'Epistle to Mary', *Collected Poems and Songs*, p.152.

[109] See *The Armstrong Nose*, pp.198-202; p.202.

[110] A rendering of 'The Ould Orange Flute' by Hamish Henderson, recorded in Stonehaven in 1955, can be heard on <www.tobarandulchais.co.uk/fullrecord/18717/1>.

[111] Quoted in Neat, vol.1, p.225.

[112] Owen Dudley Edwards, 'Sectarian Songs', p.161.

VII

Just before the outbreak of violence, in 1967, Hamish published in *Chapbook* a new song called 'Paddy's Hogmanay – or the Shamrock and the Thistle'.[113] It harks back to those happier days when he was a frequent passenger on the boat between Glasgow and Belfast.

> On several trips from Belfast (where I was working) to Glasgow on the Burns-Laird steamers in the late '40s, I collected from fellow steerage passengers a number of fragments of a song with the theme of 'Paddy's Hogmanay'. It seemed to be about a party of Ulster Orangemen who crossed the water to enjoy the festive season a good few years ago, but the song – like the party itself, maybe – had become a bit chaotic. Although he fragments could clearly be sung to a number of 'come all ye' tunes, they were always given as spoken rhymes. One of these contained the Scots expression 'a dram or twa', and this started me off on a reconstruction of the song.
>
> In the process of re-singing it into shape, most of the already existing fragments fell away, and the song, as it stands, is nearly all my own work. The only collected stanza which I was able to work in unchanged was the penultimate on ('For the Scotsmen have their thistle...') ....[114]

'Re-singing it into shape' – what a wonderful expression! And, as we started with a reference to Christmas in the Spanish Civil War song, way back in the Duke of York in Belfast, let us conclude by at least progressing as far as Hogmanay in Glasgow:

---

[113] The song did not make the cut for the *Complete Poems and Songs* – either overlooked or not deemed worthy of inclusion by Hamish and Raymond Ross.

[114] 'Paddy's Hogmanay or The Shamrock and the Thistle, a new song by Hamish Henderson', *Chapbook*, Vol 4, No 5 (1967), pp.3-4.

'Paddy's Hogmanay' or, 'The Shamrock and the Thistle'

Oh come all ye true-born Glasgow boys, and listen to my song
I'm going to speak of Hogmanay, it won't detain you long
And I've made this little tune for youse, I played it on my whistle
And I think the name I'll give to it is the shamrock and the thistle.

Aboard the 'Royal Ulsterman' we had a dram or twa
When daylight broke, we all awoke, and saw the Bromielaw.
The journey o'er, we went ashore, our friends they raised a cheer,
And soon the word was going round, 'the Irishmen are here'

We were not rash, we wore no sash, we sang no party lay
For we had come to join the fun, a real cotch Hogmanay.
We marched up to Argyle Street, we bought whisky, stout and rum,
And the songs we sang were 'Sweet Strabane' and 'Brigton, here we come'

A welcome rare we soon got there, it was a glorious spread.
Bill Thompson cried 'Get that inside! I see you're needin' fed.'
So when we had a tightener, we were feelin' in good trim
Bob said 'Come on, I'm for the Tron,' so we went along with him.

Now many's the hooly we've been at, at home across the sea,
And at New Year, with stout and beer, we go upon the spree.
But you Scots don't just make whoopee, or have drinks with Mum and dad
On the 31st of December, boys, you all go roaring mad!

Forgive me friends for being rude, I'm not, you will agree
The Irish too are a crazy crew – just look at Bob and me!
But a Scotsman seeing the New Year in is a sight for gods and men,
And it takes an Irish Paddy to be equal with him then

For the Scotsmen have their thistle, and the Welshmen have their leek,
The English have the rose, my boys, and lots of flamin' cheek.
The Irish have their shamrock, and they hold it very dear
But you'll find it with the thistle in old Glasgow at New Year.

Now my little song is ended, boys, I made it just for you
There is a moral to it, and I'm tellin' you it's true.
The Scots folk and the Irish are as one, you will agree,
And the only thing between them is the dear old Irish Sea.[115]

How different the sentiment from Dominic Behan's 'The Sea Around Us', where Ireland and Britain are separated rather than linked by water:

The sea, oh the sea is the *gradh geal mo croide* [great joy of my heart]
Long may it stay between England and me
It's a sure guarantee that some hour we'll be free
Oh thank God we're surrounded by water.[116]

Hamish had a life-long love affair with Ireland. Irishmen and -women both in Ireland (North and South) and in Britain were part of his network of friends: people like the traditional singer Paddy Tunney, who was born in Glasgow; the Dublinman Frank Harte who, like Hamish, always 'celebrated and demonstrated

[115] The Corries recorded it on *Kishmul's Galley* (Fontana STL5465, 1968). Hamish Henderson's lilting (or diddling) of the tune can be heard on <tobarandulchais.co.uk/fullrecord/36745/1>, recorded in 1964.

[116] In 1966, 'The Sea Around Us', recorded by the Ludlow Folk Trio (featuring Jim McCann, Margaret O'Brien and Sean Loughran), became the first folk record to get to number one in the Irish charts.

paddy's hogmanay

or THE SHAMROCK AND THE THISTLE
a new song by Hamish Henderson

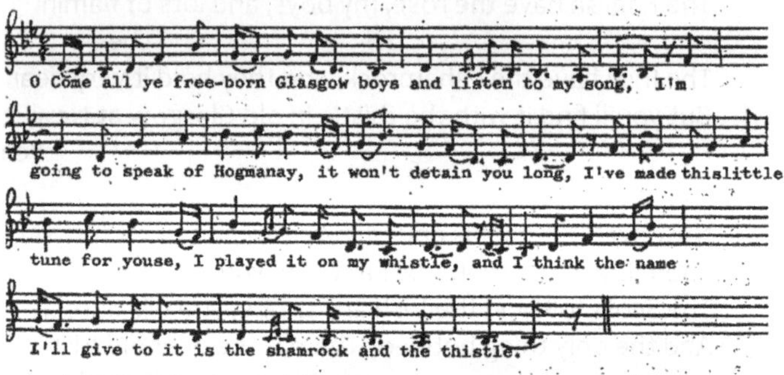

O Come all ye free-born Glasgow boys and listen to my song, I'm
going to speak of Hogmanay, it won't detain you long, I've made thislittle
tune for youse, I played it on my whistle, and I think the name
I'll give to it is the shamrock and the thistle.

O come all ye true-born Glasgow boys, and listen to my song;
I'm going to speak of Hogmanay, it won't detain you long.
I've made this little tune for youse, I played it on my whistle,
And I think the name I'll give to it is the Shamrock and the Thistle

Aboard the "Royal Ulsterman" we had a dram or twa.
When daylight broke, we all awoke, and saw the Broomielaw.
The journey o'er, we went ashore, our friends they raised a cheer,
And soon the word was going round "the Irishmen are here."

We were not rash, we ore no sash, we sang no party lay,
For we had come to join the fun, a real Scotch Hogmanay.
We marched up to Argyle Street, we bough whisky, stout and rum,
And the songs we sang were "Sweet Strabane" and "Brigton,
here we come."

A welcome rare we soon got there, it was a glorious spread.
Bill Thomson cried, "Get that inside! I see ye're needin' fed."
So when we'd had a tightener, we were feelin' in good trim.
Bob said "Come on, I'm for the Tron," so we went along with him.

Now many's the hooly we've been at, at home across the sea,
And at New Year, with stout and beer, we go upon the spree.
But you Scots don't just make whoopee, or have drinks with Mum and Dad,
On the 31st of December, boys, you all go roaring mad!

Continued on Page 4

3

'Paddy's Hogmanay, or The Shamrock and the Thistle', *Chapbook*, vol.4, no.5 (1967), p.3.

the essential oral nature of the tradition,'[117] from the Reverend Allan Armstrong in Dry Drayton and Maurice Craig and Louis MacNeice at Cambridge through the Behans, John Hewitt and Davy Hammond in Dublin and Belfast, Hayden Murphy, Andy Boyd, Margaret Barry, Garech Browne and Paddy Moloney, Robin Morton and Cathal McConnell to folk- and song-collectors like Séamus Ennis, Sean O'Boyle, Séamus Delargy, Seán Ó Suilleabhainn, Tom Munnelly and Len Graham (who all paid repeated visits to the School of Scottish Studies' archive). At the funeral of Tom Munnelly, Ireland's greatest music collector, in Miltown Malbay in 2007, Jerry O'Reilly led all assembled in 'The Parting Glass', after which both he, Bob Blair and Terry Moylan sang the 'Freedom Come-All-Ye'.

Hamish Henderson's various Irish experiences helped to form his poetics, his song-writing and his politics. But did it amount to, as Tim Neat contends, Hamish's 'Irish destiny'? Tim seems outraged that Edward Lucie-Smith, the editor of *British Poetry since* 1945 (Penguin, 1970), hails the Northern Irish poets without mentioning Hamish Henderson. Thus, in Neat's view, he neglected Hamish's 'cultural influence on Ireland'.[118] Tim does his case no favours by citing, as proof of the eight-year-old Hamish's awareness of his 'Irish destiny', an 'Irish joke' jotted down by Hamish in his mother's recipe book in 1928, in which a football punter on the stands wonders why 'he, of all the 51,000 folk in the stands, has been picked on by a pigeon.'[119] It also does not help Neat that Hamish himself, in the autobiographical 'Ballad of the Twelve Stations of My Youth'[120] name-checks Devon, London, Brighton, Berlin, Cambridge and Oldham – but not Ireland.

And yet, Ireland was a constant presence in Hamish's life and work. It was woven into the rich tapestry of his life. He knew Ireland well, from his travels and encounters and collaborations, from its folklore, its stories and songs. He was, in short, more aware of Ireland than Ireland was of him. Ireland exercised more influence on him than he did on Ireland. It was, we might say, a case of Hamish Henderson's Ireland rather than Ireland's Hamish Henderson.

---

[117] Geordie McIntyre, 'Frank Harte: A Man in Touch', *Living Tradition*, issue 46 (January 2002).

[118] Tim Neat, vol.2, p.252.

[119] *Ibid.*

[120] *Collected Poems and Songs*, pp.23-24.

7:84 Theatre Company, *The Cheviot, The Stag and The Black Black Oil* by John McGrath

Viva la Gillie More: Hamish Henderson, Gramsci and Subaltern Scotland

Ray Burnett

Introduction

I first became aware of Hamish Henderson around 1963, my final school year in Edinburgh, as a name and presence on the folk scene, cultural nationalism and the left. As my own political engagement developed, we occasionally shared company at leftist events – the Connolly Centenary 1968, the Springboks Tour 1969 – but not conversations. And when I first read and wrote of Gramsci in Aberdeen in 1968 I was quite unaware of Hamish's previous work on his *Prison Letters*, far less his involvement with and knowledge of the Italian left. This changed in 1970, and our shared interest in Gramsci's life and writings and their relevance to Scotland deepened substantially over the next few years and continued till the end. Reflections on those brief few years of the early 1970s are the substance of this 'stone on the cairn' of the memory of Hamish.

Most personal reflections hitherto have understandably come from the perspective of song, poetry, the oral tradition and the folk revival. This is about politics, discussions and representations of politics, political beliefs and ideas. It is also about history, the memory and the record of the past, in this case as it relates to the life of one of the most outstanding figures in Scotland in the twentieth century. It is based around a querying of the historical account of the period by others whose contributions are much more significant than my own, but it should not be construed as an assault or even a desire to engage in a mild 'flyting' – only an alternative reading of a few aspects of one brief period in a very full, complex and occasionally contradictory life.

Part I

In dealing with the man deemed Hamish's 'incompatible rival', his biographer Tim Neat relates an anecdote regarding Alan Bold at an event I organised in Aberdeen in which Hamish also participated. This is expanded on to briefly discuss my own friendship with Hamish in the early 1970s with particular regard to my involvement in Northern Ireland.[1] Unfortunately, in every respect bar one, Tim Neat gets it all wrong.

The Aberdeen Teach-In to which Bold had been invited was in 1970, the conference with which it was conflated was in Edinburgh in 1973. Both gatherings were of significance in relation to Hamish but they were two quite distinct events. The facts on my personal background, my involvement with the North of Ireland, the actual content of my conversations with Hamish on the latter and the chronology of events over the period as they relate to Hamish are, in every respect but one, incorrect.[2] Only by prising apart these two conflated events and bringing out Hamish's role in each of them do we gain a better understanding of the importance of Hamish's influence over this period. In between, the nature of the conversations we actually did have at the time regarding Ireland and the role of *Scottish International* in providing, for both of us, a platform for the promotion of a Gramscian perspective on Scottish culture, history and politics can also be usefully clarified.

A Scottish Left

One of the initiatives of the student left in Aberdeen in the '68 era was to stand for election for the university 'Debater' whereby we could use the latter's generous

[1] Timothy Neat, *Hamish Henderson: a Biography, Vol. II Poetry Becomes People*, Edinburgh: Polygon/Birlinn, 2009, pp.183-184.

[2] Contrary to what Tim Neat states: my mother was not Irish, all my family is Scottish, I have no relatives in Northern Ireland and my involvement in the latter was not 'through protests organised by the Provisional IRA' but through People's Democracy and the civil rights movement in the spring of 1969, well before the Provos had even come into existence. As a Scot, the focus of my involvement has always been primarily on Scottish complicity and I have never had any desire or inclination to 'throw in my lot' with any Irish organisation, least of all, as my own writings and those I commissioned on the subject make perfectly clear, the Provisionals.

funding and large capacity facilities to run a series of 'Teach-Ins', awareness-raising gatherings, in a format that would attract the widest possible audience and the best possible participation.[3] In October 1969 I organised one on Northern Ireland. The second, in February 1970, was on 'The Culture of Scotland, past, present, future'.[4]

The broad purpose was to explore Scotland's history, culture and traditions and to discuss present-day cultural activity in relation to the furtherance of a Scottish left, organically rooted in Scotland, as opposed to a left in Scotland. In May 1968, a not inappropriate moment, I had launched a small student magazine, *Inklins*, which contained an article in which I tried to 'translate' some of the left's critical thought on cultural issues from its overwhelming anglocentric focus to bring out its pertinence to Scotland.[5] It also quoted another theorist whose ideas increasingly featured in New Left thought, making the point: 'Reflections made by Antonio Gramsci in the 1930s on the Italian educational system, have a direct bearing on Scotland's history in 1968.'[6]

This interest in Scotland' history and culture was largely motivated by a long-standing commitment to the notion of an independent socialist Scotland that drew inspiration from James

---

[3] The 'Debater' was the oldest student society in the University and the first of its kind in Scotland. It ran a well-funded programme of formal parliamentary-style debates for aspiring politicians but, unlike its Glasgow cousin, it was low-calibre with poor attendance. The Socialist Society had good attendance but meagre funds.

[4] It was simultaneously billed as 'Weekend Teach-In, Scottish Culture' and 'The Culture of Scotland, past, present, future. An Open Conference'.

[5] R. S. Burnett, 'To Found Society Anew', *Inklins*, No. 1, May 1968, pp.11-15. The two main cultural writers drawn on were Alasdair MacIntyre and Raymond Williams. I think this was the first article to draw on Gramsci in relation to Scotland, although the unattributed quotation that appeared in an editorial in *Scottish International*, No 2, April 1969 should also be acknowledged. It most probably came from Hamish (see below). Neil Davidson would have been understandably unaware of this *Inklins* article or the related 1970 Teach-in (see below) when discussing my own part in the introduction of Gramscian thought to Scotland. See N. Davidson, 'Antonio Gramsci's Reception in Scotland', in N. Davidson, *Holding Fast to an Image of the Past: Explorations in the Marxist Tradition*, Chicago: Haymarket Books, 2014, pp.253-286, originally published in *Scottish Labour History*, 45 (2010).

[6] R. S. Burnett, *ibid*. p.14.

Connolly and John MacLean. This felt need for a Scottish left, as opposed to a left in Scotland, was accentuated at the time by the suffocating anglocentrism in all matters relating to history, culture and intellectual thought on the Anglo-Brit left.[7] There were few unmediated extracts of Gramsci's thought available in English.[8] But for the most part, as in the stimulating exchanges on the culture and intellectual history of 'British' Labourism, a subject of obvious key importance to Scotland, it was not just the writings of Gramsci that had to be 'translated'.[9]

Tom Nairn's scintillating polemic on the new resurgent nationalist movement had thrown up a myriad of challenges and questions as to how all of us, regardless of our professed political alignment, would benefit from a rigorous re-examination of our intellectual and cultural past.[10] But against the prevailing

---

[7] This is more fully discusse in R. Burnett, 'When the Finger Points at the Moon', in J. D. Young (ed.), *Scotland at the Crossroads: A Socialist Answer*, Glasgow: Clydeside Press, 1990, pp.90-110.

[8] A. Gramsci, 'The Formation of Intellectuals', in Antonio Gramsci, (trans. and ed., L. Marks), *The Modern Prince and Other Writings*, New York: International Publishers, 1970, pp.118-125; A. Gramsci, 'The Organisation of Education and Culture', in Antonio Gramsci, (trans. and ed., L. Marks), *The Modern Prince and Other Writings*, London, 1957, pp.126-132. The edition referred to in 1968-70 was the 1957 Lawrence and Wishart, London edition.

[9] For two of the core articles of the 'Nairn-Anderson thesis' see Perry Anderson, 'Origins of the Present Crisis', in P. Anderson and R. Blackburn (eds.) *Towards Socialism*, London: Collins, 1965, 11-52; and Tom Nairn, 'The Nature of the Labour Party' in *ibid.*, pp.159-217. The term 'Nairn-Anderson thesis' was coined by E. P. Thompson in his polemical response, 'The Peculiarities of the English', in Ralph Miliband and John Saville (eds), *The Socialist Register* 1965, New York: The Merlin Press, 1965, pp.311-362. The longer, original version was later published in E. P. Thompson, *The Poverty of Theory and Other Essays*, London: Monthly Review Press, 1978. The persistent anglocentrism of the approach was further confirmed by Anderson in the titles of his subsequent collections, *Arguments within English Marxism*, London: Verso, 1980, and *English Questions*, London: Verso, 1992, both ostensible on 'British politics, history and culture'. An important context for the challenge we faced was contained in P. Anderson, 'Components of the National Culture', *NLR*, I/50 (July-August 1968), pp.3-57.

[10] T. Nairn, 'The Three Dreams of Scottish Nationalism', *New Left Review* I/49 (May-June 1968), pp.3-18. A slightly reformulated version appeared later in Karl Miller (ed.), *Memoirs of a Modern Scotland*, London: Faber & Faber, 1970, pp.134-154.

discursive backdrop it stood out as much for its splendid isolation as for its scintillating content and thought. But at that time its author was a strange, distant figure on the metropolitan and chic European left. Legendary North East isolationism perhaps, but at the time it never occurred to anyone that he actually might be Scottish. We preferred to concentrate on 'wir ain folk' and, by enlisting the aid of Bob Tait's *Scottish International*, we were able to put together a programme that reasonably related to all of Scotland.[11]

The weekend opened with a debate on a motion condemning the SNP 'as a pedlar of myths'. Given the numerical strength of the Aberdeen student left at the time and the strong antipathy to the SNP for its resolute resistance to class-based politics, the motion was comfortably carried. This was the sideline affair that Tim Neat chose to focus on because of the discourteous behaviour of the bold Mr Bold.[12] But the real purpose of the weekend was not to focus on what divided us but to concentrate on Scotland and on what brought us together: a collective curiosity in the social, cultural and intellectual history of our country, a common past that had made our shared present.

The first day was on the past, from the early medieval era to the modern Scottish Renaissance, with each session's theme set as a question. The Gramscian tenor of the theoretical underpinning of the programme, a focus on the 'national-popular', the formation and role of 'intellectuals', the 'common sense' of each era, is readily discernible in the theme wording. 'Had there at any point', in early Scotland, 'been an artistic and cultural totality

---

[11] It was, however, overwhelmingly male. 'Aberdeen University Debater, Open Conference on the Culture of Scotland, February 20-22nd 1970'.

[12] The motion was meant to have been proposed by Alan Bold, seconded by myself and opposed by Michael Grieve, seconded by Donald Bain. When Bold arrived off the train from Edinburgh he demanded his fee and immediately disappeared into the pub. I was left to propose the motion myself with the bold Bold only turning up later when proceedings were well underway. It was this incident that Tim Neat chose to focus on in his biography, in a passage where he was mainly concerned with cataloguing all the incidents that substantiated his negative presentation of the character of Bold in relation to Hamish. Unfortunately this over-eager focus on the misdemeanours of Bold also led him to confuse the 1970 event with a quite separate event four years later and to completely misunderstand the significance of Hamish's presence and participation in Aberdeen at that time.

which could be meaningfully termed Scottish *Culture*?' Between 1560 and 1830, 'had there been a qualitative break between the past and the present so that it was no longer accurate to refer to a Scottish cultural tradition?' And in relation to the Scottish Renaissance, a movement in which all of the named participants had also been players, 'to what extent did the emergent movement develop out of the past?'

Although only billed as a participant in the middle session, Hamish made a significant contribution to them all.[13] In every case his contribution raised the history beneath the surface, the voice of the subaltern, the challenge to the received common sense of Scottish historiography. At the heart of the key session on 1560-1830 was the familiar and contentious question of the extent to which the Reformation, the Union, the Enlightenment, or all three as essential aspects of the same process, had resulted in a 'qualitative break' in the continuity of the Scottish cultural tradition. This was the session in which Hamish was a named participant, along with David Buchan and Chris Smout.[14] Clashes along not unfamiliar lines were expected. Instead there was an unanticipated shift to a contingent terrain when Hamish sought to make the case for the continuity of a distinctive Scottish tradition by setting it in a wider European cultural setting, with Scotland absorbing and assimilating ideas and practices from the latter context in its own specific and peculiar way.

Hamish also contributed to the final session on the recent past of the Scottish Renaissance but the billed participant from the folk revival aspect of the movement was Archie Fisher, a popular and 'weil-kent' voice in Aberdeen. As I recall, Hamish was more than happy to leave it to Archie to demonstrate how the folk revivalists of Aberdeen, and its hinterland, were the living

[13] So did several others, notably Sorley MacLean.

[14] David Buchan, the distinguished ballad scholar, was at that time based in his native Aberdeen and researching the ballad tradition, the fruits of which were soon to appear in *The Ballad and the Folk*, London: Routledge and Kegan Paul, 1972. The session took its dates directly from those in Chris Smout's recently published social history of Scotland, an indication of the importance attached to its publication, T. C. Smout, *A History of the Scottish People 1560-1830*, London: Collins, 1969. Chris Smout also served on the editorial board of *Scottish International* and was a solid supporter of its more radical issues and projects.

answer to the question as to how, in terms of song at least, the living movement had developed directly out of the past.[15]

On the second day, on the contemporary situation, the thematic question asked 'what is the merit of present day artistic and intellectual activity in Scotland if it is unrelated to the Scottish people?' And the event closed with a final session on the issue of 'the communication of art to people'. The question of the relationship of the arts to the people led to a feisty exchange between the poet Alan Jackson and Hamish, with Jackson arguing against any form of commitment or political alignment, not only an artistic alignment with nationalism. Hamish was also vocal in his support of Murray Grigor and others in their withering criticisms of the Scottish media and broadcasting for their serious shortcomings as to the promotion of both the past and the present of Scotland's culture and history.[16]

Overall the event was a revelatory experience. It exposed a powerful, rich, textured culture, a long, multi-layered history and a shared commonality of identity. But, in their general unresponsiveness, it also confirmed the deep disdain on the political left not just for nationalism but for any promotion of a Scottish perspective on culture and history. Conversely, while there was a high response from the student nationalist ranks it was marked by the weakness of the intellectual as opposed to the emotional engagement. One of the most intriguing aspects was the strong response from the student folk scene in Aberdeen, testimony perhaps to the quiet presence and influence of

---

[15] The Teach-In coincided with the university rectorial campaign in which the left candidate was Robin Blackburn, *New Left Review*, and member of staff at the LSE disciplined for his support of the student occupation. Archie Fisher was also a candidate, nominated, as I recall, by the Folk Club with AUSNA, the Scottish Nationalists Association, support. When Archie heard Blackburn put his case for democracy within the universities, Archie withdrew his own candidacy and gave his support to us and to Blackburn. On reflection, I think it should have been the other way round. In the event the establishment candidate, Jo Grimond, won.

[16] It is salutary to note how pertinent the concerns raised then concerning the Scottish film and broadcasting media are to those raised today. See the two articles by A. Marwick, 'A Plea for Free Movement' and Bill Williams, 'BBC Scotland' that accompanied Hamish's 'Alias McAlias' in the 'Controversy' section of *Scottish International*, 6 (April 1969), and the report on that section of the proceedings in 'Aberdeen Search Part Hunts for "Scottish Culture"', in *Scottish International*, 10 (May 1970), pp.7-9.

Hamish.[17] Not just through his endorsement of the project, but in his active participation and intellectual engagement, Hamish confirmed and validated the pertinence and applicability of a Gramscian approach to the history, culture and politics of Scotland.

One lasting legacy of the Teach-In was the part it played in promoting and raising awareness of the poetry and cultural writings of Sorley MacLean whose acceptance of my invitation to participate was a key element in giving the event its enduring significance.[18] The extended interview with the latter, in which Hamish played a key role and which was subsequently published in *Scottish International* alongside an extended report on the Teach-In itself provided an insight into a whole new dimension of the radical tradition in Scotland. It was a crucial contributory factor to further developments on this theme a few years later.

A Scots Perspective on the North of Ireland

Later in 1970 we moved from Aberdeen to Kintail and a teaching post under Sorley MacLean at Plockton H.S.[19] I continued to see Hamish regularly in Edinburgh and I also maintained my contacts with the North of Ireland. These had begun in early 1969 through People's Democracy and the civil rights campaign and had developed in Derry in the 'Battle of the Bogside' and subsequent. My friends and acquaintances were mainly unaligned left but, as the situation worsened with increased state repression, 'special power', mass detentions, internment without trial, militarisation, there was a move towards left Republicanism. After the Bloody Sunday killings, several had taken up with the Official IRA and their military campaign, the left-orientated Republicans from whom the

[17] Amongst them, there was particular strong support from Peter Hall, of Aberdeen Folk Club, editor of *Chapbook* and a fellow B.Ed. student and, of course, Arthur Argo.

[18] I discussed this in some detail in a paper to the Sorley MacLean UWS/SMO conference, R. Burnett 'Sorley MacLean and the Quest for *Alba Aigeannach nan Saor*', *Ainmeil thar Cheudan*: A Centenary Celebration of Sorley MacLean (1911-2011), Sabhal Mòr Ostaig, 2011.

[19] The chronology and sequence of events given in Tim Neat, *op. cit.*, pp.183-84 is all wrong.

Provisionals had split.[20] When Bloody Sunday occurred and a young civil rights marcher I had known was among the unarmed civilians killed, I went over to report on the killings and on the wider situation behind the barricades of 'Free Derry' for *Scottish International*. This was the context in which I had several conversations regarding 'the North' with Hamish.

As a Scot, approaching the situation from a Scottish perspective, my primary focus was on awareness-raising and to counter the misinformation in the media as to what the minority community was up; the counter-insurgency techniques being deployed in our name. Above all my interest was in Scottish complicity. It all brought vividly to mind the 1920 campaigning of Hamish's 'great John Maclean' on *The Irish Tragedy: Scotland's Disgrace* in an earlier period when state repression and Scottish complicity were at their height.[21] Now the focus was on the timidity of the two main strands of Scottish politics, Labour and the SNP, to take a stand against what was being done to defend an indefensible sectarian Orange state and the legacy of gerrymandered partition.

In conversation with Hamish I was well aware of his antipathy to Orangeism and its promotion of sectarian strife, the rottenness of the Stormont regime, but also his contempt for what partition's 'carnival of reaction' had created in the south.[22] I also became increasingly familiar with his time in Northern Ireland, his regards for both sides in the rural communities, above all for his frequent hankering back to the memory of '98 and the

---

[20] Here also the chronology of my involvement and the acount of my political alignment as given in T. Neat, *op. cit.*, pp.183-4 is completely wrong. See the actual accounts in R. Burnett, 'The Killing of James Wray' *Scottish International* (March 1973), pp.17-19; and R. Burnett, 'The Politics of the Resisting Minority', *Scottish International* (April 1972), pp.16-18.

[21] John Maclean, *The Irish Tragedy: Scotland's Disgrace*, Glasgow: John Maclean Society, 1970.

[22] It was James Connolly who had predicted that partition would lead to a 'carnival of reaction' in J. Connolly. 'Labour and the Proposed Partition of Ireland', *Irish Worker*, 14 March 1914, in Peter Beresford Ellis, (ed.), *James Connolly: Selected Writings*, Harmondsworth: Penguin, 1973, 274-5. It was a comment both of us often returned to. Orangeism was also a subject Hamish frequently took up in the letter columns of the *Scotsman* over the 1970-73 period; see A. Finlay (ed.), *The Armstrong Nose: Selected Letters of Hamish Henderson*, Edinburgh: Polygon, 1996, pp.193-5, 198-202.

courageous Presbyterian leaders of the United Irishmen.[23] On all of this there was much concurrence. His connections, however, with the Labour and trade union movement in Belfast involved an understandable alignment with a strand within the political community of 'the North' that had a different perspective and position to that with which I was aligned. Where differences arose, however, we always ensured that we did not fall out.

We also discussed, and sometimes sang, songs old and new. But, for myself at least, the most important of these conversations dealt with the choices facing those I knew who were active and committed within a community such as 'Free Derry'. The reports for *Scottish International* were significantly sub-edited to cover the extent of my friendship with individuals who had chosen to become directly involved in 'the movement'.[24] Their situation and the choices they faced was, and remains, the closest I have come to the issues of war, the ethics of armed conflict, the intensity of comradeship, the demands on personal and family relationships involved – and on conscience. The scale was vastly different, but in essence the issues were not all that dissimilar to those that had faced so many of the *partigiani* Hamish himself had known in his youthful years in northern Italy, the array of terrible choices and dilemmas arising from the peculiarities of their own bitter and communal conflict.[25] Hamish was the only person I knew with whom these issues could be raised and talked through. The fact that we did so over so many years without rancour or ill-feeling, despite our various points of disagreement, was a testimony to the deep humanitarian spirit that is so evident in his own war poetry and observations.

Scottish International not only provided a platform to raise awareness on Northern Ireland. It also provided a platform on which to write about the ideas and theoretical concepts of Gramsci in a specifically Scottish context, as in the November 1972 issue which carried an article by myself on 'Scotland and

---

[23] For a flavour of this see sleeve notes of P. Ó Conluain to Robert Cinnamond, *You Rambling Boys of Pleasure*, Topic Records, London, 1979, and the 2013 interview with Len Graham, <www.mustrad.org.uk/articles/l_graham.htm>.

[24] B. Tait to R. Burnett, 7 February 1972, 5 March 1972.

[25] For an excellent introduction to this whole subject see Claudio Pavione, *A Civil War, A History of the Italian Resistance*, London: Verso, 2013.

Antonio Gramsci'.[26] It was only after it appeared that I was first made aware of Hamish's early translation work on Gramsci's prison letters and his fruitless attempts to get them published.[27] Hamish was delighted to see its appearance. To mark the occasion he presented me with a framed photograph of a bust of Gramsci that he had previously been given by Piero Sraffa, Gramsci's friend in Cambridge who had helped supply him with books throughout the prison years.

Two months later Hamish also contributed a long essay on 'The Oral Tradition' in which he discussed at length David Buchan's recently published work, *The Ballad and the Folk.*[28] It remains, in my view, one of Hamish's best essays, covering a range of issues within its broad theme, including his thoughts on why Jacobite songs remained so popular in Scotland, or on the factors involved in the survival or otherwise of political song. It underlines an often overlooked aspect of Hamish's writings, namely his deep insightful grasp of Scottish social history, and it has a superb core section on 'The Great Underground of Bawdry'. Apart from a concluding and illuminating section on 'the Horseman's Word' he builds his argument on such unlikely historical sources as the anonymous songs on the 'strapping hizzie' in 'The Wanton Trooper', the stanzas on the 'grand farter' of a 'duke's daughter' and the citation of a literary 'scatological squib' by James 'Balloon' Tytler with the glorious title, *The Farto-Turdoniad, A Ballad addressed to Alexander Tumbleturd Esq.* There is no reference to Gramsci, no open reference to his concepts, yet the deployment of Gramscian ideas in the whole framework of the essay, to bring out the presence and the potency of the subaltern 'voice' concepts, is palpable.[29]

---

[26] R. Burnett, 'Scotland and Antonio Gramsci', *Scottish International* (November 1972), pp.12-15.

[27] Ironically, although I made reference to the *New Reasoner* in relation to the background roots of the 'old New Left' I was quite unaware that Hamish's translations had already appeared in the latter, although, as the extracts concerned now make clear, his role was presented as the secondary one of translator.

[28] H. Henderson, 'The Oral Tradition', *Scottish International* (January 1973), pp.27-32; D. Buchan, *op. cit.*, 1972.

[29] The essay became better known when it later appeared under a slightly different title but with only very minor textual changes relating to Jeannie Robertson as H. Henderson, 'The Ballad, the Folk and the Oral Tradition' in E. J. Cowan (ed.), *The People's Past*, Edinburgh: EUSPB/Polygon, 1980.

What Kind of Scotland?

In February 1973 Hamish and myself both participated in the third 'Aberdeen Teach-In' on the theme of 'Regionalism'. Hamish addressed 'The balladry and folk tradition of the area' [Aberdeen and the North East] and I spoke on 'Aspects of the folklore and social history of the region' (the Gaidhealtachd).[30] Although enjoyable and informative, it was clear that the student scene was changing. As the theme seemed to implicitly suggest, there was a sense of withdrawal from the wider engagement of the cultural and intellectual with the political, a retreat into the academy, the confines of disciplines, a narrowing off primary focus from culture and politics to literature and poetry.[31] *Scottish International*'s report back made oblique reference to myself and film-maker Douglas Eadie talking about his project for a film on Sorley MacLean.[32] As in anything involving Sorley, Hamish was an enthusiastic supporter.[33] I think we both saw it as another small but worthwhile application of Hamish's notion of 'Gramsci in action', promoting the subaltern history of Scotland from within its cultural and spatial diversity.[34] Crucially, however, it was a tangential, individual project, an offshoot from 1970. The Aberdeen Teach-In was no longer a platform for such initiatives.

The intention to take up the role had already been prepared by *Scottish International*. Its February issue had announced plans for a forthcoming major conference on the theme 'What Kind of Scotland?' This was the gathering that Neat conflates with the earlier Aberdeen event. An anonymous article in the February issue outlined what the more radically inclined of its readers were hoping for:

> It should particularly appeal to those who wonder why a kind of canny conventional wisdom so far outweighs

[30] '1973 Scottish Literature Teach-In, Aberdeen, Regionalism. Programme.'

[31] See the profile of the event in 'Aberdeen Scottish Teach In 1973', *Scottish International* (February 1973), p.7.

[32] 'Aberdeen Teach-In 1973', *Scottish International* (March 1973), p.7.

[33] The film duly appeared as *Sorley MacLean's Island*, Douglas Eadie (dir.), 1974.

[34] This notion of 'Gramsci in action' was first used by Hamish in relation to his work on the Edinburgh People's Festivals in the early 1950s (see below).

> provocative, uninhibited and speculative debate. It is especially for those who want a kind of Scotland where speculative debate is public and sustained.[35]

The way of seeing the challenge, the tenor of the argument, the language in which it was presented, all suggested that what had been argued for by myself and exemplified by Hamish in previous contributions was being picked up by some, at least, of the 'sceptical and hopeful'. In Gramscian terms, it outlined a challenge to the prevailing hegemony of received 'common sense' through the provision of a platform for the subaltern voice, that of those the author described as the 'missing constituency, lost and often presumed dead'. If the proposed conference could prove that this 'missing constituency' lived, then 'it will have been worth it for that reason, whatever else it achieves'.[36]

In the April issue the conference received further support in an open letter from Tom Nairn.[37] Apologising for his inability to take up an invitation to attend, Nairn took the opportunity to review the whole subject of culture and nationalism. Looking back on *Scottish International*'s own distinct role as a platform for debate in this field, he picked up on my own contribution on Gramsci with favourable comment and from this presented a broad critique of nationalism set in the context of Europe which was, in itself, also a critical allusion to his powerful criticisms of myopic 'Brit' Labourism he had presented elsewhere.[38]

This role of *Scottish International* in encouraging critical debate around nationalism, a discourse that was moving on to a different level, set in a different intellectual framework than hitherto, provides the real context for Hamish's exchange with Tom Scott in early April 1973.[39] Hamish made clear that in his view:

---

[35] 'What Kind of Scotland?', *Scottish International* (February 1973), pp.10-14, p.10.

[36] *ibid.* p.10

[37] Tom Nairn, 'Culture and Nationalism', *Scottish International* (April 1973), p.7.

[38] T. Nairn, 'The Left Against Europe', *New Left Review*, 75 (September-October 1972). It subsequently appeared in book form under the same title in 1973.

[39] Neat gives the date of Hamish's letter to Tom Scott as '13 April 1973', but as the conference was held over 6-7 April, a date of 1 April would seem more likely.

> The conference on 'What Kind of Scotland' will be useful and fruitful – an attitude which postpones a discussion of these issues until after the achievement of independence is absolutely crass.... The time to change Scotland is now..... [40]

The acerbic comments Hamish made in the letter on Ireland and its 'pseudo-independence' were part of an argument about Scotland, not Ireland, not the conflict in 'the North', and certainly not myself, as Neat suggests.[41] They related to a deep, fundamental difference the two friends had over the way forward to the shared goal of independence. There had been a long-standing antipathy towards *Scottish International* from a significant section of nationalist writers, a hostility Hamish tried constantly and unsuccessfully to overcome.[42]

When the gathering did take place, many of us left feeling disappointed, depressed, but also elated. The division of subject left no room for a panellist such as Hamish, no space for the oral tradition, history.[43] 'Culture' was not discussed as a contested terrain of felt experience and ideas, but a matter of institutions and structures. This focus on agencies and policies led, almost inevitably, in the political culture of the time to a familiar inbred factionalism. The simple fact that the event and panellists reflected a significant nationalist/SNP orientation was like a challenge to their presumed natural right to shape all debate, determine all agendas, that was impossible to endure for the disciples of Labourism present. Any suggestion of more Scottish content in education, the media, or broadcasting could only invoke pronounced reluctance or open hostility. The process of 'Britification' of Scottish labour had worked well.

The 'missing constituency', the organisers acknowledged, had not materialised. There had, however, been glimpses, most notably in the response to the theatrical events, in particular to the Saturday night first reading of 7:84 and John McGrath's new play, *The Cheviot, the Stag, and the Black, Black Oil*. This was the

---

[40] H. Henderson to T. Scott, 13 April 1973, quoted in T. Neat, *op. cit.*, p.183.

[41] *Ibid.*

[42] A glimpse of this is revealed in the reply of Hamish to a letter in the *Scotsman* by Tom Scott, concerning *Scottish International* and the resignation of Bob Tait in 1973. See A. Finlay, *op. cit.*, pp.214-215.

[43] See the detailed programme accompanying the unattributed precursory promotional article, 'What Kind of Scotland?', in Scottish *International* (February 1973), pp.10-14.

moment when all the questions as to 'What kind of Scotland?' began to find answers:

> all the recognitions came together like a series of flashes in the long night. There they all were, the problems, the needs, the people, the treacheries, the latent radicalism, the vision of possibilities.[44]

Significantly, the performance of *The Cheviot* was also the moment when the much sought-for sense of common cause and unity of purpose became evident. All of us present and involved that night still retain that enduring sense of a Scotland united – a radical Scotland united.

Perhaps, in part, it was because it came at the hands of an 'outsider'; perhaps, to a degree, because it occurred through the fun and sorrow of theatre. But I think the main reason lay in the perspective that John McGrath brought to bear on his understanding of Scottish history and culture – one that was consciously and unmistakeably Gramscian. Both Hamish and myself were involved in the play, Hamish as an early consultant, myself as a roped in contributor of research as John McGrath's script emerged from a collective creative process. And the John McGrath we both knew, an aspect of his writing that is too often overlooked, was a playwright well-versed in the writings and ideas of Antonio Gramsci. Letting the voice of the subaltern be heard, challenging the received authority of Highland historiography, challenging the common sense of capitalist political economy, these were ideas often discussed by the three of us as much in relation to Gramsci's *Prison Notebooks*, or the Gramscian writings of Raymond Williams, as in terms of events in the Highland past or the 'oil boom' present.

Part 2

The demise of *Scottish International* left the capital and the country without a platform from which an engagement with history and culture could be promoted from an unaligned

---

44 [Bob Tait], 'What Kind of Conclusions?', *Scottish International*, May 1973, pp.13-15, 31, at p.15. See also the report of fellow organiser, SNP member and writer John Herdman, 'What Kind of Scotland? A View of the Conference', *Scottish International* (May 1973), pp.10-13.

left position.[45] This was the vacuum in which *New Edinburgh Review*, a student quarterly with a rotating editorship and no specific political orientation circulated. *NER* was a published by EUSPB (Edinburgh University Student Publications Board), and it was in *NER* in 1974 that Hamish's translations of Gramsci's prison letters were published. The following year EUSPB also published *The Red Paper on Scotland*, edited by Gordon Brown. Hamish was due to be a contributor but was unable to do so due to illness.

The involvement of Hamish in both of these publications has been discussed both by Tim Neat in volume II of his biography and Owen Dudley Edwards in his 2011 Hamish Henderson Memorial Lecture. This was a period in which I was also quite involved with Hamish, both in relation to these publishing events and to other related ventures. From my own recollections I would like to present an alternative interpretation to that given by Tim Neat of events surrounding the *NER* publication of Hamish's translations of Gramsci's *Prison Letters* and to that given by Tim Neat and Owen Dudley Edwards as to Hamish's association with *The Red Paper on Scotland.* As with the matters discussed in Part I, these are integral parts of the Hamish story. It is as a contribution to the memory of the latter that these clarifications and alternative interpretations of events are made.

New Edinburgh Review

Owen Dudley Edwards has put forward the notion of a joint plan devised by Hamish and the then Edinburgh University student Rector, Gordon Brown, to promote a Gramscian perspective and practice in Scottish political and culture life which first involved the publication of the *Prison Letters* in the EUSPB quarterly magazine, *New Edinburgh Review.* The plan was jeopardised, according to Edwards, by the *NER* editor, whom he describes as a 'truculent Trotskyite' and 'an anchorite cocooned in self-protective vituperation.'[46] However, a closer look at the sequence of events and the political affiliations of the key people involved tell a very different story.

---

45 Other than *Scottish Marxist* which had appeared in 1972 as the journal of the Scottish Committee of the Communist Party of Great Britain, and the small duplicated broadsheets, *Scottish Vanguard* and *United Scotsmen.*

46 Owen Dudley Edwards, 'Sectarian Songs', in E. Bort (ed.), *At Hame Wi' Freedom': Essays on Hamish Henderson and the Scottish Folk Revival*, Ochtertyre: Grace Note Publications, 2012. pp.151-196; pp.153, 156.

The *NER* editor in question was Charles Keith 'Chic' Maisels, who assumed the editorship in 1973.[47] At the time Maisels and his editorial assistant were active members of the British & Irish Communist Organisation (B&ICO), one of the myriad groupuscules on the Stalinist-Maoist anti-revisionist left, best known for its 'two nations' theory in relation to Ireland.[48] Maisels was resolutely opposed to any form of 'nationalist obfuscations' in Scotland that would in any way weaken the 'single, indivisible proletarian collective body' of the working class in the British state.[49] In August 1973, Maisels and his B&ICO associate edited their first *NER* issue, a special Festival issue on folk song and the folk tradition.[50] The content included 'Resurgimento', an interview with Hamish by Geordie McIntyre, articles on important Scottish collections and on the work of Robin Morton, but the tenor, style and interpretation of the editorial context these were set in were the antithesis of the views and approach of Hamish.[51]

In early 1974 Maisels and his Edinburgh associates seceded from the B&ICO for having succumbed to 'revisionism', to form their own British and Irish Communist Organisation. It not only believed in a pan-British working class but in the indivisibility of all the British Isles. There were six founders. Maisels and his editorial assistant on *NER*, Jennifer Nussey, were two of them. Their next issue of *NER* was now on the special theme of 'Working Class Culture and Consciousness'.[52]As the alignment of

47 He is described at the time as 'a student in the Chinese Department'.

48 The B&ICO developed out of the ICO which had been formed in 1965 as an anti-revisionist organisation of Irish emigrants. With the adoption of its 'two nations theory' in 1970 it changed its name to B&ICO. It was a prolific pamphleteering organisation with an input in the North of Ireland that far outweighed its numbers. For further details on this byzantine world see <www.marxists.org/history/erol/ireland/index.htm>.

49 C. K. Maisels, 'Nationalism and the Proletarian Revolution', *The Marxist*, 15, 1970.

50 *NER*, 23 (August 1973). It was A3 in format. That was the whole point of his statement of being different.

51 'Resurgimento', Geordie McIntyre's interview with Hamish, one of the most informative in print, was republished in the programme for the 5th Carrying Stream Festival, Edinburgh, 2006 (and is included in this volume).

52 *NER*, 25 (December 1973/January 1974). The number and date is not given but is based on the advertising of Proletarian Publishing, the imprint of COBI which was not formally established until 1 January 1974.

contributors, anglo-brit emphasis of the content, presentation and layout, advertising of their Proletarian publications and the heavy political line of the editorial all confirmed, *NER* was now firmly in the hands of a miniscule Stalinist-Maoist sect.[53] The magazine would now be used as to advance the aims of the COBI whose first declared statement of principle was to work towards 'the comprehensive development of operational theory for the working class to become sufficiently conscious to seize and maintain power as the ruling class by crushing the bourgeoisie.'[54]

Contrary to Edwards' impression, this was a groupuscule with a resolute antipathy to Trotskyism. However, even a cursory glance at the contents of the issues of *NER* produced under Maisel's control, his observation that *NER* was now in the hands of an editor ensconced on a 'self-admiring throne' is confirmed as entirely apt. This was the context in which Hamish took up the opportunity to finally see his translations of Gramsci's *Prison Letters* out where they belonged, in the public domain.

Gramsci's Prison Letters

In January 1974, when replying concerning a proposal we had been discussing for a replacement platform for *Scottish International*, Hamish announced the development:

> I quite agree with you about the sad decline of S. I. – it's a hellish shame, when you consider all the hard work Bob Tait put into it. (However, I'm glad to be able to tell you that the New Edinburgh Review is going to do two Gramsci double numbers shortly – both containing swatches of my translations of the prison letters. I'll send you a copy when the first one comes out – which will be in February I think).[55]

He was delighted that his labour of love was about to see the light of day – and in Scotland. However, the covering statements of the *NER* editorial team, the balance of the content, even the

[53] The contributors included Paul Cockshott, COBI founder; and other material from Leicester where there were other founder member links.

[54] 'Statement of Principles', *Proletarian* 1, 1974, p.5. <www.marxists.org/history/erol/ireland/richards-bico.pdf>.

[55] H. Henderson to R. Burnett, 17 Jan 1974.

presentation of the material made it very clear that the last thing on their mind was what the Gramsci prison letters or the translations meant for Hamish. Fresh seceders from the anti-revisionist seceders of B&ICO, the elect few had a programme to present to the proletariat of the world. Alongside the large advert informing readers, 'If you have a serious interest in the themes of this *NER* then you must get *Proletarian*, journal of the Communist Organisation in the British Isles', there was a short message from the Editor. There would be no editorial to introduce the material, only a few 'technical remarks', the first of which declared:

> In two volumes we shall have completed publication – the first in English – of all the 218 letters in the Einaudi collection of 1947 translated by Hamish Henderson and set in context by the essential analytical history of Prof. Gwyn A. Williams. This we believe to be by far the most comprehensive study of Gramsci to be made by a British Author.'[56]

There would be no introduction to the letters by Hamish, no background details of his first encounter with the memory of Gramsci amongst the *partigiani* of wartime Italy, no assessment of their importance, drawing on his own leftist credentials or his own informed scholarship. Hamish, in short, was being used to set up the authoritative position of fellow COBI follower, Gwyn Williams. Hamish, in short, was being used. The contributor that mattered, complete with full-page portrait, was their fellow founder, Prof. Gwyn Williams.[57] The *NER* Gramsci issues were never intended to promote Hamish. His delay in securing publication was portrayed as evidence of the resistance of publishers to any publication of Marxist material. Now, however, with Gramsci, even Marx himself, having become 'highly fashionable', it was time to act:

[56] *NER*, 26/I, 'From the Editor', p.1.

[57] The insistent use of his professorial title by the Editor was deliberate, as was the inclusion of the excellent, but necessarily dense and scholarly musicological notes on a Sardinian song on the inside front cover by Ailie Munro. It flagged up the COBI emphasis on high standard intellectualism. (Everyone accepted for membership of the elect had to learn at least one other language to be a member, etc). Hamish may have had the languages, but he did not have the status of a 'professor' – richly ironic given Gramsci's penetrating work on the actual role of traditional intellectuals in capitalist and bourgeois society.

> as with all things fashionable, we must be on or guard. It is to give a real scientific basis for evaluation of Gramsci (and indeed Bordiga) that we publish this otherwise unobtainable material.[58]

The long contribution by Williams, as his own introductory notes acknowledged and the title makes clear, was part of an ongoing research project of his own into Gramsci's Turin years of 1919-1920 and early Italian communism. None of it had been written to 'set in context' the prison letters.[59] Difficulties ensued when Maisels failed to attach any of its acknowledgements and footnotes to the first article. Williams had drawn heavily on the unpublished research of Martin Clark, now in post at Edinburgh. It led to legal exchanges, the payment of legal expenses, an apology in the second issue and the withdrawal of the second part of the essay.[60] Instead of the remaining chapters of the original essay, the second contribution consisted of translated passages of Gramsci's writings in *Ordine Nuovo* with attendant comment by Williams.[61]

A short 'Editorial' continued to maintain that:

> The work of analysis/commentary, and, above all, interpretation, remains, made much more productive by the invaluable notes and commentary of our two main contributors, which takes the material out of the realms of narrowly academic history.

The content told a different story. Other than a scattering of explanatory footnotes there was no interpretative commentary by Hamish, and two thirds of the issue were devoted to the contribution of Gwyn Williams. His concluding essay on

---

58 *Ibid.*

59 Gwyn A Williams, 'Proletarian Forms: Antonio Gramsci, the Turin movement of factory council and the origins of Italian communism', *NER*, 26/I 1974, pp.52-76.

60 See the note by Gwyn Williams in *NER*, 26/II, p.47 for the apology and explanation. For fuller details see the correspondence on the issue in the *TLS*, M. Clark, 'Letter to the Editor', *TLS*, 23 August 1974; G. A. Williams, 'Letter to the Editor', *TLS*, 27 September 1974.

61 Gwyn A Williams, 'Proletarian Forms. Gramsci, Council, Communism, 1919-20: a documentary analysis', *NER*, 26/II, 1974, pp.48-116.

'Proletarian Forms' was suitably accompanied by an advert for *Proletarian*, the COBI journal, with their 'Programmatic Documents' and 'Clarification of Premises' required further reading.[62]

When the *NER* Gramsci double issues were published, an anonymous comment appeared in the *TLS*.[63] Its assertion that 'no steps were taken' to publish Henderson's 1948-50 translations for 25 years, 'until Gramsci became a subject of interest – indeed almost a cult figure – among the English speaking left' drew an immediate response from Hamish, making clear his frustrated efforts to secure publication.[64] The anonymous commentary made no comment on the quality of the translations. Instead it merely noted that Henderson's version of the letters had 'one great disadvantage', as a selection from the much better Italian edition of 1965 was soon to be published.[65] It highlighted *NER*'s inclusion of 'the bonus of a major contribution to Gramsci studies by Gwyn Williams' whose 'characteristic blend of personal commitment and professional criticism' had brought Gramsci 'more convincingly to life than any other treatment in English'. The observation that the double issue contained sufficient material that it 'could well fill two substantial books' revealed the reality. The editorial focus was never intended to be on the Prison Letters, their significance and the distinctive qualities of the translations. The Gramsci issues had two elements. And in the hands of Maisels and his associates the emphasis was firmly on Williams as an exemplar of the line they promoted. Hamish was merely a means to an end.

It was left to the already aggrieved specialist on Gramsci and the early Italian left, Martin Clark, to write to the *TLS* commending them for the 'welcome publicity' they had given 'to Hamish Henderson's splendid translation of Gramsci's Prison Letters in

---

[62] *NER*, 26/II, p.116.

[63] 'Prison Testament', *TLS*, 5 July1974.

[64] H. Henderson, 'Letter to the Editor', *TLS*, 23 Jul 1974. The letter is reprinted in A. Finlay, *op. cit.*, p.219.

[65] The reference was to the Lynn Lawner translations which appeared in 1975. Hamish had acknowledged their forthcoming appearance in Gramsci I (*NER*, 26/I, p.3). Lawner, however, failed to make any acknowledgement or reference to Hamish's earlier work in her own edition. See A. Gramsci, (L. Lawner, ed.), *Letters from Prison by Antonio Gramsci*, London: Quartet Books, 1979.

the current issues of the *New Edinburgh* Review'.[66] As Tim Neat has revealed, back in April, Clark had already written privately to Hamish, highly praising the translations but also referring to the 'first class row' he was having with Gwyn Williams for having 'plagiarised much of my Ph.D thesis' for his own *NER* article.[67] He was keen to point out that 'the row is between me and Williams – and that I think your stuff is splendid.' Now, with publication, the row was in the open. Clark's letter to the *TLS* evoked a reply from Williams in which he stressed that all his footnotes and his acknowledgements, including that to Clark for the use of his research, had been held over from the first to the second issue by the *NER* editor and that this had been done without his prior consent or knowledge.[68]

Initially Hamish had anticipated and assumed that the publication, at last, of his translations would be used as a springboard to promote interest in Gramsci and, in particular, an appreciation of his substantial relevance to Scotland. In his letter of January informing me that his translations would soon be appearing in *NER*, Hamish had suggested: 'What about writing an article on "Gramsci in Scotland" yourself for the second of the two NER Italian numbers? (Elaborating on the one you did for the SI)'.[69]

In his response to the *TLS* in reply to Martin Clark, Williams had also revealed that the second issue had been scheduled to coincide with a symposium on Gramsci and that Clark was to have been invited.[70] A more open second issue and an open symposium to accompany it was evidently what Hamish anticipated, a conference that would allow discussion of his translations in the context of our own specific situation. Given his encouragement I promptly wrote to *NER*, referring to Hamish's suggestion and

66 M. Clark, 'Letter to the Editor', *TLS*, 23 August 1974.

67 T. Neat, op. cit., p.244, where Neat wrongly refers to Gwyn A. Williams as 'Glyn Williams'. Clark had submitted his thesis on the factory councils at Reading where he also published a pamphlet on *The Failure of Revolution in Italy*, 1919-20, this being the material Williams acknowledged using. Clark then moved to Edinburgh and his thesis work was subsequently published as M. Clark, *Antonio Gramsci and the Revolution that Failed*, New Haven: Yale University Press, 1977.

68 G. A. Williams, 'Letter to the Editor', *TLS*, 27 September 1974.

69 H. Henderson to R. Burnett, 17 January 1974.

70 G. A. Williams, 'Letter to the Editor', *TLS*, 27 September 1974.

offering precisely what he had proposed. I received no reply or acknowledgement.

With two-thirds of its content given over to Gwyn Williams, there was no room in *Gramsci II* for any other contributions. Instead, a third Gramsci issue was promised as a final volume that would 'deal fully with the background to, and interpretative aspects of, the prime material.' It also announced that it would contain the papers to be delivered at the First National Gramsci Conference, a revised version of the originally planned symposium. As the event drew nearer Gordon Brown also wrote, in relation to preparations for *The Red Paper* (see below), adding 'I hope to meet you at the Gramsci Conference on June 22nd.'[71] When the plans for a conference and a third issue had emerged, I had written again to Maisels asking for details and repeating my offer of a paper, but to no avail.

It was the papers from this conference that Edwards refers to as having to be 'finally gouged out' of Maisels to provide the content for the last *NER* issue under his editorship. The reason why I had received no reply to my offer of a paper soon became apparent when the bizarre 'Gramsci III' issue finally appeared. Owen Dudley Edwards has claimed that this Gramsci conference and the attendant publication of conference papers was all part of a strategy by Hamish to promote a 'nationalist Gramsci' and that by late 1974:

> the Gramsci infection had already been sped on its way by Hamish many years before, and he had succeeded in godfathering a Gramsci conference under EUSPB, with the promise of publication well before the SNP had more than one seat. [*i.e.* before the February 1974 election, R.B.].[72]

But from the content and design of *Gramsci III* it is quite clear that neither Hamish nor Gordon Brown nor anyone else outside the Maisels coterie had any influence or control over the magazine's production. With its Maoist covers, centre page spread and liberal scattering of pictures and slogans from China's anti-revisionist 'Cultural Revolution' it was a contemptuous last issue farewell to the 'gaggle of arty-farties' around EUSPB and the 'insestuous [*sic*] vacuosity of literaries talking to themselves', a disdainful

[71] G. Brown to R. Burnett, 30 May 1974.

[72] O. D. Edwards, *op. cit.*, p.156.

display of true-path righteousness to an *NER* that would now 'fall back into the lowest common-denominator stakes.'[73]

Apart from a cursory 'thank you' for having opened the conference there was no further reference to Hamish or to his *Prison Letters* translations, no paper by him and instead of the promised 'evaluative editorial', postponed by Maisels from the first two issues, there was no editorial summing-up of the content of *Gramsci I* and *II*. Instead, the article by Maisels focused entirely on a pre-prison Gramsci, the politics of the Second International era and the internal disputes within the early PCI. The only references back to *Gramsci I and II* were to Gwyn A. Williams, his comrade in the revolutionary elect, in a contribution that was little more than a thinly disguised promotion of the 'Proletarian Programme' of the Communist Organisation of the British Isles.[74]

Predictably, however, there was a further paper by Gwyn A. Williams. Ironically, given his subsequent rich contribution to the cultural and political history of Wales, his essay insisted that there could be no room for consideration of any 'national peculiarities' in the discussion of a people's history or culture – only proletarian internationalism.[75] Later, in the book publication of his own *NER* contributions, Williams thanked Maisels for having introduced him to Hamish, whom he described as 'a Sorelian diremption in his own right'.[76] But in his summary of the important collections

---

[73] *NER*, 26/II, 1974. Sub-titled 'The Struggle for Hegemony', the cover photo was of the masses gathered on a Chinese hillside. The centre spread picture (pp.16-17), was of a mass workers' gathering under the heading 'The Broad Democracy of the Proletariat', with appropriate quotations from Mao below, of which the quotation from 'On the Correct Handling of Contradictions Among the People', 1957, was a good indicator of the context in which Gramsci and Hamish's translations were being utilised: 'Our educational policy must enable everyone who receives an education to develop morally, intellectually and physically and become a worker with both socialist consciousness and culture.'

[74] C. K. Maisels, 'Gramsci between Two Internationals', *NER*, 27, 1972, pp.24-29.

[75] G. A. Williams, 'The Making and Unmaking of Antonio Gramsci', *NER*, 27, 1974, pp.7-15. The notable works by G. A. Williams, subsequently a member of Plaid Cymru, on Welsh culture and history include *The Welsh and Their History* (1982) and *When Was Wales? A History of the Welsh* (1985).

[76] G. A. Williams, 'Preface', *Proletarian Order: Antonio Gramsci, Factory Councils and the Origins of Communism in Italy, 1911-21*, London: Pluto Press, 1975, p.8.

of Gramsci's writings, including the *Prison Letters*, he made no mention of the translations by Hamish which had accompanied his own 'prime material' in *Gramsci I and II*.

Two other contributors also made no reference to the translations and focused entirely on the same aspects of revolutionary party organisation and policies and a pre-prison Gramsci as Williams.[77] A third was Labriola, resurrected from history for the perceived validity of his political line. Only V.G. Kiernan, Hamish's friend and colleague, came obliquely close to Hamish. His essay on 'Gramsci and the other Continents' did not refer to the translations. But in its style, content and emphasis it brought out the essential qualities of Gramsci as someone deeply interested in the human condition, expressing it in a series of insightful enquiries into the culture, folklore, religion and history of an array of peoples across the world. It was, and remains, the only apt accompaniment to the Gramsci revealed in translation by Hamish from the whole *NER* saga.[78]

On looking back over the whole sorry episode, it is difficult to avoid the conclusion that Hamish was shamefully exploited and that the *NER* publication of his translations was a tragic missed opportunity. Far from it having led to Hamish 'godfathering' a Scotland-orientated conference with 'appropriate scholarly discussion' of Gramsci, it led to the translations being buried in the wrappings of a tiny sect with a deep antipathy to any notion of national culture whose sense of self-importance was in inverse proportion to their political significance. It would be a further fourteen long years before the translations were to be published in an appropriate book form with a fine introduction by Hamish, presenting them through an informed Scottish-Italian prism in his own inimical style.[79]

---

[77] The contribution by Victor Kiernan was in marked contrast to the others. It shared Hamish's appreciation of the human dimension of Gramsci's life and writings and in its stimulating range across the culture, folklore, and religion of the peoples of five contents as discussed by Gramsci it remains fascinating reading. V. G. Kiernan, 'Gramsci and the Other Continents', *NER*, 27, 1974, pp.19-24. Kiernan's essay was subsequently published in V. G. Kiernan, *Imperialism and Its Contradictions,* ed. and introduced by Harvey Kaye, London: Routledge, 1995, pp. 171-90.

[78] *Ibid.*

[79] See the perceptive observations on this in Corey Gibson, '"Gramsci in Action": Antonio Gramsci and Hamish Henderson's Folk Revivalism' in E. Bort (ed.), *Borne on the Carrying Stream: The Legacy of Hamish Henderson,* Ochtertyre: Grace Note Publications, 2010, pp.239-256; pp. 240-243.

The Red Paper on Scotland

Tim Neat has maintained that the story of the *NER* publication of Hamish's translations of the *Prison Letters* is important, 'not least because of the part played by the young Gordon Brown.'[80] This is followed by an account of Hamish's involvement with *The Red Paper on Scotland*, the collection of essays published under Brown's editorship in 1975. Both were publications of EUSPB, a body in which Brown had a role in his capacity as the university's second student rector.[81] This association between Henderson and Brown has since been presented by Owen Dudley Edwards as being of major significance in forming the basis of a shared plan for the promotion of a Gramscian approach to politics and culture in Scotland, an interpretation that has been uncritically accepted by Bort in his own discussion of the politics of Hamish.[82]

According to Edwards, the publication of the translations of the Gramsci Prison Letters in *NER* was the necessary precursor and first stage in this plan. The gathering together of contributions over 1974 and eventual publication in 1975 of *The Red Paper on Scotland* was the second. In the preceding, I have argued for a different interpretation of events in relation to Hamish, the translations and the *NER* Gramsci issues. In this concluding section I would like to suggest that this is also an

---

80 T Neat, *op. cit.*, pp.243-244. There are several factual inaccuracies in this account. The Gramsci issues were not published over '1973-1974', the first did not appear until early 1974; the translations of the prison letters only appeared in the first two issues, not 'in three consecutive issues'; they were not published 'with illustrations' of the original mss.; and, as noted above, there was 'no major appreciation by the Welsh academic Glyn [*sic*] Williams.' The latter's contributions made no reference at all to the translations.

81 There are further factual errors in Tim Neat's account regarding Edinburgh University Student Publications Board (EUSPB). It was not 'set up' by Gordon Brown as a post-grad, but was first established in 1969; the Gramsci Letters were not EUSPB's 'first publication'. There had been at least two as early as 1972; the translations were not published as '*The Prison Letters of Antonio Gramsci*' but simply as *New Edinburgh Review GRAMSCI special double issue* and *New Edinburgh Review GRAMSCI II*.

82 See O. D. Edwards, *op. cit.*, pp.153-157, and E. Bort, 'At Hame Wi' Freedom': The Politics of Hamish Henderson', in Bort, 2012, *op. cit.*, pp.197-216; 204.

untenable interpretation of events regarding Hamish, Gramsci, Gordon Brown and *The Red Paper,* with a brief word on two other Gramsci-inspired projects both Hamish and I were involved in to provide context.

After its reading at the *Scottish International* conference, *The Cheviot, the Stag and the Black, Black Oil* went on tour. I was involved in different ways. I wrote the Programme introduction to the play that accompanied it on tour. Our house in Dornie was a west-coast base where John McGrath and his family and the company could take a break from the gruelling tour schedule. It was also the base when the play was restaged and the interior scenes were shot when the TV adaptation was filmed.[83] Apart from incorporating Hamish's song, 'Ballad of the Men of Knoydart',[84] the play and its performance, were, in all sorts of ways, Hamish territory. There were songs old and new, an emphasis on common cause, Highland and Lowland, urban and rural, an emphasis on the role of women in Highland resistance, above all giving a platform for the history and the 'voice' of the subaltern to be presented.

This work of John McGrath and 7:84 (Scotland) was to continue with a range of other productions, and my work with McGrath and the company continued both in terms of researching material and, latterly, as a Board member. Several, such as *The Game's A Bogey, Joe's Drum, There Is A Happy Land*, touched directly on Hamish's political aspirations, his contributions, and his knowledge. And I remember several enjoyable discussions with Hamish over content and issues on a number of occasions. Hamish loved the whole idea of raising awareness of Scotland's radical history and the importance of the contribution of the oral tradition to the promotion of that 'people's past'.

As mentioned, John McGrath was well versed in Gramsci. Being older, and with his roots down south, he also had connections to other playwrights, scholars and leftists who were part of Hamish's wider circle. And just as Hamish's promotion of the People's Festivals in the 1950s can be seen as 'Gramsci in action', I think, in the work of John McGrath and 7:84 (Scotland) at its best, it was hard not to also think of Gramsci – and, as the shows

---

[83] See J. McGrath, 'The Year of the Cheviot', pp. v-xxix; and R. Burnett, 'Have the Clearances stopped?' in John McGrath, *The Cheviot, the Stag and he Black, Black Oil,* London: Methuen, 1981 pp.75-6.

[84] H. Henderson, *Collected Poems and Songs*, ed. Raymond Ross, Edinburgh: Curly Snake Publishing, 2090, pp.128-130.

and the performances rooted themselves in the communities of Scotland, to think of Henderson.[85]

A Gramscian Perspective?

This allusion to *The Cheviot* serves as a reminder as to how people, activities and cultural and political currents in the early 1970s overlapped. It also highlights some of the key aspects that a Gramscian approach might manifest itself, providing a yardstick by which to assess *The Red Paper* as an associated project and the extent to which it reflected the Gramscian mission of Henderson and Brown as has been suggested. In shorthand, schematic terms, such cultural political projects can be seen as involving the stimulation of a challenge to 'common sense'; the promotion of a sense of class and an awareness of power; a focus on the social relations of production as a site for the contestation of power; culture, language, the institutions of civil society as a significant and crucial terrain of struggle; and the organic rooting of this challenge in the subaltern history of Scotland.[86]

Owen Dudley Edwards maintains that while James Connolly, John Maclean and Hugh MacDiarmid all had an influence on Hamish they were not the principal motivation for his felt need to root his cultural and political activity in Scotland. Rather. '... the massive nationalist impact on Hamish was made by the letters of Antonio Gramsci which Hamish translated over the next two decades, and to which he converted Brown.' And from this, Edwards claims: '*The Red Paper* came into existence because the Henderson text of Gramsci had shown Gordon Brown that

[85] For Hamish's original use of this term for his work in Edinburgh in the early 1950s, see H. Henderson, 'The Edinburgh People's Festival, 1951-1954', in A. Croft (ed.), *A Weapon in the Struggle The Cultural History of the Communist Party of Great Britain*, London: Pluto, 1988, pp. 163-170. Reprinted in E Bort (ed), *'Tis Sixty Years Since: The 1951 Edinburgh People's Festival Ceilidh and the Scottish Folk Revival*, Ochtertyre: Grace Note Publications, 2011, pp.35-44.

[86] This, of course, is only one aspect of Gramsci. It should not be forgotten that, first and foremost, Gramsci was a revolutionary Marxist. Much of his life and a great deal of his writings were concerned with issues of agency, class, relations of production, and the other dimensions of the contestation of power.

nationalism was compatible with socialism.'[87]

A shared Gramscian political perspective and joint authorship of the project, it is claimed, led Hamish and Gordon to solicit contributions that would 'extend and enrich intellectual discussion whence the best conclusions could be drawn'.[88] This attribution of a key and highly influential role for Hamish in the whole gestation and delivery of the project is endorsed by the Henderson scholar 'Paddy' Bort, who concurs that: 'Hamish's influence on Brown, as Owen Dudley Edwards shows in his chapter in this volume, must not be underestimated'.[89]

But is this a valid reading of *The Red Paper* and its genesis? It raises a series of questions: i) to what extent was it consciously planned as a Gramscian project and who was actually in charge of the proposal and its content? ii) where can we actually find Gramsci in *The Red Paper*? Is he there by name and citation or is he discernible in coded language, or in private correspondence with contributors and others? iii) who actually deploys Gramsci, directly or by inference, in their contributions? iv) what does Gordon Brown actually mean in his own referencing of Gramsci? v) to what extent does the final structure of the publication confirm or otherwise, a Gramscian perspective? As only one of the several actual and intended contributors and with not all the sources necessary for consultation readily available at the time of writing, I can only give preliminary answers to these self-imposed questions. But on that provisional basis I would argue that:

i) the evidence is not yet forthcoming for *The Red Paper* to be considered as a project in the shared ownership of Hamish and Gordon Brown. In my own case, I knew Hamish and had discussed Gramsci in relation to Scotland with him on several occasions, as noted, but the invitation to contribute did not come from Hamish but from Gordon Brown, whom I knew, of course, but at that stage had never met. On 30 April I received a letter containing a lengthy outline of the project using the same sentences as quoted by Neat from Brown's similar letter to Hamish. Turning to the invitation to contribute, he continued: 'Hamish Henderson has just informed me of your proposed Scottish Political Quarterly

---

[87] O. D. Edwards, *op. cit.*, p.155.

[88] *Ibid.* 156.

[89] E. Bort, op. cit., p. 204.

and I have read with interest your contributions to "Scottish International".'[90]

A list of already confirmed contributors followed, including 'and several others'. Brown was 'particularly anxious' to include 'articles on "The Left in Scotland Today"' in the form of 'an analysis of the ideologies, policies and support for the various political groups in Scotland from the Labour Party leftwards' and another 'analysing present Scottish Nationalist policies from a Socialist standpoint.' He then concluded by asking if I would 'consider contributing on one or other of these suggested themes.'[91] If Hamish had been in such a leading role as has been suggested, I would have expected the invitation to have come directly from himself, as it had done in relation to the *NER* Gramsci project. Yet curiously, Hamish was not even mentioned as one of the confirmed contributors – an oversight, perhaps? More significantly, given that Brown acknowledged that he had read my contributions to *Scottish International*, one of which had been specifically on Scotland and Gramsci and flagged up by Tom Nairn in that regard, if the project was indeed part of a Gramscian mission then it is odd, to say the least, that he was not even referred to in the invitation.

A reply to my offer to contribute the desired analysis of SNP policies discussed in some detail how this would fit in with the other relevant contributions:

> The outline of the framework of your article analysing the S.N.P. which you provide sounds ideal and fits in well with previously agreed contributions. Both Tom Nairn and Bob Tait have agreed to write on the nationalist-internationalist debate in the context of Marxist theory, and we have attracted a series of articles on Scottish social, economic and cultural problems. Where I think the Red Paper needs strengthening is in its analysis of present Political developments and I am still hopeful of attracting three articles – one on the devolution debate in the context of demands for industrial democracy and community power, one on the concentration of wealth and power in Scotland today (and how this would have to be tackled), and one on the left's strength and weaknesses in the present Scottish situation.

---

[90] G. Brown to R. Burnett, 20 Apr 1974.

[91] *ibid.*

> So, the analysis of the S.N.P. which you suggest is of vital importance, fitting in as a necessary sequel to the dialogue between Tom Nairn and Bob Tait on what attitude the left should take to nationalism, in the light of Marxist theory.[92]

Again, although there was specific reference to 'Marxist theory' and two other contributors, there was no reference to either Gramsci or to Hamish.

The initial outline had referred to a section on 'a study of Scottish society and culture with articles on Class Relationships in Scotland, the Radical Tradition in Scottish Education, Scottish Literature and Scottish folk culture', and when further details were sent in July Hamish was named as a contributor on 'The Oral Tradition' but in none of this was there any clear indication of a specifically Gramscian perspective.[93]

ii) Perhaps a sense of a Gramscian approach could be taken from the passage in the initial letter to myself, as in that sent also to Hamish referring to:

> A Red Paper on Scotland whose aim is to sketch, analyse and comment upon, from a left-wing point of view, the live elements of the Scottish radical cultural and political tradition and the socialist possibilities arising from the current Scottish political and economic situation.[94]

The first part, as quoted by Neat, with its reference to 'the live elements of the Scottish radical cultural and political tradition' could perhaps be read as a coded reference to Scotland's subaltern legacy – what Raymond Williams, building on Gramsci, referred to as 'residual culture'. But the latter part of the sentence, the part Neat does not quote, is perhaps the more significant, with its reference to the 'possibilities' within the 'current' Scottish situation, a limiting of vision to the accepted constraining framework of parliamentary socialism in the Scottish Labourist tradition.

iii) The proposition that *The Red Paper* was the outcome of a Gramscian crusade by Hamish and Gordon Brown is most severely tested when the actual deployment of Gramsci in the final

[92] G. Brown to R. Burnett, 30 May 1974.

[93] G. Brown to R. Burnett, 20 April 1974 and 3 July 1974.

[94] G. Brown to R. Burnett, 20 April 1974.

published contributions is examined.[95] According to Edwards, by 1974:

> between the two of them, Hamish and Gordon sent Gramsci-consciousness seething through Edinburgh University staff and students alike, and recruited others already versed in Gramsci but celebrating him chiefly in little-read publications.[96]

The only two of the 28 contributors who specifically discussed Gramsci were Tom Nairn and myself.[97] There was a footnote reference to my Gramsci article in *Scottish International* in the contribution by Bob Tait, the former *SI* editor, and a short quotation and oblique allusion through reference to my own contribution in that of John McGrath.[98] There were references to the Gramscian-inspired *The Cheviot* by David Craig, Ian Carter and James D. Young, and an extract from an article of my own concerning popular opposition to oil developments in Wester Ross in the contribution of David Taylor, but none of these oblique references entered into any discussion or application of Gramscian ideas.[99] Amongst the great majority of the contributors making no reference to Gramsci, notwithstanding

---

[95] There are further factual errors in Neat's account as to the schedule and date of publishing. The initial plan was to publish in October 1974, not 'early 1975', Neat, *op. cit.* p246. And the actual date of publication was not 'February 1975', but 21 March 1975, G. Brown to R. Burnett, 20 March 1975.

[96] O. D. Edwards, *op. cit.,* p.156. The reference to celebrating Gramsci in 'little-read publications' is curious. The only left publication in which discussion of Gramsci in English-language publications occurred at that time was in *New Left Review*, a prestigious journal with an international readership.

[97] T. Nairn, 'Old Nationalism and New Nationalism', pp. 22-57 and R. Burnett, 'Socialists and the SNP', pp. 108-124, in G. Brown (ed.), *The Red Paper on Scotland,* Edinburgh: EUSPB, 1975.

[98] B. Tait, 'The Left, the SNP and Oil', pp.125-133 and J. McGrath, 'Scotland Up Against It', pp.134-140, in G. Brown, *op. cit.*

[99] D. Craig, 'The Radical Literary Tradition', pp.289-303; I. Carter, 'A Socialist Strategy for the Highlands', pp.247-253; J. Young, 'The Rise of Scottish Socialism', pp.282-287; D. Taylor, 'The Social Impact of Oil', pp.270-281, in G. Brown, *op. cit.*

their political alignments or the topics of their contributions, were John Foster, writing on Scottish capitalism, Alex Ferry, writing on workers' control, David Craig on the radical literary tradition, and David Gow on devolution. Nor, as it happens, did Owen Dudley Edwards, who seems to have been uninfected by the 'Gramsci-consciousness seething through Edinburgh University staff' that was apparently prevalent all around him.[100]

iv) Where Edwards is, I think, correct in his reflection on *The Red Paper* is that the reference to Gramsci by Gordon Brown in his own introductory essay was more than just an obligatory name-check on a passing intellectual fad. He did have, as I found at the time, a genuine interest in Gramsci and the applicability of some, at least, of his ideas to an analysis of the political situation in Scotland.

'Gramsci's relevance to Scotland today,' Brown wrote, in an advanced, industrialised Western economy was in his emphasis that:

> the transition to socialism must be made by the majority of people themselves and a socialist society must be created in the womb of existing society and prefigured in the movements for democracy of the grass roots.[101]

At first glance it may seem difficult to understand how, from a reformist position ultimately at odds with that of the committed Marxist Italian revolutionary, Brown could see a connection, and (from a contemporary viewpoint in Scotland 2015 it may seem impossible!). What tends to be forgotten however, is the extent to which the sheer breadth and imaginativeness and undogmatic style of Gramsci's writings could make his ideas, theoretical concepts and analytical insights so stimulating and attractive to readers of a non-Marxist and reformist position, but with an enquiring intellectual interest in political thought and ideas addressing the social, cultural and political formations of advanced liberal Western democracies. In the early 1970s Scotland, there was a widespread interest in ideas relating to community politics, radical educational ideas, industrial

---

[100] O. D. Edwards, 'Scotland: Lessons from Ireland', pp.304-316, in G. Brown, *op. cit.*

[101] Gordon Brown, 'Introduction', in Brown, *op.cit.*, pp.7-21; p.18.

democracy, and the politics of the self, as well as the more familiar terrain of the debate on the left around the agency of socialist advancement, the role and structure of the political. The key to Brown's interest in Gramsci lies as much in the ideas of Lucio Magri and Paolo Freire, the other thinkers he cites alongside Gramsci as the sources of his interest and readings on these issues.[102]

v) In July, 1975, as the final list of contributors and topics became clearer, a revised pre-publication profile of the project was released. To re-align its ambition to the reality of its content, *The Red Paper* was now re-defined as 'a political tract', and the purpose of its publication more prosaically set in the confines of Scottish party politics than in the more inspiring realm of intellectual enquiry in political culture and thought. The scope was less visionary, the framework more constraining, any sense of a Gramscian perspective was only visible by its absence:

> The objectives of the Red Paper on Scotland is to provide socialist perspectives for the debate now being conducted about the future of Scotland, in the light of the political impasse reached through the Kilbrandon and Crowther Hunt papers, the recent SNP successes, the forthcoming regionalisation, the discovery of oil and the increasing shift of investment from West to East in Scotland.[103]

The purpose of *The Red Paper* was no longer to debate the political philosophy and theory around the 'dichotomy' between nationalism and internationalism but: 'to provide a socialist *corrective* to the present futile dichotomy between nationalism and anti-nationalism in the debate about Scotland's future. (*my italics*). It was no longer to engage with and build on 'the live elements' of our subaltern past but merely 'to *comment* upon the radical cultural and political tradition.' (*my italics*)

When publication finally arrived there was, I recall, a curious sense of anticipated disappointment in the air. Back in July 1974,

---

[102] The works cited are A. Gramsci, *Prison Notebooks*, 1971; L. Magri, 'Problems of the Marxist Theory of the Revolutionary Party', *New Left Review* 1970, pp.97-128; P. Freire, *Pedagogy of the Oppressed*, 1972, and *Cultural Action for Freedom*, 1972.

[103] Attached EUSPB press release, in G. Brown to R. Burnett, 3 July 1975.

Gordon Brown had attached a covering note to the publisher's release saying: ' It may be that we shall be able to launch the book with a conference in early October and I raise the possibility in the hope that you might be interested in taking part.'[104] But by the eventual eve of publication day, any idea that *The Red Paper* might serve to promote debate and generate ideas above and beyond the dialogue of the deaf that internecine party politics in Scotland inevitably invoked was long gone. A thank you letter from Gordon Brown enclosing a copy of the book said it all: 'To some extent it is unwieldy because it will not readily be apparent to the reader, that, for example, a study of industrial democracy or the origins of Scottish socialism is crucial to the present debate.'

Whatever Gramscian perspective there might have initially been was so feint as to be imperceptible. The revised purpose of the project was now capitalised to be made clear:

> you cannot study Scotland without looking at both the inequalities which disfigure present day society and the cultural and historical factors which have a bearing on the opportunities for the Labour movement to take up the challenge in Scotland today.

A handwritten postscript anticipated my reaction to the project's diminution to the service of 'Labour' and the high hopes for a platform with transformative potential:

> P.S. I don't know if you'll like it — I'm not sure about it on a whole but here it is!
> Best wishes,
> Gordon

Perhaps ill-health in the ranks had been an omen. There was no contribution from Hamish.

[104] G. Brown to R. Burnett, 3 July 1975.

The Rebel Underground of Folk

An eventful decade saw Hamish heavily involved in The Edinburgh Folk Conference of 1979, a painful but pivotal year for Scotland. The papers were subsequently published, and both Hamish's role and his own contribution are discussed by Tim Neat and Owen Dudley Edwards. It is fitting to conclude this essay on a note of harmony and agreement by readily concurring with both as to the importance and significance of the latter.[105] Hamish's key essay I have already referred to in its original *Scottish International* guise.[106] However, it is the shorter introductory essay that is an even finer, arguably the finest, exposition of his Gramscian approach.[107]

It is no accident that in his study on Hamish and Gramsci in relation to the folk tradition and the folk revival, Corey Gibson refers to this essay for evidence he rightly regards as important and illuminating in relation to Hamish's method in regard to his notion of 'Gramsci in action'. Commenting on the 'conspicuous absence' of any explicit reference to any of the familiar key Gramscian concepts in any of Henderson's writings, Gibson observes: 'Gramsci's influence on Henderson is, rather, coded into the texture of his work, and invested in his own referential frameworks.'[108]

In a contribution to an evening of 'Tribute to Hamish Henderson' in Edinburgh's Central Library in 2011 I made a similar point in regard to Hamish and Gramsci in the context of the appropriation of Gramsci within the academy. There were 'many Gramscis', I observed, across the road on the shelves of the National Library. Yet through several prolonged conversations on various aspects and issues of the subject, from the early '70s onwards, it had been very evident to me that as the avalanche of work on Gramsci cascaded out and the multiplicity proliferated, with a diversity of positions all laying claim to the legacy, Hamish had a good awareness of this growing fog of interpretations.

---

105 T. Neat, *op. cit.*, pp.317-318; O. D. Edwards, *op. cit.*, pp.158-159.

106 H. Henderson, 'The Ballad, the Folk and the Oral Tradition', E.J. Cowan (ed.), *The People's Past*, Edinburgh: EUSPB, 1979, pp. 69-107.

107 H. Henderson, '"It Was In You That It A' Began": Some Thoughts on the Folk Conference', in Cowan op. *cit.*, pp.4-16.

108 C. Gibson, *op.cit.*, p.253.

Ray Burnett at 'Tales of One City: A Tribute to Hamish Henderson', Edinburgh Central Library, 17 February 2011 <www.flickr.com/photos/talesofonecity/5616105027/in/set-72157626370903125>.

And, I suggested, there was a way to see through all this obfuscation. For us, at least, in relation to our own situation and future, deriving not least from his own personal engagement with Gramsci's life and times, the languages, culture, history and politics of Gramsci's Italy, the exposition of Gramsci's most illuminating theoretical concepts and methodology in relation to Scotland could be reduced and embodied in two coded words – 'Hamish Henderson'.

In his introductory essay to the published conference papers, Hamish ranges across historical place and period, songs and singers, writers and tradition-bearers, collectors and scholars to present his argument. The latter are drawn on as sources, support and exemplars in the presentation of an essay that is permeated with Gramscian notions of organic intellectuals, the subaltern, the national-popular, political resistance, insurgency, manoeuvre and war of position.[109] For, like Gramsci, his favourite field of exposition was history – oral tradition, popular culture and collective memory in relation to key social and political moments and events.

Apart from regarding it as the best example of Hamish's application of a Gramscian approach, Hamish's essay 'It Was in You that it a' Began' also has a special personal significance, an importance that relates directly to the point where I began – the May 1968 aspiration 'to build society anew', in our own specific place, by rooting that aspiration in the politics, history, culture and legacy of Scotland.

In an absorbing passage discussing the survival, or otherwise, of political song, Hamish refers to the crucial role of the collector, pointing to the distinct paucity of 'overtly' political songs, or anything remotely resembling the bawdy, in the Greig-Duncan Aberdeenshire collection, from which he flags up a fragment of a song from the French Revolutionary era:

> Viva la new convention
> Viva la Republican
> Viva la America
> For it was in you that it a' began.[110]

Hamish notes the song's links to the Irish street political ballad, 'Rouse Hibernians', celebrating the 'united heroes' of 1790s and the '98 Rising ':

> Erin's sons be not faint-hearted,
> Welcome, Sing then "Ça Ira".
> From Killala they are marching
> To the tune of "Viva la".[111]

---

109 For a lucid discussion of these 'many Gramscis', particularly with regard to his postcolonial appropriation and the need to go back to his life, times and original writings, see Timothy Brennan, 'The Southern Intellectual', in T. Brennan, *Wars of Position, The Cultural Politics of Left and Right*, New York: Columbia University Press, 2007, pp. 233-272.

110 A fragment he was alerted to by Emily Lyle, H. Henderson, *op. cit.*, p.10.

111 Georges Denis Zimmerman, *Songs of Irish Rebellion*, London: Folklore Associates, 1967.

And he provides further details revealing that its tune was of Scottish origin and that it was also used later by the Young Ireland poet Thomas Davis, for his stirring song 'Clare's Dragoons' on the Irish 'wild geese' who fought in France, which also has a 'viva la' chorus:

Viva la, the rose shall fade,
  And the shamrock shine for ever new.[112]

These songs and their links are introduced in the context of a notion of the folk tradition of which he argues that 'Folk – the "Folk" that matters – has always in fact something of the rebel underground about it,' a point he develops with particular regard to the range of political song and the enduring appeal of Jacobite song. It is a passage which impressed me then and impresses me still.[113]

I remember raising it a few years later, after a Scottish Assembly event in the old Royal High, and the most engaging long discussion that followed.[114] With the Calton Hill's monument to Thomas Muir and Scotland's 'Political Martyrs' etched on an Edinburgh sky and the 'auld toon' rising below from the Canongate to the Castle, I told Hamish that I thought his observations on this song had been really important and that for me they evoked the memory embedded in the Edinburgh landscape around us of the 1790s, the 'United Men' and the stirrings of political awareness in the town and across Scotland in that era.[115] It had reminded me of the other glimpses of these radical sentiments contained in Meikle, another of the sources Hamish had cited: the seal inscribed with '*Ça Ira*' that had contributed to Muir's conviction

---

[112] Patrick Galvin (ed.), *Irish Songs of Resistance*, London: Oak Publications, 1962.

[113] H. Henderson, 'It Was in You that it a' Began', in E. J. Cowan (ed.), *The People's Past*, Edinburgh: EUSPB/Polygon, 1980, pp.4-11.

[114] A thoughtful, 'listening-in', Angus Calder was also with us for part of the way on that happy and memorable meander through the city.

[115] For an account of this radical tradition within the Edinburgh landscape see R. Burnett, 'In the Shadow of Calton Hill', in E. Bort (ed.), *Commemorating Ireland: History, Politics, Cultuere*, Dublin: Irish Academic Press, 2004, pp.133-166.

and transportation at his infamous trial;[116] the popular crowd at the Edinburgh theatre who had drowned out the playing of the Hanoverian anthem with their revolutionary cries of '*Ça Ira*' and their 'rebel' singing of the Jacobite favourite, 'The Sow's Tail to Geordie';[117] the soldiers up in the Castle with their toast to 'George the II and last, and a damnation to all crown heads';[118] and the verse of Thomas the Rhymer that had circulated in all Scotland in 1794:

> A mild winter, a cold spring,
> A bloody summer, and no king.[119]

Along the way by 'the Bridges' and Chambers Street to Sandy Bell's or later, we shared our sense of common cause with that subaltern 'Embro' of James Connolly, his commemorations of the Year of '98 shortly after leaving his native city for Dublin and his celebrated early writings to the Belfast newspaper whose title evoked the old '98 song — the *Shan Van Vocht*:

> Oh the French are in the Bay,
> They'll be here by break of day
> And the Orange will decay,
> Says the Shan Van Vocht.[120]

We were recalling and dwelling on a sense of empathy that at times was almost palpable in that part of town with the ties and aspirations of that area when the delegates of the United Irishmen returned to Belfast from Edinburgh and raised a toast to 'Mr Muir' and to: 'the swine of England, the rabble of Scotland, and the wretches of Ireland.'[121] Songs of that era were certainly amongst Hamish's favourites, from those like 'Henry Joy

---

[116] H. W. Meikle, *Scotland and the French Revolution*, Edinburgh, 1912, (reprint London: Routledge, 1970), p.133.

[117] *Ibid.*, p.147. For 'The Sow's Tail to Geordie', see G. S. MacQuoid (ed.), *Jacobite Songs and Ballads*, London: Walter Scott (The Canterbury Poets edition), 1884, pp.62-63.

[118] *Ibid.*, p.113.

[119] *Ibid.*, p.147.

[120] Galvin, *op. cit.*

[121] Meikle, *op. cit.*, p.140, fn.1.

McCracken' commemorating the Protestant United Irishmen of Antrim and Belfast in the North to those of the rising in Wexford and Fr. Murphy's 'Boolavogue' in the West.[122]

Hamish's essay and its stirring of the memory of all these songs also struck a personal chord. As a young lad in the Edinburgh of the 'sixties, songs like 'Clare's Dragoons' and the 'Shan Van Vocht' were alongside 'Killiecrankie', or 'Sic a Parcel of Rogues' as part of the repertoire. We sang them, not because they (or we) were Irish, but because they were 'rebel', along with the other 'rebels' in our received Scottish/British history – the Jacobites. So we sang their songs as well. For my part they were all components of the 'live elements of the Scottish radical, cultural and political tradition' that Gordon Brown had identified as a core element of the Scotland that his *Red Paper* of 1975 was to foreground and explore.

But there was also a strong feeling of personal connection to that tradition. Hamish's essay had brought it out vividly in its awakening of the subaltern culture of the Edinburgh of my mother's family in the Cowgate of Connolly, and that of the Aberdeenshire of my father's family and the farmland chiels of Buchan. Recollecting all these conversations and sessions, it is clear that it was through Hamish that the felt experience and the nascent ideas of that residual culture gained meaning, intellectual validity, direction and purpose. And it was through Hamish that the sort of discourse I had been tentatively advocating in May 1968, and taken the first faltering steps toward in the Aberdeen Teach-In of 1970, and subsequent projects, through 7:84 and other channels promoting awareness of our radical history and culture, could be seen as small, modest contributions to the emergent and challenging culture of the present. To appropriate one of Hamish's own creations in application to himself, and adding my own personal chorus to the 'viva la' tradition:

> Viva la Gillie More
> *It was in you that it a' began.*[123]

---

[122] For the version of 'Henry Joy McCracken' as sung by Dick Gaughan, see: <www.dickgaughan.co.uk/songs/texts/henryjoy.html>; for the version of 'Boolavogue' as sung by Luke Kelly and the Dubliners, see *The Dubliners Songbook*, Dublin: Heathside Music, 1974.

[123] For Hamish's 'Song of the Gillie More' see H. Henderson, *Collected Poems and Songs*, pp.137-138.

O horo the Gillie More
Here's a weld'll wear for ever
Oor grup they canna sever
O horo the Gillie More
Ane's the wish yokes us thegither
Ane's the darg that lies afore
You an' me the man the brither!
Me an' you the Gillie More.

Hamish Henderson, 'Song of the Gillie More' (Jan Miller, 2015)

Hamish and Madiba: Hamish Henderson, Nelson Mandela, and the Fight Against Apartheid in South Africa

Eberhard Bort

They have sentenced the men of Rivonia
Rumbala rumbala rumba la
The comrades of Nelson Mandela
Rumbala rumbala rumba la
He is buried alive on an island
Free Mandela Free Mandela
He is buried alive on an island
Free Mandela Free Mandela[1]

2013: EUL Acquisition of Hamish Henderson Archive

On 7 August, a public announcement was made at the Edinburgh University Library that the Library had purchased the Hamish Henderson Archive which was now to be curated by the University Library and made available for *bona fide* researchers.[2] That was great news. Not only does that collection contain over 10,000 letters, there are also notebooks, diaries, newspaper cuttings, and other materials which will be

---

[1] It was an honour and a pleasure to be invited to speak about Hamish Henderson and Nelson Mandela at the 2013 People's Festival in Edinburgh – a festival once founded by Hamish Henderson and now organised in his memory. This is the edited version of the Edinburgh People's Festival Hamish Henderson Memorial Lecture, given at Word Power Books on Wednesday, 7 August 2013, the day Edinburgh University Library announced its acquisition of the Hamish Henderson Archive. Hamish Henderson, 'Rivonia', in *Collected Poems and Songs*, edited by Raymond Ross, Edinburgh: Curly Snake, 2000, pp.150-51.

[2] Brian Ferguson, 'Edinburgh university buys Hamish Henderson Archive', *The Scotsman*, 8. August 2013.

a fantastic resource for people who are studying the life and work of Hamish Henderson (1919-2002), his poetry, his work in the School of Scottish Studies and in the field as a collector of songs, ballads and stories, as well as his political campaigns. It offers a tremendous opportunity for all who are interested in the contemporary history of Scotland.

Steve Byrne, the convener of the Hamish Henderson Archive Trust, is to be commended for facilitating the negotiations between the Library and the Henderson family – it resulted in a splendid outcome, which was also visualised in an exhibition at Edinburgh University Library – and all who made it possible must be congratulated on their achievement!

When Nelson Mandela died last December, it was astonishing that in all the acres of print which commemorated the life, work and legacy of this most extraordinary of statesmen, no one seemed to make the connection, at the UK or at the Scottish level, between Mandela and Hamish Henderson. 2014 was the fiftieth anniversary of the Rivionia trial, which prompted Hamish to write 'The Men of Rivonia'. It was, as far as I could make out, not mentioned in any of the accounts and appreciations.[3]

1993: 'Mandela Danced in the Square'

Three years after his release from prison in 1990, Mandela came to Glasgow to collect his Freedom of the City – which Glasgow had bestowed on him in 1981, the first city in the world to do so, against a lot of opposition. On 9 October 1993, Mandela was in Glasgow to thank the people of the city for the honour and their role in supporting the fight against apartheid. During the visit, the man who would become South Africa's first black president a year later, Nelson Mandela received not just the Freedom of the City of Glasgow, but also of a further eight municipalities of the UK – Aberdeen, Dundee, Midlothian, Hull, Sheffield, Greenwich, Islwyn and Newcastle. And he spoke to a crowd of around 10,000 people in George Square. He told them:

---

3 Only David Calder in the online *Caledonian Mercury* (6 Dec 2013) used Hamish's 'The Freedom Come-All-Ye' in his short celebration 'RIP Nelson Mandela – Freeman of Glasgow' <http://caledonianmercury.com/2013/12/06/nelson-mandela-freeman-of-glasgow/0043502>.

> The people of Glasgow were the first in the world to confer on me the Freedom of the City at a time when I and my comrades in the ANC were imprisoned on Robben Island serving life sentences which, in apartheid South Africa, then meant imprisonment until death.[4]

In his acceptance speech in the splendour of the Banqueting Hall of the City Chambers, Mandela said:

> Whilst we were physically denied our freedom in the country or our birth, a city 6000 miles away, and as renowned as Glasgow, refused to accept the legitimacy of the apartheid system and declared us to be free.'[5]

On that day, Hamish Henderson was in Glasgow, invited by the ANC. From a stage erected in George Square, Hamish sang 'Rivonia', written 29 years earlier, one of the first of about 200 songs worldwide about Nelson Mandela.[6]

In the City Chambers, after the ceremony attended by 400 guests, there was a reception, where the chief anti-apartheid campaigner Brian Filling – now Honorary Consul of South Africa – introduced Hamish Henderson to Nelson Mandela. They embraced fondly. That was the only ever meeting between these two remarkable personalities.

Arnold Rattenbury, when reviewing Hamish Henderson's *Collected Poems and Songs* for the *London Review of Books*, said that 'around such a figure myth and legend quite naturally swirled and, sometimes with his own help, stuck.'[7] So, Timothy Neat and I have written about Hamish and Mandela appearing together

---

[4] 'Nelson Mandela's memorable 1993 visit to Scotland', *STV News*, 18 July, 2008, <http://news.stv.tv/scotland/30271-nelson-mandelas-memorable-1993-visit-to-scotland/>.

[5] David Pratt, 'Inside Track: Scotland and Mandela ... a real cause for pride', *The* Herald, 10 July 2013.

[6] Ian Walker remembers that Eurydice, the Glasgow Women's Socialist Choir, sang his anti-apartheid song 'Hawks and Eagles' while sharing a stage with Mandela on that memorable Glasgow occasion – in conversation with the author, 21 August 2013.

[7] Arnold Rattenbury, 'Flytings', *London Review of Books*, Vol. 25 No. 2, 23 January 2003, pp. 26-28.

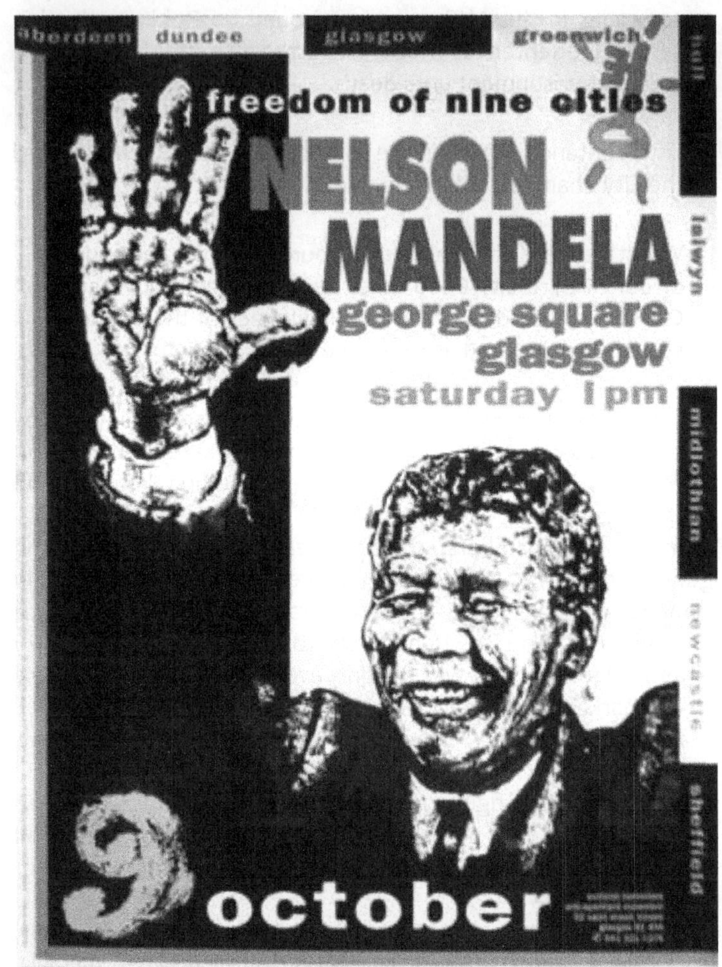

Poster for Glasgow Rally on 9 October 1993

on the balcony of the City Chambers, when, as Brian Filling tells me, Hamish never actually was on that balcony. Memory can play tricks, particularly when larger than life characters like Hamish Henderson are invoked.

'Mr Mandela's freedom of the city was a hard won battle,' as the journalist and prominent Scottish anti-apartheid activist David Pratt recalls

> that had its heroes and villains both close to home and far overseas. It was when Glasgow Lord Provost, David Hodge, hosted a controversial lunch for the South African ambassador Matthys Botha in September 1978 that the level of activism across Scotland really began to hot up.
>
> In the years that followed Glasgow's Conservative group remained among the most vociferous opponents of the Anti-Apartheid Movement, consistently trying to block the city's association with Mr Mandela and the African National Congress (ANC).
>
> Undeterred, Scotland on the mainstream level of boycotts, pickets, rallies, concerts and calls for sanctions threw itself behind the anti-apartheid cause. Much less widely known, however, was the role played by Scottish activists within a covert movement.
>
> Ordinary Scots acted as couriers, procured documents, established safe houses in Glasgow for those ANC activists in exile; some were even involved with arms smuggling to the ANC in South Africa.[8]

Denis Goldberg, a fellow Rivonia trialist of Mandela who served more than 22 years in an apartheid prison before later coming to Scotland after his release in 1985, added:

> These were Scots, quite heroic young people who went in and out of South Africa delivering documentation, delivering money... they played a role which showed the essential humanism of human beings who are going to help others.[9]

---

[8] David Pratt, 'Inside Track: Scotland and Mandela ... a real cause for pride', *The Herald*, 10 July 2013.

[9] *Ibid.*

Mandela's visit to Glasgow has been amply commemorated. Ian Davison was inspired to write his African Calypso song 'Mandela Danced in the Square':

> We'd sung about him for years,
> And there were speeches everywhere.
> But I'll never forget the cheers,
> When Mandela danced in the square.[10]

And Blair Douglas composed the mighty tune 'Nelson Mandela's Welcome to the City of Glasgow' in honour of the occasion – it can be found on his album 'A Summer in Skye'. Simple Minds' rather syrupy 'Mandela Day' was preferred by STV for their commemorative collage to Hamish's 'Rivonia'.

1947: The Royal Tour

So, Hamish and Nelson Mandela met in 1993 – the year Mandela received the Peace Nobel Prize. But Hamish's involvement in the struggle against apartheid goes back much further. The plight of the Black people in South Africa under Apartheid was a life-long concern of Hamish Henderson. In 1947 he protested against the Royal Tour of South Africa, when the King extolled South Africa 'as giving an example to the world in harmonious living together of diverse peoples'. Hamish countered in a speech for the Highland Independence Party published in *Voice of Scotland*: 'The fact of the matter is that there is no place on earth where the back people are worse treated.' He also lamented the fact that only one Scottish MP – William Gallagher, Communist MP for West Fife – had protested against the tour of the King, Queen and Princesses.[11]

Hamish's opposition to apartheid was rooted in his World War II experience. During the Alamein campaign he had been attached to the 1st South African Division. Hailing their bravery, he said (in a letter to the *Scotsman*):

---

[10] <https://myspace.com/iandavisonsongs/music/song/mandela-danced-2618291>.

[11] Quoted in Timothy Neat, *Hamish Henderson: A Biography*, Vol.1, *The Making of the Poet* (1919-1953, Edinburgh: Birlinn/Polygon, 2007, pp.195-96.)

> There was no question of apartheid on the battlefield. The South Africans were glad enough to have the support of the 4th Indian Division on their left flank on the night of 23 October 1942! And I never heard any objections, either from Springbok or Pommie, to the presence on our side of the New Zealanders' Maori battalion under its half-Maori CO, Fred Baker.[12]

That was written in 1969, and Hamish notes that the then Prime Minister of South Africa was at the time of Alamein interned as a Nazi sympathiser. Along with 'a prize assortment of malignant racialist crackpots, the ideologues and political strategists of the Broederbund, the secret society that now effectively runs South Africa.'[13]

In 1960, Hamish wrote 'The Freedom Come-All-Ye', with the lines

> Black an white ane-til-ither mairriet
> Mak the vile barracks o thair maisters bare

And

> An yon black boy frae yont Nyanga
> Dings the fell gallows o the burghers doun.[14]

That was not a reference to Mandela, as Hamish confirmed, but to the township of Nyanga, one of the oldest and poorest black townships in the Cape Town area, and in the media at that time as one of the hot spots of anti-apartheid protests.[15]

In 1960, there was also the Sharpeville Massacre. On 21 March 1960, at the police station in the South African township of Sharpeville in the Transvaal, South African police opened fire

---

[12] Hamish Henderson, *The Armstrong Nose: The Letters of Hamish Henderson*, edited by Alec Finlay, Edinburgh: Polygon, 1996, p.183.

[13] *Ibid.*

[14] Hamish Henderson, *Collected Poems and Songs*, edited by Raymond Ross, Edinburgh: Curly Snake, 2000, p.143.

[15] I think that Hamish knew that Nyanga means moon in Xhosa, and that 'the black boy frae yont Nyanga' could be read as the man from beyond the moon.

on a crowd of about 5,000 to 7,000 black protesters, killing 69 unarmed people. The government declared a state of emergency – and outlawed the ANC.[16]

1964: Rivonia

On 11 June 1963, on the Liliesleaf farmstead of Rivonia, near Johannesburg, a police raid yielded eight suspected leaders of Umkhonto we Sizwe (Spear of the Nation), the 'militant wing' of the ANC, founded in 1961 as a departure from the non-violent history of the ANC: Denis Goldberg, Rusty Bernstein, Raymond Mhlaba, Bob Hepple, Govan Mbeki, Arthur Goldreich, Ahmed Kathrada, and the man the police considered their prize catch of the day, ANC leader Walter Sisulu. Mandela himself was at that time already in a Pretoria jail, serving a five-year prison term for leaving the country without a passport and inciting a strike. They were arrested and charged with treason, potentially facing the death penalty. In the 'Rivonia Trial' (1963-64), eleven leaders of the ANC (sometimes called the 'Rivonia 11'), including Mandela, were tried for conspiracy and 235 acts of sabotage.[17]

On 20 April 1964 – standing in the dock at the Palace of Justice in Pretoria, Nelson Mandela delivered his famous 'speech from the dock'. In a quiet voice, he laid out his arguments for four hours. He began by telling the story of his life and the reasons why he joined the struggle for racial equality, the history of the ANC, how he gradually arrived at the conclusion that non-violent protest must give way to more violent approaches if the goals of a multi-racial democracy in South Africa were ever to be achieved:

> we believed that as a result of Government policy, violence by the African people had become inevitable, and that unless responsible leadership was given to canalise and control the feelings of our people, there would be outbreaks of terrorism which would produce an intensity of bitterness and hostility between the various races of this country which is not produced even by war. Secondly, we felt that

[16] See Tom Lodge, *Sharpeville: a massacre and its consequences*. Oxford: Oxford University Press 2011.

[17] Douglas O. Linder, 'The Nelson Mandela (Rivonia) Trial', 2010, <http://law2.umkc.edu/faculty/projects/ftrials/mandela/mandelaaccount.html>.

> without violence there would be no way open to the African people to succeed in their struggle against the principle of white supremacy. All lawful modes of expressing opposition to this principle had been closed by legislation, and we were placed in a position in which we had either to accept a permanent state of inferiority, or to defy the Government. We chose to defy the law. We first broke the law in a way which avoided any recourse to violence; when this form was legislated against, and then the Government resorted to a show of force to crush opposition to its policies, only then did we decide to answer violence with violence.
>
> But the violence which we chose to adopt was not terrorism. We who formed Umkhonto were all members of the African National Congress, and had behind us the ANC tradition of non-violence and negotiation as a means of solving political disputes. We believe that South Africa belongs to all the people who live in it, and not to one group, be it black or white. We did not want an interracial war, and tried to avoid it to the last minute.[18]

He points out that, even in the face of widespread violence against the black population, the ANC stuck with its policy of non-violence. Only in 1949 did it endorse unlawful demonstrations, until then it had been strictly constitutional. But it remained committed to non-violence. The turning-point came in 1960:

> In 1960 there was the shooting at Sharpeville, which resulted in the proclamation of a state of emergency and the declaration of the ANC as an unlawful organisation. My colleagues and I, after careful consideration, decided that we would not obey this decree. The African people were not part of the Government and did not make the laws by which they were governed. We believed in the words of the Universal Declaration of Human Rights, that 'the will of the people shall be the basis of authority of the Government', and for us to accept the banning was equivalent to accepting the silencing of the Africans for all time. The ANC refused

[18] Nelson Mandela, 'Statement from the dock at the opening of the defence case in the Rivonia Trial', 20 April 1964, <www.anc.org.za/show.php?id=3430>.

> to dissolve, but instead went underground. We believed it was our duty to preserve this organisation which had been built up with almost fifty years of unremitting toil. I have no doubt that no self-respecting White political organisation would disband itself if declared illegal by a government in which it had no say.
>
> In 1960 the Government held a referendum which led to the establishment of the Republic. Africans, who constituted approximately 70 per cent of the population of South Africa, were not entitled to vote, and were not even consulted about the proposed constitutional change.[19]

Umkhonto we Sizwe was formed in November 1961. Mandela was imprisoned in 1962 but, as he states in his speech, the dominant idea at the time of the Rivonia raid remained 'that loss of life should be avoided'. When Umkhonto was formed,

> the ANC heritage of non-violence and racial harmony was very much with us. We felt that the country was drifting towards a civil war in which Blacks and Whites would fight each other. We viewed the situation with alarm. Civil war could mean the destruction of what the ANC stood for; with civil war, racial peace would be more difficult than ever to achieve.[20]

He then sets out the thinking behind Umkhonto:

> Four forms of violence were possible. There is sabotage, there is guerrilla warfare, there is terrorism, and there is open revolution. We chose to adopt the first method and to exhaust it before taking any other decision.
>
> In the light of our political background the choice was a logical one. Sabotage did not involve loss of life, and it offered the best hope for future race relations. Bitterness would be kept to a minimum and, if the policy bore fruit, democratic government could become a reality.[21]

---

[19] *Ibid.*

[20] *Ibid.*

[21] *Ibid.*

> The decision and 'initial plan', he continues, were based on a careful analysis of the political and economic situation of our country. We believed that South Africa depended to a large extent on foreign capital and foreign trade. We felt that planned destruction of power plants, and interference with rail and telephone communications, would tend to scare away capital from the country, make it more difficult for goods from the industrial areas to reach the seaports on schedule, and would in the long run be a heavy drain on the economic life of the country, thus compelling the voters of the country to reconsider their position.
>
> Attacks on the economic life lines of the country were to be linked with sabotage on Government buildings and other symbols of apartheid. These attacks would serve as a source of inspiration to our people. In addition, they would provide an outlet for those people who were urging the adoption of violent methods and would enable us to give concrete proof to our followers that we had adopted a stronger line and were fighting back against Government violence.
>
> In addition, if mass action were successfully organised, and mass reprisals taken, we felt that sympathy for our cause would be roused in other countries, and that greater pressure would be brought to bear on the South African Government.
>
> This then was the plan. Umkhonto was to perform sabotage, and strict instructions were given to its members right from the start, that on no account were they to injure or kill people in planning or carrying out operations.[22]

Then, Mandela gives a detailed history of the activities of Umkhonto, and his involvement in them, followed by a rebuttal of accusations that the ideology of the ANC was dominated by the Communist Party, explaining that co-operation with the Communists was down to 'a common goal – in this case the removal of white supremacy – and ... not proof of a complete community of interests.'[23] He then defines his own position as an 'African patriot':

---

[22] *Ibid.*

[23] *Ibid.*

> I am attracted by the idea of a classless society, an attraction which springs in part from Marxist reading and, in part, from my admiration of the structure and organization of early African societies in this country. The land, then the main means of production, belonged to the tribe. There were no rich or poor and there was no exploitation.
>
> It is true, as I have already stated, that I have been influenced by Marxist thought. But this is also true of many of the leaders of the new independent States. Such widely different persons as Gandhi, Nehru, Nkrumah, and Nasser all acknowledge this fact. We all accept the need for some form of socialism to enable our people to catch up with the advanced countries of this world and to overcome their legacy of extreme poverty.[24]

And he expresses his admiration for Western democracy:

> From my reading of Marxist literature and from conversations with Marxists, I have gained the impression that communists regard the parliamentary system of the West as undemocratic and reactionary. But, on the contrary, I am an admirer of such a system.
>
> The Magna Carta, the Petition of Rights, and the Bill of Rights are documents which are held in veneration by democrats throughout the world.
>
> I have great respect for British political institutions, and for the country's system of justice. I regard the British Parliament as the most democratic institution in the world, and the independence and impartiality of its judiciary never fail to arouse my admiration.[25]

Finishing his speech, Mandela gets to the core of what the struggle was all about: equality in South Africa:

> Africans want to be paid a living wage. Africans want to perform work which they are capable of doing, and not work which the Government declares them to be capable of. Africans want to be allowed to live where they obtain work,

[24] *Ibid.*

[25] *Ibid.*

> and not be endorsed out of an area because they were not born there. Africans want to be allowed to own land in places where they work, and not to be obliged to live in rented houses which they can never call their own. Africans want to be part of the general population, and not confined to living in their own ghettoes. African men want to have their wives and children to live with them where they work, and not be forced into an unnatural existence in men's hostels. African women want to be with their menfolk and not be left permanently widowed in the Reserves. Africans want to be allowed out after eleven o`clock at night and not to be confined to their rooms like little children. Africans want to be allowed to travel in their own country and to seek work where they want to and not where the Labour Bureau tells them to. Africans want a just share in the whole of South Africa; they want security and a stake in society.
>
> Above all, we want equal political rights, because without them our disabilities will be permanent. I know this sounds revolutionary to the whites in this country, because the majority of voters will be Africans. This makes the white man fear democracy.
>
> But this fear cannot be allowed to stand in the way of the only solution which will guarantee racial harmony and freedom for all. It is not true that the enfranchisement of all will result in racial domination. Political division, based on colour, is entirely artificial and, when it disappears, so will the domination of one colour group by another. The ANC has spent half a century fighting against racialism. When it triumphs it will not change that policy.[26]

He sums it up in his final few sentences:

> This then is what the ANC is fighting. Their struggle is a truly national one. It is a struggle of the African people, inspired by their own suffering and their own experience. It is a struggle for the right to live.
>
> During my lifetime I have dedicated myself to this struggle of the African people. I have fought against white domination, and I have fought against black domination. I have cherished the ideal of a democratic and free society in

[26] *Ibid.*

> which all persons live together in harmony and with equal opportunities. It is an ideal which I hope to live for and to achieve. But if needs be, it is an ideal for which I am prepared to die.[27]

In *The Long Walk to Freedom*, Mandela cast his mind back to the moment he sat in that Pretoria courtroom: 'The silence seemed to stretch for many minutes. But in fact it lasted probably no more than thirty seconds, and then from the gallery I heard what sounded like a great sigh, a deep, collective 'ummmm,' followed by the cries of women.'[28] On 4 June 1964, 'the men of Rivonia' were sentenced to life imprisonment. Nelson Mandela would spend the next eighteen years in a prison on Robben Island, just off Cape Town.

Hamish was hugely impressed by Mandela's speech. And his song 'The Men of Rivonia' came together very quickly. He used the tune of the Spanish republican Civil War song 'Viva la Quince Brigada' with its refrain 'Rumbala, rumbala, rumba-la' – which reminded him of African drums.[29] He sang it first in Athens at a conference, then in the pubs and clubs closer to home; Dolina Mclennan sang it in Edinburgh's Waverley Bar – and by September 1964 Pete Seeger had taken it up across in America.

Hamish sent the song to the ANC office in London. And Raymond Kunene acknowledged it – 'greatly appreciated' on 13 October[30] – It was published in America, in Italy, in the British folk magazine *Sing*. He had Roy Williamson and Ronnie Brown of the Corries record it, and sent several copies of the recording to Kunene.[31] On 22 January, Hamish received a much more enthusiastic letter from

[27] *Ibid.* Lord Provost Michael Kelly quoted this last paragraph at the Freedom of the City award ceremony of 4 August 1981, adding: 'It is for this idealism that Mandela is awarded the Freedom of Glasgow.' Quoted in Brian Filling, 'Nelson Mandela and the Freedom of Scotland's Cities', in Brian Filling and Susan Stuart (eds), *The End of a Regime? An Anthology of Scottish-South African Writing Against Apartheid*, Aberdeen: Aberdeen University Press, 1991, p.295.

[28] Nelson Mandela, *The Long Walk to Freedom*, p. 354.

[29] Timothy Neat, Hamish *Henderson: A Biography, Vol.2, Poetry Becomes People*, 1952-2002, Edinburgh: Birlinn/Polygon, 2009, p.188.

[30] *Ibid*, p. 190.

[31] Hamish Henderson, 'Rivonia', in Brian Filling and Susan Stuart (eds), *The End of a Regime?*, p.281.

Raymond Kunene, after the song had been forwarded to the ANC headquarters in Dar es Salaam – reporting there were 'ecstatic comments from all the friends there'.[32] It spent five months in the Tanzanian hit parade. And it reached as far as Robben Island where Nelson Mandela heard it. As well as the Corries, the South African group Atté recorded it. And it is sung to the very day, by the likes of Arthur Johnstone and Geordie McIntyre.

Brian Filling tells me that Hamish was rather surprised when he introduced him to Denis Goldberg – who is name checked in the song:

> Verwoerd feared the mind of Mandela
> Rumbala rumbala rumba la
> He was stifling the voice of Mandela
> Rumbala rumbal rumba la
> Free Mbeki Goldberg Sisulu
> Free Mandela Free Mandela
> Free Mbeki Goldberg Sisulu
> Free Mandela Free Mandela[33]

Hamish had apparently thought that 'The Men of Rivonia' were all black freedom fighters. But Goldberg was white – and imprisoned in a separate prison from the others until his release in 1985.[34] Apart from Goldberg, Lionel Bernstein, Bob Hepple, Harold Wolpe, James Kantor and the owner of the farm, Arthur Goldreich, also were white Jews.

> The crime of the men of Rivonia
> Rumbala rumbala rumba la
> Was to organize farmer and miner
> Rumbala rumbala rumba la

---

[32] *Tim Neat, vol.2, p.191.*

[33] Hamish Henderson, *Collected Poems and Songs*, pp.150-51.

[34] Was that why Goldberg, in his 2011 Mandela-Tambo lecture in Glasgow – in which he praised Hamish as the 'Workers' Poet Laureate' and gave a full translation of 'The Freedom Come-All-Ye" (including a mild rebuke for Hamish's use of the colonial 'black boy') – did not even mention 'Rivonia'? Maybe he felt, somehow, that it was not written for him, despite the reference to his name? Or maybe he was just too modest and did not want to draw attention to the fact that Hamish had written a song that mentions his name?

Against baaskap and sjambok and keerie
Free Mandela Free Mandela
Against baaskap and sjambok and keerie
Free Mandela Free Mandela[35]

Nelson Mandela was kept prisoner on Robben Island, where he worked in a lime quarry and was allowed one letter and one visitor every six months, until 1982, when the authorities transferred him and four other Rivonia trialists (Sisulu, Mlangeni, Mhlaba, and Kathrada) to Pollsmoor Prison in suburban Cape Town. Douglas O. Linder sums up the rest of the Rivonia story – the trial that changed South Africa:

> The winds of change began to sweep South Africa in 1985. Denis Goldberg became the first of the Rivonia defendants to be released from prison. President P. W. Botha offered Mandela a deal: renounce violence and be freed. Mandela refused the offer: 'Only free men can negotiate--a prisoner cannot enter into contracts.' In November of 1985, the National Party government entered into secret negotiations with Mandela for what, it was hoped, might be an eventual transition to a multi-racial government.
>
> By the beginning of 1990, only Mandela among the Rivonia defendants remained imprisoned, now at a bungalow in Victor Verster prison where he continued his secret negotiations. In February 1990, President F. W. de Klerk announced the release of Nelson Mandela. The next year, Mandela was elected president of the ANC.
>
> In April 1994, South Africans of all races went to the polls. The ANC won 62% of the vote and on May 10, Nelson Mandela took the oath of office as the first black President of South Africa.[36]

Set free the men of Rivonia
Rumbala rumbala rumba la
Break down the walls of their prison
Rumbala rumbala rumba la
Freedom and justice Uhuru

---

[35] *Collected Poems and Songs*, p.150-51.

[36] Linder, art.cit.

Free Mandela Free Mandela
Freedom and justice Uhuru
Free Mandela Free Mandela[37]

1969: Battle of Murrayfield

The anti-apartheid movement in South Africa's strategy of internal sabotage was matched by efforts of boycott externally. In response to an appeal by Albert Luthuli, the 'Boycott Movement' was founded in London on 26 June 1959 at a meeting of South African exiles and their supporters – under the leadership of Archbishop Trevor Huddleston.[38] Its purpose was explained by Julius Nyere:

> We are not asking you, the British people, for anything special. We are just asking you to withdraw your support from apartheid by not buying South African goods.[39]

The movement attracted widespread support from students, trade unions and the Labour, Liberal and Communist parties. On 28 February 1960, it launched a 'March Month, Boycott Action' at a rally in Trafalgar Square. After Sharpeville, the organisation changed its name to the 'Anti-Apartheid Movement'. At that time, the UK was South Africa's largest foreign investor, and South Africa was the UK's third biggest export market. [40]

South Africa was forced to leave the Commonwealth in 1961. A year later the United Nations General Assembly passed a resolution calling on all member states to impose a trade boycott

[37] *Collected Poems and Songs*, pp.150-51.

[38] Brian Filling, 'Nelson Mandela and the Freedom of Scotland's Cities', in Brian Filling and Susan Stuart (eds), *The End of a Regime?*, p.294.

[39] Abdul Minty, 'The Anti-Apartheid Movement – what kind of history?', *South African History Online*, <www.sahistory.org.za/archive/anti-apartheid-movement-what-kind-history>.

[40] Christabel Gurney, '"A Great Cause": The Origins of the Anti-Apartheid Movement, June 1959-March 1960', *Journal of Southern African Studies*, Vol.26, No.1 (March 2000), pp.123-144.

against South Africa. In 1964, South Africa was suspended from the Tokyo Olympic Games.

The anti-apartheid campaign became an issue in the 1964 UK General Election. But the disappointment was palpable when the newly elected Labour government under Harold Wilson rejected trade sanctions.[41]

In Scotland, there were branches supporting the anti-apartheid movement throughout the 1960s and '70s in Glasgow and Edinburgh.

> The Committee was formally established in 1976 as the Scottish Committee of the Anti Apartheid Movement and the minutes begin from 8 May 1976. It had a certain degree of autonomy within the UK structure. Brian Filling remained in the Chair and John Nelson remained Secretary of this Scottish Committee for its complete existence and went on to hold the same positions in Action for Southern Africa, ACTSA, Scotland. After the elections on 27 April 1994 and the victory of the ANC and Nelson Mandela, apartheid came to an end. The last Annual General Meeting of the Scottish Committee took place on 3 December 1994 when it was dissolved and its assets transferred to the Scottish Committee of Action for South Africa (ACTSA).[42]

The British and Scottish campaign came to a boil anent the Springbok Rugby Union Tour of late 1969. The protests were organised UK-wide under the leadership of Peter Hain and his fellow anti-apartheid campaigners. They generated a lot of publicity, and Hain became known as 'Hain the Pain', as his ploys, including pitch invasions, lobbing orange smoke bombs and even gluing the locks of the players' hotel rooms, began to bite. In Edinburgh, Gordon Brown signed responsible as the campaign's local organiser.[43]These militant demonstrations of 1969-70 against the Springbok tour 'sounded the death-knell for major sporting

---

[41] Roger Fieldhouse, *Anti-Apartheid: a history of the movement in Britain*, Pontypool: The Merlin Press, 2004.

[42] Carole McCallum, 'Anti-Apartheid Movement in Scotland Archive', Glasgow Caledonian University Archives, 2009, <www.gcu.ac.uk/archives/aams/>.

[43] See Peter Hain, *Outside In*, London: Biteback Publishing, 2012.

links between Britain and South Africa.'[44] Hamish Henderson was involved – to a degree – in what would become known as 'the battle of Murrayfield'.

Here is his own vivid description of the event, as given to his biographer Timothy Neat: After a few hours in Sandy Bell's, he says:

> We set off late. And with the crowds we got delayed! So, I arrived at the gates of Murrayfield at one minute to three. Everybody else was in the ground – so the stewards, seeing this tall, rugby-looking gent shambling towards them, waved me on straight through the gate and I just kept going. Suddenly there I was – with the whole arena before me – and the first bars of 'God Save the Queen' were sounding. That was our signal for the pitch invasion! Barricades of sleepers had been erected all round the pitch, with sandbag platforms on the inside – so that the defending police could hammer-down anyone attempting to leap or climb over. My God, forget the Queen, I thought, I'm at the barricades, and on I went! Being tall, I gave the police an advantage – they only had to aim a loose kick and get me in the head! So first in first out, I was pole-axed and slumped at the base of the barricade. This was just as all the other protesters surged forward. Naturally they climbed over us early casualties and soon enough there I was at the bottom of the pile. With the weight of the bodies I felt I was losing consciousness and this single thought came into my head: 'This is it! I'm going to die – for this great human cause!' A feeling of exhilaration swept through me. I hoped to shout 'Victory for the ANC!' before I died, but I was content – I felt my life hadn't been lived in vain.[45]

Before he knows what's happening, he finds himself outside the stadium, clearly miffed at not being arrested.

Great story. But is it true? Raymond Ross remembers having met Hamish first in late November 1969 in the Meadow Bar:

---

[44] Mike Terry, 'The British Anti-Apartheid Movement: 30 Years of Boycotting', *South African History* Online, 1989, <www.sahistory.org.za/archive/british-anti-apartheid-movement-30-years-boycotting>.

[45] Timothy Neat, *Hamish Henderson: A Biography*, Vol.2, p.192.

'We're in the "Mildew" to help organise, in our own wee way, the Anti-Apartheid Demo that December at Murrayfield...' But he then goes on:

> I don't think Hamish actually makes the Murrayfield rammy or the 'illegal' march back along Princes Street to demo outside the High Street Polis Station do demand the released of those arrested.[46]

Ray Ross said he had written this from memory, but confirmed he had not spotted Hamish at Murrayfield.[47] On the other hand, there were quite a few protesters, and even a prominent figure like Hamish might have slipped Ray's observant eye.

Where we have corroborated evidence is what followed. Later in the evening, no doubt after a few refreshments in Bell's, Hamish and Stewart McLennan, Robert Waugh and A H Caldwell protested at the High Street police office. They were told to move, but refused, and were, eventually, bundled into a cell. They were released the next morning, pending trial. In January, they were all fined £30 each for 'causing an obstruction outside Edinburgh City Police Station after the Scotland South African rugby international.'[48] The poet Helen B Cruickshank, fearing that the fine would eat into Kätzel's housekeeping money, sent a – no doubt welcome – sub, to be 'spent on the family.'[49]

Margaret Thatcher and Ronald Reagan, fierce in their belief in Free Trade, were adamantly opposed to sanctions. And they saw South Africa as a bulwark against communism.[50] In 1987, Margaret Thatcher called the ANC "a typical terrorist organisation", and her spokesman Bernard Ingham said, whoever believed that the ANC

---

[46] Raymond Ross, 'Hamish: the Tombstone and the Halo', in Steve Byrne (ed.), *The Hamish Henderson Papers: A Commemorative Collection of Essays*, Edinburgh: The Hamish Henderson Archive Trust, 2013, pp.53-61; p.58.

[47] Raymond Ross, in conversation with the author, 7 August 2013.

[48] *Edinburgh Evening News*, 29 January 1970, quoted in Timothy Neat, *Hamish Henderson: A Biography*, Vol.2, p. 194.

[49] Quoted in Timothy Neat, *Hamish Henderson: A Biography*, Vol.2, p.194.

[50] Josh Brooman and Martin Roberts, *South Africa 1948-1994: the Rise and Fall of Apartheid: The Rise and Fall of Apartheid*, London: Longman, (3rd ed.) 2001, p. 102.

would overthrow the South African government lived in 'cloud-cuckoo land.'[51] But both Thatcher and Reagan kept communicative channels open, and repeatedly demanded the release of Nelson Mandela.[52]

While Glasgow bestowed the Freedom of the City on Nelson Mandela in 1981, the Labour group in Edinburgh never got the two-thirds council majority for a similar proposal until well after Mandela was released. In 1986, Glasgow council renamed St George's Place as Nelson Mandela Place – a stroke of genius, as that was the location of the South African Consulate. 'Suddenly,' as Pete Sansom put it, 'the consulate's authority was undermined by its own address.'[53] Michael Kelly, who drove the campaign together with Brian Filling, said:

> We were one of the first to do that in the world. Beyond Africa, Mandela wasn't particularly well known then. It was controversial at the time and took a lot of bravery from the council. There was a lot of debate over why we were doing things like renaming places after an unknown African. That is why it was important because we helped to raise his profile and caused people to look at the man behind the stories.[54]

In Edinburgh, having failed in the Freedom of the City stakes, instead, there was a campaign to name the new square at Lothian Road Nelson Mandela Square – it lost to Festival Square in 1986 (in anticipation of the 40th anniversary of the Festival in 1987) – ah well, had they at least named it the People's Festival Square! But it was graced by Ann Davidson's statue 'Black Mother and Child' (the first publicly funded statue of a black woman in Britain) – as a memento for the victims of apartheid and oppression.

> Ann Davidson won the competition run by the Council, and her statue 'Woman and Child' was made to represent

---

[51] 'Thatcher, the ANC and the "cloud cuckoo land" misquote', *Politicsweb*, 9 April 2013, <www.politicsweb.co.za/politicsweb/view/politicsweb/en/page71619?oid=368489&sn=Marketingweb+detail>.

[52] Max du Preez, *The Rough Guide to Nelson Mandela*, London: Rough Guides, 2011, p.175.

[53] Peter Sansom, 'Nelson Mandela's Place', <www.qmunicate.com>.

[54] Annie Brown, 'Glasgow led the world in awarding Nelson Mandela Freedom of the City', *Daily Record*, 13 February 2010.

and to honour all those killed or imprisoned for their stand against apartheid. The woman and her child stand in front of a sketch in bronze of a shanty. The statue was unveiled on 22nd July 1986 by Suganya Chetty, a member of the African National Congress then living in exile in Edinburgh.[55]

1988: Nelson Mandela Freedom March

Hamish, though not at the forefront of these campaigns, was involved in the Edinburgh anti-apartheid committee (1980-1992). He can clearly be spotted on the STV Mandela Montage, marching in Glasgow on 12 June 1988, striding through the picture chanting 'Free Mandela' through a megaphone.[56] That march followed the Wembley Stadium concert on 11 June (a week before Mandela's 70th birthday) which changed his image from 'terrorist outlaw' to revered icon.[57] 600 million watched the birthday bash, which featured, among others, Stevie Wonder, Simple Minds, Dire Straits, Sting, George Michael, The Eurythmics, Eric Clapton and Whitney Houston, as well as Miriam Makeba and Hugh Masekela from South Africa. The march that had started on Glasgow Green reached London a week later, on Nelson Mandela's 70th birthday.[58] Twenty months later Mandela was free.

---

[55] 'Mandela Square that never was', *Looking at Edinburgh*, 30 October 2008, <http://edinburghlook.wordpress.com/2008/10/30/mandela-square-that-never-was/>.

[56] Nelson Mandela's memorable 1993 visit to Scotland', *STV News*, 18 July, 2008, <http://news.stv.tv/scotland/30271-nelson-mandelas-memorable-1993-visit-to-scotland/>.

[57] See Simon Hooper, 'The rock concert that helped spring Mandela', *Al Jazeera*, 10 June 2013, <www.aljazeera.com/indepth/features/2013/06/20136101243646806.html>.

[58] The Canadian filmmaker Jason Bourque's documentary film *Music for Mandela* (2011) charts the role of music in Mandela's life and in the struggle against apartheid. Bourque was inspired by the 70th birthday concert at Wembley. See Tim Masters, 'Mandela documentary examines power of music', *BBC News online*, 20 August 2013, <www.bbc.co.uk/news/entertainment-a rts-23285366>. U2 wrote a new Mandela song – 'No Ordinary Life' – for the biopic *Long Walk to Freedom*, released in the autumn of 2013. See Laura Butler, 'No ordinary life – U2 write new song for Mandela story', *Irish Independent*, 23 October 2013.

> On the day, in 1990, when Nelson Mandela's forthcoming release was announced, a round-robin of phone calls produced an impromptu demonstration of joy by scores of people in Festival Square, Edinburgh. I think everyone knew what would happen when Hamish Henderson stood up on a convenient plinth – he would lead us in his anthem 'Rivonia'...[59]

Power to the heirs of Luthuli
Rumbala rumbala rumba la
The comrades of Nelson Mandela
Rumbala rumbala rumba la
Spear of the Nation unbroken
Free Mandela Free Mandela
Amandla Umkhonto we Sizwe
Free Mandela Free Mandela[60]

Mandela and Megrahi

Subsequently, Nelson Mandela could pick up his nine freedoms of the city in Glasgow in 1993. In 1997, when he attended the Heads of Commonwealth Conference in Edinburgh, he also received, at long last, the capital's Freedom of the City. But there was, this time, no meeting between Hamish and Mandela. He had, though, a brief encounter with Conservative councillor Daphne Sleigh – and asked after the well-being of Margaret Thatcher. 'I have always had a great deal of admiration for Mrs Thatcher. I was touched by her concern for me.' He explained to the leader of the Conservative group how kind Mrs Thatcher had been to him when he met her. In the ensuing few moments of conversation Mandela told her how Mrs Thatcher had urged him to conserve his energy 'because your country needs you.'[61] We may not like it, but Nelson Mandela seemed quite smitten with the Iron Lady – after meeting

---

[59] Angus Calder, 'Obituary: Hamish Henderson', *The Independent*, 12 March 2002.

[60] *Collected Poems and Songs*, pp.150-51.

[61] Cameron Rose, '1997: Nelson Mandela in Edinburgh', *The Edinburgh Reporter*, 27 June 2013, <www.theedinburghreporter.co.uk/2013/06/1997-nelson-mandela-in-edinburgh/>.

her in 1990. As Elleke Boehmer wrote, he 'expressed admiration'' for her, hastening to add: 'her political determination as a woman prime minister, not her politics.'[62] Mandela himself noted that, while he could make *'no impression whatsoever* on the question of sanctions,' he found her 'charming':

> She was very warm, you know; she was just the opposite of what I was told... I was ... tremendously impressed by her ... *strength* of character – really an iron lady...[63]

He also got on well with John Major, and even better with Tony Blair – after all, there had always been more support for the anti-apartheid cause from the Labour Party. But that did not stop him 'from blasting Blair for his decision to join the US in the invasion in Iraq.'[64] As Jim Murphy remarked, 'he never saw any contradiction in being both an anglophile and an anti-imperialist.'[65]

Nelson Mandela also took great interest in the fate of Abdel Basset al-Megrahi, the suspected Lockerbie bomber. As early as 1992, he informally approached President George Bush, proposing a trial in a third country. Bush, President Mitterrand and King Juan Carlos of Spain responded favourably. In November 1994, six months after his election as president, Mandela formally proposed that South Africa should be the venue for the Pan Am Flight 103 bombing trial. At the Commonwealth Heads of Government Meeting in October 1997, Mandela warned: 'No one nation should be complainant, prosecutor and judge.' A compromise solution was then agreed for a trial to be held at Camp Zeist in the Netherlands, governed by Scottish law.[66]

Megrahi was, eventually, convicted and sentenced to 27 years of imprisonment in Scotland. He appealed against the verdict, but

---

[62] Elleke Boehmer, *Nelson Mandela: A Very Short introduction*, Oxford: Oxford University Press, 2008, p.141.

[63] 'From a Conversation with Richard Stengel about Contracting Pneumonia', in Nelson Mandela, *Conversations With Myself*, Basingstoke: Macmillan, 2010.

[64] du Preez, p.245.

[65] Jim Murphy, 'The myth of Mandela worked marvels, because every bit of it was true', *The Scotsman*, 6 December 2013.

[66] 'South Arica: Nelson Mandela – a Living Legend', *The Daily Observer*, 28 July 2008, <http://allafrica.com/stories/200807250785.html>.

his initial appeal was turned down in March 2002. Mandela, by then ex-President, paid him a visit in Barlinnie prison on 10 June of that year.

> 'Megrahi is all alone,' Mandela told a packed press conference in the prison's visitors room. 'He has nobody he can talk to. It is psychological persecution that a man must stay for the length of his long sentence all alone. It would be fair if he were transferred to a Muslim country, and there are Muslim countries which are trusted by the West. It will make it easier for his family to visit him if he is in a place like the kingdom of Morocco, Tunisia or Egypt.'[67]

Mandela did not officially endorse the Scottish government's release of Megrahi in August 2009, when the Scottish government sought international backing for Kenny MacAskill's decision to let Megrahi return to Libya . The response was 'that Mr Mandela does not want to be involved in public issues any more but that he 'sincerely appreciates' the move.'[68]

Dr Henderson of Lovedale

To say that Hamish Henderson and Nelson Mandela were 'lifelong friends' or bosom buddies, as Colin Fox's invitation to this lecture seemed to imply, might be called a wee exaggeration. There are no letters in the Hamish Henderson archive from Nelson Mandela. There was no meeting between the two nigh-contemporaneous figures – Mandela born in 1918, Hamish in 1919 – when Mandela came to Edinburgh in 1997. And there is no mention of Hamish in any of the books by or on Nelson Mandela that I have consulted.

Mandela does, incidentally, refer to a Henderson: 'Dr Henderson of Lovedale'.[69] He was a Scot – James Henderson

---

[67] *Ibid.*

[68] Brian Swanson, 'Mandela's Lockerbie snub to Nats', *The Scottish Express,* 8 December 2012, <www.express.co.uk/news/uk/363278/Mandela-s-Lockerbie-snub-to-Nats>.

[69] 'Address of Nelson Mandela, President of the African National Congress on Receiving an Honorary LLD Degree at the University of Fort Hare', 9 May 1992, <www.anc.org.za/show.php?id=4128>.

(1867-1930), educated at Edinburgh University and New College.[70] He emigrated in 1895 to Malawi to join the Livingstonian Mission; then, in 1906, he became principal of the Lovedale Institution in the Cape Colony, 'the most important centre of African education in the southern hemisphere.

> Almost as soon as he arrived, he was involved in the foundation of Fort Hare University College. He continued to keep Lovedale at the forefront of African education and a center of ecumenical cooperation. He edited the *South African Outlook*, in which Africans could express their opinions on any subject to do with Christianity or society in South Africa. At the time of his death he was still actively seeking to give South Africa an educated Christian African leadership whether the state wanted it or not.[71]

Lovedale, on the Tyhume River in Alice, Eastern Cape, had been founded by John Bennie of the Glasgow Missionary Society of Scotland, named after one of its leading members, Dr John Love. Its first principal was Rev. William Govan, born in Paisley and ordained in Glasgow. Govan Mbeki, the former president of the African National Congress, was named after him. He paid tribute to William Govan:

> He firmly believed that Africans had the same right to a full and proper education as whites. He and his successors such as Neil McVicar, Dr Stewart, Alexander Kerr and the Reverend Shepherd never accepted the prevailing racist's attitudes that Africans were not suited to receiving an education equal to that of whites. Govan and his immediate successor, Dr Neil McVicar, turned Lovedale into a powerful and immensely influential educational institution. It was the

[70] Paul B Rich, 'The Appeals of Tuskegee: James Henderson, Lovedale, and the Fortunes of South African Liberalism, 1906-1930', *The International Journal of African Historical Studies*, Vol.20, No.2 (1987), pp,271-292.

[71] Andrew C Ross, 'Henderson, James', in Gerald H. Anderson, *Biographical Dictionary of Christian Missions*, Grand Rapids, Michigan: W. B. Eerdmans Publishing Company, 1998, p.288.

> pride and joy of African people in many parts of Southern Africa.[72]

In an age when higher level study was the near exclusive preserve of whites, over the decades, Lovedale and Fort Hare trained the great majority of educated blacks in South African. Amongst them were Albert Luthuli, Govan Mbeki, Steve Biko (who died at he age of 30 from police brutality in custody on 12 September 1977[73]), Thabo Mbeki, Joshua Nkomo. Desmond Tutu and Robert Sobukwe. Seretse Khama, the first President of Botswana, Julius Nyerere, President of Tanzania, Robert Mugabe, President of Zimbabwe, and Kenneth Kaunda, the first President of Zambia attended Fort Hare. Oliver Tambo, Nelson Mandela and Chris Hani, the leader of the South African Communist Party who was assassinated in 1993, all were enrolled, but expelled for their political activities before they could obtain their degrees. Mandela studied at Fort Hare when Dr Alexander Kerr, a graduate of Edinburgh University, was Principal, continuing the great Scottish educational tradition of Lovedale and Fort Hare, from John Philip of Kirkcaldy who arrived at the Cape of Good Hope in 1819 through John Campbell, James Fairbairn (the editor of he progressive *The Cape Commercial Advertiser*), Thomas Pringle (a poet and acquaintance of Sir Walter Scott) and Robert Moffat, the father-in-law of David Livingstone, who himself plaid a radical part over the ten years he stayed in South Africa.[74] Mandela recalled:

> Fort Hare ... was a beacon for African scholars from all over Southern, Central and Eastern Africa. For young South Africans like myself, it was Oxford and Cambridge, Harvard and Yale, all rolled into one.[75]

---

[72] Govan Mbeki, 'Culture in the Struggle for a New South Africa' (Address to the Sechaba Conference, Glasgow, 23 September 1990, in Brian Filling and Susan Stuart (eds), *The End of a Regime? An Anthology of Scottish-South African Writing Against Apartheid*, Aberdeen: Aberdeen University Press, 1991, pp.216-23; p.216. Mbeki ended his address by quoting the last verse of Robert Burns's 'A Man's a Man', p.223.

[73] See Xolela Mangcu, *Biko: A Life*, London: I.B. Tauris, 2013

[74] See Andrew C Ross, 'Scotland and South Africa: Blessed Be the Tie That Binds?', in Brian Filling and Susan Stuart (eds), *The End of a Regime?*, pp.3-13.

[75] Nelson Mandela, *Long Walk to Freedom*, p.51.

Despite its predominantly black intake, Lovedale resisted all attempts by the apartheid regime to segregate it. In 1991, with momentous changes underway in South Africa, Commonwealth Secretary General Emeka Anyaoku said, 'When all the passions of this moment have subsided, Lovedale will stand forth as Scotland's lasting contribution to the regeneration of South Africa and indeed Africa as a whole.'[76]

Thus, as Andrew Ross wrote:

> Scots played a significant part in the creation of a non-racial tradition in South Africa, indeed they played a vital role in its being institutionalised in the constitution of the Cape Colony, which tragically did not survive the creation of the Union of South Africa by a British Liberal administration.[77]

But he also mentions the dark side. Referring to Robert Knox (the recipient of Burke and Hare's victims) and Thomas Carlyle, he contends: 'Scots and the Scottish academic tradition also played a key role in the formulation of scientific racism with its appalling impact not only on South Africa but the world.'[78]

At Hame Wi' Freedom

Although Mandela references only the 'other' Henderson, the names of Hamish Henderson and Nelson Mandela have, certainly since 'Rivonia', and at least here in Scotland, been inextricably linked. And justifyably so. As Kätzel Henderson affirmed, Mandela was one of the 'underdogs' Hamish championed, in a long list including Paul Robeson and Julius and Ethel Rosenberg.[79] And in paying tribute to the phenomenal achievement of Nelson Mandela, it is entirely appropriate to spend some time praising Hamish for his life-long efforts in support of the anti-apartheid cause.

For Mandela, the fight against apartheid has been his life, and he received support from many in many parts of the world; for Hamish, resistance to the apartheid regime was an important

[76] www.gcu.ac.uk/archives/gcuia/WGovan.html

[77] Ross, 'Scotland and South Africa', p.9.

[78] *Ibid.*

[79] Kätzel Henderson, in conversation with the author, 7 August 2013.

part of his political activism, encompassing many causes, from the anti-nuclear campaigns to the anti-poll tax protests, from his ant-sectarianism to his promotion of gay rights, his support for the Clyde shipbuilders, his solidarity with Chile after the overthrow of Salvador Allende, for Ian Hamilton Finlay's 'Little Sparta', his fight for Home Rule and for his home, the School of Scottish Studies (he even wrote to Winnie Mandela in the 1980s to solicit a story in support of the School,[80] which was then threatened by Thatcherite cuts).[81]

Nelson Mandela's birthday falls on 18 July, and the call goes out every year for people everywhere to celebrate his birthday by acting on the idea that each person has the power to change the world. The idea of Mandela Day was inspired by Nelson Mandela at his 90th birthday celebrations in London's Hyde Park in 2008 when he said: 'It is time for new hands to lift the burdens. It is in your hands now.'[82] Mandela's last public appearance was at the closing ceremony of the World Cup Finals in 2010, after the tournament had been successfully hosted by South Africa. Hamish Henderson died in 2002.

Nelson Mandela's 95th birthday celebrations on 18 July 2013 were overshadowed by his critical health condition. He had been in hospital for seven weeks with a severe lung infection, held alive by machines. By August 2013, as we were gathering in Edinburgh to celebrate him and Hamish, his condition seemed a bit more stable.[83] But on 5 December 2013 Nelson Mandela died at home in Johannesburg, surrounded by his family. 'Our nation has lost its greatest son,' South Africa's president Jacob Zuma announced on national TV: 'What made Nelson Mandela great was precisely what made him human. We saw in him what we seek in ourselves.'[84]

---

[80] Timothy Neat, *Hamish Henderson: A Biography*, Vol.2, p.346.

[81] See Eberhard Bort, 'At Hame Wi' Freedom: The Politics of Hamish Henderson', in E Bort (ed.), *At Hame Wi' Freedom: Essays on Hamish Henderson and the Scottish Folk Revival*, Ochtertyre: Grace Note Publications, 2012, pp. 197-216.

[82] 'Mandela joins stars at London gig', *BBC News Online*, 28 June 2008, <http://news.bbc.co.uk/1/hi/entertainment/7475717.stm>.

[83] David Dolan, 'Nelson Mandela condition improving says daughter', *Scotland on Sunday*, 11 August 2013.

[84] 'South Africa's Nelson Mandela dies in Johannesburg', *BBC News online*, 5 December 2013 <www.bbc.co.uk/news/world-africa-25249520>.

The world mourned one of the great leaders of our time – a man of peace, freedom and reconciliation – the man his fellow South Africans fondly called by his clan name, Madiba, a sign of respect and affection.

The Scottish Parliament paid its respects to Nelson Mandela on 10 December 2013. And Rob Gibson MSP lodged the following motion:

> That the Parliament seeks to celebrate the people of all lands who joined the struggle to fight apartheid in deeds, words and music over the decades that it took for the release of Nelson Mandela and for South Africa to emerge as the rainbow nation; especially recalls the role of songs and music in spreading the anti-apartheid message and, in particular from Scotland, it praises the part played by Hamish Henderson, the folklorist, poet, soldier and anti-racist activist whose life view echoed Mandela's message at the Rivonia trial in 1964 that 'Freedom is never, but never, a gift from above; it invariably has to be won anew by its own exercise'; further recalls that Hamish Henderson wrote his song, Rivonia, using the republican Spanish civil war tune, Viva la Quince Brigada, to carry his anthem of solidarity with Nelson Mandela and the leaders of the ANC who were starting several decades of prison sentences after their trial, and reminds today's celebrants of Mandela's life that this song was recorded privately in 1964, sung by the Corrie Folk Trio, and was sent to South African freedom fighters, sung in the fields and ultimately sung before Nelson Mandela himself.[85]

Famous quotations by Nelson Mandela are legion. This one comes by way of Confucius and Ralph Waldo Emerson: 'The greatest glory in living lies not in never falling, but in rising every time we fall.' He also said: 'Do not judge me by my successes, judge me by how many times I fell down and got back up again.'[86] I doubt

---

[85] S4M-08584: Scotland and South Africa, Rivonia Remembered, <http://www.scottish.parliament.uk/parliamentarybusiness/28877.aspx?SearchType=Advance&MSPId=2675&SearchFor=AllMotions&DateChoice=3&SortBy=DateSubmitted>.

[86] Nelson Mandela, *Conversations With Myself*, Basingstoke: Macmillan, 2010.

whether Mandela knew a song Hamish loved: 'Sae Will We Yet' by Walter Watson (1854), sung by the Corries, Jock Duncan and by Tony Cuffe, and recently recorded in a fine version by Mick West – with the memorable line which, I am sure, Hamish would have been delighted to sing to him with a glint in his eye (after all, the getting up here refers to a tumble after a dram or twa):

> When we fell we aye got up again,
> and sae will we yet.[87]

Nelson Mandela and Hamish Henderson were both 'at hame wi' freedom.' Freedom, for Mandela, is the highest good. 'The sun never set on so glorious a human achievement,' he said: 'Let freedom reign.'[88] Freedom, he maintained, 'is indivisible; the chains on any one of my people were the chains on all of them, the chains on all of my people were the chains on me.'[89] He further elaborates: 'For to be free is not merely to cast off one's chains, but to live in a way that respects and enhances the freedom of others.'[90] And: 'There is no such thing as part freedom.'[91]

'Freedom and whisky gang thegither,' Hamish would perhaps have quoted the Bard.[92] And, from the fourteenth century, John Barbour's famous lines from *The Brus*,

> A! Fredome is a noble thing!
> *Fredome mays man to haiff liking.*
> *Fredome all solace to man giffis,*
> *He levys at es that frely levys!*[93]

87 John Ord, *Ord's Bothy Songs and Ballads of Aberdeen, Banff and Moray*, Edinburgh: John Donald, 2nd ed., 1995, p.371.

88 Nelson Mandela, *Long Walk to Freedom*, p.747.

89 *Ibid.*, p.751.

90 *Ibid.*

91 Jennifer Crwys-Williams (ed.), *In the Words of Nelson Mandela*, London: Profile Books, 2010, p.41.

92 Robert Burns, 'The Author's Earnest Cry and Prayer', *The Canongate Burns: The Complete Poems and Songs of Robert Burns*, edited by Andrew Noble and Patrick Scott Hogg, Edinburgh: Canongate Classics, 2001, p.25.

93 'Freedom is a noble thing! / Great happiness does freedom bring. / All solace to a man it gives; / He lives at ease that freely lives.' John Barbour, *The Brus*, edited and translated by Archibald A H Douglas, Glasgow: William MacLellan, 1964, p.53.

To which he would probably have added, in the way Rob Gibson alluded to, and with a view of the lessons we can learn from Nelson Mandela's life: 'Freedom is never, but never, a gift from above: it invariably has to be won anew by its own exercises.'[94] Ah, would the two had met for a wee 'impromptu colloquium'[95] in Sandy Bell's – and would we could have been there to eavesdrop...

Nelson Mandela in George Square, Glasgow, 9 October 1993 (photograph: David Pratt)

[94] *The Armstrong Nose*, p.186.

[95] Angus Calder, 'Introduction to the First Edition' (1992), in Hamish Henderson, *Alias MacAlias: Writings on Songs, Folk and Literature*, edited by Alec Finlay, Edinburgh: Polygon, 2nd ed., 2004, p.xiii.

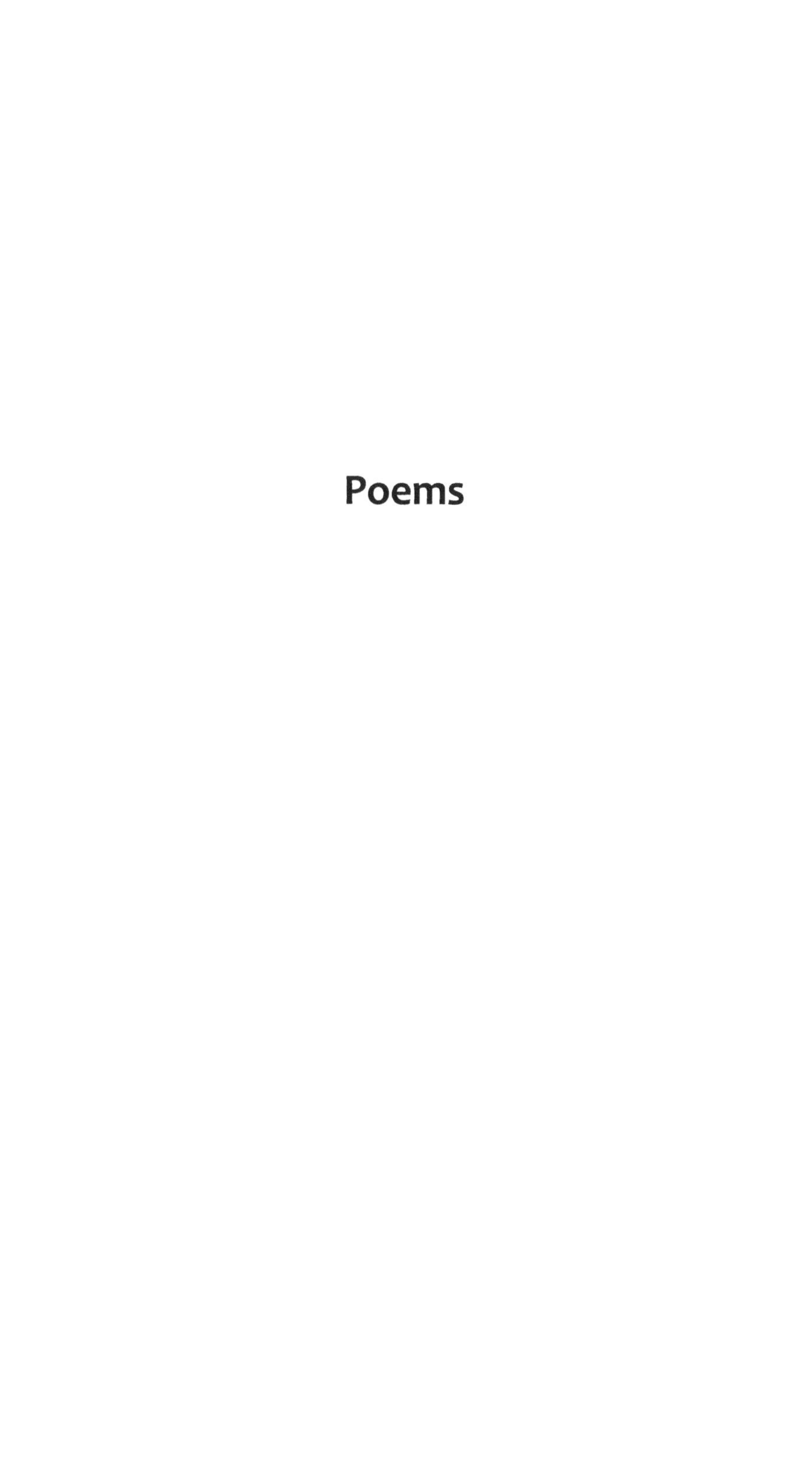

Poems

Archie Fisher at Edinburgh Folk Club (photograph: Allan McMillan)

George Gunn at the Scottish Storytelling Centre (photograph: Allan McMillan)

Interrogations

(*after Intelligence reports by Hamish Henderson*)

A glassy blue stare from the brutish face
of SS Colonel Herbert Kappler,
with his *Schmisse* prominent,
trying to outstare me. How pathetic!

Despite his duelling scar, the man
lacked all honour: as reprisal
for a Partisan ambush in Rome,
he ordered 335 hostages murdered:

men and women of all ages, classes,
and walks of life, in the Ardeatine Caves.
To stir his conscience, if he had one,
I read to him 'Lament for the Son',

Corrado Govoni's elegy for Aladino,
his son, shot dead. But it was no use,
he only made my blood freeze
with his obscene response:

'An old father's grief is for me
something sacred.' Less onerous
was interrogating a Lance Corporal
in the *Afrika Korps*, defeated,

but an enemy whose honour
did not depend on a duelling scar.
He resisted every query stating
name, rank and serial number.

However much of a pain,
I don't think he was a Nazi
true-believer, merely
human, all too human.

Mario Relich

Alang wi' Hamish

I never thocht that I wad be
Amang the aristocracy.
Or listed in the company
O' rich an' famous;
But noo at last I bear the gree
Alang wi' Hamish.

O Hamish, wale of Scotland's drinkers,
Your sangs are sung by toffs an' tinkers,
By usquebaugh an' tankard sinkers
At Sandy Bell's;
But ilka Scot who wears nae blinkers
Fa's for your spells.

While Scots detest their Tory rule,
While Nicky Fairbairn plays the fool,
While Lizzie Lochhead plays it cool
– A lass o' pairts –
Still Hamish Henderson will rule
O'er Scottish hairts.

David Daiches

Only the best Burns suppers avoid boring pomposity. After some unedifying roll-throwing, haggis-spillage and rude interjections at the Scotch Malt Whisky Society event in Leith, Conservative intellectual Michael Fry was assisted to an early departure, his toast to the lassies undelivered. Liz Lochhead replied nevertheless. There will be no return bout.

Another high spot was the presentation of a life membership scroll to David Daiches by Hamish Henderson, the previous year's recipient. Prof Daiches responded in Bardic verse, and here are three elegant stanzas.[1]

---

[1] Tony Troon, *The Best of The Scotsman Diary*, Edinburgh: Mainstream, 1992, pp.12-13.

Man and Boy

for Hamish Henderson

One One May morning, a little boy,
I crept out early to the glistening dew.
But as I climbed the glen
Mist wrapped itself around me
Like a tattered standard, and the high hills
Peeked over cloaks of cloud.
The burn dodged and twisted, clambering
Till lost into a borderland of marshy tussock.
Near the source I ran aground
And stopped to watch the valley clear.
Looming through the mist
A giant figure stretched his early morning
Shadow to my side. A rollicky tilt,
Hands flailed then sank into the pockets
Of a wrunkled cardigan, matching hat on head,
A collie dog at heel and steel eyes
Glittering behind lopsided spectacles.
"How are you laddie?" "All right."
Strands of loose white hair spreadeagled
In the breeze on ruddy cheeks.
"What are you doing up here?" "Thinkin."
"Aye, just so. On a May morning."
We listened in his silence
To the music of the curlew and the plover
As the mist dispersed before a laverock air.
"Gaelic" he said, "they sing in Gaelic,
The language behind the speech."
Then abruptly he was off with louping stride
And I scuttled after to keep up.
"Time for travelling" he intoned.
"We've dragged our feet for far too long."

Two Level at the rucksack eyes
Rise and falling with his breath
White haired, bonneted and cropped.
A long stride shortens the road
Off the path, splash through the stream
Because this was Adomnan's ford
Columba's light in a leather satchel
A long stride shortens the road
Down amongst the littered rocks
Finn's band hunted Diarmid stretched
His length against the prickly boar
A long stride shortens the road
Rest a moment at the hillside cairn
The Gregarach proscribed and torched
Rob Roy battleless from Sherrifmuir
A long stride shortens the road
Tumbledown of wet grass, boulders
Mark the deserted townships clearing
Crofters to the margin, emigrants world wide
A long stride shortens the road
The burgh's sentryless by day
Boots clashing on the stony setts
Together cross the Lowland bridge
A long stride shortens the road
Shoulder to shoulder past the Tolbooth court
Tree hung for liberty, life,
Raps for death at the castle gate.
A long stride shortens the road
Fields of battle are spread below
Scots with Bruce and Wallace bled
Can sing Mandela's anthem now
A long stride shortens the road.

Three The single decker crawled interminably
Through linear villages that broke their banks
With regimented houses and breeze blocks
Spilling shapelessly across the land.
Grey country on a lowering afternoon
Lit by brazen signs reflected in plate steel,
Lurching towards a devolution referendum.
As we overcame the crest of Lanarkshire

The valley rolled successive folds below
With smoky chimneys and repeating waves
Of urban sprawl, high rise stacks and factories
Sealed securely to let none in.
I leaned my forehead against the glass
Peering down towards the river
Marked only by the lowest line
The eye could reach amidst the concrete mass.
This city gave me birth and hope,
Here to return and cast a vote.
As we began the downward climb
The bus began to fill with folk.
Two miners from the Welfare,
A woman going to shop in town,
Youngsters on their way to disco
And a head-scarved gaggle fresh from bingo.
Suddenly he was up into the aisle
No longer dozing by my shoulder,
But towering to the rooflights
Leaflets flourished in his hands from nowhere.
"Have you voted yet today?
Ladies, it's your parliament at stake.
Scotland's right belongs to you as well.
Aye, look around you, lads,
Nationless, the workers' cause unwon.
For King and country, mam?
I fought to beat the fascists,
Now I want to win the peace,

For us and for the nations of the world."
He had the bus alight and laughing.
Then he set them singing,
Clydeside red, the weavers' ballads
Polaris and the CND, with bawdy numbers in between
Then unexpectedly the bus arrived.
"Jesus Christ," the driver spat contentedly,
"Will you be on my shift the morn?"
Men shook his hand, women hugged.
"God." He said, "But I could use a drink."

Donald Smith

Seumas MacEanraig

Duine ard cràiceach
le oiteag Bhlàr Ghobharaidh
  air anail
agus dualchas Ghlinn Sìdhe
  na anam,
na sheasamh na chraoibh
ann an coille nan linntean,
's e ag èisdeachd ri faghaid
Dhiarmaid 's an tuirc,
  na gadhair ris an leathad
's Fionn na shuidhe gu gruamach
fo sgàil Bheinn Ghulbainn.

Cuimhnichidh mi air
's mi a' coiseachd
am measg tulchain a' ghlinne,
an abhainn bhog ri monbhar
  fon drochaid chloiche ann an Cille Mhicheil,
's sgeulachd Dhiarmaid is Ghrainne
  is Sheumais
na ceòl biothbhuan nam chluasan.

  Gum biodh sìth dha fhèin
Anns a' ghleann.

Donald Meek

Hamish Henderson

A tall, tousled man
with the breeze of Blairgowrie
  on his breath
and the heritage of Glenshee
  in his soul;
standing as a tree-trunk
in the forest of the ages,
hearing the hunt
of Diarmad and the boar
  and the hounds cresting the hill
and Fionn sitting sulking
in the shade of Ben Gulbainn.

He comes to mind
as I walk
among the knolls of the glen
the river soft murmuring
  under the stone bridge of Kirkmichael,
the tale of Diarmad and Grainne
  and Hamish
as undying music in my ears.

  May he himself have peace
In the glen.

Donald Meek – translated by **Bill Innes**

The Bones of Scotland

(For Alison McMorland)

One morning a man walked out of the sea
he lay down & became
the bones of Scotland
the wind which was his voice blew
along the endless shifting strath of dream
& he said
"Yes these are the open hillsides
of your old new land calling you home
these are the hayfields freshly cut
a sea of grass flowing towards you yes
the cream & yes the purple flowered potato drills
yes these are the yellowing barley parks
pulling the Sun out of the ground
yes these are the hazel trees rising with sap
ready for the Travellers to coppice in the Winter
the mountains you say are steep hard & beautiful yes
& yes the firths can be deep & fierce
the rivers broad & yes in spate
but these remember are your bones also
here between hill & island
between the early morning & the end of time
yes you too have walked out of the sea
you also are the voice in the wind
amongst the yellowing iris flags & yes the birches
with the people moving out from their sleep
like birds in the morning air yes
yes you!"

George Gunn

Abhainn

We first met cowping pints together
in Sandy Bell's one afternoon,
I did not understand the half of what you meant,
Skiving lectures from David Hume.
Allt a' ghlinne bhig, Allt fearnach, Brerachan:
The bluid o the ages, skailan, flawan.

While Sorley mourned his sabbaths of the dead
and MacDairmid growled; "Not Burns - Dunbar"
You celebrated and sang all four's DNA
With Johnny Faa beneath the stars.
Borthwick, Earnscleugh, Wauchope, Allan:
The bluid o the ages sweelin, flawan.

I played at a Ceilidh in Leven for you
where we sang our hearts out in your praise
But your kind eyes rested some place else
Near the ending of your joyous days.
Garbh uisge, Eas gobhain, Ardoch, Keltie, Devon:
the bluid o the ages pirlin, flawan.

On the sad morning after referendum
I thought of you and the chances gone:
Though the burghers' gallows did not fall,
There can be no end to this old song.
Millden, Eigie, Blairton, Ythan:
The bluid o the ages tummlin, flawan.

William Hershaw

Stella of Rose Street

(in memory of Stella Cartwright, 1938-1985)

"Dear George, it is so strange, our souls seem to fly together joyously over mountains and seas while each of us in our mutual way suffers agonies."
(Stella Cartwright)

"An orgasm with Miss Cartwright was metaphysical, transcendental, like nothing else you can ever imagine. She seemed built for love."
(Stanley Roger Green)

"You placed me on a pedestal / according to my lights / but what you didn't know, my dear / I have no head for heights."
(Norman MacCaig)

It was so much gabble,
fantasies of genius in the Little Kremlin.
Once, I fell for it myself,
tottering along the red carpet,
poetry dribbling into my own vomit,
or maybe it was Hugh's,
all mixed up
in the whisky of empty promises.

I talked in Milne's Bar to a shop steward
who'd help build MacDiarmid's bog.
He said the workmen had their tea in Grieve's posh wee cups
and saw the reckoning in the leaves.
He yapped as auld poets glowered from their photos
and we downed chilled ale
to drown the memories of a Juniper Green girl
with a pint of that Muse again.

They must have seen joy in you our Stella
to wrench them from their word play,
to take a lovely shag to brighten up their anxious lines.
Och the happiness and the pain
of drinking
that smiler with the knife
comes to get us all.
And that lonely honey George
must have driven you nuts
romancing you in the Pentland Hills
and kissing you full on your lips
one damp Saturday afternoon
by the Water of Leith.

They say 'the best poem is silence'
but you were a shriek in the ecstasy
of loving and of agony,
a naked drunken howl.
The saintly saviour of hurt animals
and a shopper for the sick,
you wanted to wrap yourself around
something you could trust,
wanted a photograph of a true poetry lover
held to your lovely breasts
to make a change from the piss
of Milne's Bar
and the daily Abbotsford drivel.

What you found was madness in a Zimmer Frame at thirty,
splashes of alcohol and tears lit
by the sudden flashes of beautiful orgasms,
the sunshine today
in all the muck
along Rose Street.

Keith Armstrong

The Divided Self

'When'er my muse does on me glance, I jingle at her.' (Robert Burns).

Such an eye in a human head,
from the toothless baby
to the toothless man,
the Edinburgh wynds
bleed whisky.
Through all the Daft Days,
we drink and gree
in the local howffs,
dancing down
Bread Street.
Like burns with Burns
these gutters run;
where Fergusson once tripped,
his shaking glass
jumps
in our inky fingers,
delirium tugs
at our bardish tongues;
dead drunk,
we dribble down
a crafty double
for Burke & Hare,
heckle a Deacon Brodie
gibbering
on the end
of the hangman's rope.

In all these great and flitting streets
awash with cadies,
this poet's dust
clings
like distemper to our bones.
We're walking through
the dark and daylight,
the laughs
and torture

of lost ideals.
Where is the leader of the mob Joe Smith,
that bowlegged cobbler
who snuffed it on these cobbles,
plunging
from this stagecoach pissed?
Where is the gold
of Jinglin' George Heriot?
Is it in the sunglow on the Forth?
We're looking for girls of amazing beauty
and whores of unutterable filth:
'And in the Abbotsford
like gabbing asses
they scale the heights
of Ben Parnassus.'

Oh Hugh me lad
we've seen some changes.
In Milne's, your great brow scowls the louder;
your glass of bitterness
deep as a loch:
'Till a' the seas gang dry, my dear
And the rocks melt wi' the sun.'

Oh Heart
of Midlothian,
it spits on
to rain
still hopes.
Still hope in her light meadows
and in her volcanic smiles.
And we've sung with Hamish
in Sandy Bell's
and Nicky Tams
and Diggers,
a long hard sup
along the cobbles
to the dregs
at the World's End:
'Whene'er my muse does on me glance,
I jingle at her.'

Bright as silver,
sharp as ice,
this Edinburgh of all places,
home to a raving melancholia
among the ghosts
of Scotland's Bedlam:
'Auld Reekie's sons blythe faces',
shades of Fergusson in Canongate.

And the blee-e'ed sun,
the reaming ale
our hearts to heal;
the muse of Rose Street
seeping through us boozy bards,
us snuff snorters
in coughing clouds.

Here
on display
in this Edinburgh dream:
the polished monocle
of Sydney Goodsir Smith,
glittering by
his stained inhaler;
and the black velvet jacket
of RLS,
slumped by
a battered straw hat.

And someone
wolf whistles
along Waterloo Place;
and lovers
kiss moonlight
on Arthur's Seat:
see Edinburgh rise.

Drink
from her eyes.

Keith Armstrong

Interviews

We are the music makers
And we are the dreamers of dreams
Sunday January 30th 2011
CEILIDH
& Howard's 81st birthday bash
Howard T Glasser Archive
Claire T Carney Library
UMD Library Archives & Special Collections

On Sunday, 31 January 2011, Dartmouth Archives and Special Collections hosted a ceilidh to celebrate the 81st birthday of Howard T. Glasser – friend, artist, and founder of the SMU/UMD Eisteddfod.

RESURGIMENTO!
An Interview with Hamish Henderson

Geordie McIntyre

Geordie McIntyre: The thing which most interests me in this context, Hamish, is the extent to which the revival was consciously architected in the beginnings. Can you tell us if there was in fact any such conscious motivation?[1]

Hamish Henderson: I felt in Italy particularly, with the Highland Division originally and with other units, that local cultures that we were encountering seemed to add, for certain people, a tremendous enjoyment to the war. I mean the war needed some enjoyment added to it and that was part of it. For example in Sicily it was great to see, at the very start of the Sicilian Campaign, the Jocks getting taken over by the local Sicilian families. In the evening they would put chairs outside the house: there would be the Jock, sitting in the middle with the old granny and the family sitting round and there you would hear the odd song being raised. And this particular mixing of cultures really did seem to me at the time to be a thing with a future to it. I liked the idea of Scotland contributing something to Sicily, or elsewhere for that matter. People generally seemed to enjoy and like this. I go back to that because this is the point from which I so to speak begin – I mean begin in that I was doing something to steer it together in a concrete way.

GM: In other words you saw this intermingling of cultures in a concrete situation and you presumably then were intellectually aware of the changing communication pattern and the likelihood of an increasing trend in this direction, for good or ill, in the future and you wanted in some sense to direct this trend.

---

[1] From: 'Folk Song and the Folk Tradition' Festival Issue of the *New Edinburgh Review* (August 1973), here reproduced with the kind permission of Geordie McIntyre.

HH: Well, that's rationalising it with extremely powerful constricting rays, as you might say. A great deal of this was just joy and fun, Geordie. I mean I am a writer, I have written songs and one of the things I personally liked was the coming together of these various cultures. I had a prejudice from early times that Scotsmen could do this better than their 'auld enemies': that they could make contact with the other people. On a political basis I enjoyed it because I have always felt that the more human beings know about each other the better, and we were fighting a war against Fascism at the time and the more communication that existed between the troops – the more they understood each other – the more they were able to come together the more there was a practical dynamic to the situation.

GM: You see this on a broadly humanistic level, then?

HH: Yes, quite. As far as I was concerned it goes back to the Spanish Civil War as well, when I was a schoolboy and I came in contact in 1937 with people who had been in Spain and also people who were going to Spain. As far as I was concerned the pattern is a kind of conscious anti-fascist pattern, to put it bluntly.

GM: What intrigues me about the general points you've raised there Hamish, is the fact that, obviously, it is a complex situation we're dealing with and there are a number of motives. We're not dealing with any single-cause motives in any field of human behaviour. But nevertheless, going on just a little bit from the war period – was there any broad consensus between yourself and others as to a conscious creation of a revival in Scotland or Britain?

HH: I don't think that one could claim that it was very conscious, Geordie, except that I wanted and always have wanted to spread around the best of the oral culture that I could. In the army, for example, I was singing Italian songs and things like that and immediately after World war Two I did the same thing in Scotland. But long before that I was interested in the nature of oral culture as opposed to what often seemed to be the kind of 'fossilisation' of print. I liked the free-flowing oral thing. I remember that the idea of writing songs, that is poems with tunes, occurred to me as a definite weapon. I don't think that's expressing it too strongly. I was very conscious of the fact that many of the things that I liked were music – were song in fact.

GM: From what you've said already, Hamish, you did see yourself as part of an ongoing tradition, a continuing movement.

HH: I felt myself as part of an ongoing movement certainly. Nobody on earth felt more Scottish than I did at Cambridge. And I found that the Socialist students at Cambridge were delighted with the folk-song when I wet up there in 1938. The phrase 'Scots Ballads' would link with them quite clearly and would conjure up the idea of a popular culture that was enjoyed by a wide section of people. They had the mythological view of this being some sort of classless society of the past.

GM: There is a definite romantic component, then?

HH: Well there always is a romantic component, let's face it. The idea of a classless society is in itself a romantic idea; but nevertheless it might be a rewarding and even a possible idea. It is an idea which might be a figment – nevertheless it's a perfectly tenable ground on which to proceed.

GM: There was quite a lot of borrowing from America on Clydeside in the '20s and '30s. American tunes and Wobbly[2] songs were sung at climbing clubs, cycling clubs and such. It seems that in your work of the period you were recognising this global culture and drawing on any source.

HH: As far as the hobo songs were concerned they were floating around in the '30s. In the mid-30s Alastair Cook (the same as the 'Letter from America' Alastair Cook) dipped into the John A Lomax collection in the Library of Congress and produced a series of programmes called 'I Hear America Singing'. In this series he used hobo and wobbly songs, chain-gang songs; in fact the Lomax collection of the time. These appeared on the radio to the intense interest of everybody. I notice that Ewan MacColl refers to them in a recent issue of 'Folk'. These programmes were of tremendous importance. The international thing. Well, take France for example. France has never really needed a folk song revival, they have always had clubs and cafes for singing. In the summer of '38 I was earning a bit of money by singing in the Y.M.C.A. in Paris and they thoroughly enjoyed Scots ballads. But certainly what we were doing could be seen, in retrospect particularly, as relating to something of social significance. I don't think anyone could have forecast the strength and exuberance of

[2] wobblies = Industrial Workers of the World, formed in 1905 in Chicago.

the revival as it really developed. I didn't and I was in it from quite an early stage.

GM: You could not, obviously, forecast the revival, but yet a lot of the songs created at this time have a 'missionary' element – a wish to communicate wider ideas in song together with an awareness of past material.

HH: Well, the best example of what you call the 'missionary' element is the preface to the People's Festival Ceilidh of 1952. I can do no better than to quote what I wrote then: 'Although Scotland's heritage of folk-song is justly famed for its richness and variety, very few Scots ever have a chance of hearing the old songs given in the authentic traditional manner. This is a great pity, because on the lips of concert-hall performers most folk-songs completely lose their character – what was robust becomes insipid, and what was simple becomes artful in the worst sense.' Or again: 'The emphasis this year will be on young singers who are carrying on the splendid tradition in its integrity.' And how's this for missionary: 'We are convinced that it is possible to restore Scottish folk-song to the ordinary people in Scotland, not merely as a bobby-soxer vogue, but deeply and integrally.'

GM: Could you give us some concrete examples of these young singers you mention there?

HH: We had quite a few young traditional singers: several people from Glasgow, from Maurice's clanjamfray. They came and sang, mostly mimicking the older singers. Young people from the East had a more obvious continuity and there was great enthusiasm for what was happening. Of course, then, there was skiffle too and for a while the kids were sort of battering the songs into the ground – including singers who eventually turned into really good singers.

GM: These singers remained fundamentally revivalist singers but they had clearly transcended the role of mimic to a stage of understanding and interpretation. Can we take it that implicit in the idea of understanding there is an awareness of the people who created these songs, the individuals, the groups and the particular social background they came from? In other words, the mimicry was transcended only when the singers developed an understanding of the socio-economic structure which created these songs?

HH: I think that's largely true. The abandoning of mimicry to a large extent means the achieving of understanding and empathy. This obviously means that if the young singers concerned have the opportunity of making contact with the actual environment of people like Jeannie Robertson, then their understanding of and feeling for the songs will be increased tenfold.

GM: This understanding should embrace the fact that someone like Jeannie is obviously a woman of the twentieth century. She has included in her own repertory material songs from other cultures – one thinks of the American songs which were commented on in a recent issue of *Scottish Studies*.

HH: This brings us, of course, to the whole question of the name 'revival' – of what is happening. When I was a kid, as I've pointed out, the hobo songs appeared on our horizon. To a very large extent the tradition in Scotland was luckier than in some other places because the sort of mixing and turbulence that existed in the revival in Scotland only mirrored what happened naturally in the tradition at any time. If you look at the eighteenth century collections you can see quite clearly that to call the Scottish folk-song tradition Scots is often a misnomer. Songs came flooding in from the South and from Ireland and if you go back far enough with the big classic ballads you've got a concatenation of motifs and tunes and texts that cover Europe. So that the international thing that I was referring to earlier on and the consequent stepping up of this owing to the mass media, the L.P., television and all the rest of it – this isn't in a sense two things at all: it's one long stream.

GM: Have you any hopes that the revival should be countercultural? In a sense, of course, it opposes the gimcrack, the artificial, and in that sense it's a radical expression.

HH: Well, that's stated quite explicitly in that Preface, isn't it?

GM: There has been some confusion among people that a folk-song scholar like yourself is solely concerned with antiquarianism. Such people are accused of being concerned with the past for its own sake. Of course, as someone who has been actively involved in the revival, you could not be further removed from antiquarianism.

HH: Antiquarianism is just a word that can be thrown like a brickbat. Quite a lot of people may genuinely feel that some scholarly work does not have as much contact as it might have with the experience of ordinary people. But this is surely a very short-sighted and philistine view, as we agree. But it is easy to understand how some people could have it. Naturally, the comments on the revival and upon the whole folk-song scene mirror people's predilections – their own advantage too, if you like. It's easy enough for them to accuse scholars of antiquarianism if they have no scholarly advantage. I have got a scholarly advantage and I am also tremendously interested in the songs and ballads and the stories too of course. These stories are fascinating and if they give an added richness to your feeling for the songs then certainly a ballad singer could hardly fail to profit from a study of the stories.

GM: One of the things that interests me, Hamish, is that given the undeniable presence of the revival one of the most obvious effects has been the high level of commercialism that now exists. Performers are in a sense gearing their music to a market. I personally am not pessimistic about this since I think there are now a great many outlets for both songs and poems where few were open formerly, but I'd like your general comments on this. Also, have all these younger singers, with all the pressures now on them, fulfilled their earlier promise? Have they fulfilled your expectations in their development as communicators?

HH: Well, you've got to face the reality of the media; how people are living and working and entertaining themselves at the present time. One can't wish that out of cognisance and because of that it's inevitable that quite a number of the good young singers will in fact be communicators, entertainers, on that level. Again I've never been pessimistic on this count, far from it, although on a purely personal level one can regret certain things. People that one might have thought would have been more fertile, more creative, turn out to be content to churn out the same old stuff time and time again. They can sing to an old folk's home and get the occasional T.V. spot and show not the least spark of creativity – no names, no pack drill! But it seems to me that to counterbalance folk whom you can truthfully say have entered a kind of slough of despond – the filthy lucrative slough of despond – for them you have a still larger number of people who are creative. About the radio I remember arguing years ago. People were saying, you know, that 'old

Maggie Henderson was singing before she bought that old gramophone and now they're only putting on 'Ramona' and the like.' Well, this seemed to me from the start a lot of codswollop. It just wasn't true. People were still singing their own songs, the old songs. To a large extent now T.V. is a problem, but by and large the situation is much the same. Then again, there's always about folk-song something of the rebel, of the underground, something reacting against something else and to that extent some of the most fruitful of the younger singers have had periods in which they are reacting against the commercialisation of the song. To that extent folk-song is only operating along the old traditional rebel lines.

GM: You have said that the People's Festivals were extremely successful. Why then did they cease? Was it felt that there was no longer a need for them?

HH: On the contrary; they became more and more necessary. But after the '52 Festival the Edinburgh Labour Festival Committee was banned by the Labour Party (which was a considerable backer). As it was a prescribed organisation we quickly found that there was a limit to what anyone could do without subsidy. It's amusing to note that a sub-committee of the Labour Party has recently recommended tat the ban be lifted – after 20 years. In many ways that programme of the '52 People's Festival is my finest work of art.

GM: These Festivals were very formative for people who were to become active in the revival, people like Morris Blytheman and Norman Buchan.

HH: Oh, Norman Buchan was bowled over by the first one in 1951 – and so was Janey. They didn't know much about my work at that time and I think it came very new, to Norman particularly.

GM: Are there any particular areas of the revival which you are less optimistic about? Any developments which you deprecate?

HH: I would deprecate anything that artistically falls below par. I deprecate people who are turning out shoddy instead of the genuine article.

GM: The academic criterion of what is a folk-song is, then, irrelevant?

HH: Artistic criteria only. I'm talking in terms of actual aesthetic value – it seems to me that this is the only criterion of genuine reality.

GM: The classic definition of a folk-song irrelevant?

HH: It is. There is no classic definition of a folk-song.

GM: Well – there are some one or two generally accepted definitions.

HH: Exactly – there are approximations to definitions of a folk-song. But there is hardly a definition which, in the long run, will not yield to manipulation. In this area of the oral shared culture, the criterion is an artistic one: is it pleasing, does it have its own artistic integrity. If not, then we can truthfully deprecate it. Basically the folk culture is oral, not printed.

GM: Your own songs have been printed. I presume that the ideal would be that the singer learns the song, then throws away the paper and sings it?

HH: The essence of the whole revival is oral. I've often been criticised for not printing more, but this is an idea that I have – that it should not primarily be printed. This is not Fifth Monarchy Man nonsense any more than the revival was Fifth Monarchy Man nonsense. The revival exists in reality. It is not something that exists in cloudcuckooland. It was something that could take shape, that could happen. The folk-song revival is the most powerful, enjoyable shared happening of European culture to date. It affects by far the widest number of people. The British movement is being enjoyed all over Europe today. In that it corresponds to the Romantic of the eighteenth and nineteenth centuries when all sorts of boundaries were broken down by what was then a genuine rediscovery of folk-song too. To that extent the revival today repeats as wide pleasure what was then antiquarian enjoyment.

GM: We have undoubtedly seen enormous political and social changes in the period of the present revival and these changes have been reflected in the songs of the revival. So do you think that, together with the romantic element, there is a higher level of social awareness in this particular movement?

HH: Oh, undoubtedly. If I underplayed this at the beginning, it's because it is all too easy, in retrospect, to see the thing as too organised. It's necessary to start where all the ladders start. But one can't deny that most of the people involved were, to a greater or lesser degree, Marxists. To a certain extent the revival is an aspect of anti-fascism, a rejection of what was already being planned for Europe – a kind of 'high heid yin's paradise' – the revival is 'a man's a man for a' that' and no wonder therefore that Scotland played a part in it. There is this powerful democratic tradition. You could say that Burns was the Ewan McColl of the eighteenth century. But seriously, there was much in Burns of the conscious revivalist: nearly the last decade of his life was devoted to song. That, without doubt, is the greatest compliment ever paid to Scottish folk-song.

GM: The influence of the revival is obvious in contemporary songs. Is this another indication of the success of the revival?

HH: Absolutely. The revival will sink or swim by its capability to throw up new and constantly fresh thinkers and writers who will be open and free to take and adapt anything. The health of the whole set-up depends on the maximum freedom of movement.

Scottish Studies: A *Melody Maker* Interview with Hamish Henderson

Andrew Means

Hamish Henderson, of the School of Scottish Studies at Edinburgh University, is one of the revival's most revered songwriters, collectors and authorities.[1]

His compositions, such as 'Freedom Come-All-Ye', 'Farewell to Sicily', 'The John Maclean March' and 'The Men of Knoydart', have spread far and wide. They have, in some instances, been absorbed into the repertoires of traditional and revival singers alike, and he has even been in the position of collecting his own song from a traditional singer while on collecting expeditions.

Since he initiated the School of Scottish Studies in the early fifties,[2] it has grown into an outstanding organ of research into folklore. Although it has been criticised as an insulated academic institution, the School has always maintained that its function is to provide the groundwork for others' practical development rather than taking an active position in the revival itself.

It has grown from an early concentration on song and tales to envelop a place name archive, a film programme, a thriving undergraduate course, the periodic publications *Scottish Studies* and *Tocher*, and a series of LPs of which the first three – *Bothy Ballads, Music from the Western Isles* and *Waulking Songs from Barra* – were released on Tangent last year.

---

[1] This article, written by the music journalist Andrew Means, based on an interview with Hamish Henderson, appeared on 17 March 1973 in the *Melody Maker*, Britain's leading music paper until it was merged with the *New Musical Express* in 2000. It is here reproduced with the kind permission of Andrew Means.

[2] Hamish Henderson was not the founder of the School of Scottish Studies, but its first hired researcher in 1951; he was on its staff from 1955 to 1987.

I

As might be expected from a man who has seen the folk revival develop from conception, Hamish is extremely articulate in expressing his opinions. Softly spoken and with an appealing sense of humour, he is one of the few able to see the present revival in historical and national perspective.

Consequently he began the interview by pointing out, half-seriously, that he represents a contradiction of an old Scottish pre-occupation – to emigrate.

'In fact the Scots have been trying to get out of it for years. I represent a quite extraordinary throwback in all this – I was always trying to get back into it.

It was difficult enough in my case because the Scots, having extruded all the people that can be exported, therefore were exceptionally difficult about letting others in. Anybody who doesn't face up to the established Presbyterian ethos, doesn't fall in with it – I'm now talking about intellectually – is in a difficult position. Now it's much better, everything's much better, partly due to the folk revival.

'The folk revival has been a tremendous catalyst in all this, releasing new energies, giving place for new feelings and creative imagination and everything, in breaking this terrible hard, coarse mould, this uncouth mould of the old Kirk thing which lays so heavily on Scotland you can't believe it.'

How much has the revival affected the Highlands?

'I should imagine very little, except that the revival in the Highlands is an extraordinary sort of two edged thing. All of Scotland, Presbyterian Calvinist Scotland, consists of this upper crust and a wonderful underground. The firmer the upper crust is, the livelier and more ribald the underground.

'So that folk music in Scotland right from the time of the Reformation onwards and even before has been a kind of protest movement. If you were a folk singer in the seventeenth century, the odds were that you might find yourself in front of the Kirk session, and at worst you might find yourself blazing on the castle esplanade. People imagined that folksong was something to do with the witch cult.

'The witch cult trials show clearly that the people who were in command at that time regarded folksong, singing the old bawdy songs particularly, and playing them on jew's harps or any other instrument at the disposal of the people, as something that made it very credible that you were in league with the Devil. So what has really pulled us through is the evil.'

Since Margaret Murray's famous book *The Witch Cult in Western Europe* was published in 1921, it has become fashionable to regard witch covens as congeneric fragments of a pre-Christian pagan religion. Hamish disagreed with this theory, asserting that the Kirk – in common with the Church elsewhere – created an organised witch cult in order to have an excuse to tighten its control of the populace.

'The way it was, unorganised, is the way everything should be. It represented a certain layer of human experience which will always be with us. As you might say, the anti-computer layer of experience. That is what it represented, and that to a large extent is also what folksong represents.

'That is why, whether people like it or not, folksong is important to them, why in modern, highly organised ... great big block buildings and polluted atmosphere ... the great city, Europe, America, the World, the folksong and folksong revival has been so very important. It goes back to this particular level of experience.

'It also goes back talking in terms of recent politics, to protest – protest in the political sense of the 1930s and indeed of World War Two, but particularly the 1930s. That was a period in which capitalism really seemed to get itself very well organised in that it had come to power in a gross, aggressive form in two countries, namely Italy and Germany – particularly, of course, Germany. This was a direct assault upon all the achievements, blundering and mixed up achievements, of mankind.

'There's no coincidence in the fact, it seems to me, that it was in the United States, which was itself growing into this tremendous capitalist society, this bloodstained Goliath ... that you got the beginnings of the present folksong revival.

'It was exactly in America that represented this enormous threat – reacted against by Ginsberg and folk like that now – to natural, ordinary human living, it was in exactly America where you had at that time the very beginnings of he antidote.'

Just as capitalist America represents a modern social struggle, so in the thirties the Spanish Civil War symbolised a similar political phenomenon. Its repercussions were widespread.

'The Spanish Civil War plus the American experience played a very large part in my own personal experience. Plus indeed, of course, Scotland and Ireland. I knew both countries fairly well.

'I was first in Ireland when I was quite a small bairn, and always have liked and loved Ireland. I hope that it finds its way to political peace and unity, which is what it needs. Unity on the basis of the abolition of sectarian preference in both parts of Ireland, specially in the south where the tyranny of the Catholic Church has been one of the main obstacles to the unity of Ireland. But also the abolition of bloody sectarianism in the north of Ireland, one of the most obscene things in the politics of Europe.

'But Scotland, my own country, to which despite of everything I have a strong attachment, always seemed to me, even from the time when I was a very small kid, to be rather an interesting country as far as this mixture of folk and literature [goes].'

II

On various occasions during the conversation Hamish mentioned the influence of the radio on his early ideas about folksong. In one instance he spoke of a series of reports from America by Alistair Cook, utilising material collected by John Lomax. In another he referred to W.B. Yeats's street ballads which were once broadcast. Yeats wished for his own ballads to enter the common folk repertoire and for their authorship to be forgotten. The idea had intrigued Hamish.

Since then his own songs have achieved anonymity in many cases. Several times he has heard his songs sung by singers who have either not known the writer of them or else have strenuously denied that it could have been Hamish Henderson.

It is indeed strange that a songwriter and poet of his repute should have had no comprehensive collection of his work published or recorded.

'This is the whole point of the way I function, or try to function. If there's one thing I've tried to do, it is to operate with, through and by other people. I've got philosophical ideas about this. My own feeling was, and still is, that literacy had created too great, exorbitant individualism, that what we needed – what everyone needed in the context of modern industrial civilisation – was a return to a shared way of life and shared culture.

'Now this might be regarded, if I put it as simply as that, as a kind of Fifth Monarchy Man nonsense or something of that sort, but I can assure you that this is what I felt and what I think to a certain extent has been justified by events.

'I can truthfully say that, from my heart, although I do print things, even then I as often wanted to say them or sing them. Then I was naturally faced with the problem if I don't print them other people will. Then copyright rears its usually ugly head...

'... Nevertheless, how I was trying to operate, on the level of the shared culture, was to a certain extent antagonistic to ordinary commercial and money values. Therefore, when you say they don't exist as a sort of centralised depot of my own writings, this is exactly their whole strength, do you see. This is what I want to maintain.

'In so far as I am a writer and conscious of the fact that I can contribute something as an individual, I've got the pardonable wish to have this remembered and acknowledged, and it would be quite wrong of me to deny it. But that is by far the least important of the planes on which I operate, the one to which I personally give least importance.'

Could he foresee in the thirties the aims which the revival has assumed in the last twenty years?

'Oh no. I certainly couldn't dream, a lot later than the thirties, that it would become so vast. I did certainly foresee that something was going to happen. But I don't think honestly that anyone could have foreseen the tremendous, exuberant success of the revival.

'The success of the revival of course is rather a two-edged thing. You've got aspects of the revival that are not so fruitful as others. And naturally of course the revival has spawned its own gogeterism, its own commercialism. One has got to take that in one's stride, and understand it, even play along with it, give it its head. After all, singers need bread, like poets. One's got to give one to take another. This is one of the facts.

'Nevertheless the enormous spread of the revival is in my opinion one of the most interesting psycho-cultural phenomena of the mid-twentieth century.

'It sprang out of the period of the civil war in Spain, in my opinion, and out of World War Two, out of the realisation to what terrible extent of horror and inhumanity technological progress could lead. It could lead to Auschwitz on the one hand and to Hiroshima on the other. I think, personally, that this folk song revival is part of this human defence against a gross assault on humanity.'

Is there any series of experience or any period of time in which your own songwriting and your interest in folksong in general crystallised?

'I was always very interested in folksong. I find that an exceptionally hard question to answer. The War, I think, more than anything else.

'When people were coming back at the end of the Spanish Civil War, there was one fellow from Clydebank particularly. If there was anything that ignited my interest, it was that, hearing this chap and one or two others singing Spanish songs on the Spanish Civil war. This thrilled me completely – this was in 1939.'

III

In the early months of the War Hamish was a sergeant commanding a section in the Pioneer Corps. During this time he began to write songs based on the routine of army life.

'It was obvious to me that this sort of set-up – an army, with people moving from one unit to another, especially with the sense of urgency that existed with the fact that the war had to be won – was an incubator for anyone making songs that could be folk songs.'

At the end of 1941 he was commissioned and transferred to the desert, where he was 'virtually attached' to the First South African Division as an intelligence officer.

'The South African Division was the most liberal thing that ever came out South Africa, there's no doubt about it. It was out of that division and various units like it that were in the desert that a great deal of the organised resistance against apartheid spread after the War.'

In 1942, when the allied forces were retreating from Libya towards Alamein, he wrote 'The Taxi Driver's Cap'. The refrain – 'because he smokes a pipe and wears a taxi driver's cap' – was originally a line written by Maurice James Craig, referring to Josef Stalin.

Hamish can rarely resist singing a song that has been mentioned in conversation. For 'The Taxi Driver's Cap' he used the tune of 'The Lincolnshire Poacher'. The song is an interesting reflection of a frame of mind current within the army at that time, as illustrated by the first verse:

O Hitler's a non-smoker
and Churchill smokes cigars
and they're both as keen as mustard
on imperialistic wars.
But your uncle Joe's a worker
and a very decent chap
because he smokes a pipe and wears
a taxi-driver's cap.[3]

As the army advanced through Italy, the 51st Highland Division was transferred to join troops preparing for the invasion of France. The division's departure from Sicily was the occasion for another song – 'Farewell to Sicily'.

As with his famous post-war composition, 'Freedom Come-All-Ye', it is written in dialect and set to a pipe tune ('Farewell to the Creeks' in the case of 'Farewell to Sicily' and an adaptation of 'The Bloody Fields of Flanders' in the case of 'Freedom Come-All-Ye').

The first singer to record 'Farewell to Sicily' was Ewan McColl, on a Riverside recording called *Barrack Room Ballads*, in 1956. Hamish and Ewan McColl had met just after the war, when the latter visited Edinburgh with Theatre Workshop – one of the first fringe events of the Edinburgh Festival.

It was in the early fifties that Hamish founded the School of Scottish Studies at Edinburgh University.[4] His hope was that an academic body such as Edinburgh University or Aberdeen University, where the Gavin Greig collection is kept, would realise that value of recording material still available.

Through the late Sir Alexander Grey, economist, poet and translator of the Danish ballads, Hamish made contact with members of the staff of Edinburgh University.

'Though they were very nice, courteous and civil to me, I got the strong impression that they would have had more respect for me if I was going to set about collecting old carpet tacks.'

Edinburgh University was finally convinced of the value of a School of Scottish Studies by the intervention of Alan Lomax.

To retrace the events leading up to this, in 1947 Hamish published a book of ballads that he had collected during the

---

3 Hamish Henderson, *Collected Poems and Songs*, edited by Raymond Ross, Edinburgh: Curly Snake, 2000, pp.96-97.

4 See footnote 2.

war called *Ballads of World War Two.* The Scottish poet Hugh McDiarmid had suggested that he take his collection to the Caledonian Press and in order to avoid having to bowdlerise the ballads, it was published under the bogus name of The Lili Marleen Cub of Glasgow, available to subscribers only.

It was this collection that led Lomax to Henderson. The two met in 1950. In the intervening years Hamish had been working in Ireland and Italy.

On St Patrick's Day 1949 he was with the Behans in Ireland when he received the news that he had won a Somerset Maugham award for an anthology entitled *Elegies for the Dead in Cyrenaica.*

'The conditions of the Somerset Maugham Award – I don't know what they are now, but what they were then – were that you had to spend I think it was at least six months overseas, not even in Ireland.

'I held it then as being really a very sophisticated conspiracy to get me out of Britain, probably connived by all sections of the community.'

Hamish decided to go to Italy to translate into English *Letters from Prison* by Antonio Gramsci, 'who is one of the most interesting Marxist thinkers of all time.' Contact with Italian partisans during the wartime had acquainted him with the name and reputation of Gramsci, if not he writing.

IV

Alan Lomax arrived in Scotland just as Hamish was returning from Italy, and Ewan MacColl introduced them to each other. Lomax had been commissioned by Columbia to record a series of LPs on 'folk and primitive music,' and he asked Hamish to assist him in Scotland.

They recorded such singers as Flora MacNeil, Annie Johnston and her brother Calum – who was the piper at Compton MacKenzie's funeral in Barra not so long ago, and died himself as a result of turning out in the severe weather conditions of the occasion – John Strafford, Jimmy MacBeath, Ewan MacColl, and Hamish himself.

When the project was completed, Lomax presented a copy to Edinburgh University which in its turn realised the value of such collecting work. Eventually this new-found interest took root in the form of the School of Scottish Studies.

On paper it was formed in 1951, but the school had no resident building until two years later. The original staff consisted of Hamish and Calum MacLean. They worked in close cooperation and friendship until Calum's death from cancer in 1960.

'The early days as far as I was concerned – some of them – were not all that happy. In the early days of an institution like the School of Scottish Studies usually there are teething troubles.'

The alliance of Henderson and MacLean was all the more remarkable as Maclean was a converted Catholic while Henderson – although he respected the other's belief – admits to always having been 'very much anti-religious.'

One of Hamish's most fortunate achievements was the discovery of Jeannie Robertson. To some extent it was the result of calculation, in that he had traced the source of most of the major ballad collections of Scotland to Aberdeenshire.

Furthermore, just as Child had taken a comparatively large proportion of his 'A' texts from Mrs Brown of Falkland, Hamish felt that there was a strong likelihood that a major ballad singer in the same tradition was in existence somewhere in the area in the early fifties.

The resulting search failed to meet expectations until he was advised to try the market at Castle Gate, Aberdeen. Previously, the idea of looking for his envisaged singer in a city hadn't occurred to him, but on his first day at the Castle Gate he found Jeannie.

'In Buckie we found Jessie Murray who had beautiful versions of classic ballads and quite a number of other fine songs, but we did not have somebody who could be compared with Mrs Brown of Falkland.

'Now, it was in 1953, beginning to record among the travelling folk of Aberdeen, that I discovered Jeannie. It became obvious to me within a single evening's recording that not only was she, as was immediately obvious, a most magnificent ballad singer, but also she had a tremendous fund or depth of song that was there to be explored.

'As it was, I did in fact continue recording her until in about five or six years of her being discovered, through records and so on, she was known throughout the length and breadth of the world of people listening to song.

'She herself was perfectly well aware that she was a good singer, but she had never sung in what one would term public before. She was well known as a good singer to people, relatives of hers, travelling people living in Aberdeen, and that was it.

'To be acknowledged as a famous ballad singer, as she now is, I'm sure was far from her thoughts.'

Hamish Henderson and Jeannie Robertson

'Opening Up the Lore of the Travelling People' – A *Textualities* Interview with Hamish Henderson

Jennie Renton

The enmeshed traditions of written and spoken word in Scotland fascinated Hamish Henderson, whose zeal in collecting folk song, ballad and tale helped pioneer an upsurge of interest in Scotland's oral tradition, and bring into the public eye the wonderful oral heritage of the travelling people. Our conversation was punctuated with much hilarity, Hamish throwing back his head and barking with laughter in sheer joy at his subject. He provided me with a number of chapbooks from his large and dearly loved collection to illustrate this interview.[1]

Even among the giants of Scottish literature it's sometimes hard to distinguish original work from what has been drawn from common tradition.

Some of the finest works of Scottish literary culture have been a fusion and interpenetration of the written and the oral tradition. Many of our greatest art poets, Burns, Hogg, Byron and Scott among them, foraged in the communal bin, and sometimes they would howk out something that they would silently pass off as their own. It's not only among the folk poets that you find this interchange. There's this continual link, the serpent swallowing its tail.

James Hogg is a beautiful case in point. There are arguments to this day about the various versions of border ballads which he said he'd got from his mother and passed on to Sir Walter Scott. How much was from Margaret Laidlaw, his mother, and how much was from other informants and how much was Jimmy Hogg himself? In his *Jacobite Relics* are a number of songs he'd written himself and silently passed off as folk songs. 'Donald MacGillivray' is one of them. Some of the most famous things in Scottish literature

[1] The interview was first published in 1987 – <http://textualities.net/jennie-renton/hamish-henderson-interview/> – and is here reproduced with Jennie Renton's kind permission.

inhabit this border zone between literature and oral traditions.

James MacPherson's famous bogus epic, which purported to be a translation of the poems of the warrior-bard Ossian, was his own work, and a work of some genius. It had a tremendous affect upon European letters. But he tried to palm it off as a traditional epic, and, as a result, Celtic scholars have been shelling peas at it ever since. Sir Walter Scott spent most of his life hiding his very copious personal identity under a bulging fig leaf, namely 'The Author of Waverley'. On a visit to Trinity College, Dublin he was welcomed as The Author of Waverley, to which Scott rather sniffily said 'Who?', although it was by then common knowledge that he had written The Waverley Novels.

The type figure in all this rather strange business is 'MacAlias', a name invented by Moray McLaren. In an article for the *New Statesman*, he pointed out how many Scottish writers have adopted pseudonyms, noms de plume or noms de guerre, to use the more appropriate style for characters like Hugh McDiarmid. Some, like James Hogg the 'Ettrick Shepherd', are better known by the soubriquet than by their real name. I would suggest one reason for this peculiarly Scottish literary phenomenon is that so many people, even great art poets, owed so much to other people.

Could another reason be the impact on the Scottish identity of Scotland's relationship to England?

That can be exaggerated. Scotland's increasingly dependent state on England, and the natural ill effects of this are possibly part of the picture, but not really a very important part. I think the sooner we come to grips with our own problems right here in Scotland, the sooner both political life and, in my view, literature and culture will benefit. You'll cease to have so many writers, and people working in the Arts generally, who are keeping a wary eye cocked at the big neighbour over the border, and as often as not kowtowing to his prejudices.

McGonagall couldn't be accused of that!

McGonagall is much better than some people think. You can only understand McGonagall properly, as you can only understand Scott properly, if you realise that he is – among other things – part of the oral tradition. His curious, uncouth, lopsided, formless lines and quatrains are very like the Anglo Irish poems composed by Irish speaking poets as eulogies to the new jumped up Anglo Irish landlords that had come in. They used the same metres as the old Irish poems written in honour of the clan chiefs, but, written in English, it's astonishing how McGonagallese some of them read. McGonagall's parents were Irish. He and James Connolly were born within a cripple's crawl of each other in Candlemaker Row and the Coogate in Auld Reekie. This was virtually an Irish ghetto, and when he was a kid he must have heard hundreds of these 'Come-all-ye' songs which used the same tunes and the same metric forms as the Gaelic songs from which they took their cues. I'll give you an example, not a Catholic one but an Orange one – that's six of one and half a dozen of the other where this particular phenomenon is concerned. 'David Brown's Farewell to Kilmood Lodge 541':

> Farewell ye Carrickmannon boys, adieu unto Forth Hill,
> No more I'll share your social joys, when I think on you my heart does fill.
> But when I land at Quebec a glass of water I will call,
> And drink to the boys that I love best, the elders in the Protestant Hall.

You can see the link between that and McGonagall?

Even the best Scottish poets run the gamut between the excellent and the very poor. MacDiarmid in this sense was very much the man 'whaur extremes meet'. I doubt if any major poet has written on the one hand so brilliantly well, and on the other, so catastrophically badly. Burns wrote some of the most beautiful lyrics in Scots or in any language, and he was also capable of writing unmitigated rubbish. Admittedly, the rubbish was mainly in English, but he should have known better. Scott was a special case. Much of what he wrote, especially in later life, was scrawled in double quick time in order to meet creditors.

Apparently, he wrote so fast, his writing is very hard to decipher. Edinburgh University Press is producing a new edition of Scott, which will correct the hundreds of compositors' errors in existing editions.

A similar case is James Joyce's *Ulysses*. The original edition produced in Paris by Sylvia Beach had thousands of errors, not just hundreds. Of course, Joyce was writing in a somewhat esoteric style, or rather styles. It was such an extraordinary, innovative work that a certain number of printer's errors could be understood. The Penguin edition of 1969 corrected many of these, and introduced a new one. On the jaunt out to Glasnevin

Cemetery to bury little Paddy Dignam, someone tells a story about two drunks who visited a grave in the cemetery:

> 'They asked for Mulcahy from the Coombe and were told where he was buried. After traipsing about in the fog, they found the grave, sure enough. One of the drunks spelt out the name: Terence Mulcahy. The other drunk was blinking up at a statue of our Saviour the widow had got put up... And after blinking up at the sacred figure, *Not a bit bloody like the man*, says he. *That's not Mulcahy*, says he, *whoever done it.'*

In the 1922 Sylvia Beach edition, published by her company Shakespeare and Son, the drunk blinks up (as here) at the 'sacred' figure, but in the 1969 Penguin edition, he blinks up at the '*scared*' figure. I dropped the firm a note, drawing attention to the error, and added the plaintive comment 'Is nothing sacred'... In the next impression they took the hint.

Moving on now to your work as a folklorist...

I was inspired greatly by the work of Gavin Greig, the North East dominie. He and the Reverend James Duncan of Lynturk made a fantastic collection of Scots ballads and folksongs. When I was quite a kid, I learned that his manuscripts were in the University Library at Aberdeen and I got in to see them. I was thrilled by the sight of this enormous collection. Greig had a powerful humane intellect. He not only knew a great deal about his songs, he published among his versions of classic ballads songs which had just been written by George Bruce Thomson: songs which have now entered the oral tradition like 'McGinty's Meal an' Ale' and 'The Wedding of McGinnis and his Cross-eyed Pet'. Greig was knowledgeable enough and thoughtful enough not to exclude them from his collection. He had a proper Gramscian idea of folk culture.

Gramsci looked at folklore from a social/historical standpoint. Is that your own approach?

Very much so. Lawrence and Wishart recently brought out a volume of the cultural writings of Gramsci. His ideas about folklore, his insights, are fascinating. From prison he sent his wife Giulia a Sardinian folk tale; he told her: This is the bare bones of it, when you tell it to the children you must put flesh on it. As a folklorist, he was looking with a keen eye at the make-up of the communities in which the stories were told. The social/historical facts of the matter. Really, the most suggestive remark of Gramsci's about folksong – the most pregnant insight – is in his fifth prison notebook. (There were 33 altogether). This is how it goes:

> What distinguishes folksong in the context of a nation and its culture, is neither the artistic fact nor the historic origin; it is a separate and distinct way of conceiving the world and life, as opposed to that of 'official' society.

Here in Scotland, seventy years earlier, Campbell of Islay expressed the same general idea in somewhat different terms: 'In the Highlands, as elsewhere, society is arranged in layers, like the climates of the world. The dweller on the Indian plain little dreams that there is a region of perpetual frost in the air above him; the Eskimo does not suspect the slumbering volcano under his feet; and the dwellers in the upper and lower strata of society, everywhere know as little of each others' way of life, as the men of the plain know of the mountains in the snow.' – That's from *Popular Tales of the West Highlands.*

If you want to find the touchstone of the truth of these remarks of Gramsci's and Campbell's, you'll invariably find it in the field if sex – which is naturally one of the most hoodoo-ridden zones of society. If you want to locate the most fundamental characteristic attitudes of any social group, that's where to look for them. Authentic folksong- the folksong of the people from whom Herd, Burns and Peter Buchan collected – was never afraid of the 'Merry Muses' – or 'the secret songs of silence', which was Peter Buchan's collection. It never had any use for the conventional hypocrisies and taboos of respectable bourgeois society. It handled (and handles) the joys, miseries and above all the comedy of sex with medieval directness. Needless to say, this has never endeared it to the Holy Willies (and the groaning Jonahs) of Scottish life.

The comic folktales – the so-called *Schwänke* – are the same, whether they come from Buchan or Byelo-Russia. They always call a spade a spade!

What do you think of Jung's ideas to account for the correspondence of content of folktales from every part of the world?

I'm afraid these ideas have engendered a good deal of escapy other-wordly nonsense, particularly in Germany and the German-speaking countries. It's very attractive and seductive to wreath and swathe yourself around with all sorts of mystical ideas. Yet I would hesitate to denounce them totally. I've just been reading that fantastic book by Bruce Chatwin *The Song Lines* about the Australian aborigines and their attitude to their sacred lands and the way that they sung their whole continent into being. They have *sung* Australia into being. What a wonderful concept. Now there you are dealing with Aboriginal feelings and ideas and compulsions which may possibly underlie much of the prehistoric background of folk tales.

1890 saw an upsurge of interest in folklore – David Nutt, Joseph Jacobs, etc.

…and of course, Andrew Lang. That was a time more of editing than collecting, although Lang did collect some stories. But basically these collections he made were from other sources. It was a great period of consolidation. Many of these very fine folklorists of that time tended to be pessimistic about the survival of the folk tale, especially in England. Probably a lot more of the tales lingered on than we know. English folklorists didn't do the work among the folk story tellers that people like Cecil Sharp did among the singers.

How do you feel about Anglicised versions of Scottish folk tales?

If you Anglicise Scottish tales the sun goes out of them. Take the collection of North East tales made by Peter Buchan in the early nineteenth century. They are identifiable as genuine folktales, but with an eye to what would be commercial he translated them into such stilted English he crucified them. He called them 'Tales as Told by the Ancient Sybils of the North Countrie'. Old Mrs McPhee or old Mrs Mutch had to be turned into 'ancient sybils' in order to go down with the Waverley Novel reading clientele.

On the other hand, John Francis Campbell of Islay, regarded throughout Europe as the most important nineteenth century Scottish folklorist, gave most of the stories both in English and vivid, idiomatic Gaelic. He was a great Highland laird. A good Gaelic scholar. His mother was English but his parents made sure he learned Gaelic. He eventually learned a number of languages and so had a comparative basis from which to look at folklore. He collected often through other people, schoolmasters, and so on, especially in Argyll. The first volume of his *Popular Tales of the West Highlands* was published in 1860.

Very vigorous language is used in A Thorn in the King's Foot, *stories of the Scottish travelling people by Duncan and Linda Williamson.*

In *A Thorn in the King's Foot*, Duncan's wife Linda has made the most meticulously accurate transcriptions of the language in which Duncan tells his stories. These stories of the Scottish travelling people or 'tinkler gypsies' have been passed on through countless generations of story tellers and contain the most ancient aboriginal motifs. Yet even though there are supernatural events in them, they do correspond to the thoughts and feelings of modern Scots – possibly the majority. Why shouldn't they, when they have been borne forward on the lips of tradition-bearers like Duncan?

Some of the basic folk tales of the human race have probably not only like Ariel circumnavigated the world once, but several times, gaining new impetus from different versions that have been sparked off at different times. There are countless interweavings of these connections. It's true of stories among the settled people. How much more true of the tales of the travellers! One of the real achievements of the School of Scottish Studies has been opening up the lore of the travelling people which had been almost totally neglected by previous folklorists. Back in the fifties, I first became aware of this untapped wealth of stories through Jeannie Robertson in Aberdeen, a miraculous singer with a wonderful store of classic ballads and folk song of every description. When I first joined the School of Scottish Studies, the idea that storytellers and singers from traditional backgrounds deserved a place in the 'art hierarchy' was nonsense to some people.

Changed days.

It's a dialectical process. Or you might just say, one good think leads to another. I've put my shoulder to the wheel and naturally it gives a lot of pleasure to see it moving. I love storytelling and singing sessions, not geared to any fixed function or entertainment. That's the cream of human life. Especially if you've got a living, bounding oral tradition, as we still have in Scotland.

'For Our Own and the Others': Hamish Henderson

Colin Nicholson

Do not regret
that we have still in history to suffer[1]

For many years, at any number· of the folk festivals organised up and down the country, Hamish Henderson has helped the occasion to swing. A ceilidh has hardly seemed a ceilidh without his enthusiastic participation. His repertoire has entertained the dedicated and the curious alike. From the bawdy to the sophisticated, from lyrical to lullaby, from pensive to agitational, from ducal to proletarian, it came to seem that his memory was inexhaustible. And to it all he has brought a singular, some might say gargantuan appetite for enjoying himself which ensured that the proceedings went not with a whimper but a bang. Henderson's dedication to the preservation and promulgation of Scotland's popular culture has inspired generations of younger people, and at Edinburgh University's School of Scottish Studies he has contributed to the assembling of a unique archive of the nation's song and story. His achievement as one of our leading cultural anthropologists is exceptional, and developed from an early, clear-eyed choice as to where his intellectual, social, political and literary responsibilities lay. Temperamentally, these things began at an early age.

Born in Blairgowrie, Perthshire, in 1919, Henderson's first memories are of a cottage at the Spittal of Glenshee where there was a lot of singing, in both Gaelic and Scots. Although his mother was not a native Gaelic speaker, she had developed a love of the

[1] Hamish Henderson, *Elegies for the Dead in Cyrenaica*, London: Lehmann, 1948; reprinted Edinburgh: Polygon, 1990, p.22. Subsequent quotations are given parenthetically. This interview appeared first in Colin Nicholson, *Purpose and Place: shaping identity in contemporary Scottish verse*, Edinburgh: Polygon, 1992, and is here reproduced with the kind permission of Colin Nicholson.

old language from North Highland forbears, and had learned enough to compete at the local Mod.

[HH] *Nowadays Perthshire is hardly thought of as a Gaelic County, but in the twenties there were quite a number of native speakers, even in the eastern glens. The area must have been the extreme periphery of the Gaelic world at that time. But anyway, both my grandmother and my mother were singers and my grand mother had a great store .not only of songs but of stories and poems too. She could recite the whole of Walter Scott's 'Glenfinlas' from end to end: a fantastic memory for anything in metre, and up to a point I think I've inherited that.*

What he doesn't say is that he composed a tune for 'Glenfinlas', for ·he thought it needed one. But he does note that the local mountain in Glenshee, Ben Gulbainn, meaning Curlew Mountain, is the same as Ben Bulben in Sligo, Éire , celebrated by Yeats. In both places, a mountain of that name is associated with the boar hunt that led to the death of Diarmid.

[HH] *As in many cases the anglicisation in Ireland is more distorting than we have in Scotland. When I began reading Yeats I realised how much there was in common between the experiences of Anglo-Ireland and the sort of semi-Gaelic world that I grew up in.*

His arrival in the School of Scottish Studies, where he was to spend the rest of his academic life, was typically unconventional. Expelled from Italy (where he had been translating Antonio Gramsci) for addressing the Partisans for Peace as the Cold War intensified, he arrived in London to find a letter from Ewan McColl informing him that the noted American folklorist Alan Lomax was over to make a series of recordings for the World Albums of Folk and Primitive Music. McColl's overriding concern was that Lomax should be kept away from the mandarins at the BBC, who had – at that time – little regard for genuine traditional music.

[HH] *He recorded me singing a few songs and then asked would I act as his field guide for a Scottish tour. Afterwards I suggested that for security's sake he should deposit copies of all the tapes we had collected with the School; which of course he did. At that time, though it was very much being discussed, the School existed only on paper. But Lomax and I had amassed an enormous and impressive collection of material, and eventually I was approached to undertake my first collecting tour alone.*

In 1938 Henderson had gone up to Downing College, Cambridge; where he studied German and French as well as developing an interest in Italian first nurtured in him when he was a child. He had also engaged in clandestine anti-fascist activity in Nazi Germany just before the war.

[HH] *I was enlisted in the summer of 1939 by someone who had heard me deliver a speech against fascism in the Cambridge Union ... someone who was associated with a Quaker group. I was given a list of addresses which I memorised, and what I had to do was take letters, put them in different envelopes and post them as from within Germany. I never read what was inside them, I thought it safer not to. My cover was a trip to read Hölderlin at the University library in Göttingen where I was lodged with a Jewish family, which I thought was crazy. But it was just a double-bluff; that the authorities wouldn't suspect someone staying with a Jewish family of doing this kind of thing.*

An answer to one of the questions on an interminable form for a residence permit led to a brush with the Administrative Police.

[HH] *Following my instructions, I made no secret of my anti-fascist feelings and when asked whether I had any Jewish relations or whatever, I wrote down* leider nicht *(unfortunately not). But the interview with them was not difficult, and that evening I posted my first letter. I brought back with me a little Jewish boy from the family I was staying with. This was perfectly legal, and I left Germany on August 27th, 1939.*

Rejected as a volunteer because of his poor eyesight, Henderson was drafted into the Pioneer Corps in the summer of 1940 and spent the bitterly cold winter of that year erecting tubular steel anti-tank defences along the East Sussex coast. So he jumped at the opportunity when his Company notice board announced that the Intelligence Corps was looking for people with foreign languages.

[HH] *In due course I was sent to an Intelligence Depot at Winchester, and there they really put us through it. My Jasus, the discipline and drilling was something else again! But eventually I was recommended for a commission at the end of 1941 and was sent straight out to Egypt.*

Active service took him right across North Africa as the Desert Army advanced, and on to Sicily and the invasion of the toe of Italy. He was on the Anzio beachhead in 1944 and subsequently elsewhere on the peninsular as the allies moved north.

An inveterate collector even then, Henderson found time to gather soldiers' songs which he published in 1947 as *Ballads of*

World War Two.[2] Hugh MacDiarmid had originally suggested that they be published, though in the public prints in 1964 he .and Henderson were hotly to contest the value of popular culture.

[HH] *I know, I know. It's not a very consistent attitude. Just after the war, of course, none of us had any idea that there was going to be such a revival of folk -song.*

But whatever else his reasons for publication may have been, for Henderson these ballads were recorded evidence of a subaltern culture voicing itself in active opposition to officially sanctioned norms, as his foreword makes dear:

> The state radio in time of war does not encourage divergence from the straight patriotic line.... For the army balladeer comes of a rebellious house. His characteristic tone is one of cynicism. The aims of his government and the military virtues of his comrades are alike target for unsparing (and usually obscene) comment. Shakespeare, who ran God close in the matter of creation, knew him well and called him Thersites. (B p. iii)

One of the more widely remembered parodies of 'Lili Marlene' is 'The Ballad of the D-Day Dodgers' which Henderson had put together.

[HH] *I had heard fragments of it sung, and I remember thinking 'Oh, we're going to make a good song out of this.' It's a genuine folk-song to the extent that it was suggested by a tune very common at the time, and different fragments had been reaching me.*

But the 'Ballad of the Big Nobs' is Henderson's own, and its last verse makes reference to military leaders of the time:

> We had two Hielan laddies –
> Now we've got two Irish paddies.
> Let's hope they're some fuckin' use
> to the Eighth Ar-mee. (B p.12)

---

[2] *Ballads of World War Two* (Glasgow, 1947), collected by Hamish Henderson. Subsequent quotations are marked B and given parenthetically.

[HH] *The Hielan laddies were the Scots Field Marshal Sir Claude Auchinleck who took over command of the Eighth Army after the fall of Tobruk, and Major-General Neil Ritchie, who immediately preceded him in that command. The Irish were Alexander and Montgomery, who were both Northern Ireland Protestants.*

Characteristically, 'Ballads' includes songs from German and Italian troops as well as French Tunisians. 'Giovinezza Tedesca', a satirical song against the Italians made by serving German soldiers, and sung to the tune of the Fascist anthem, was garnered by Henderson from two Viennese prisoners on the Anzio Beachhead.

[HH] *I was questioning prisoners because we wanted to know what the immediate plans of the Germans were. But after the interrogations were finished I often used to ask them if they had any gossip or any songs – just to enliven the proceedings.*

Constructing a rough but affectionate tribute to Stalin, another of Henderson's own compositions, the 'Ballad of the Taxi-Driver's Hat', speaks to attitudes long since demolished.

[HH] *I remember somebody saying in the desert 'I wish we had a platoon of Russians here,' and the prevalent idea at the time was that the Russians were very good troops and that eventually we would beat the Germans together. Consequently the troops felt very good about Stalin. After the Russians had withstood the tremendous initial onslaught of the Germans in 1941, the general feeling was that they were going to pull it off. And this feeling persisted. Remember that Stalingrad coincided with Alamein; two crucial battles being waged at the same time.*

Perhaps the best-known of Henderson's ballads is the 'Highland Division's Farewell to Sicily', which he began writing just after the Sicilian campaign. Its shaping of a response through domestic Scots imagery was subsequently to structure other writing:

> Then fare weel ye dives o' Sicily
> (fare ye weel ye shieling an' ha')
> And fare weel ye byres and ye bothies
> Whaur kind signorinas were cheerie.
>
> And fare weel ye dives o' Sicily
> (Fare ye weel ye shieling an' ha')
> We'll a' mind shebeens and bothies
> Whaur Jock made a date wi' his dearie. (B p. 16)

[HH] *Yes. That was the whole point of it – a kind of fusion of Scotland and Sicily in my mind. This was quite conscious and I was first given the idea of it by a Sergeant in the Highland Div. who said to me, seeing an old woman there with a black shawl over her head, 'My God, we might be in Lewis'. I took the idea and developed it.*

Over the years Henderson has developed his own ideas and skills in the writing of song-poems, with several of his compositions now firmly inscribed in popular consciousness. One of these, 'The John MacLean March,' was written for a commemorative meeting held in Glasgow to mark the twenty-fifth anniversary of MacLean's death, while 'The Gillie Mor' also owed its conception to a particular occasion.

[HH] *I was Literature Secretary of the Scotland-USSR Society at the time, attending a conference at which messages from Scotland to various USSR groups were being read out. One of them was from the blacksmiths of Leith to the blacksmiths of Kiev, and this at once had an almost physical impact on me. Two such marvellous names. In many of these trades you have the idea of a superhuman individual who is really the sum total of the work force.* Gille Mòr *just means big fellow in* Gaelic *– in clan societies he might be the chiefs armour-bearer – so strong man. I transposed it to a different context.*

Active during the anti-Polaris campaign of the 1960s, Henderson produced what is probably his most celebrated song, 'Freedom Come-All-Ye'; celebrated enough, anyway, to be frequently invoked as Scotland's 'other' anthem.

[HH] *I've just written an obituary for Roy Williamson* [of 'The Corries'] *and his song 'Flower of Scotland' is an effective alternative to the so-called 'national' anthem. But to be quite honest, I have always privately opposed the idea of 'Freedom Come-All-Ye' becoming an anthem because if there's one thing I don't think would do that song any good at all would be for it to become official. The whole idea is that it is an alternative to 'official' attitudes.*

A very different 'hero' ballad is 'Rivonia', with its activist refrain 'Free Mandela! Free Mandela!'

[HH] *Rivonia is the name of the farm in South Africa where African National Congress Leaders had taken refuge and where they were captured. Their trial was usually referred to as the Rivonia trial. I composed the song just after Nelson Mandela made that magnificent speech from the dock in 1964.*

Bridging differences, whether of country, culture, class or community remains an abiding concern and when, in his Introduction to Gramsci's *Prison Letters,* Henderson suggests parallels between Sardinia and Scotland, he goes on to quote approvingly words of the American Joe Gould which in turn reflect accurately upon much of Henderson's own work:

> What we used to think was history-all that chitty-chat about Caesar, Napoleon, treaties, inventions, big battles – is only formal history and largely false. I'll put down the informal history of the shirt-sleeved multitude – what they had to say about their jobs, love-affairs, vittles, sprees, scrapes and sorrows.[3]

At the end of the Second World War, Henderson won the Somerset Maugham Award for his volume of war poetry, *Elegies for the Dead in Cyrenaica:* an early response to the literary gifts he displayed there, recognising that a hitherto unknown Scot had produced eloquent and moving witness to the experience of global conflict. *Elegies* enshrines cross-cultural perceptions of radically unusual kinds.

Wilfred Owen rose compellingly above the racial hysteria of World War One to reach across no-man's land and imagine the 'melancholy army' of opposing German soldiers as clouds strung out on the dawn of battle in 'ranks on shivering ranks of grey.'[4] That humane gesture also lies at the heart of Henderson's poetry, lending credibility to his claim that a 'remark of a captured German officer ... first suggested to me the theme of these poems. He had said: "Africa changes everything. In reality we are allies, and the desert is our common enemy"' (p.59). Certainly *Elegies* displays considerable inventiveness in its various descriptions of a relentlessly hostile terrain. This 'landscape of half-wit / stunted ill-will' is a 'dead land ... insatiate and necrophilous' (p.17). Its 'limitless; shabby lion-pelt' (p.19), becomes a 'malevolent bomb-thumped desert' (p.20) which generates a 'sow cold wind' (p.23). 'The unsearchable desert's moron monotony' is an 'imbecile wasteland' (p.25), whipping up

---

[3] *Gramsci's Prison Letters* (London, 1988), translated and introduced by Hamish Henderson, p.12.

[4] *Collected Poems of Wilfred Owen* (London, 1964), edited by C. Day Lewis, p. 48.

'tourbillions of fine dust' (p. 27) across a 'benighted deadland' (p.45). Imagery of the Crucifixion is transposed into the secular lot of ordinary serving soldiers. As it construes the dying thoughts of conscripts, the First Elegy alludes to the spear in Christ's side:

> and their desire
> crucified itself against the unutterable shadow
> of someone
> whose photo was in their wallets.
> Then death made its incision.

Both the scourging and the crown of thorns appear as the military lot of everyman in 'Opening of an Offensive':

> The thongs of the livid
> Firelight lick you
> jagg'd splinters rend you. (p.28)

But it is the motif of the desert itself which perverts redemptive imagery, in effect diabolising Christian tenet:

> vile three in one of the heretic desert,
> sand rock and sky. (p.23)

Other witnesses have testified to the desert's aesthetic appeal, but this is nowhere evident in *Elegies*.

[HH] *It is not. Just as Robert Burns never mentions what he must have seen a· thousand times: the mountains of Arran. But it is because the desert meant to me at that time an enemy, though in the Prologue there is a phrase 'a sensuous austerity' which to a certain extent is also a reflection of the desert, and I do remember the moon and incredible skies at night.*

When and where had Henderson first begun to think in terms of a related sequence of poems?

[HH] *I first began to write the elegies in Libya, during the Highland Division's advance, though parts of 'Seven Good Germans'* [Seventh Elegy] *were earlier still, to my recollection.*

Towards the end of March, 1943, half-way through the Tunisian campaign, Henderson fell ill and was in a field hospital for three days.

[HH] *I was lying in bed and the first part of the First Elegy more or less came to me. 'There are many dead in the brutish desert, / who lie uneasy / among the scrub.' I thought of it originally as a kind of prose line, and then it suddenly began to become poetry. I was looking at the landscape and could actually see the scrub.*

This opening of the sequence registers two of the most impressive themes of the volume as a whole; a recognition of the commonality of the combatants living or dead, and a transfiguring of desert war in terms of Scottish reference and experience:

> There were our own, there were the others.
> Therefore, minding the great word of Glencoe's son,
> that we should not disfigure ourselves
> with the villainy of hatred; and seeing that all
> have gone down like curs into anonymous silence,
> I will bear witness for I knew the others. (p.18)

[HH] *It comes from a story told to me in my childhood by my grandmother, a sentimental Jacobite to whom the Jacobite Episcopalian tradition meant a great deal and for whom the Glencoe massacre had brought great shame upon Scotland. She said that when the Jacobite troops occupied Edinburgh in 1745, a son of old Glencoe, who must have been an old man himself at that time – it was either his son or grandson – asked permission of the Prince to guard the house of the Master of Stair. The Master of Stair was a kind of secretary of state for Scotland, and he was thought of as having organised the Glencoe massacre. In seeking such permission the son or grandson had said that he did not want his family to be 'stained with the villainy of hatred'. I thought what a wonderful phrase; if ever there was a heroic, magnanimous statement, here it was. And I thought it applied to us in the desert. Why should we hate this enemy? Don't misunderstand me: I went right through the war trying to be instrumental in killing as many Germans as possible. But the two feelings could co-exist.*

The Second Elegy, 'Halfaya', is dedicated to Luigi Castigliano, a cadet officer in the Italian army who deserted and joined the allies on the Anzio Beachhead.

[HH] *I used him as an interpreter and delegated to him jobs I couldn't do myself. He was a James Joyce scholar, and after the war*

I sent him books from the Cambridge University library, so that he could complete his thesis.

·Pursuing the relationships between the living and the dead during war, 'Halfaya' ponders sleep permanent and temporary:

> The dreamers remember
> a departure like a migration. They recall a landscape
> associated with warmth and veils and pantomime
> but never focused exactly. (p.19)

[HH] *It's a recalling of childhood memories, I can remember in the desert having fantastic dreams in which all kinds of childhood memories surfaced.*

'Leaving the City', the Third Elegy, speaks of the obliteration of rank and hierarchy among 'the proletariat / of levelling death':

> See our own and the opponents
> advance, meet and merge: the commingled columns lock,
> strain, disengage and join issue with the dust (p.22)

Seeing both sides as comrades in arms, 'Leaving the City' inserts lines from Cavafy's 'The God Leaves Anthony', a poem in which the City of Alexandria symbolises life itself. Henderson's elegy then conjures a recurrent mirror-image in which one side becomes the other. The overwhelming question here centres upon:

> these, advancing from the direction of Sollum
> swaddies in tropical kit, lifted in familiar vehicles
> are they mirage- ourselves out of a mirror?

[HH] *As I say in the preface, people captured equipment from each other so that everything, tanks, armoured vehicles, lorries, might be used coming in the opposite' direction. Both sides, up to a point, were living off each other, so it was a kind of mirror-existence.*

> ... this odd effect of mirage and looking-glass illusion persisted, and gradually became for me a symbol of our human civil war, in which the roles seem constantly to change and the objectives to shift and vary. (p. 59)

For such reasons, and due in part of Henderson's habitually historicised perceptions, the Fourth Elegy assumes a catholic awareness:

> Therefore reflecting
> the ice-bound paths, and now this gap in the minefields
> through which (from one side or the other) all must pass
> shall I not speak and condemn? (p.24)

It is a catholicity which incorporates native geography, in 'Highland Jebel', as part of the sequences's philosophical concerns, uniting 'a metaphysical Scotland with a metaphysical desert' (p.67). Lines from Hölderlin open his Fifth Elegy, in which a metaphor of migrating birds carries the flight of memory from war-torn desert to battle-scarred Scottish history. What is being suggested here is as much a sense of separation as of connection. Seeking refuge from present stress, the imagination of these Scots soldiers takes off from the surrounding sand to seek the shorelines of home. There, it:

> found the treeless machair,
> took in bay and snub headland, circled kirkyard and valley
> till, flying to its own,
> it dashed itself against the unresponsive windows. (p. 25)

This distance leads to sombre historical reflection as the waiting troops hear, from beyond horizon, a more immediately threatening 'murmur of wind-borne battle'. A Scottish soldier fighting far-off wars in defence of England's imperial interest suffers particular tribulations as:

> Burning byres
> come to my mind. Distance blurs
> motive and aim. Dark moorland bleeding
> for wrong or right. (pp. 25-6)

A remark in Henderson's Foreword, referring to the sleepers of the Second Elegy, is instructive both for 'Highland Jebel' and for a motif across the volume:

> It is true that such moments are intended to convey a universal predicament; yet I was thinking especially of the Highland soldiers, conscripts of a fast vanishing race, on whom the dreadful memory of the clearances rests, and for whom there is little left to sustain them in the high places of the field but the heroic tradition of *gaisge* (valour). (p. 60)

So Henderson will include Gaelic phrases as the war triggers domestic associations in 'this highland's millennial conflict'. This process then dilates to incorporate wider associations, linking the Trojan Wars with the war-cry of the MacLeans who died in defence of their chief · at Inverkeithing. Still alert to the participation of opposing troops in an allusive web tracking war and civilisation back to Greek origins, the mythic structure assembled here enables the Highland Clearances to take their place in an unfolding process towards a final assembly beyond the constraints of any single creed:

> Aye, in spite of
> the houses lying cold, and the hatred that engendered
> the vileness that you know, we'll keep our assignation
> with the Grecian Gael. (And those others). Then foregather
> in a gorge of the cloudy jebel
> older than Agamemnon. (p.26)

Midway through the sequence comes 'Interlude', a poem called 'Opening of an Offensive'. An interlude in more than one sense, it is itself an incitement to rise and fall upon the enemy with all due ferocity, and with a famous phrase from Scottish mediaeval history, 'Mak siccar!' (Make sure!) as battle-cry. Ancestral voices prophesying war are turned to contemporary account.

[HH] *The idea is that there are moments when you have to cut the Gordian knot – rather, I should say – stick a dagger into the enemy. So I felt that a kind of ruthlessness was appropriate there. If you are engaged in war there's no point in repining. The thing has to be carried through. It just won't do to become a conscientious objector half-way through the heat of battle.*

The battle in question was El Alamein, preceded by the largest artillery barrage hitherto laid down, with 750 guns pounding the enemy on a front of five kilometres:

> Is this all they will hear, this raucous apocalypse?
> The spheres knocking in the night of heaven? (p.28)

That discordant music is expertly inscribed as Henderson pumps his lines with alliterative onomatopoeia, to transmit the surge of battlefield exhilaration. Through the sound of the bagpipes local pride orchestrates the destiny of nations:

> tell
> me that I can hear it! Now – listen!
>
> Yes, hill and shieling
> sea-loch and island, hear it, the yell
> of your war-pipes, scaling sound's mountains
> guns' thunder drowning in their soaring swell!
> – The barrage gulfs them: they're gulfed in the
> clumbering guns,
> gulfed in gloom, gloom. Dumb in the blunderbuss black –
> lost – gone in the anonymous cataract of noise.
> Now again! The shrill war-song: it flaunts
> aggression to the sullen desert. It mounts. Its scream
> tops the valkyrie, tops the colossal artillery. (p.28)

[HH] *It's an astonishing thing. To this day, even in the city here, the pipes have an electric effect on me. There are many Scots who do respond to the pipes in this way. Imagine the effect of this, and all that it means in Scottish history, to hear the tunes we all know so well being played in the desert, and to know that Scottish troops were there. In that situation it was the ideal recipe for courage.*

Returning to its central requiem for 'the dead, the innocent' (p.18), part two of *Elegies* takes as overture the ironic pity of Sorley MacLean's musings on a dead German youth in the desert, 'Death Valley'. The Sixth Elegy, 'Acroma', brings a more corrosive irony to bear upon the sterile platitudes which Staff Officers (and the speaker too) habitually use to detach and distance themselves from the victims of war. Perhaps casting a mordant glance at the original version of Auden's 'Spain', 'Acroma' presents an image of the ordered lay-out of military cemeteries. The pattern of death extends both to the immediately opposing forces and, further back in time, to highland experience:

All barriers are down: in the criss-crossed enclosures
where most lie now assembled in their aching solitude
those other lie too – who were also the sacrificed
of history's great rains, of the destructive transitions. (p. 33)

The best-remembered example of song obliterating the dividing lines between contending armies is the German melody 'Lili Marlene', popular with both sides during the war and since. It becomes an echo from beyond the grave, memorialising 'Seven Good Germans' 'as once' they were:

Seven poor bastards
dead in African deadland
(tawny tousled hair under the
issue blanket)
wie einst Lili
dead in African deadland
einst Lili Marlene

The seventh of these imagined figures: 'Riding cramped in a lorry / to death along the road which winds eastward to Halfaya,' had 'written three verses in appeal against his sentence / which soften for an hour the anger of Lenin' (p.37).

[HH] *It was because verses of that kind bring ordinary basic humanity into harsh historical necessity. Here's a young man going to be in the desert instead of having a girlfriend, raising a family; instead of living an ordinary life. So harsh political or military reality interferes with his whole existence. This existential aspect is at the heart of the matter for everyone.*

The Seventh Elegy was the one which brought the sequence into being.

[HH] *I was thinking that I'd known Germans before the war and it struck me as most peculiar that these essentially, it seemed to me, almost sheepish and pacific people should be such ferocious fighters and should be the slaves of this infernal, demonic despotism. These things were churning around in my head and I was thinking 'Who are these people?' I had come to know some of them as prisoners I was interrogating, and the seven characters in the poem were based imaginatively upon those experiences and upon my pre-war memories. The first title I had was 'The German Dead at Eleba', and it was from that poem that the larger idea gradually developed.*

'Karnak' is the most richly allusive poem in the sequence. Its intellectual reach also makes it one of the most rewarding, with myth and irony mingling to epiphanous effect. As a connective thread weaves one civilisation to another, Ancient Egypt vying with Greece, and Greece with contemporary Germany, the poem traces German and English literary intertexts. Rival deities, and the rise and fall of imperial aspirations leave Scottish resonance to register unspoken relevance, as the poem records a visit to the Valley of the Kings.

There can be little doubt that Henderson's prolonged exposure to the brute fact of death inculcated a deep suspicion towards the longing for immortality implied in Karnak's stupendous architecture of the afterlife. Recording his first impression of the place early in 1943, Henderson remarked: 'This civilisation was filled, so great was its unshaken complacence on this earth, with a profound death-longing – it longed, dreamed, lusted, went a-whoring after death' (p. 52):

> Yes, here among the shambles of Karnak
> is Vollendung unknown to the restless Greeks.
> Here, not in Elis and Olympia,
> are Edle Einfalt and Stille Grösse. (p.38)

'Karnak' ironically transfers such notions to Egyptian architecture in the German line Henderson includes, usually translated as 'noble simplicity and serene grandeur'. In a further ironic turn this is then transferred to the contemporary desert with: 'There is *Schwerpunkt*, not here.'

[HH] *It's a military term meaning 'point of main effort'. At Alamein the* Schwerpunkt *was to the north, in a frontal attack against well-prepared, dug-in, wired and mined positions. I was bringing that military term to bear upon the notion that the central point in those Egyptians' lives was death, and the massive preparations for death.*

The lines:

> But the envious desert
> held at arm's length for millennia
> had its own way at last – (p.38)

inevitably echo Shelley's testimony to artistic survival over pride's decay. The name inscribed upon the pedestal which in Shelley's epitaph for the vanity of kings still carries 'Two vast and trunkless legs of stone', is Ozymandias, Greek for Pharaoh Ramses II, whose statue may still be seen at Thebes, and who completed the great hypostyle hall at Karnak. Shelley's poem reproduces the desired epitaph for Ramses: lines which provoke Henderson's own response:

> 'My name is Ozymandias, king of kings;
> Look on my works ye mighty and despair!'
> Nothing beside remains. Round the decay
> Of that colossal wreck, boundless and bare
> The lone and level sands stretch far away.[5]

Henderson's poem presents a paradoxical image of permanence, punning syllabically as it denies 'die eine', and reaching towards a great nineteenth-century representation of the nation whose armies are now knocking at the city's gates:

> Synthesis is implicit
> in Rilke's single column, (die eine)
> denying fate, the stone mask of Vollendung.

[HH] *Rilke has a poem in one of his 'Sonnets to Orpheus' where he refers to 'die eine in Karnak', the one in Karnak, the single pillar which survives to live beyond the near-eternal temples. I walked for hours all over Karnak to see if I could find a definite pillar.*

Against the backdrop of the Valley of the Kings, the poem refers to the Ancient Egyptian symbol of resurrection. Osiris, judge of the underworld, has already made an appearance; now sun god and chief deity embodies archetypal renewal:

> The sun-boat travels through the hours of darkness
> and Ra mounts heavenwards his chosen path. (p.40)

In antique defiance of life's brevity, art inscribes its own continuities. The carved friezes of Karnak transform themselves into an animated tapestry of perennial human activity. For this, a shaping legacy is Keats' Grecian Urn which leaves 'not a soul to tell why thou art desolate':

---

[5] *The Complete Poetical Works of Percy Bysshe Shelley* (Oxford, 1965), edited by Thomas Hutchinson, p.550.

What men or gods are these? What maidens loth?
  What mad pursuit? What struggles to escape?
        What pipes and timbrels? What wild ecstasy?[6]

Henderson's variations on Keats' Grecian theme bring ancient civilisation through Romantic references to connect with the observer's own preoccupations in the North African desert:

Will patient labourers work the shadouf?
Is fruit on the branch: and will ripe pomegranates
be shipped to Thebes? Will rough Greeks land on Pharos?
Will prisoners of war drive the shaft for tomb? (p.40)

Finally, the interrogative litany turns to imagine the living king on his return to Thebes at evening after a day's hunting, blithely unaware of:

the long ambiguous shadow
thrown on overweening temple
by the Other, the recurrent
the bearded
the killer – the rhythmical tragedy
the heir – the stranger. (p.41)

Nor can Moslem invasion look to unchanging permanence: the last two lines pre-scribe divisions within Islam:

Welcome O Hussein
When you enter Karbala. (p.42)

[HM] *This signals the origin of the Shi'ite Moslem heresy – at least, it was a heresy for the Sunnis. Hussein was the grandson of the prophet Mohammed, and I imagined him entering Karbala in Iraq where he was killed and the whole Shi'ite alternative to the more massive Sunni Moslem tradition began. Those closing lines touch, too, upon Christ entering Jerusalem, shortly before the crowds turn on him and crucify him. Behind that part of the poem lies the fact that I had visited the old traditional Moslem university at Al*

[6] *The Poetical Works of John Keats* (Oxford, 1939), edited by H. W. Garrod, p.260.

Azhar and saw the students rocking to and fro with the Imam in the middle, teaching them the Koran. In some ways it put me in mind of the Gaelic psalm-tunes from a different, Calvinist fundamentalism up there in the Islands.

From this sweep of changing civilisations, the Tenth, and final Elegy, 'The Frontier', looks forward in time to project airline passengers 'crossing without effort the confines / of wired-off Libya' (p.44). The shadow cast this time is that of their aircraft, and they are as mindless of the human cost of the North African campaign as the pharaohs were of their own historical demise. Classical epic suffers the same displacement as recent desert heroism:

> Still, how should this interest the airborne travellers,
> being less real to them than the Trojan defence-works
> and touching them as little as the Achaian strategies?
> (p.45)

Rejecting this unconcern, the writing fleetingly resurrects dying soldiers. A combination of German (*brennpunkt* means 'burning point' in a battle), Italian (Buonconte figures in Dante's *Inferno*) and Scottish (a coronach is a funeral lament), symbolises the alliance between the living and the dead. This is further emphasised by the reappearance here of Rilke's single pillar at Karnak as a 'solitary column' – Scots-German emblem of a mutually constructed 'cairn of patience' (p.20):

> Run, stumble and fall in their instant of agony
> past burnt-out brennpunkt, along the hangdog dannert.
> Here gutted, or stuck through the throat like Buonconte,
> Or charred to grey ash, they are caught in one corral.
> We fly from their scorn, but they close all the passes:
> their sleep's our unrest, we lie bound in their inferno –
> this alliance must be vaunted and affirmed, lest
> they condemn us!
> Lean seedlings of lament spring like swordsmen around us'
> the coronach scales the white aretes. Bitter keening
> of women goes up by the solitary column. (p.45)

In a culminating intertext the apocalyptic figure who confronts Bunyan's hero metaphorically combines nightmare and reality, the living and the dead, which have been concerns across the sequence:

> Run, stumble and fall in our desert of failure,
> impaled, unappeased. And inhabit that desert
> of canyon and dream – till we carry to the living
> blood, fire and red flambeaux of death's proletariat.
> Take iron your arms! At last, spanning this history's
> Apollyon chasm, proclaim them the reconciled. (p.46)

[HH] *Apollyon appears in* The Pilgrim's Progress, *the demonic being with flames coming out of his belly, who faces Christian. It was a play on the word appalling also. After all, this is about the dead, and how are we going to reconcile the survivors with the dead except by facing up to the problems they would have faced had they been alive?*

In 1947, not yet thirty years old, Hamish Henderson went to stay with Naomi Mitchison at Carradale to put the finishing touches to his volume. 'Heroic Song for the Runners of Cyrene' reconstructs an epic context of archetypal dimensions; fitting coda for *Elegies for the Dead in Cyrenaica*:

[HH] *There was a dispute between Tripolitania and Cyrene as to where the boundary between them lay. They decided, in civilised fashion, to mark the boundary where runners from each side happened to meet. The faster the runner, the greater the amount of territory that could be claimed. When the runners met, though, those from Tripolitania accused those from Cyrene of having cheated. To settle the dispute, and to prove that they themselves had run an honourable race, the runners of Tripolitania agreed to be buried alive at the spot where they claimed the frontier should be. However, to me, Cyrene meant more in terms of civilisation than its rival ever could, so I dedicated the heroic song to them.*

The notion of running to meet a fate enabled Henderson to include a metaphor which effectively bridges the opposing forces – ('And those other too') – that have structured his sequence:

> neither slower nor faster
> but as yet out of sight
> behind plateau and escarpment
> is history the doppelgänger
> running to meet them (p.49)

'Ceilidh is an Excellent Word' A *Travelling Folk*-Interview with Hamish Henderson

Archie Fisher

Archie Fisher: There's a kind of gap in the legend of the Hamish Henderson story. What were your first contacts with what we now call the Tradition, Hamish?[1]

Hamish Henderson: Well, I suppose it was almost, as the saying goes, from the cradle because my mother sang. She had a bonnie voice. And my granny also sang – she hadn't got a bonnie voice! So they had me listening to plenty of songs and my mother had inherited some of these. She sang some big ballads. They both could sing Gaelic songs; in fact my mother was very fond of Gaelic songs. She sang versions of songs that were in the collections published by the Comunn Gaidhealach like *Coisir a' Mhoid* and things like that.

AF: How did they come down to her? Had they come down by word of mouth inside her own family?

HH: Oh no, these people around there were all interested in Gaelic at that time. The idea that it was a Lowland place, at any rate as far as we were concerned, is quite wrong. And, in fact, this year of course, the big Mod, the National Royal Mod was in Blairgowrie, and people were astonished to see that all the streets – it's the first place, I think in Scotland

[1] Originally broadcast on BBC Radio Scotland. From the references to Martyn Bennett's use of 'Floret Silva Undique' on his first album ('Martyn Bennett', Eclectic, 1995), Margaret Bennett's retirement from the School of Scottish Studies (1996), Archie having met Hamish Henderson at Celtic Connections, and the closing of Edinburgh University's Staff Club, the interview may be dated to the autumn of 1997. Although the Mod at Blairgowrie was in 1996.

that's had this – all the streets had names both in English and in Gaelic. And from my own childhood this would be by no means extraordinary, you know, because there were old people that were native Gaelic speakers and also, up in Glen Shee, where I spent part of my childhood, which is a really beautiful place, Archie, and old native speakers were still there at that time. So that's one answer to your question. I can't remember what the other one was!

AF: The tradition as I said, as we now call it, wasn't, of course, a conscious thing with these people at that time. The academics had put it into books. The Folk revival hadn't kicked in yet, it hadn't started. What was the function of these songs? Were they for informal sessions, and for weddings?

HH: Enjoyment, pure enjoyment, Archie. And, of course, all the other things you mention. If a wedding was appropriate then no doubt, a good song would be sung at it. So I think it's very much a mistake to try and put dockets on all these things for this and for that. We just had them, that's all. I was very lucky in a way. I mean, a lot of the old folk around there sang big Lowland ballads, for example, including some that had quite evidently come down I should think from the North East. For example, the great ballad about the blood feud between the Gordons and the Farquharson. It lasts just three verses but in a sense it tells the whole story:

The Burning of Auchindoun

As I came in by Fiddichside on a May morning
I spied Willie MacIntosh an hour before the dawning
'Turn again, turn again, turn again I bid ye
If you burn Auchindoun, Huntly he will heid ye'

'Heid me, hang me, that shall never fear me
I'll burn Auchindoun ere the life leave me'

As I came in by Auchindoun on a May morning
Auchindoun was in a blaze an hour before the dawning
'Crawing, crawing, for all my crouse crawing
I've lost the best feather in my wing
For all my crouse crawing'[2]

HH: Well, it's a blood feud ballad; it doesn't relate to Perthshire, but all the place names and so on have longer versions related to Aberdeenshire.

AF: You picked out the high action parts there.

HH: Well, it tells the story in three verses in a sense. Well, we thought it did anyway – one of my granny's songs.

AF: When did you actually become aware that the tradition was outwith your family; that it was still living in areas like the North East? Was that in your academic research, or was it in your family?

HH: Well, just when I was a schoolboy. I was a schoolboy in England, Archie, and luckily there were one or two teachers there who were very interested in Scottish balladry. The German master rejoiced in the name of Arthur Stewart Macpherson. I remember him introducing me – he was one of the two teachers there, or was it three? – who knew something of Hugh MacDiarmid's poetry at that time. So we were exceptional in that way I think. I mean, sometimes in Scottish schools it took them a long way further to get acquainted with MacDiarmid's work, you know. The other one was Guts Gayford. Guts was a wonderful bloke. He was a member of the English Folk Dance and Song Society. And he was the first person who mentioned to me the name of Gavin Greig and said what wonderful work he had done up in the North East. I doubt in fact if there were many schools which would have had this sort of mention at that time. So on holidays, when I was about seventeen, I took my hat in my hand or whatever, and tried to see the notebooks of Gavin Greig which were lodged in the strong room of King's

---

[2] Norman Buchan and Peter Hall, *The Scottish Folksinger*, Glasgow: Collins, new edition, 1979.

College in Aberdeen, in the library there. And so I was *allowed* to look at the age of seventeen. What a privilege! So I was quite sure – My God! – it wasn't all that time since Greig had been collecting. He died in 1914, and this was 1937 or something like that and there were plenty of these [ballads] around. So that gave me an idea that at some point, when I could get the money and get, maybe, some sort of academic backing, to do some collecting.

AF: So it wasn't just little nuggets scattered around Scotland; it was a rich seam of the tradition there?

HH: Absolutely, it's the biggest single collection of traditional song, certainly in the British Isles, ever made. There's the great Gavin Greig and James Duncan of Linturk collection and in the old days, always the Gavin Greig collection. But now it's - and quite rightly – it's the Greig Duncan collection.

AF: The current buzz word is 'Celtic', but back in the early days you were aware of the parallels of the Celtic culture and the Scottish culture, especially in Brittany?

HH: Oh absolutely, I mean, Celtic – I saw a letter there jibbing at the use of the word 'Celtic', but the word 'Celtic' is excellent. It is, in fact, the most appropriate single word to use, whether you're talking about, of course, the great Gaelic tradition in the West and North, but the Lowland tradition too. I remember talking to Ewan McColl and Bert Lloyd one time – the first time that ever I had the chance of speaking with the two of them at the one time – and we were discussing.... I mean, I've been a bit, sort of, chauvinistic about the number of folk songs to be encountered in Lowland Scotland for example. And many more, I was saying, than you would get at a place like Yorkshire. And I remember Bert Lloyd venturing the idea: this is because of the great Celtic hinterland. There's a thought to give! And it has always seemed to me quite likely that this is true. That in fact, we are rich in that sense because there's the two major lines of tradition, the Gaelic one and the Lowland one, but the one, I think, owes a lot to the other. In areas like Perthshire where I was brought up it isn't very far back to find areas where Gaelic was the principal tradition. Not just one of them, but the principal tradition.

AF: And what were the parallels with Brittany and the Gaelic cultures of Scotland?

HH: Well, Brittany is a great melting pot of folklore, songs, traditions, ideas. In the Middle Ages modern folklore has shown that it quite clearly was, you might say, the contact point between various cultures. Take folk tales, for example: the folk tales that have bobbed up in France and also in Scotland and England, in many cases one can trace through analysis their Breton connections. And one can well understand this because it was, in fact, the ideal place where such a fusion could take place. So I've always been highly interested in Brittany and gone to Brittany as often as I could – not as often as I should have done maybe, but quite often, all the same. In Brittany there lives a marvellous woman called Claudine Mazéas, half ancient Breton aristocracy, half Jewish. She still wears the Star of David at her throat, and during the War she was in a Camp. And she was such a proud and magnificent looking woman that she intimidated the Nazi guards according to eye witnesses. She survived the War and she was a great boon apparently to children and others that were incarcerated the same time as she was. Anyway, Claudine is the major folklorist, probably, in Brittany at the present moment, and when I went across to see one of the films that Tim Neat had made, shown in Douarnenez, Brittany, I got a little note from her saying: '*Claudine Mazéas suette le visite*.' She was asking for a visit – who could turn that down, Archie? I had a wonderful time with Claudine and I've still kept in touch with her. We've been hoping – that's Tim Neat who made the films, and myself – to make a film about Brittany; the contacts between Breton culture and Scottish culture.

AF: The most obvious one that comes to ear, you might say, is of course, the bagpipes? [*plays Breton pipe tune*] A Breton mirror image, perhaps, Hamish, of the old feuds between Scotland and England. What was that one called?

HH: It's called 'Le Siege de Gangon.' Guingang is, in Breton, the White Camp, and so it is a mirror image, maybe – or a mirror sound of Scotland versus England, or in this case, Brittany versus France.

AF: Is that political side to folk music in Britanny – the political freedom – the thing that freed the music as well?

HH: Oh yes.

AF: But we didn't quite need that, did we?

HH: Well, I think, in the main, Archie, in spite of occasional statements to the reverse, we've been very lucky. In the eighteenth century after the Act of Union – well, the Act of Union in many ways, I think, gave a great boost to Scottish traditional music and Scottish arts of all sorts. People realised that they could maybe lose something and so they came right back on the rebound. And they were lucky, of course, too, to have poets and collectors. Burns, of course, is the great name that occurs to everybody, but [there was also] Alan Ramsay and David Herd. The more you look at these, the more you realise there are North East connections, even if there are people working in Ayrshire, you know. Well, I don't need to mention Burns's North East antecedents. But David Herd was born at St Cyrus, although he lived most of his life in Edinburgh. And several others – Robert Fergusson, the great poet whom Burns called his 'elder brother in the muse,' was also of immediate North East stock. So I think we owe a lot to the North East, just as we owe a lot to the Gaeldom.

AF: There was, perhaps, one occasion in this long history of your association with traditional music. It was the first, what was called 'The People's Festival' in the wake of the new Edinburgh Festival when you brought traditional singers from a' the airts and pairts together for the first time. This had a tremendous effect on the urban people interested in the tradition.

HH: Yes it did. The People's Festival was a landmark in my life, needless to say, because it enabled me to bring down from the North East, or to invite Gaels who happened to be in the Lowlands, together to celebrate life and music and everything. Also to show that a Festival didn't need to be the high heid yins of famous opera in foreign pairts – not that I've anything against them – but, all the same, the big Festival was obviously going to overlook Scottish traditional culture. We decided in the People's Festival, to do something else. When the idea of an Edinburgh Festival started, Hugh MacDiarmid wrote a vitriolic article in a magazine called *The Galliard*. In that he was sort of denouncing it as a plot to suppress Scotland, and suggested almost, in so many words, that it should be boycotted or destroyed. Well, our idea was, in the People's Festival, we used to say: 'There's no need to do that. All we do is do something else.' And so at the People's Festival, the main item of entertainment was what was called the Ceilidh, a very good word; just like Celtic, ceilidh is an excellent word, better than concert. It expresses things that 'concert' cannot express. So the first Ceilidh, which was in 1951, I think... Oh, the first Ceilidh was fantastic. I mean, everyone who was there, for example, Joan Littlewood who was working with Ewan McColl in Theatre Workshop, she was absolutely, what's the word, 'gobsmacked' by it. I could see her party stunned afterwards, and she said: 'This is what we all need.' Needless to say, and we took it from there. The second one also got a great deal of attention in the press. The third one was the one that introduced Jeannie Robertson to the world, more or less. Jeanne had been discovered a little while previously. 'Discovered' is the right word, she was known by a heck of a lot of people up there in Aberdeen but, still, as far as Edinburgh was concerned, and the wider world, she was discovered. And needless to say, I need hardly tell you, Jeannie became the great star of the whole idea of the People's Festival.

AF: A word that's often misused nowadays is the term 'Diva' but Jeannie Robertson was a true traditional diva, wasn't she?

HH: She certainly was. Nothing wrong with the word 'diva'. It's like all these words that people turn up their noses at, in a sense like Celtic. Celtic is an excellent word and expresses so much more than many other words about Scotland and Ireland or, indeed, Brittany can do. Anyway, as you say, Jeannie was the supreme diva of the early People's Festivals. Later on, of course, there were the Stewarts of Blair, Belle Stewart and Sheila Stewart her daughter, who made a great impression naturally, when they came down. They hadn't been in 1953, as you might say, 'discovered'. It was in that year that Maurice Fleming in Blairgowrie, acting (I have to make a slight boast here) on a suggestion of my own, looked around in Blair for singers. I'd given him a whole list of things that I thought he might find. He found every single one of the songs, according to him, in Berrybank. Berrybank was the place where these wonderful Stewarts, with all their guests, were assembled at the berry picking time. I went up there quite often at the berry picking time. I remembered that again from my childhood. My God! I picked berries when I was about six. So, wasn't I lucky, Archie, in many ways; both up in the Glen and in Blair? We had so much song on the doorstep, as you might say, or in the berryfields' dreels.

AF: It took another decade for that event to have its full repercussion and for the folk song revival in the early '60s to gather momentum. But in that time, in these ten years, was this the sort of core of your work with the School of Scottish Studies? Was this the foundation that was going to feed the revival up till now, in fact?

HH: Yes, I think that's perfectly true. People listened to songs. They came along to the School of Scottish Studies.

AF: Who were the stars of the day?

HH: What sort of stars...?

AF: I'm not talking about the people who were listening, but the people they were listening to. Some names come to mind like John Strachan who has not perhaps been acclaimed as highly as he should have been.

HH: Oh, John of course was a great star. He was well known in Aberdeenshire. He was well known on the radio. I first heard his voice, to tell you – I don't think I've said this to anybody else, Archie – in the desert because we occasionally got programmes during the War. It wasn't all 'Lily Marlene' or 'The D- Day Dodgers'. It was also John Strachan. I heard him singing the very song that I've always liked of his – 'Rhynie' – in the Western desert!

Rhynie

At Rhynie I sheared my first hairst,
Near to the foot o' Bennachie;
My maister was richt ill to fit,
But laith was I to lose my fee.

Lilten lowren lowren addy,
Lilten lowren lowren ee.

Rhynie's work is ill to work,
And Rhynie's wages is but sma'
And Rhynie's laws are double strict
And that does grieve me worst of a'.

Lilten lowren lowren addy,
Lilten lowren lowren ee.

Rhynie it's a cauld clay hole,
It's far frae like my faither's toon;
And Rhynie it's a hungry place;
It doesna suit a lowland loon.

Lilten lowren lowren addy,
Lilten lowren lowren ee.

But sair I've wrocht and sair I've focht,
And I hae won my penny fee;
And I'll gang back the gait I cam,
And a better bairnie I will be.

Lilten lowren lowren addy,
Lilten lowren lowren ee.[3]

AF: There was another important American intervention, in a sense, when Alan Lomax came over. He brought not only his knowledge in the technique of recording, but that bit of hardware which wasn't as readily available. Did that help you in your collecting?

HH: Oh enormously! I'd never seen anything like it. It was called a 'Magnicorder'. Never did a machine earn a name better… I mean, Alan Lomax: I first met him in London. Ewan McColl had made the contact there. Alan Lomax hired me as a guide when he was going to collect in the North East. I didn't realise that he was actually hiring me, in the main, as a Coolie. Because this Magnicorder came in two enormous halves, and I used to carry one of them. Alan would actually hump the other one. Still, it was great to have these and to find wonderful – I had never heard anything like it – such accurate and beautiful recordings!

AF: What had you been using prior to that?

HH: Oh, I never used… I mean, my ears and my tongue, that was all.

AF: Easily transported!

HH: Easily transported, exactly.

AF: So what did that contribution, did that era with Alan Lomax make to disseminating and assimilating the traditional music of Scotland?

HH: Well, I naturally got copies of all the recordings we had made together, and I got him to lodge them with the University of Edinburgh. The Professor of Music, Professor Sydney Newman – he is dead now, but he did a great deal eventually for the School of Scottish Studies –, he was

[3] John Strachan, *Songs from Aberdeenshire* (The Alan Lomax Portrait Series, 2002).

delighted to hear these recordings and he made available copies then so that I could play them in my little cubicle. We were hired by Edinburgh University, very nicely, to transcribe these things. When I say 'We' – one was Francis Collinson (who is dead now), a fine scholar. The other one was James Ross, who also is dead, a Skye man, a brilliant man, and there was me, sitting here now.

AF: Were you a minority group, were you a pressure group, or was what you were doing really appreciated? Did you have to struggle for funding?

HH: Well, I won't say that we were absolutely voluminously funded, Archie, but we got along. Certainly I think there was a lot of prejudice against us at the start. People, I think, didn't really realise that what we were doing was academically respectable. And, in a way, I suppose it wasn't academically respectable – that's the whole point of it! But in the evening we had three cubicles there; three of us, we'd be transcribing during the day. It was in a great disused warehouse where the Staff Club is now – or was (I think the Staff Club has changed its colours, the University Staff Club). Anyway, there was plenty of space and we just had ceilidhs in the evening. We'd invite students. They came – Highland students, North East students. It was wonderful.

AF: Was this the embryo of the Edinburgh University Folk Club – the first Folk Club in Scotland?

HH: Yes, I think it was. Certainly there were other things flowing into it but that certainly was one of them. It's hard now to disentangle all the various strands. Certainly that was one of them. We had great old times and of course, we'd bring in drink, carefully, and there was dancing going on in the evenings – plenty of room in this great disused warehouse and there were our cubicles where we could play the music.

AF: I suppose this was the time that I ran into you, round about the 1960s. Up till then music has been pouring into the School in terms of collections. Then there's the turn of the tide; and music starts to pour out and young singers start to emerge like Jean Redpath.

HH: That's right; Jean, of course... I remember the first evening I heard her stunning voice and realised what an addition to the whole scene was there. But the actual University Folk Song Society had started by that time. That must have been the second, or even the third year of its existence when Jean was first on the scene. I mean, if there's one thing in life that I think, in a manner of speaking, I'm entitled to be proud of, it's the fact that I introduced Serge Hovey to Jean Redpath – and what a magnificent outcome of all that, with this fantastic series of records.

AF: There was a time in the '70s that you referred to people as being 'Folkniks', in some of your letters. Were these people the American element of the revival or were there people in this country, in Scotland – were there people exploiting the tradition and the songs of the source singers?

HH: Well, I mean, people, needless to say, they do what they can. I mean there were some people – no names, no pack drill – who obviously latched on to the growing folk song movement; some successfully, others not so successfully. But this was bound to happen – wouldn't have it otherwise. I mean, if it hadn't been for them, so to speak, you wouldn't have the other side of the picture.

AF: In retrospect, looking back now, was that just a passing phase? It didn't do that much damage on the ground, did it?

HH: No, it didn't do that much damage on the ground. I think that one thing one can say for Scotland is it usually does find its feet in these things, you know, and the progress, the real progress, the emergence of genuine people interested in the thing, and in many cases, able to use it, that has been far more important than the various things you mention.

AF: Well, I could hardly call you blinkered, Hamish, especially in one recording that has come to my ears recently. It's the culmination of your poetry and the music of young Martyn Bennett. How did this come about?

HH: Well, I've known Martyn since he was a bairn of course. He is the son of the fine Gaelic singer Margaret Bennett who was for quite a long time on the staff of the School of Scottish Studies, and is now like me, a retired craitur. And she was living for quite a long time in Badenoch, Kingussie, and so Martyn has got a real central Highland background. But I have known him all these years, and Margaret told me that on one occasion in their house in Strathearn Road in Edinburgh, Martyn came in and said with some triumph: 'I've found a poem I can use.' And it turned out to be my poem 'Floret Silva Undique'. It's a goliardic poem from the Middle Ages – 'The wood is flowering all about. You know these poems usually have bits of Latin stuck in them. So I wedded it to the beautiful Durham English anonym 'The lily of the rose, the rose I lay.' It seemed to me the two went together very well.

Floret silva undique
The lily, the rose, the rose I lay.

Floret silva undique
Sweet on the air till dark of day

The bonniest pair ye iver seen
Play chasie on the Meedies green.

Floret silva undique
The lily, the rose, the rose I lay.[4]

AF: You'd almost call that 'New Age', Hamish.

HH: I like it personally.

AF: There have been, of course, young musicians and singers that have come through the contacts with you. I am thinking in particular of Andy Hunter who has gone on to the academic side of the traditional arts as well now.

---

[4] Hamish Henderson, *Collected Poems and Songs*, edited by Raymond Ross, Edinburgh: Curly Snake, 2000, p.1441-142.

HH: Absolutely. Andy, of course, well there again, I've known him since he was – well, not a bairn exactly, well he was a bairn; he was a schoolboy in Allan Glen's School in Glasgow.

AF: That was an important centre for a while during the revival, wasn't it?

HH: It certainly was, because of Morris Blythman, the school teacher there who was a king pin of many things, including the revival in Glasgow. Other things were, of course, the anti Polaris songs and the Scottish rejection of nuclear weapons and all that.

AF: And 'The Wee Magic Stane'. I remember being rather surprised at that house session, I think it was at Norman Buchan's, to see a lad in an Allan Glen's uniform singing 'If it wasnae for the work o' the weavers.'

HH: Oh, Morris was a wonderful bloke. There again, Morris is dead now, alas. But he certainly was a wonderful central figure in the Folk Revival in Glasgow. When Alan Lomax came, on one occasion, I brought him in and he had a fantastic time. I remember him sitting in a chair and looking with mesmerised eyes at what was going on, you know. Well, there were various people like the Fishers, for example...

AF: ... a nefarious clan. I suppose I had been doing something that hadn't been done in in the Revival before. We started to reconstruct songs and write songs in the idiom. I am thinking particularly of the Jacobite ballad 'King Fareweel'.

HH: Well, I could almost write (maybe I should) a history of the evolution of that into Andy's marvellous version. I first heard it down in the Queen's Park here. I used to go there every summer for the Miner's Gala day because some of the miners I had actually known in the Army. One of the years, if I remember rightly, it would be about '63 or '64, I met a chap, McAlistair, whom I had met in the Army. He invited me up to a ceilidh in one of the pubs at the top of the High Street; just opposite the Ensign Ewart, to be exact – we went across there occasionally – anyway, there was a very well conducted Miner's ceilidh. You know, many of the miners here, just as in Wales, have got wonderful voices, but their repertoire was not all that interesting. It was more like 'Two lovely black eyes', etc. And I wondered if an elderly gent sitting in the corner was going to [sing] – I was wondering: who is he? I thought at first the Master of Ceremonies was possibly going to pass him over. Luckily he didn't. He rose to his feet. His name was Jock Cameron, he was a retired miner and he sang this previously unrecorded Jacobite song, 'King Fareweel', which came straight out, as you might say, of the Miner's Gala day. So there now, Jacobite songs previously unrecorded... Though this one actually is a version of things that had appeared earlier on, but still it was, as you might say, it was of itself, a separate song. Anyway, I went up and spoke to him afterwards and he invited me to come to his house and I recorded quite a lot from him. But it was this 'King Fareweel' that struck Jeannie Robertson's attention. I was playing some of these back to her – talk about miscegenation, if that's the right word. Things were going from the one to the other. Jeannie, who was learning songs hand over fist at that time, and one of the songs she did learn, in fact, was that old version of 'King Fareweel'. There was a family of Robertsons, traveller Robertsons, Shepherd Robertson was the name of the father. They had a separate version because Jeannie had to learn 'King, Fareweel' from the tape. She sang it while Shepherd Robertson was there and he then brought out his own version. So it's obvious that it is much more widespread than I had previously thought. These things I naturally played to Andy and eventually, in the fullness of time, he produced his fantastic version, 'King, Fareweel' – which is the finest Jacobite song of all, in my opinion.

King, Fareweel

A big Prince landed in the North,
A' they lads o' the hills were at the ready;
An' the folk they cam frae far and near,
Tae view the lad in his tartan plaidie.

Refrain: King fareweel, hame fareweel,
A'tae bid oor King fareweel.

When wee King Geordie heard o' this,
That the Prince laid claim tae the land o' his daddie,
Sir Johnnie Cope he sent tae the North
Tae catch the lad in the tartan plaidie.

When Cope he came tae Inverness
They tellt him the Prince was South already,
That Perth and Falkirk and Stirlin too,
Had viewed the lad in the tartan plaidie.

Noo a big Prince cam tae Edinburgh toon,
And he wisnae a wee wee German lairdie
For a far better prince nor ever he was
Layed oot in the heather in his tartan plaidie.

At Prestonpans they laid their plans,
And the Heilan lads they were lyin ready,
Like the wind frae Skye they bid them fly,
And monie's the braw laddie lost his daddy.

Noo London Toon wis on her knees,
But the Heilan Lads they were far from cheerie,
And they left for hame through the want o men,
And they waved fareweell tae yon London ladies.

At Glesca Toon they found their shoon,
But the merchant folk they grat richt sairly,
The Prince turned roon - said he'd burn their toon
Locheil said. "Nae", and the Prince he daurnae.

On Culloden Moor they made their stand;
The brave Locheil and the braw Glengarry,
Cumberland cursed and he swore an oath,
He wad gar their bluid fill the sheughs in the valleys.

Wi' your feather beds and your carpet ha's,
Could ye no pit doon a wee German laidie?

For a better Prince nor ever he was,
Laid oot in the heather in his tartan plaidie.[5]

AF: Andy Hunter's monumental version of the Jacobite ballad 'King Fareweel', and a very interesting process to put it together as well from Hamish. Hamish, can we have a quick glance through the two way mirror of time and say, 'How would you like to be remembered and who would you like to remember you?'

HH: Oh, you wait to this moment to ask me an unanswerable question! Well, I think I'll go straight to the point: I'd like to be remembered as the discoverer of Jeannie Robertson. I don't think that she would have been found, at any rate not at that time, but for me. So – that's it.

AF: I saw you this year in Celtic Connections. A lot of water has gone under the bridge since the People's Festival and an event like Celtic Connections. Has it been flowing in the right direction?

HH: I think so. I don't think you can turn back water if it decides to go one way or the other. No, I'm very much in favour of – you know, with a few reservations, Archie, which I wouldn't like to express. I think the water has flown excellently. If there have been occasional spurts going here and spurts going there, you would expect that. The main thing is that, in my opinion, the central current has joined the Carrying Stream.

---

[5] Andy Hunter on his LP *King Fareweel* (1984), Lismor LIFL 7002.

Howard Glasser and Hamish Henderson: Creative Collaboration and Kinship

Margaret Bennett

When asked about his vocation as an internationally renowned calligrapher and graphic artist, the American Howard Glasser would generally speak also of his 'avocation' – a passion for traditional Scottish folk-music. He had heard Alan Lomax's records in the mid-fifties, and he was hooked on Scottish traditional singers, though his first visit to Scotland was to collaborate with Scottish calligrapher Tom Gourdie. Howard later became known in Scotland for his calligraphy of Hamish Henderson's 'The Flytin o' Life and Daith' and in 1996, when I was one of several Scottish singers at his festival 'The Eisteddfod' in Dartmouth, Massachusetts, I asked him about his first meeting with Hamish. Eight years later, he sent his diary notes on his last meeting with Hamish. In between the first meeting and final parting were over forty years of friendship between two kindred spirits.

MB: How did you meet Hamish?

HG: There was a big calligraphy exhibition at the National Museum of Scotland in 1960, and I was staying with Tom Gourdie, the calligrapher, in Kirkcaldy. Every day I would go in to Edinburgh because it was the time of the Festival, and I had tickets for various things, which ultimately I never used, when I met Ray Fisher. Anyway [laugh] I would go in on the train, to go to these different events, and I noticed in the paper there was an ad for a little concert in some little theatre, and it listed Hamish Henderson, Jeannie Robertson, Jimmy MacBeath, and Arthur Argo, and these were people whom I knew from the Lomax records, these Columbia records of Primitive music. And I thought, 'These are all the voices from the records!' Oh, I was in heaven! These were all people up on my pedestals, you know, and so I got there really

by Hamish Henderson

Quo life, the warld is mine
The floo'ers and trees, they're a' my ain.
I am the day, and the sunshine
Quo life, the warld is mine.

Quo daith, the warld is mine
Your lugs are deef, your een are blin.
Your floo'ers maun dwine in my bitter win'.
Quo daith, the warld is mine.

Quo life, the warld is mine
I hae saft win's, and healin' rain,
Aipples I hae, an' breid an' wine
Quo life, the warld is mine.

Quo daith, the warld is mine
Whit sterts in dreid, gangs doon in pain.
Bairns wantin' breid are makin' mane.
Quo daith, the warld is mine.

Quo life, the warld is mine
Your deidly wark, I ken it fine
There's maet on earth for ilka wean.
Quo life, the warld is mine.

Quo daith, the warld is mine.
Your silly sheaves crine in my fire
My worm keeks in your barn and byre.
Quo daith, the warld is mine.

Quo life, the warld is mine
Dule on your een! Ae galliard hert
Can ban tae hell your blackest airt.
Quo life, the warld is mine.

Quo daith, the warld is mine
Your rantin' hert, in duddies braw,
He winna loup my preeson wa'.
Quo daith, the warld is mine.

Quo life, the warld is mine
Though ye bigg preesons o' marble stane
Hert's luve ye cannae preeson in
Quo life, the warld is mine.

Quo daith, the warld is mine.
I hae dug a grave, I hae dug it deep
For war an' the pest will gar ye sleep.
Quo daith, the warld is mine.

Quo life, the warld is mine
An open grave is a furrow syne.
Ye'll no keep my seed frae fa'in in.
Quo life, the warld is mine.

Howard Glasser · scribe

Howard Glasser, 'The Fyting o' Life and Daith' by Hamish Henderson

early. I remember it was very windy, and church bells were ringing, big, wonderful, church bells. I was an hour early, because I get lost wherever I go, so an hour early I was standing outside of this theatre. It looked like an old movie theatre at one time, and I'm freezing, standing there, and a young man comes out and he says, 'Oh, are you waiting for the concert?' he says, 'it's awfu early. D'you wanna come in to get warm? Come on in.'

So, I went in, and I was all excited. And I'm standing in the back, and there's some people sitting in the front row, and somehow or other I said, 'Is Hamish Henderson there?'

He says, 'Oh yeah, yeah just go up and talk to him.'

So I stood about ten feet away, and I walked up to these people sitting in the first row just talking, and it was Jeannie, and she looked over, and she says, 'Hamish, that young man looks like he wants to talk to you!'

I shyly introduced myself and he said, 'Oh, oh, great, ok!' I said why I was in Scotland and so on, and it was Sunday, and he said, 'Come round to the School of Scottish Studies tomorrow, and come and see me.'

MB: So you met Hamish, Jeannie Robertson, Jimmy MacBeath, probably Davy Stewart all in the one go?

HG: No, Davy Stewart wasn't there but, anyway, on Monday I went around to the School of Scottish Studies, which is a very interesting place. I was ushered into a room which had a great long table and, down at the other end of the table, there was Hamish and all of these people sitting round, and included were Ray Fisher and Arthur Argo. I don't think Jean Redpath's mother was there, but she was sorta around too – it was a very interesting group, and Jimmy [MacBeath] was there. And I walked in, right in the middle of a conference about what they were gonna have – you see, there was the great International Edinburgh Festival, where they brought in the greatest orchestras and theatre companies from around the world and then, the School of Scottish Studies would take advantage of that audience to put on, to make their pitch – and hopefully maybe to make a dollar and a half or so, or a pound or two, whatever. And so they would put on these little ceilidhs and things, and Hamish was wonderful in getting the traditional musicians from all over the country to sort of come down for that week, and he had all these people down, and they were organising these little ceilidh sessions. So Hamish was organising this with the help of these young people, like Arthur Argo. I've got an old photograph somewhere, from the newspaper, with all these people... Anyway, at one point old Jimmy MacBeath, who was this wonderful singer, and his collar was up like this [Howard demonstrates] and sitting there, anyway, he goes 'Bleh, Bleh, Bleh' [Howard demonstrates a hacking cough] and he says: 'Ah, I need my fags! I'm outta cigarettes, I don't have any cigarettes.' So I, feeling like an intruder actually, I said: 'Tell me where to go and I'll go get them. I'll be the errand boy'. And Ray Fisher, now don't tell her I told you this, she grabbed me by the hand and she says, 'C'mon, we'll both go!' And she took me out to find the cigarettes, and the clouds opened up and it poured rain. It would, it could come on quickly and leave just as quickly. But it was a wonderful time, and it was a time when it was very exciting to be in Edinburgh, with the revival stuff that was going on. Young people like Jean Redpath, and that crowd – it was wonderful.

MB: Was it during this visit you also went to the Outer Hebrides?

HG: Yes, well, I went to Ullapool and to Gairloch and down to Oban and then I hopped on a boat, MacBraynes ... and eventually to Barra. I'd spoken to Hamish before I went there, and he gave me the name of somebody, a Miss Campbell, and also the name of this wonderful lady who did the waulking songs and the –

MB: Canntaireachd? Was it Mary Morrison?

HG: Mary Morrison! She's on the Lomax record! How can you forget a name like that? Anyway, I went to see Mary in a thatched cottage.... She was standing in front of her cottage with her little black and white collie dog and I came up with my camera and of course I had heard her from the Lomax records and she looked at me and she said, 'Och, I suppose you've come to take a photograph of my thatched cottage!' And of course that completely threw me, and I said, 'Of course not, I came to hear you and to talk to you,' and so on. So I never did take the photograph, but I made a sketch of it. I made a drawing of it, but I was in it. I wanted a photograph of her and I ended up, it hadda be from memory, in the sketch, but it was wonderful, wonderful.

MB: Did you have any memories even of what it was like going through the door of a thatched cottage for the first time, with a peat fire burning?

HG: I was really quite surprised with, you know, the inside was so cosy and so nice and warm, and when she sat, and she started singing, and she closed her eyes, and her hands started going, and I could picture the table with all the women sitting around. She was all by herself when she did this and it was wonderful, just wonderful. Of course I had heard those wonderful primitive sounding chants. ... I think one of the things, the reasons why I was treated so well, is that I didn't know anything. So I didn't even know what question to ask, but I remembered, like, a phrase of Gaelic and I said, 'Och, do you know the one? *Ho ro mo nighean donn bhoidheach*?' You know, a very common song everybody knows, so common nobody really wants to sing it. So there were a couple of things like that I'd come up with, and they would light up, knowing, ah ha, he really is interested. So they were very willing to share.

Howard Glasser and Hamish Henderson, 2000

MB: Were you aware when you recorded people like Mary Morrison just how important the recordings would become?

HG: Well yeah, in a way... it wasn't immediately obvious; for instance, the first ceilidh I went to was on Iona, and there was a man got up and he was singing like Paul Robeson [imitates in a deep voice] 'Ol' Man River'. And then somebody got up and recited 'The Face on the Bar-room Floor'. Then there was somebody else would sing a song that was maybe from a Scandinavian kind of legend, and it made no difference to them, between one song and another – a funny Bothy song or even 'The ants went marching one by one' or whatever that song is about! But I was grateful for everything I found, music hall, stuff.[1] You know, old – I really was in search of old ballads but then I found all this great music hall stuff that I didn't know anything about, and I didn't know anything about the religious music.

I stayed at Miss Campbell's, as Hamish had mentioned, and I remember, I destroyed her Tilley lantern... I touched the mantle on the Tilley – of course it was gone! I felt so badly about it ... And they had no electricity and there were a couple of telephones around the town, the crank kinda phones.

MB: I have a folklorist question: What kind of a machine did you use for these recordings?

HG: The first time I went to Scotland, it was an American machine, it was called a 'Steelman' and it was one of the very first small portable machines, but half the time it didn't work. I used to say it was made of rubber bands and chewing gum. But then, the second time I came, in 1963, I used one that Hamish recommended, a reel to reel. They were using a German machine, a U-H-E-R. A small machine, reel to reel, using acetate tapes, and powered by battery where they had no electricity...

---

[1] Howard is referring to the complete range of his recordings, which include children singing, as the whole family would be at home. This particular reference is from a recording made in Ullapool with Peter Stewart whose family were all Gaelic-speakers, though the children had to learn English songs at school. Howard's recordings of this particular family of travellers cover a remarkable range of material as well as the unique setting of their fireside.

While this represents only a small part of the interview, it gives the background to Howard's meeting with Hamish, the start of a forty-year friendship, which led to a network of friendships, as many singers will tell you. Though Howard made no claim to be a professional folklorist, yet, when faced with the obligatory task of writing fieldwork notes, (neglected by too many fieldworkers), Howard's work excels. Here is the first page of his Ullapool fieldwork notebook:

August 4th – Thursday – Lochinver – Low clouds, dull & drippy

& on for a time in Ullapool

Took a last look around Lochinver. Found my new friends waiting at the car – One at a time they came up to say goodbye – I, almost, hated to leave –

Although the distance to Ullapool was short, dodging sheep & cattle on the narrow winding road, through the bleak & barren coastal moors and fortress like hills of rock proved quite tiring. As the mist and haze closed in, my eyes searched the gray stretches of water for a glimpse of Lewis or Harris in the Outer Hebrides, which, I knew loomed out on the invisible horizon.

On to Ullapool – a lovely setting – a small village on Loch Broom – This is really the Gaelic Highlands and looks exactly as it should – stray sheep grazing in the streets – a misty grayness hovering around the tops of the mountains across the lovely bay – a fishing boat coming in – sea gulls – children playing – an old fisherman – a few English tourists – the sounds of Gaelic voices.

I was sent from house to house in search of a bed & breakfast place. I had visited almost every house and became thoroughly discouraged. I felt a difference in the people – not the open trusting people of the places more south & east. Could this be my first encounter with the highland temperament?

I believe I got the last accommodation in the village at Mrs. MacGregor's and two minutes later someone else came by enquiring about a 'single' – but I had it!

Mrs. MacGregor, an elderly woman, with a bristly white mustache, seemed polite & friendly but some what reserved.

In the intervening years, Howard welcomed many Scottish singers to America, forging connections between folk on both sides of the Atlantic, though Hamish never visited the USA. When Howard returned to Scotland in 2000, I had the pleasure of driving him here and there while he was in Edinburgh. Naturally he visited Hamish who was at home in his top floor flat. Howard made his way slowly up the stairs for what was to be their last meeting together, and Howard's last visit to Scotland:

> I huffed and puffed my way to the top of his stairwell. I don't know how Hamish managed. Kätzel was with Hamish when I arrived, but after a warm greeting she left us alone for our visit. Hamish had a lively sparkle in his eyes that, despite his frail body, reflected excitement and energy. He had a broad, happy smile. As we talked about his new book and other things, he said he wouldn't mind if I made a recording... He sang a Yiddish song with gusto. He had learned it in North Africa during the Second World War... I spent three hours which I shall always cherish. Hamish had a passion for the talents and creative powers of 'ordinary' people. He was a man of courage and principle. He was an unselfish and loyal friend. Hamish had always been concerned that it should be the young that kept the traditions alive, and not commercial interests or mass media.
>
> My life was changed in 1960 when I found many answers to some of a young person's quest for their own truths. I was fortunate to be in Scotland at that time, to know, and to record Hamish, Arthur Argo, Jeannie Robertson, Donald, Isaac and Lizzy Higgins, Jimmy MacBeath, Lucy Stewart, Tina Stewart, Cameron Turriff, Peter Stewart, Alec & Belle Stewart, Willie Scott, Matt McGinn, Mary Morrison, Calum Johnson.... They're all gone now... they are somewhere at the ceilidh of ceilidhs... and I expect Hamish is sleeping in his chair with his empty glass on its arm and Sandy is sleeping at this feet.

Timothy Neat, 'The Dying Hamish'

Contributors

Keith Armstrong, the 'Jinglin' Geordie' from Whitley Bay, has worked as a community development worker, poet, librarian & publisher. He has been a self-employed writer since 1986 and completed a doctorate on Newcastle writer Jack Common at the University of Durham in 2007, where he received a BA Honours Degree in Sociology in 1995 and Masters Degree in 1998 for his studies on regional culture in the North East of England. His poetry has been extensively published in magazines such as *New Statesman, Poetry Review, Dream Catcher, Other Poetry, Aesthetica, Iron, Salzburg Poetry Review* and *Poetry Scotland*, as well as in the collections *The Jingling Geordie, Dreaming North, Pains of Class* and *Imagined Corners*, on cassette, LP & CD, and on radio & TV.

Margaret Bennett is a folklorist, writer, singer and broadcaster, brought up in Skye, Lewis and Shetland before studying in Glasgow. In the mid-sixties, the legendary Hamish Henderson inspired her career choice. In 1968 she emigrated to Canada to study Folklore at Memorial University of Newfoundland, after which she spent a year in Quebec as a folklorist for Canada's Museum of Civilization. From 1984 to 1996 she lectured at The University of Edinburgh's School of Scottish Studies and now teaches part-time at the Royal Conservatoire of Scotland. A prize-winning author, she has written ten books, contributed to over 40 others, featured on media productions and several musical collaborations with her son, Martyn Bennett (1971–2005), including the National Theatre of Scotland's acclaimed production, 'Black Watch'. Recipient of many national and international awards for contributions to literature, folklore and culture, she is widely regarded as 'Scotland's foremost folklorist'.

Eberhard 'Paddy' Bort works in the Academy of Government at he University of Edinburgh and chairs Edinburgh Folk Club and the Carrying Stream Festival. His most recent publications are *View from Zollernblick: Regional Perspectives in Europe* (Grace Note Publications, 2013) and *The Annals of the Parish: A Decade of Devolution 2004-2014* (Grace Note Publications, 2014).

Ray Burnett is a Honorary Research Fellow at the Scottish Centre for Island Studies at the University of the West of Scotland and Director of the Dicuil Institute of Island Studies on Benbecula in the Western Isles. His *Benbecula* (Mingulay Publishing, 1986) is a comprehensive survey of the island, its history, and its culture,

David Daiches (1912-2005) was a leading and long-standing authority on Scottish literature, the author and editor and introducer of books on Robert Fergusson, Robert Burns, James Boswell, Walter Scott (whom he is credited with reviving), Robert Louis Stevenson and Hugh MacDiarmid, as well as writing such influential books as The Paradox of Scottish Culture (1964).

Lesley Duncan is a journalist and poetry editor who also writes poetry. She is poetry editor of *The Herald* and for more than 15 years has had the pleasure of choosing the paper's 'Poem of the Day'. Her collection, *Images Not Icons*, was published by Kennedy and Boyd in association with *The Herald*.

Archie Fisher is an avid horseman and master guitarist, singer and songwriter – one of Scotland's foremost Folk music troubadours. He is well-known for his 27-year tenure as the host of BBC Radio Scotland's award-winning 'Travelling Folk' show. Recognised for his contributions to Scottish folk music, he was inducted into the Scots Traditional Music Hall of Fame and in 2006.

Howard Glasser first began providing the setting and inspiration for his Ceilidhs at the Carnegie Institute of Technology in Pittsburgh, PA in 1961. Subsequently, he arranged informal gatherings, concerts and Eisteddfod Traditional Arts festivals and collected recordings of performances and interviews of hundreds of traditional and folk musicians in the United States and Scotland. Already an avid folk music enthusiast, he was inspired by a three-month sojourn in Scotland where he collected recordings and interviews of musicians performing traditional songs for their own entertainment, at informal family and community gatherings. By trade, Howard Glasser is an internationally renowned graphic artist, calligrapher and teacher. In fact, his graphic art infuses the folk music material, where he has lent his skill to creating striking posters, logos, programmes, advertisements, tickets, and banners. He spent 30 years of his career at the University of Massachusetts Dartmouth (once known as SMU), before retiring in 2001. In 1972, at SMU, the weekly Ceilidhs grew into the Eisteddfod Festival of Traditional Music. Under Glasser's guidance the Eisteddfod flourished for 24 years, and broadened to include workshops, exhibitions, seminars and other programs.

George Gunn was born in Thurso where he still lives. He has been a deep-sea fisherman, a driller for oil in the North Sea and a journalist – he contributes to local and national papers and journals and sends a fortnightly column, 'From The Pictish Navy', to the *John O Groat Journal*. From 1992 to 2010 he was Artistic Director of Grey Coast Theatre Company, which he co-founded; he also tutors in drama at North Highland College. He has published a number of pamphlets and small collections over the years, including *Black Fish* (Scotia Review, 2004), *Winter Barley* (Chapman, 2005) and *The Atlantic Forest* (Two Ravens Press, 2008).

William Hershaw was born in Newport on Tay. Both sides of the family had a coal-mining background, although his father joined the Fire Brigade. He is a poet, musician and songwriter, and Principal Teacher of English at Beath High School, Cowdenbeath. His works in Scots and English include *Fower Brigs Tae A Kinrik*, published by Aberdeen University Press, and *The Cowdenbeath Man* published by the Scottish Cultural Press. In 2013, he published his first novel, *Tammie Norrie: The Hoose Daemon of Seahouses*, and in 2015 *Postcairds Fae Woodwick Mill: Orkney Poems in Scots* (both Grace Note Publications).

Tom Hubbard is a Scottish novelist, poet and itinerant scholar who has worked in many countries. His permanent home is in his native Fife. He was the first Librarian of the Scottish Poetry Library, from 1984 to 1992. His first novel *Marie B.* (Ravenscraig Press, 2008), based on the life of the Ukrainian-born painter Marie Bashkirtseff, was longlisted for a Saltire Society book award. His recent book-length poetry collections are *The Chagall Winnocks* (2011) and *Parapets and Labyrinths* (2013), both from Grace Note Publications, as well as a pamphlet collection, *The Nyaff* (2012), from Windfall Books of Kelty, Fife. In 2014, he published his second novel, *The Lucky Charm of Major Bessop* (Grace Note Publications). As a visual artist, he contributed writers' portraits to Mario Relich's first poetry collection, *Frisky Ducks and Other Poems* (Grace Note Publications, 2014).

John Lucas is Professor Emeritus of English at the universities of Loughborough and Nottingham Trent. Among his many critical and scholarly books are studies of Dickens, Elizabeth Gaskell and Arnold Bennett. He is the author of *England and Englishness: Poetry and Nationhood 1700-1900*, *Modern English Poetry: Hardy to Hughes*, and *The Radical Twenties*. John Lucas has also translated the poems of *Egil's Saga* and is the author of six collections of poetry, most recently *A World Perhaps: New and Selected Poems* (2002), *The Short of It* (2004) and *Flute Music* (2006). Since 1994 he has been the publisher of Shoestring Press.

Richie McCaffery lives in Stirling and has recently completed a PhD in Scottish Literature at the University of Glasgow, where he was a Carnegie scholar researching the Scottish poets of World War Two. His essays have appeared in *The Scottish Literary Review*, *The Dark Horse*, *Northwords Now*, *Fras* and *Etudes Écossaises*. He is the author of two pamphlets – *Spinning Plates* (HappenStance, 2012) and *Ballast Flint* (1013) – and the collection *Cairn* (Nine Arches Press, 2014). He has recently finished his PhD thesis in Scottish Literature, looking at the Scottish poets of World War Two.

Geordie McIntyre is a Glaswegian of Highland and Irish descent. His lifetime involvement in song, ballad and poetry is reflected in his singing, collecting and songwriting. His early years as a radio and television technician and later as a Modern Studies teacher, coupled with his passion for the outdoors, have in diverse ways fuelled and complemented his central interest in folk music. Geordie has an extensive repertoire of sngs and has sung at clubs and festivals in most corners of Britain and Ireland and more recently in the USA.

Dolina Maclennan from the island of Lewis is a well known singer, actress, and storyteller of national and international renown. In 1962, she was part of *Plain Songs and all that Jazz* – the first appearance of Folk and Jazz at the official Edinburgh Festival. The next official Festival event she took part in was in the 1972 production of *Fin McCool*. She was a member of the original cast of *The Cheviot, The Stag and the Black Oil*, the seminal work by playwright John McGrath which toured in the 1970s. In 1970, Dolina broke new ground by singing for Stuart Hobb's production in the Scottish Ballet *An Clo Mòr* and brought Gaelic lessons to people's home with *Beagan Gaidhlig* under the direction of George Reid. She was part of the Gaelic soap *Machair* since its inception in 1992. Dolina won the Fletcher of Saltoun Award for her significant contribution to Scotland's life and culture in 2012.

Allan McMillan, occasional singer and former EFC vice chairman, is Edinburgh Folk Club's resident photographer and the manager of the Club's Facebook pages. Allan has his own flickr page: <www.flickr.com/photos/allan_mcmillan/>.

Alison McMorland came to wider public notice in the early 1970s and since then has been active as a collector, performer, teacher editor and publisher. Not least has been her single-minded commitment to developing the traditional arts within the community both in England and in Scotland. This wider concern and perspective has embraced pioneering and innovative work in oral history and reminiscence, children's folklore, as well as voice workshops and Arts for Health. Songs and singing have been and remain at the heart of what she is about. In the wrds of Hamish Henderson, she 'stands out as one of the principal modern interpreters of an ancestral ballad singing tradition, breathing new life into ancient memorials by uniting scrupulous traditional fidelity with versatile and resourceful creative artistry.' Since returning to Scotland in 1989, she has shared with Jo Miller the first Traditional Arts Development position in Scotland, co-founded a community arts organisation and is a tutor on the Scottish Music Course at the Royal Conservatoire in Glasgow.

Ewan McVicar was born in Inverness. He worked as a banker in Scotland and Africa, then as a guitar teacher in the USA. On his return to Scotland, he was employed in various areas of social work before becoming a self-employed storyteller and songwriter. He has performed in over 200 schools and in castles, museums, folk festivals and other venues across Britain, as well as in Canada, the USA, Holland and Russia. He has written some 40 songs which have been commercially recorded, including 20 for the *Singing Kettle* children's show. He lives in Linlithgow.

Andrew Means grew up in Britain and lives in Arizona, on the outskirts of Phoenix. As a journalist he has written about musicians and entertainment for local and national media, including the *Melody Maker*. He has written a memoir about the country music entertainer Marty Robbins (entitled *Some Memories – Growing Up With Marty Robbins*), a biography of the rock group Pink Floyd and an introduction to novelist and essayist George Orwell. He writes fiction as A.L. Means. His works include a novel, *Shine Like The Sun*, a set of short stories entitled *Foreign Ways* and a children's story, *The Trouble Upstream*.

Donald Meek was Professor of Scottish and Gaelic Studies at the University of Edinburgh. Before that, he held the inaugural Chair of Celtic Studies at the University of Aberdeen. Professor Meek subsequently led the Ministerial Advisory Group on Gaelic which delivered the pivotal Fresh Start for Gaelic report, and became Chairman of the Gaelic Books Council. The Donald Meek Award was established by the Gaelic Books Council in 2010 to encourage and support new and established Gaelic writers. Donald Meek, a native of Tiree, is one of the best-known Gaelic scholars of his generation. During his career at Glasgow, Aberdeen, and Edinburgh Universities, he has written many books in the field of Gaelic and Highland history – seen from the inside. He has also been prepared to become engaged in policy matters to make a difference to the lives of ordinary people in the Highlands and Islands.

Jan Miller from Penicuik is an artist working with many materials, but she is particularly well-known for her papier-mâché statues, many connected with the Scottish Folk Revival – Jeannie Robertson, Jimmy MacBeath, Davy Stewart. Her Robert Burns graces Cy Lawrie's pub in Glasgow. In 2002 Jan made the Hamish Henderson Bust, commissioned by Edinburgh Folk Club – which is now in the 21st Century Gallery of the National Museum of Scotland. Her sketches for that bust were published in the first Carrying Stream Festival brochure (2002). Jan has worked for Glasgow University as a medical illustrator, followed by ten years illustrating for the Scottish Exam Board. Since 1995, she has worked as an adult education tutor in the Lothians, teaching painting, drawing, stained glass, and papier-mâché sculpture. Jan has always been interested in the Scottish ballad and poetry culture, learning 'The Wife of Usher's Well' as a poem aged 7. When she realised it was a song, she was hooked. She also makes amazing cakes and clootie dumplins – raised two lovely daughters, both fine singers – has written some poems/songs – and done a little housework!

Timothy Neat is a writer and film maker who, after sixteen years as a lecturer in the History of Art at Duncan at Jordanstone College of Art in Dundee, gave up teaching (in 1988) to work in the independent sector. Brought up in Cornwall, he has lived all his adult life Scotland – supplementing his literary income with work as a migratory beekeeper, wild mushroom hunter and salmon netter. His books have a strong visual component, and his films have a strong literary and musical emphasis. He writes poetry, takes photographs, and draws. Close friendships with Hamish Henderson, John Berger, Sorley MacLean and Ian Hamilton Finlay have strongly influenced his ideas and work. In 2007 and 2009 he published his massive two-volume biography of Hamish Henderson (Birlinn).

Colin Nicholson was Professor of Eighteenth-Century and Modern Literature at the University of Edinburgh, whose interests span both the eighteenth century and modern literature, as well as Scottish, Canadian and postcolonial topics. During the 1990s, he edited the *British Journal of Canadian Studies.*

Mario Relich, born in Zagreb and brought up in Montreal, has lived for most of his life in Edinburgh and has been an Associate Lecturer in English Literature and Film Studies at the Open University in Scotland for many years. He is also Secretary of the Poetry Association of Scotland and a member of the executive committee of Scottish PEN. His first poetry collection, *Frisky Ducks and Other Poems* (Grace Note Publications) was published in 2014.

Jennie Renton is the owner of Main Point Books, which is an independent bookshop in Edinburgh. She is also a founder of Textualities.net, a website dedicated to books and writing, and a freelancer involved in production, editorial and publicity activities.

Donald Smith is a storyteller, novelist, playwright and performance poet. He was born in Glasgow to an Irish mother and was brought up in Edinburgh, Glasgow and Stirling. He is a founding member of the Scottish Storytelling Forum and of Edinburgh's Guid Crack Club, and is Director of the Scottish Storytelling Centre at The Netherbow. He chaired the Committee that established the National Theatre of Scotland and became a founding Director. He is the author of numerous books, including a novel set in Edinburgh at the time of Robert Burns, *Between Ourselves* (Luath, 2008), *God, the Poet & the Devil: Robert Burns and Religion* (Saint Andrew Press, 2008), and the collection of poetry, *A Long Stride shortens the Road: Poems of Scotland* (Luath, 2004).

Sheena Wellington was born in Dundee into a family of singers and jute workers. She is a singer, very occasional songwriter and lifelong enthusiast for traditional song. When she sang 'A Man's A Man For a' That' at the opening of the first Scottish Parliament in nearly 300 years on 1 July 1999, it was widely seen as the highlight of that very special day. In November 2009, she was inducted into the Scottish Traditional Music Hall of Fame.

Lightning Source UK Ltd.
Milton Keynes UK
UKOW06f1958091115

262404UK00008B/149/P